PUBLISHER'S PREFACE TO THE STUDY EDITION

Since the publication of the first English translation of *Church Dogmatics I.1* by Professor Thomson in 1936, T&T Clark has been closely linked with Karl Barth. An authorised translation of the whole of the *Kirchliche Dogmatik* was begun in the 1950s under the editorship of G. W. Bromiley and T. F. Torrance, a work which eventually replaced Professor Thomson's initial translation of *CD I.1*.

T&T Clark is now happy to present to the academic community this new *Study Edition* of the *Church Dogmatics*. Its aim is mainly to make this major work available to a generation of students and scholars with less familiarity with Latin, Greek, and French. For the first time this edition therefore presents the classic text of the translation edited by G. W. Bromiley and T. F. Torrance incorporating translations of the foreign language passages in Editorial Notes on each page.

The main body of the text remains unchanged. Only minor corrections with regard to grammar or spelling have been introduced. The text is presented in a new reader friendly format. We hope that the breakdown of the *Church Dogmatics* into 31 shorter fascicles will make this edition easier to use than its predecessors.

Completely new indexes of names, subjects and scriptural indexes have been created for the individual volumes of the *Study Edition*.

The publishers would like to thank the Center for Barth Studies at Princeton Theological Seminary for supplying a digital edition of the text of the *Church Dogmatics* and translations of the Greek and Latin quotations in the original T&T Clark edition made by Simon Gathercole and Ian McFarland.

London, April 2010

HOW TO USE THIS
STUDY EDITION

The *Study Edition* follows Barth's original volume structure. Individual paragraphs and sections should be easy to locate. A synopsis of the old and new edition can be found on the back cover of each fascicle.

All secondary literature on the *Church Dogmatics* currently refers to the classic 14-volume set (e.g. II.2 p. 520). In order to avoid confusion, we recommend that this practice should be kept for references to this *Study Edition*. The page numbers of the old edition can be found in the margins of this edition.

CHURCH DOGMATICS

For further resources, including the forewords to the original 14-volume edition of the *Church Dogmatics*, log on to our website and sign up for the resources webpage: http://www.continuumbooks.com/dogmatics/

KARL BARTH
CHURCH DOGMATICS

VOLUME III

THE DOCTRINE
OF CREATION

§ 48–49

THE CREATOR AND HIS CREATURE I

EDITED BY
G. W. BROMILEY
T. F. TORRANCE

t&t clark

Published by T&T Clark

A Continuum Imprint

The Tower Building, 11 York Road, London, SE1 7NX
80 Maiden Lane, Suite 704, New York, NY 10038

www.continuumbooks.com

Translated by G. W. Bromiley, J. W. Edwards, O. Bussey, Harold Knight, J. K. S. Reid, R. H. Fuller, R. J. Ehrlich, A. T. Mackey, T. H. L. Parker, H. A. Kennedy, J. Marks

British Library Cataloguing-in-Publication Data
A catalogue record for this book is available from the British Library

ISBN13: 978-0-567-16427-8

Typeset by Interactive Sciences Ltd, Gloucester, and Newgen Imaging Systems Pvt Ltd, Chennai
Printed and bound in Great Britain by CPI Antony Rowe, Chippenham, Wiltshire

CONTENTS

§ 48–49

THE DOCTRINE OF PROVIDENCE, ITS BASIS AND FORM

The doctrine of providence deals with the history of created being as such, in the sense that in every respect and in its whole span this proceeds under the fatherly care of God the Creator, whose will is done and is to be seen in His election of grace, and therefore in the history of the covenant between Himself and man, and therefore in Jesus Christ.

1. THE CONCEPT OF DIVINE PROVIDENCE

We have dealt with the work of creation as such in the first part of the doctrine of creation, and with man as the creature of God in the second. In this third part we now compare and contrast the Creator and the creature. We thus take up the doctrine of what is called providence, *de providentia Dei*[EN1]. Mediaeval scholasticism treated it as part of the doctrine of the being of God. Post-Reformation dogmatics brought it into very close relation with the doctrine of creation. We follow the latter tradition, and our first question is how far it is correct and meaningful to take this course.

By "providence" is meant the superior dealings of the Creator with His creation, the wisdom, omnipotence and goodness with which He maintains and governs in time this distinct reality according to the counsel of His own will.

The word "providence" requires clarification. It is derived—and this derivation is materially important—from Genesis 22[14], [8]—the passage in which Abram called the spot where he had been prevented from offering up Isaac, and where God's path and man's had so unexpectedly crossed, Jehovah-Jireh, in remembrance of Isaac's question concerning the lack of a burnt offering and his own answer: *Elohim jireh*[EN2], or, according to the Vulgate: *Deus providebit*[EN3]. This text gives us exegetical reasons for avoiding the view that providence means only foreknowledge. It is no *nuda et otiosa rerum praescientia et cognitio, sed actuosa et efficax rerum omnium*[EN4] (Bucanus, *Instil, theol.*, 1605, 14, 2). In this passage "to see" really means "to see about." It is an active and selective predetermining, preparing and procuring of a lamb to be offered instead of Isaac. God "sees to" this burnt offering for Abraham. A

[EN1] on the providence of God
[EN2] God will see
[EN3] God will provide
[EN4] bare and passive foreknowledge and understanding of events, but active and efficacious with
   respect to all things

modern term like the German *Vorsehung*[EN5] needs to be expressly filled out in relation to the unity of the divine knowing, willing and acting. In earlier German *providentia*[EN6] was more strongly and accurately translated as *Fürsehung*[EN7] (e.g., in *Qu.* 28 and 29 of the *Heidelberg Catechism*). For the world, for men and for the Church God sees to that which in their earthly lot is necessary and good and therefore planned and designed for them according to His wisdom and resolve. And as He does so, He cares for them, and therefore sees to the fulfilling of His own purpose for them and to His glory in face of them. The proposal of the Saxon theologian S. F. N. Morus (1789) to use *procuratio*[EN8] instead of *providentia*[EN9] showed a correct appreciation. The "for" does, of course, include the fact that the eternal God does basically see "before" His temporal creatures what they at best can only see afterwards, as in verse 13 of this passage Abraham saw the ram. In view of this active meaning of the word, it may be asked why *praedestinatio*[EN10] should not be preferred to *providentia*[EN11]. There was a certain tendency to do this in the older Reformed theology: *utroque nomine idem significatur*[EN12] (A. Heidanus, *Corp. Theol. chr.*, 1686 I, 347). But the difference in content between predestination, election, the covenant and its history on the one hand and providence, i.e., the preservation and overruling of the creatures as such on the other, should not be obliterated, even linguistically. Predestination is more than a special example of the general divine government of the world. It is not a *quaedam pars providentiae*[EN13] (Thomas Aquinas, *S. theol.*, I, *qu.* 23, 1c). Nor can we accept the statements of Zwingli: *Est autem providentia, praedestinationis veluti parens … Nascitur praedestinatio … ex providentia, imo est ipsa providentia*[EN14]. (*De vera et falsa religione, Sch. u. Sch.* III, 282f.). Predestination is rather the presupposition, and its fulfilment in history the constitutive centre, of God's overruling, and the basis and goal of its realisation. In predestination we certainly have to do with the creature under God's lordship, but with the creature, i.e., man, as the object of the original, central and personal intention of God, with man as the partner in the covenant of grace made by God in and with creation. In providence, on the contrary, we have to do with the creature as such and in general; with God's active relation to the reality created by and therefore distinct from Himself. For this reason it is better not to use *destinare* but *videre* or *curare*, both of which stress the reality of the distance between the Creator and His creation, and emphasise the reality of the latter. The only thing is that if we keep the word *providere* we must remember that this is the divine seeing, and therefore we must not interpret it except as filled out in that dynamic and active sense. It has been simply defined in this purified and fuller sense as ἡ ἐκ θεοῦ εἰς τὰ ὄντα γενομένη ἐπιμέλεια[EN15] (John Damascene, *Ekdos.*, 2, 29), or God's *cura rerum creatorum*[EN16] (Quenstedt, *Theol. did. pol.*, 1685, I, 13, sect. I, th. 5); and more fully as *actualis et temporalis omnium et singularum rerum, quae sunt et fiunt iuxta decretum Dei aeternum immutabile et liberrimum conservatio, directio et deductio ad finem ab ipso*

[EN 5] lit. "seeing things ahead of time"
[EN 6] providence
[EN 7] lit. "seeing to things"
[EN 8] provision
[EN 9] providence
[EN10] predestination
[EN11] providence
[EN12] both terms mean the same thing
[EN13] a particular part of providence
[EN14] For providence is, as it were, the source of predestination … Predestination is born … of providence, and, indeed, is providence itself
[EN15] the care God has for existing things
[EN16] care for created beings

determinatum sapientissime et justissime facta ad ipsius gloriam[EN17] (*Syn. pur. Theol. Leiden*, 1624, *Disp.*, 11, 3), or as *aeterna et omnipotens illa Dei vis seu voluntas, quae juxta aeternum decretum de rebus in tempore futuris se exerit, ut ilia, quae apud Deum constituta sunt, ita existere faciat, sicut Deus voluit et porro conservet, quamdiu decrevit, et gubernet, dirigat et ordinet in fines a se constitutos ad suam gloriam*[EN18] (A. Heidanus, *l.c.*, 348).

Our first task is to see why we cannot follow the example of the Scholastics and treat the subject denoted by this word, like predestination, in the context of the doctrine of God. On this point it is to be observed that in predestination it is a matter primarily and properly of the eternal election of the Son of God to be the Head of His community and of all creatures. It is a matter of the divine resolve and action, of the eternal decree, which does not presuppose the act of creation and the existence of creatures, but is itself their presupposition. And it is a matter of the eternal decree without which God would not be God, i.e., the God who reveals Himself to the Christian Church in the witness of Holy Scripture, and is known and attested by it. He is either the gracious God of this eternal choice, or He is not this God, the true God, at all. Providence, however, belongs to the execution of this decree. It is eternal, divine providence to the extent that it is grounded in this decree. But it presupposes the work of creation as done and the existence of the creature as given. It is God's knowing, willing and acting in His relation as Creator to His creature as such. We cannot, of course, develop the doctrine of God's being and perfections, or the doctrine of predestination, without referring constantly to this relationship, because God's being and the decree of His election of grace are revealed to us only in this relationship. But we cannot import this relationship into the being of God as though the creature too were eternally in God. The root of the doctrine of predestination is to be found in the being of God. But the doctrine of providence has no corresponding root of which this may be said. On the presupposition of the finished work of creation and the given existence of the creature we can certainly say that as Creator God would be untrue to Himself in His relationship with His creature without the knowing, willing and acting described in the doctrine of providence. But He would be no less God even if the work of creation had never been done, if there were no creatures, and if the whole doctrine of providence were therefore irrelevant. Hence there can be no place for this doctrine in that of the being of God. [005]

This is the objection which we have to bring against the presentation of Peter Lombard and Bonaventura among the Scholastics. Bringing together the being and perfections of

---

[EN17] the active, temporal process whereby God to His own glory preserves, directs and leads all things (which have been formed and exist by God's eternal, immutable and utterly free decree), both individually and collectively, to that end which has been most wisely and justly determined by Him

[EN18] that eternal and omnipotent power or will of God, which operates according to [God's] eternal decree concerning events in future time, and by which God makes those things which have been ordained by Him to exist just as He has willed, then preserves them for as long as he has decreed, and rules, directs and orders them to the ends determined by Him to His glory

God and His providence, they obscure the fact that the being of God does not intrinsically and necessarily include God's knowing, willing and acting in relationship to His creature. They obscure this the more because, like Thomas, they treat the election of grace, the mark of the being of the biblical and true God, as only a particular form of this general providence. Thomas Aquinas was obviously trying to avoid obscuring this when in the context of the doctrine of God he dealt only with what was later called the doctrine of providence in the narrower sense (*S. theol.*, I, *qu.* 22), i.e., a doctrine of the *ratio ordinandorum*[EN19] eternally to be found in God, returning at a much later point (*qu.* 103f.), in direct conjunction with the doctrine of creation, to the corresponding real knowledge, will and action of God, the *gubernatio rerum in communi.*[EN20] This division of the problem is still to be found in a modern Roman Catholic dogmatics such as that of F. Diekamp. But it has been tacitly dropped in the works of J. M. Scheeben, J. Pohle and B. Bartmann. It is not really of any avail. For even an eternal *ratio ordinandorum*[EN21] cannot be described without this entailing a description of the relationship of the Creator to a creature (even if only future), and the consequent integration of this creature in the being of God. Even Thomas could not avoid this either at the first point or the second. This *ratio ordinandorum*[EN22] could belong to the being of God Himself only if it not merely did not compete but was radically identical with the election of grace in Jesus Christ, the election of grace being understood as this *ratio*[EN23], the root of the doctrine of providence. That this is the case is what has actually to be said of this relationship. But for this very reason there can be no place in the doctrine of the divine being for a doctrine of providence above or even alongside that of the election of grace. Like the doctrine of creation, and together with it, that of providence describes an outer and not an inner work of God. Like the doctrine of creation, and together with it, it rests on the doctrine of the *opus Dei internum*[EN24] which as such, while it is an *opus ad extra*[EN25] as decree, belongs to the being of God and is identical with it, i.e., on the doctrine of God's eternal election of grace.

But we have also to show positively how far it is actually connected with the doctrine of creation. And first it is only proper that we should see and maintain the difference between the two concepts. The work of creation, the positing of the reality distinct from God, its summoning forth from nothing to appropriate creaturely being, is a once-for-all act, not repeated or repeatable, beginning in and with time and ending in it. That the creature is, presupposes this finished act in all the temporal developments, extensions and relationships of this being, in all the individual forms of the creaturely world and in all the historical manifestations and modifications of its existence. It also presupposes a further action of God, namely, His activity in providence. But it does not presuppose further acts of creation. As distinct from creation, providence is God's knowledge, will and action in His relation to the creature already made by Him and not to be made again. Providence guarantees and confirms the work of creation. And no creature could be if it did not please God con-

---

[EN19] ground of those things which have been ordained
[EN20] ruling of things in general
[EN21] ground of those things which have been ordained
[EN22] ground of those things which have been ordained
[EN23] reason
[EN24] internal work of God
[EN25] work outside of God

tinually to confirm and guarantee and thus to maintain it. This does not mean, however, that He continually creates it afresh. It is presupposed that the work of creation is done, and done perfectly, and therefore concluded. What follows this unique act is first and decisively the history of the covenant which is the meaning, basis and goal of this act. It is the execution of the eternal decree of God's eternal election of grace. This is the occurrence which can be called a new creation in Gal. 6^{15} and 2 Corinthians 5^{17}. But this new creation belongs to the order of the reconciliation with God of a world in need of reconciliation. It is not a repetition of the first creation. It transcends it by a distinct and radical alteration and even transformation of the creature in which its existence as such is presupposed but not re-established. A second thing which follows that unique act, however, is the rule of divine providence which accompanies, surrounds and sustains the history of the covenant, the fulfilment of divine predestination, as what we may and must call a second history strictly related to the first and determined by it. Its necessity rests on the fact that the creaturely partner in the covenant of grace is not merely this but also a mere creature needing creaturely life, and therefore its Creator, and therefore that the Creator should manifest Himself as such, as its Lord, Preserver and Governor. If the covenant is the internal basis of creation (Gen. 2), creation is the external basis of the covenant (Gen. 1). From the second of these statements, and therefore from Genesis 1, we can see the necessity of this second history accompanying, surrounding and sustaining the first, and therefore the necessity and meaning of divine providence. The history of the covenant which follows creation also needs an external basis. Its external basis is the sway of divine providence. This does not repeat or continue creation. It corresponds to it in the continued life and history of the creature, proving the faithfulness which its Creator wills to maintain and does maintain in relation to it. Why? Because at its head, in man, the creature is the partner in His covenant, elected by His grace in Jesus Christ. Because it continually needs Him as Creator, and His action (in correspondence to the act of creation) as a confirmation of the external basis of the covenant. Because He is resolved and able and ready to meet this need. [007]

The most important biblical representation of the relationship but also the difference between creation on the one side and the covenant and providence on the other is the account of the seventh day of creation which concludes the first creation saga (Gen. 2^{1-3}, cf. *C.D.*, III, 1, pp. 213–228). "Thus," we read, i.e., with the fact that on this day God rested from all His work, "the heavens and the earth were finished." The fact that God rested means that He did not continue His work of creation. He was content with the creation of the world and man. He had planned and had now accomplished this and not another work, completing and concluding it with the creation of man. The Creator-God of the Bible is not a world-principle developing in an infinite series of productions. His freedom is demonstrated in the fact that His creative activity has a limit appointed by Himself, and His love in the fact that He is content with His creature as a definite and limited object, and has addressed Himself only but totally to it as such. To this extent the seventh day implies a break between the work of creation and all the divine work which follows—a break which we must not forget when we consider the relationship between Creator and creature. It is tempting to think that creation and providence (especially from the standpoint that the former entails the preservation of the creature) are necessarily identical *realiter, respectu Dei*[EN26], providence being only a *continuata rerum creatio*[EN27] (A. Heidanus, I c, p. 348). *Utraque enim dicit eandem Dei voluntatem seu iussionem, per quam res existunt et esse perseverant; atque eundem habet terminum nempe ipsum esse rerum*[EN28] (F. Burmann, *Syn. Theol.*, 1671 I, 43, 12). *Est enim respectu Dei eadem actio creatio et providentia, cum Deus per unicam simplicissimam voluntatem omnia operetur, ut existant, in existentia permanent et operentur*[EN29] (J. Braun, *Doctrina foederum*, 1692, I, 2, 12, 4, quoted from Heppe, *Dog. d. ev. ref. Kirche*, ed. 1935, p. 204). But this view was not so important in the older Reformed theology as Heppe maintains. Calvin did not know it, and even in the presentations of later writers it does not play any very striking, let alone a dominant role. Systematised and posited absolutely, it could only be harmful to Christian perception in this matter. It would force us to choose between not understanding creation as genuine *creatio* (*ex nihilo*)[EN30] in view of providence, and regarding providence as a series of pure creative acts in view of creation. It is true enough that creation and providence, like all the works of God, are one in their divine origin. But in God there is multiplicity and fulness as well as unity, and these are not *realiter* mutually exclusive antitheses, just as God's eternity does not exclude but includes time. Hence we do not violate the dignity of God, but properly regard it, if without denying their unity in the divine will we accept the real difference between creation and providence as seriously demanded by Gen. 2^{1-8}. In creation we have to do with the establishment, and in providence with the guaranteeing and determination, of the history of creaturely existence by the will and act of God. If the one God wills and does both, we must not say that He wills and does the same thing in both cases. We must not interpret providence as *continuata creatio*[EN31], but as a *continuatio creationis*[EN32]. The very passage in Gen. 2^{1-3} which demands a break impressively reveals this continuity and real connexion. That God rested on the seventh day, and therefore in the time created by Him, like a workman on holiday when his work is done, means that in His pure deity—and this is the crown of His work of creation and the sign of the continuation of this work on very different lines—He wholly identifies Himself with the world and man, willing to be fully immanent even in His transcendence. He has made this final day and act of the history of creation an element in His own life-act. He willed to co-exist as Creator with His creature. He has given Himself to be one with him in all the majesty of His freedom and love. And this final day in the history of creation, on which God did not make anything new, but in resting did the greater thing of giving Himself to be one with the creature in all His majesty—this seventh and last day was the first of the finished creature, and above all the first in the life of the man created on the sixth day. With this day there thus begins within the history of creation the history of the covenant, the fulfilment of the eternal election, and in connexion with this, and determined by it, this second history, the history of the general encounter and co-existence of God the Creator with the reality created by Him, the sway of divine providence.

[008]

[EN26] in reality, with respect to God

[EN27] continued creation of things

[EN28] For both terms refer to the same will or command of God, by which things both come to be and preserve their being; and each has the same import with respect to the essential being of things

[EN29] For with respect to God creation and providence are the same action, since God effects all things through a single and utterly simple act of will: both that things come into existence, and that they remain in existence and perform their proper function

[EN30] creation (from nothing)

[EN31] continued creation

[EN32] continuation of creation

1. The Concept of Divine Providence

Creation and providence are not identical. In creation it is a matter of the establishment, the incomparable beginning of the relationship between Creator and creature; in providence of its continuation and history in a series of different but comparable moments. In creation we see particularly the difference of the nature, position and function of the Creator on the one side and the creature on the other; in providence their reciprocal relationship, the address of the Creator to the existence of His creature on the one side, and the participation of the creature in the existence of its Creator on the other. The act of creation takes place in a specific first time; the time of providence is the whole of the rest of time right up to its end. Creation has no external basis apart from the free will and resolve of God, and no internal apart from the mystery of the election of grace in the divine being itself; providence has its basis not only in God's unconditioned freedom and decision and the mystery of His election of grace, but also externally in the presupposed being of the creature and internally in its neediness in relation to the Creator.

Yet we cannot speak of the difference between these two works of God without also drawing attention to their relationship. Those who sought to equate them were right to the extent that in both we have to do with the same sphere of divine action and Christian knowledge. In both, as distinct from the doctrine of God on the one side and that of reconciliation on the other, we have to do with the relationship between Creator and creature as such. In both we have to do with the unconditional lordship of the will and Word of the Creator [009] over the creature—a lordship which in both cases has its meaning in the divine election and covenant as its final secret and basis. If we cannot identify them, we cannot separate them. We cannot think of the one without the other. And the obvious reason for this is that the one does not occur without the other.

It would be a weak and poverty-stricken concept of providence which did not rest on the presupposition that the One who sees and cares for the creature is also its Creator, so that it is not to Him an alien other but His own work and most original possession for which He knows that He is directly responsible and which stands unconditionally at His disposal.

Credibile non esset curari a Deo res humanas, nisi esset mundi opifex[EN33] (Calvin, *Instit.*, I, 16, 1). The *curare* envisaged in a serious concept of providence is a radical one in the strict sense appropriate to it. It embraces its object, namely, the continuation and history of human reality, and indeed all the reality distinct from God, in every respect and throughout its whole range. If this concept is to be credible, the One who provides and cares must be the One in whom this reality has its absolute origin. It cannot be self-grounded. It must be creature. And it cannot be the creature of another. It cannot be the product of a third and alien principle. It must be the creature of the One who is its *curator*. We have not yet said with what right and necessity we have to reckon with a strict concept of providence and therefore this serious and radical *curare*. But if this is the case, we can accept the dictum of Calvin that it belongs to the concept of providence to be preceded and accompanied by that of God's

---

[EN33] That human affairs are governed by God would not be a credible proposition if God were not the maker of the world

7

creation, and to receive its meaning from it. The power of the *Deus providebit*[EN34] is that of the *Deus creavit*[EN35].

In Christian dogmatics, however, the primary emphasis has always and rightly been laid upon the opposite truth that He would obviously not be the Creator who, having willed and made the creature, left it to its own devices, and did not act towards and with it, or ceased to do so, in the sense of the concept of providence, as its Preserver and Ruler. The theological concept of Creator and creating, of creation and creature, must be kept in view. God the Creator must not be equated with a mere manufacturer, or His work with a manufactured article. The man who makes something, however noble, talented or powerful he may be, can easily leave what he makes to itself, and the more easily the more perfect it is. But the Creator cannot do this in relation to His creature. Between Creator and creature in the sense of biblical theology there is a connexion which makes it impossible for the Creator to leave His work to itself, and makes immediately necessary the reality and knowledge of a second action of the Creator following the first, i.e., His action in the sense of the concept of providence. In no sense is God a creature in Himself. He has in Himself absolutely nothing of the nature of a creature. He does not need a creature to be perfect in Himself. Alongside and apart from Him there can be nothing like Him with its origin, meaning and purpose in itself. Yet on these

[010] strict conditions of His own being this God posits Himself as Creator, and apart from and alongside Himself He posits the creature, a reality distinct from Himself. This God who confronts His creature with such transcendence obviously stands, in respect of its continuation and history, in a relationship which could only be contingent and possibly alien to a supreme being or demiurge. The majestic freedom in which the relationship of Creator and creature is grounded is the guarantee of its preservation. The eternity of God is the pledge that He will give it time so long as He wills. The conclusion is compelling when we add that this Creator is the God to whose being there belongs that eternal election of grace, that *decretum internum ad extra*[EN36] which characterises the concept of God in biblical theology, on the basis of which the covenant of the Creator with His creature is the meaning of its creation, and in virtue of which the creature has attained its reality and entered its existence with the promise of the faithfulness of God, and may thus look forward to continued existence.

"Thou hast granted me life and favour, and thy visitation hath preserved my spirit" (Job 10[12]). Calvin was thus right to begin his exposition of the doctrine of providence (*Instit.*, I, 16, 1) with the assertion that Christian thinking on the Creator is distinguished from profane by the fact that to it the presence of the divine *virtus*[EN37] is no less evident in the continuance of the world than its origin, as opposed to the cold and lifeless notion of a

---

[EN34] God will provide
[EN35] God created
[EN36] internal decree with respect to that which is outside of God
[EN37] power

momentaneus creator, qui semel duntaxat opus suum absolverit. Nisi ad providentiam eius usque transimus, nondum rite capimus, quid hoc valeat, Deum esse creatorem: utcunque et mente comprehendere et lingua fateri videamur … nec quisquam serio credit, fabricatum esse mundum a Deo, quin sibi persuadeat operum suorum curant habere.[EN38]. Similarly, J. Gerhard opened his *Locus de Providentia* (*Loci theol.*, 1610f., VI, 1) with the delimitation: *Creator omnium Deus non discessit ab opificio a se condito, sed omnipotentia sua illud adhuc hodie conservat et sapientia sua omnia in eo regit ac moderatur*[EN39]. And he adduced as his first text Jn. 5^{17}: "My Father worketh hitherto, and I work"; then Ac. $17^{24f.}$: "God that made the world and all things therein, seeing that he is Lord of heaven and earth … giveth to all life, and breath, and all things"; then Ps. $121^{2f.}$: "My help cometh from the Lord, which made heaven and earth. He will not suffer thy foot to be moved: he that keepeth thee will not slumber. Behold, he that keepeth Israel shall neither slumber nor sleep." Other sayings quoted by many in this connexion are Heb. 1^3: "Upholding all things by the word of his power," and Col. $1^{16f.}$: "For by him were all things created … and he is before all things, and by him all things consist," and (like Jn. 5^{17}) both are more important for the inner establishment of this matter than was perceived in the older Protestant theology.

This theology was primarily directed against Epicurus and his school, the "swine of the herd of Epicurus" as they were called in the clear and amiable language of the time. Epicureanism, like Stoicism, was a form of antique philosophy which had been brought back into discussion by the Renaissance. The positive point at issue could be particularly well made in this antithesis because, while the Epicurean system allowed the existence of gods, its denial of a divine πρόνοια[EN40] governing the world involved at once and quite logically a denial of creation. According to Epicurus and his followers, the world, or rather the plurality of worlds, is a free play and interplay of atoms existing from all eternity, with no need of a superior Creator or Ruler even in the form of a fate or destiny, as was strongly emphasised in opposition to the Stoics. In the spaces between the different worlds gods do exist. Formed of the finest atoms, they are like men, but with a supreme excellence and distinction, and [011] therefore to be worshipped. But it belongs to their perfection that they are ceaselessly happy in and amongst themselves. They are free of all strivings and obligations (ἀλειτούργητοι), and therefore quite unconcerned about the rest of the world, and especially the world of men. It would be beneath their dignity to be otherwise, and the innumerable contingencies of the world-process, and especially the evils which are so inconsistent with their nature, prove that they have no part in the affairs of the world and man whether by way of creation or control. From this consistently "liberal" view we can indeed see clearly that where there is no Creator, where there are only gods of this calibre, there is no Lord, Governor and Provider, and *ex opposito*[EN41] that the real Creator, the God to whose being in majesty there belongs also His *decretum internum ad extra*[EN42], is as such necessarily the Lord and Governor and Provider as well.

The more perspicacious of the older Protestant polemicists like A. Heidanus (*l. c.*, p. 350f.) thought it right to mark off themselves no less from the theology and cosmology of

---

[EN38] momentary creator, who has left off his work once and for all. If we do not reach the idea of God's providence, we do not yet rightly grasp what it means to say that God is creator, however much we may appear to understand in the mind and explain with the tongue … and no one seriously believes that the world was made by God unless he is persuaded that God continues to have care for His works

[EN39] God, the creator of all things, has not abandoned the work He established, but by His almighty power preserves it to this day and by His wisdom rules and guides all things in it

[EN40] foreknowledge, providence

[EN41] contrariwise

[EN42] internal decree with respect to that which is outside of God

Aristotle. For him the world is eternal and there can thus be no question of a creation. What then is his deity, his prime mover which is itself unmoved, his immaterial form, his actuality unburdened with potentiality, his reason which thinks itself (and therefore the best)? Does this πρῶτον κινοῦν EN43 move otherwise than as the principle and exemplary model of all other movement? Does it move otherwise than as the good and goal which has no other goal beyond itself, towards which everything else strives in virtue of the attraction which everything loved (and this unconditionally as the perfect and the imperfectly loved) exercises on that which loves, on which therefore everything depends and towards which everything must move? Does it even move, asks Heidanus, as a captain moves his ship, a conductor his choir or a field-marshal his troops? Is this prime mover of all things more and other than the law, the eternal *prius* EN44, of their movement? That in which alone the Aristotelian world-principle would resemble the God of the Christian doctrine of providence is obviously the freedom of will and movement, the sovereignty and above all the inner self-determination of a God who confronts the world as its Creator and can thus approach its movement independently and determine it from without. But since the Aristotelian mover of all things is not their Creator, it is necessarily too exalted (or from the standpoint of the Christian doctrine of providence too poverty-stricken) to be capable of this movement in relation to the reality distinct from it. The Aristotelian cosmos has a kind of god ordering it, unlike the Epicurean. But since this god is not the Creator of his cosmos, since he is not above but in it (thus finally resembling the Epicurean gods), the Aristotelian cosmos is also in fact one which is abandoned by God. The older Protestant theology was right to treat Aristotle as an adversary in this respect, and we can only wish that it had freed itself more basically and radically and generally from the spirit of this picture of god and the world, and the argumentations dictated by it.

More difficult was the discussion with those who held the view that there was indeed a creation and a divine Creator, but who like the Epicureans, although for different reasons, could not agree that this Creator had any further interest in the world which He had made. This is the view which since the 18th century has been known as Deism. According to Augustine's polemical representation (*De Gen. ad Lit.*, 4, 12), God is supposed to have acted like an architect who once he has erected and finished a house leaves it for good, and is no longer needed—the less so, the better his work. To be sure, God is more than an architect, and His creature rather different from a house which is of no further interest to Him. Yet in terms of this picture it might not unreasonably be asked why this should not be a true picture of the relationship between Creator and creature. Thomas Aquinas (*S. theol.*, I, *qu.* 104, *art.* 1, *vid.* 2) saw the force of the argument that it belongs to the perfection of a divine Creator and His work that it should be made in such a way that it no longer needs Him but can continue in motion *sua operatione cessante* EN45. For the mechanically minded 18th century a clock assembled, wound and started once and for all was the perfect work, and God was thus compared to a great clock-maker whose work exalts its maker by no longer needing him. But even the finest clock can obviously run down, and so an ingenious thinker formulated the argument as follows (according to D. F. Strauss, *Chr. Glaubenslehre*, 1841 Vol. II, 354f.): "The praise which would be accorded the human inventor of a *perpetuum mobile* EN46 is won by God only if in creation He has given the world the ability to maintain itself in motion."

The argument falls to the ground for three reasons. First, it overlooks the fact that a

[012]

EN43 first mover
EN44 presupposition
EN45 once His activity has ceased
EN46 machine capable of perpetual motion

creature independent of the Creator and maintaining itself in life and movement would no longer be His creature but a second God. It thus ascribes to God the absurdity that He can and must cease to be the one and only God. Second, it overlooks the fact that it not only belongs to the nature of the creature, but constitutes its true honour, not merely occasionally but continuously to need and receive the assistance of God in its existence. Third, it overlooks the fact that the existence of even the most perfect creature is not an end in itself, but stands under a determination in relation to its Creator whose meaning is established and conditioned by the further dealings of the Creator towards and with it. In other words, the deistic argument is void because it equates the relation between Creator and creature with that between a manufacturer and his work, and decisively because it does not take into account the fact that in this relation as understood in biblical theology we have to do with the external presupposition of the covenant, which for its part is the fulfilment of the divine election of grace which is as such a denial of God's lack of concern for being outside Himself. The God with whom we have to do at this point cannot be compared with an architect, a clock-maker or even the awaited inventor of a *perpetuum mobile*[EN47]. His praise consists in the fact that He acts very differently from the way in which a human workman either does or could: *non discessit ab opificio a se condito*[EN48]. And so the praise of His creation according to the insight of biblical theology consists in the fact that it is not present as an eternally self-subsistent and self-moved cosmic nexus, whether this is understood with Aristotle as an order ruled by supreme reason or with Epicurus as a disorder comfortably ignored by the happy gods.

The simple meaning of the doctrine of providence may thus be summed up in the statement that in the act of creation God the Creator as such has associated Himself with His creature as such as the Lord of its history, and is faithful to it as such. God the Creator co-exists with His creature, and so His creature exists under the presupposition, and its implied conditions, of the co-existence of its Creator. God does this as His free will normative in its creation, and His wisdom, goodness and power therein displayed, remain the same. He does it as He is always to the creature the One He was when it did not exist and came into being, as He continually acts as such towards and with the creature which He has called to life, as He sovereignly exercises His lordship over His work and possession in new acts and revelations of His free will, wisdom, goodness and power, and therefore as He causes the history of the creature to be the history of His own glory. He does it as—far from leaving the creature to itself and its own law or freedom, its dissatisfaction or self-satisfaction—He causes it to share in His own glory, namely, by the fact that it may serve Him in His immediate presence and under His immediate guardianship and direction, thus fulfilling its own meaning and purpose, having its own honour and existing to its own joy. Hence whatever may take place in the history of the creature, and however this may appear from the standpoint of its own law and freedom, it never can nor will escape the lordship of its Creator. Whatever occurs, whatever it does and whatever happens to it, will take place not only in the sphere and on the ground of the lordship of God, not only

[013]

[EN47] machine capable of perpetual motion
[EN48] He has not abandoned the work He established

11

under a kind of oversight and final disposal of God, and not only generally in His direct presence, but concretely, in virtue of His directly effective will to preserve, under His direct and superior co-operation and according to His immediate direction. In this history, therefore, we need not expect turns and events which have nothing to do with His lordship and are not directly in some sense acts of His lordship. This Lord is never absent, passive, non-responsible or impotent, but always present, active, responsible and omnipotent. He is never dead, but always living; never sleeping, but always awake; never uninterested, but always concerned; never merely waiting in any respect, but even where He seems to wait, even where He permits, always holding the initiative. In this consists His co-existence with the creature. This is the range of the fact that in the act of making it He has associated Himself with the creature. He co-exists with it actively, in an action which never ceases and does not leave any loopholes. And so the creature co-exists with Him as the reality distinct from Him, and in its own appropriate law and freedom, as He precedes it at every turn in His freedom of action and with His work—He its Creator, who as such must no less necessarily precede it than it must follow Him as His creature, and be directly upheld by Him in its own existence, and stand under His direct and superior co-ordination, and be directly ruled by Him. Again, it is the majestic freedom of the Creator in face of His creature which is as such the guarantee of the faithfulness and constancy with which He is over and with it.

The simple lines of J. J. Schütz are thus an exact statement of this general truth:

> "That which the Lord our God did make,
> He surely will sustain;
> O'er all the way that it may take,
> His grace will always reign."

It is obvious that the deistic view of a Creator who has no further interest in the creature when He has made it is here abandoned. The notion of a mere divine *providere* can only be dropped as one which is basically atheistic. *Providentiam vocamus, non qua Deus a coelo otiosus speculetur quae in mundo fiunt sed qua mundum a se conditum gubernat: ut non unius tantum momenti sit opifex sed perpetuus moderator. Sic providentia, quam Deo tribuimus, non minus ad manus quam ad oculos pertinet*[EN49] (Calvin, *De aet. Dei praed.*, 1552, *C.R.*, 8, 347). Zwingli made the point as follows (*De providentia*, I). It would be in conflict with the concept of supreme truth, and presuppose obscurity in God, if anything that happens were concealed from Him, so [014] that He allowed it to take place blindly. It would be in conflict with the concept of the supreme power of God if He willed good for His creature, but could not procure respect for His will or guide and help things. And it would be in conflict with the concept of His goodness if He could do this but for some reason, e.g., disgust or boredom at His work, would not do so. On all these assumptions God would not be God but a kind of demon of very doubtful

---

[EN49] We mean by providence not an indolent God looking down from heaven on what is happening in the world, but God ruling the world He established, so that He is not to be understood as a craftsman who completed His work] at some particular moment but rather as the world's perpetual governor. In this way, the providence that we attribute to God pertains to the hands no less than to the eyes

qualities. But God is the highest Good, and He is the Father, the Son and the Holy Ghost, and as such the fulness of power, goodness and wisdom, and all in inseparable unity. Thus He cannot act like that demon, but acts as the sovereign and living Lord of His creature.

2. THE CHRISTIAN BELIEF IN PROVIDENCE

Belief in God's providence is the practical recognition that things are as we have said. It is the joy of the confidence and the willingness of the obedience grounded in this reality and its perception. In the belief in providence the creature understands the Creator as the One who has associated Himself with it in faithfulness and constancy as this sovereign and living Lord, to precede, accompany and follow it, preserving, co-operating and overruling, in all that it does and all that happens to it. And in the belief in providence the creature understands itself as what it is in relation to its Creator, namely, as upheld, determined and governed in its whole existence in the world by the fact that the Creator precedes it every step of the way in living sovereignty, so that it has only to follow. And in the belief in providence this does not have the character of idle speculation, just as God's providence is not the idle onlooking of a divine spectator, but takes practical shape in the fact that the creature which enjoys this recognition may always and in every respect place itself under the guidance of its Creator, recognise its higher right, and give it its gratitude and praise.

Along these lines, the particular belief in God's providence, or the one Christian faith in this particular form, became a favourite theme, as is well known, in Christian instruction, edification and not least hymnology in the 17th and 18th centuries. Paul Gerhardt was able to give it classical and unforgettably pregnant expression. The hymns of confidence and consolation in this period, or rather that which stood behind them, the trust which was wrestled for and the joy which was attained thereby, are elements in Christian faith without which this cannot exist, and to return to which, and simply to live in them, many later and supposedly more profound or more extensively occupied periods, including our own, would be only too glad. In the sense of the Gospel there can be no doubt that to believe always means with childlike directness to accept the providence of God, to rejoice in it, and to follow its governance. And it is no accident that the Reformation with its rediscovery of the all-sufficiency of the person and work of Jesus Christ, and the true divine sonship in Him of the sinful man who may cling to the grace of God and this alone, self-evidently carried with it in all its great representatives, Calvin no less than Zwingli and Zwingli no less than Luther, a kind of re-birth of the Christian belief in providence. One witness among the many which could be adduced may be quoted *in extenso*[EN50], namely, *Questions* 26–28 of the *Heidelberg Catechism*, in which, amongst other things, the connexion between creation and providence, and between these two on the one side and grace and the covenant on the other, is finely stated, and which are most instructive in respect of the other points still to be made in this introduction. [015]

[EN50] at length

13

Question 26: What dost thou believe when thou sayest: "I believe in God the Father Almighty, Maker of heaven and earth?"

Answer: That the eternal Father of our Lord Jesus Christ, who made out of nothing heaven and earth and all that therein is, and sustains and rules the same by His eternal counsel and providence, is my God and Father for the sake of His Son Christ, so that I may trust in Him, not doubting that He will care for my every need of body and soul, and turn to good all the evil that He may send me in this vale of woe, seeing that He can do this as an almighty God, and will do so as a faithful Father.

Question 27: What dost thou understand by the providence of God?

Answer: The almighty and present power of God by which He still upholds and there-fore rules as with His hand heaven and earth and every creature, so that leaves and grass, rain and drought, fruitful and unfruitful years, food and drink, health and sickness, riches and poverty and all other things do not come by accident but from His fatherly hand.

Question 28: What fruit doth it yield to know the creation and providence of God?

Answer: That we should be patient in adversity and thankful in prosperity, and that for the future we should have confidence in our faithful God and Father that no creature will separate us from His love, because all creatures are in His hand, and none can stir or move without His will.

In the light of this statement several sharp delimitations are indispensable.

1. The Christian belief in providence is faith in the strict sense of the term, and this means first that it is a hearing and receiving of the Word of God. The truth that God rules, and that the history of existent creation in its given time is also a history of His glory, is no less inaccessible and inconceivable, no less hard for man to grasp, than the truth of the origin of creation in the will and power of the Creator. In regard to the former there is as little to discover, comprehend and maintain, as little to conceive and postulate, as little room for pious or impious, practical or theoretical ventures, as there is in the latter. In both we find ourselves in the sphere of the confession which is possible only as the confession of faith or not at all. It is quickly said, and apparently easy to understand, that the history of created being takes place in every respect and in its whole range under the lordship of God. But we have only to consider one little portion of this history of created being even in outline, let alone in its concrete differentiations and details, and honesty forces us to ask whether these are not empty words. We start back from what we say, for it obviously goes far beyond what we know from our own experience and conviction, and what we can see and know and say responsibly falls far short of what is said with this confession. Indeed, it is better not to say it if in and in spite of this hesitation we do not have to say it as we confess our faith. Sincerely? Yes, if this sincerity consists in the fact that we are directed to say it by the Word of God, but not if it rests only on our own experiences and convictions. And we have only to ask how far, i.e., how little what we say with this confession squares with a corres-ponding heartfelt trust and obedience, to be honestly arrested afresh by the question whether it is not a cheap and unimpressive saying because we have never really answered it with our lives, and never will. If in spite of this more serious hesitation we do not have to say it as we confess our faith; if we do not

[016]

know that we can say it only to our own shame, it is better not to say it. In this matter, too, Christian faith begins where the sincerity of our own experiences and convictions reaches its limit with faith, where the measure of our corresponding trust and obedience obviously does not suffice, where we must completely abandon any self-confidence. It begins where we can cling only to the Word of God, where we may cling to this Word, but may do so with the indisputable certainty which is legitimate and obligatory and even self-evident when a man looks away from himself to God, when he has to do with His gift, when he makes use of the possibility which is created by the free work of the Holy Spirit within him, within his despondent heart, his foolish and fickle thoughts, his sinful life. In this faith man must say what a Christian has to say concerning the providence of God. If it is a confession of this faith, it is *eo ipso*[EN51] a solid confession, because *eo ipso* one which has reference to this objective content and derives from the revelation of this objective content.

The notion against which we have to delimit ourselves at this point is that which regards the Christian belief in providence as an opinion, postulate or hypothesis concerning God, the world, man and other things, an attempt at interpretation, exposition and explanation based upon all kinds of impressions and needs, carried through in the form of a systematic construction, and ventured as if it were a pious outlook which has a good deal in its favour and may be adopted if we ourselves are pious. We can formulate and adopt opinions, postulates and hypotheses of this type, and sometimes abandon them again. But it is important to remember that even in the form of belief in providence Christian faith is grounded on the Word of God, and can draw its life from this alone. On this basis alone can we be sure, and on this basis we must, that it is not a non-obligatory and ultimately insecure view, and that the lordship of God over the history of created being is not therefore a problem, but an objective fact which is far more certain than anything else we think we know about this history or even ourselves. We can and must understand that the knowledge of this lordship of God can be compared only to the category of axiomatic knowledge, and that even in relation to this category it forms a class apart. If the Christian belief in this lordship were a view which ultimately had behind it only the thinking, feeling, choosing and judging human subject, both it and its confession would always be unstable. But it is not such a view. It consists in a realisation of the possibility which God gives to man. It is the freedom which God Himself has given to man for God. And as such it cannot [017] vacillate. The matter itself, God's lordship over the history of creaturely being, has spoken in the Word of God as in His revelation to man, and it no longer permits him even hypothetically to think as though it were not present and this history took place under no lordship at all, or that of another. Man has not elected himself, but is elected, to believe in the lordship of God. He has thus

---

[EN51] in itself

15

no option but to believe in it, and to confess this faith. In this sense the statement concerning providence is a statement of faith. We shall have to take pains to understand and assert it as such in all its details. We shall have to avoid the temptation of slipping back from the level of faith to the level where there can be only interpretations, opinions, postulates and hypotheses which it would be difficult to establish dogmatically.

We have already recalled with admiration the belief in providence reflected in the edificatory literature and hymnology of the 17th and 18th centuries. Its witness is still impressive as given by P. Gerhardt because in him there may still be seen clearly the Reformation connexion between "Commit thou all thy griefs and ways" and the Christmas hymn "All my heart this night rejoices." But even in him are we not astounded at the extent to which the Christian subject dominates the presentation with a depiction of his own experiences and convictions of faith? What if this tendency becomes more pronounced? What if it is forgotten that belief in providence is possible only on the basis of the living Word of God, and can be confessed only in the form of an answer to its address? What if the one who believes and confesses begins to take himself more seriously and to ascribe more power to his own view of the course of events under the sway of providence? What if hesitation at the inadequacy of what we see and know in relation to what has to be believed and confessed, and at the feebleness of our faith and obedience in relation to what this reality believed and confessed must mean in our lives, quietly disappears? What if it is no longer seen that we can believe in providence only on the basis of a Nevertheless which does not spring from our own pious hearts but is forced upon us from without, i.e., that we can only *believe* in it in the strict sense? What if it gradually becomes easier and more obvious to believe in providence than in God's triunity, or the deity of Christ, or His reconciling work? What if it is no longer grasped that the former belief is identical with the latter or it is nothing? What if the former belief is preferred to the latter, and found secure by comparison? What if it is found an excellent thing that at least in respect of belief in providence we are on the same ground as tolerable heretics and enlightened pagans? What if for the sake of simplicity we finally place ourselves on the ground of this obviously general and natural religion, and regard belief in providence as in the last resort only one of the most important ingredients in this natural religion which in the last resort is alone normative and indispensable, trying to maintain, exercise and understand the belief only in this sense? This is the great apostasy which actually took place in the 17th and 18th centuries and afterwards, i.e., from an orthodoxy which lost its inward context, by way of a Pietism which exalted the Christian subject to be the measure of all things, to the Rationalism which will listen only to the human subject as such and the expression of his own opinions, postulates and hypotheses. It is no cause for surprise that in this way the belief in providence necessarily becomes pale, indistinct, shy, hesitant and impotent. What man can think in this matter has neither colour nor contour, power, constancy nor force. The confession of belief in providence, for all that it is so unassuming as in the *Heidelberg Catechism*, is genuinely alive and happy and impregnable when it refers to

[018]

the fact that God's lordship over the creature has spoken for itself in His Word, and has seized man, or rather freed him for it, in spite of all his own thinking and feeling and knowing, and all the inadequacy of his own trust and obedience. Only in these circumstances is this the case, and not when it is a so-called world-view, even a Christian world-view. For a world-view is an opinion, postulate and hypothesis even when it pretends to be Christian.

According to A. Ritschl (*Unterricht in d. chr. Rel.*, 1875, § 60) it is the glory of faith in the fatherly providence of God that it is the Christian view of things in a nut-shell. He formulated this view as follows: "In this faith we assess our momentary position in relation to the world according to our knowledge of the love of God and the resultant superiority of every child of God above the world as this is divinely led to its goal, i.e., our salvation." Every word and connexion in this statement shows that in it we really have to do with a world-view. It is palpable that it is fashioned with reference to the naturalistic and historicist positivism which dominated the cultured world in Ritschl's age. There is thus no place for the "eternal Father of our Lord Jesus Christ" as the Creator of heaven and earth in *Qu.* 26 of the *Heidelberg Catechism*, or for the almighty and present power of God sustaining and ruling heaven and earth in *Qu.* 27. Nor can there be any place for the quiet but forceful answer to *Qu.* 28: "What fruit doth it yield to know the creation and providence of God?" All that is left is a judgment of the Christian subject, or strictly not even this, but an assertion of the way in which the Christian subject actually assesses his momentary position in relation to the world in the confession of his belief in providence. According to this assertion the self-consciousness of this subject is so astonishing that what we learn concerning the believing man in the three questions of the *Heidelberg Catechism* seems feeble by comparison. Knowing the love of God, and deducing its own position from it, it finds itself above the world. It is in possession of lordship over it, as Ritschl customarily says. And the goal to which God leads the world is its own salvation as a Christian subject. It is obvious why there is so much dubious self-consciousness in this statement. If the objective matter to which the Christian belief in providence is suppressed or no longer heard; if it has become so much irrelevant metaphysics, as Ritschl believed, then obviously there remains only the believer's confession of himself. And the assurance that as a child of God he is above the world—a world which is divinely ordered in his favour—cannot really have been given with sufficient confidence. Everything now depends on himself. Hence he cannot rate himself too highly. The belief in providence can have no other certainty but this dubious self-assurance. It is weak because it is a world-view which as such can have only this certainty. For even if the believer's confession of himself—and this has still to be proved—is genuine and meaningful; even if it is at least subjectively honest, it is always marked by the property that it can go as it comes and disappear as it arises. We must take good care, therefore, not to be guilty of aberration in this direction.

2. The Christian belief in providence is also faith in the strict sense to the extent that, with reference to its object, it is simply and directly faith in God Himself, in God as the Lord of His creation watching, willing and working above and in world-occurrence. The consolation and impulse of this faith is that it points man to God in respect of the whole history of created being including his own. The man who lives by his faith may know that in everything which may happen to him he has to do with God. And beyond his own personal situation and history, as a near or distant witness and participant in all world-occurrence in all its dimensions, he may realise and count on it that God [019] Himself not only has a hand in it all, but is in the seat of sovereign rule, so that no other will can be done than His. Whatever the distance, the heights or depths, they are all bounded by the horizon that God exists as and where His creatures exist, and that His existence as such controls theirs. God's disposing is the kernel by which faith in His providence is nourished, to which it always strives and must continually return. Much may vary in the sphere of the divine disposing. In it there is a place for prosperity and adversity, victory and defeat, peril and protection, life and death, angels and demons, even human sin and human liberation. God is Lord in all these things. He is so in very different ways. But properly and in the last resort exclusively it is He who is always Lord.

And this reference to Him is the meaning and power of the belief in providence. In face of all the variations of world occurrence the trust and obedience of this belief always have Him in view as Helper, Commander, Judge and King. They look always to His mercy, holiness, faithfulness and omnipotence. Belief in providence depends on God and God alone: on God as the One who works all in all; but only on Him and on the fact that He is Lord of all.

It does not depend, therefore, on creatures and the different determinations proper to them in the world of His control, whether in detail, so that this or that good and fine and beautiful or in some way illuminating creaturely being is its true object, or as a whole, so that even though we say God we really mean creation and its life and their goodness or beauty or some other distinction. God is not creation. Neither in detail nor as a whole is He a determination of creation. To be sure, in its various determinations creation is, in the fine phrase of Luther, the mask of God, namely, to the extent that its history is also the history of the glory of its Creator. But it is only His mask and never His face, so that in it and its determinations in detail or as a whole we never have to do with God Himself. For as the history of God's glory takes place in, with and under that of creation, it is a hidden history, which is neither felt, seen, known, nor dialectically perceived by man, but can only be believed on the basis of this Word of God. We do not now speak of the divine manifestations, particularly that which fulfilled all others as the incarnation of the Word, the becoming creature of the Creator. In divine manifestation it is a matter of the establishment of faith in which the glory of God breaks through its concealment and man finds himself in direct confrontation with God. Even here the acting subject and therefore the basis of faith is God Himself and not His creaturely appearance in itself and as such. Even as the person of Jesus Christ it is the eternal Son of the Father, and only in unity with Him the man in whom this glory is revealed. Our present reference is to faith in God's more general presence and lordship in world-occurrence. Of this it falls to be said that it is real, and takes place in the world, but is concealed in world-occurrence as such, and therefore cannot be perceived or read off from this. Its revelation is not world-occurrence itself, but the Word of God, Jesus Christ. On the basis of this Word, in the freedom created by it, it may be believed, but prior to the consummation of the time of the world it can never be seen. Hence the object of the belief in providence can only be God Himself, as God Himself in His revelation in Jesus Christ is its only basis. The object of this belief cannot, then, be a creature, or any of its variable and varied determinations, instead of God. How could this belief stand if God were to it only what this or that glorious or apparently glorious creature is, or if He were only the Lord of the good and beautiful, of light and love and life, in the cosmic process, in a process which obviously stands so largely and we might often think totally under opposite determinations? If He is not the Lord in the latter. He is not in the former, and this is not the Christian belief. The Christian belief is not directed to any crea-

[020]

ture, or any modification or aspect of the creature, but to the Creator who is the Lord of His creature in all its modifications and aspects.

But this means—and here we come to the decisive point in this delimitation—that no human conception of the cosmic process can replace God as the object of the belief in providence. Man makes such conceptions. It is inevitable that he should do so, for otherwise he would not be capable of any practical orientation and decision. It is difficult to see how to forbid this. It belongs to his very life as man to do it. Every man has some conception at least of his own life and that of his nearest fellow; a picture of his own or someone else's life-work as it has so far developed and will do so, or should or should not do so, according to his insight, understanding and judgment. His particular notion of those different determinations of creaturely being, of good and evil, right and wrong, weal and woe etc., will naturally play an important part in this. Such pictures may have a wider reference. They may be pictures of the life-process of a society, e.g., the Church, or a particular form of the Church, or a nation, or group of nations, or the whole of human history. Some standards, moral or amoral, technical, cultural, political or economic, will dominate the one who forms them, leading him to assert progress or decline, formation, reformation or deformation, and determining both his assessment of the past and his expectations, yearnings and fears for the future. And such pictures, always on the same assumptions on the part of the one who forms them, may have an even wider reference. They may embrace the whole of being known to man, perhaps as a kind of history of evolution, perhaps more modestly as an analysis and description of the eternal movement of all being and its laws and contingencies, possibly including or defiantly or gaily excluding the good God, who at bottom, subject to what the one who forms them thinks concerning Him, might well be able to call some place his own within this total picture. [021] There is no objection to man making these small and great conceptions of the course of things. Indeed, there is much to be said for it. It is itself quite definitely part of the world-process, and therefore of the history of creaturely or at any rate human being, that there should always be such conceptions, which whether small or great can never be conceived as mere pictures of history, but raise the claim, and can always make it good in some depth and breadth, to shape and actually make history. Our present point is that no such conception can replace God as the object of the belief in providence. No such picture can come in question as a picture of God. The belief in providence does not rule out such conceptions. It can allow them their specific place and right as necessary expressions and media of human life. In certain circumstances it can take them very seriously. It can sometimes, transitorily and with a particular application, see its object in the similitude of such pictures. But it will realise that even in them, in the strict sense of the concept, it has to do only with the masks of God, or more accurately with the masks through which man—not without the divine appointment, will and permission—can see these masks of God, and behind which he usually hides himself from God and his fellows (under the name and pretext of an "ism"). The belief in providence embraces these conceptions, but it also limits them. It reckons with the truth which they contain. It also reckons with the distinctive dynamic with which they do not merely reflect but shape history. But it remains free in face of them. It does not rest on any of them. It cannot do this. For it is faith in God and His dominion and judgment to which all history, even that of the spirit, even that of human conceptions of human history, is wholly subject. It cannot, then, become belief in a human system of history invented by man, even when this system is the one to which the believer himself would give the preference and his heartiest approval. When a man believes, he will understand and apply even his own system, his own more or less distinct picture of history, only as a working hypothesis, and thus maintain the humility, the humour and the freedom to modify or abandon it as occasion may demand. He will treat it as an instrument which he has fashioned or taken over from others, which he uses so long as it can be used, but which he may see himself compelled and authorised to alter or to set aside and replace by another. He may give it much *fides humana*EN52, but he will not give it any *fides divina*EN53. He will be seriously convinced of its relative truth and goodness, but he will not believe in them. He will believe in God's providence, and not in his own as documented in his system. In all that follows we must beware of any aberration in this respect.

What we have to avoid is the equation of the belief in providence and its confession with a philosophy of history.

[022] To see clearly at this point, we must refer back to our first contention that the belief in providence is not an opinion, postulate, hypothesis or world-view of the believing subject, but his freedom born of the Word of God. It is as God Himself tells man that He is the Lord of history, and man hears and accepts this from God Himself, that he believes in the providence of God. He thus believes in God. To be sure, he also reads in the book of history, whether of his own life or of the narrower or wider historical contexts in which it is lived. He makes some sense of what he reads and thinks he understands there. He forms his own opinion of it. On the basis of this opinion he sees himself forced to certain postulates. He thus works with certain hypotheses. And therefore independently, or stimulated and taught by others, he fashions with some degree of comprehension and accuracy a kind of philosophy of history. Why should he not do this? Again, and rightly again, he hazards the supposition that the rule of God's providence corresponds in some degree to his philosophy of history. But he will not think that he can really read the rule of God's providence from the book (or his own little booklet) of history. He will listen to the Word of God, and not to the inner voice which suggests that he should regard this or that historical picture as perhaps the most accurate. For in the providence of God he does not have to do with a picture but with the reality of history. And in the belief in providence he does not have to do with a tenable or probable knowledge, but with the true knowledge of this reality. If he believes in the providence of God, he does not believe in himself. He does not rely on or appeal to his own eyes which he uses to read the book of history, nor the inner voice which seems to suggest the best interpretation of what he reads, but the ears which God has given him to hear His Word. He believes in God, and therefore in the voice of truth, and therefore in the revelation and

---

EN52 human credibility
EN53 divine credibility

reality of history. He believes in the divine providence itself, not in an assertion or estimation, however well-founded, of what he thinks is perhaps its previous course, or present *kairos*, or future purpose, in short its plan.

But this entails a further step. As man believes in God, even in the form of his belief in providence he can believe only in God, and only God. This object cannot be confused with any other. As no philosophy of history can be the basis of the belief in providence, none can be its object. This faith believes that God is the Lord who rules over and in all things, not that history is the unfolding of a specific process, the execution of a specific schema, the development of a specific programme. Sometimes with all seriousness we can regard it as probable that all or many things have previously come to pass in a particular interconnexion which we think we see, that they now stand in a particular crisis, and that they will develop in a particular direction. But no matter how firmly we are convinced of this, we cannot believe in it, nor live by it, nor find comfort in it. We may receive from it our penultimate, but not our ultimate and proper directives. We cannot believe, as Lessing did, in an education of the human race, played out in history, to a moral and religious rationality to be attained in time or eternity. Nor can we believe, as Hegel did, in a self-development of the absolute spirit to be realised in history and more or less attained in 1830. Nor can we believe, as Karl Marx did, in a purpose of history worked out in the clash and counterclash of the economic classes culminating in the victory and liberation of the economically oppressed. Nor can we believe, as did Treitschke and his contemporaries, in the conflict of nations which reached its most important phase with the rise of a united Germany. Nor can we believe, as did Spengler, in history as the evolution and conflict, the rise and fall, of different cultures. Nor can we believe, as did J. Burckhardt, in history as the mounting and tragic crisis of humanity, and therefore in the pathology of world history. We can think we see many of these things. We can be very seriously determined in practice by some such view. But while we may quietly or enthusiastically accept these constructs, and count on their validity, we cannot believe in them. We cannot think that to see them is to see God. The identification of the leading [023] principles of such pictures with the God of the Old and New Testaments has never been possible. On the contrary, their inventors and champions have usually been wise enough to refrain from claiming such things for them, preferring to deny this God either directly or indirectly, and to give their principles another name (or no name at all) in accordance with their character. The fact is that we cannot believe in these principles. Unfortunately we can offer them false worship as what the Bible would call alien and false gods. But we cannot really impose them upon ourselves or others. We can absolutise them. But they can never be more than relative absolutes. We cannot really rest on them. They are not capable of any genuine faithfulness or reliable direction. They have their own dynamic. But they can reign only in part and for a time (whether a thousand years or only twelve). And at bottom they can do so only in appearance. In their place and time they, too, are naturally objects of the divine providence. But they can be confused with this providence only if we have very poor sight. We may add by way of warning that all that we have said applies fully to Christian or supposedly Christian views of history constructed with the aid of the Bible, like those championed by Gottfried Arnold or J. A. Bengel.

And now we must take a third step. In faith in God's providence man will certainly consider history with very open, attentive and participating eyes. How could it be otherwise? He exists in it, and as he does so—how else?—he has to live out and exercise his faith in the ruling God, and to show his little trust and obedience. The history of created being in its great and little consequences and connexions is the sphere over and in which there takes place the mighty and penetrating sway of this ruling God. It is in it that there is fulfilled secretly but very really the history of His glory. And so the belief in God's providence undoubtedly consists in the fact that man is freed to see this rule of God in world-occurrence, this secret history of His glory. This does not mean that faith becomes sight. It will know how to separate itself from a supposed and arrogant and certainly deceptive sight. Yet this does not mean that it is blind. It would not be faith if it were not knowledge in this respect, relative, provisional and modest knowledge in need of correction, yet true and thankful and courageous knowledge. When a man believes in God's providence, he does not know only *in abstracto*[EN54] and generally that God is over all things and all things are in His hand, but he continually sees something of the work of this hand, and may continually see God's will and purpose in very definite events, relationships, connexions and changes in the history of created being. He notes in this history disposings and directions, hints and signs, set limits and opened possibilities, threats and judgments, gracious preservations and assistances. He knows how to distinguish between great and small, truth and appearance, promise and threat. He knows how to distinguish between necessary waiting and pressing on, speech and silence, action and passion, warfare and peace. He perceives always the call of the hour, and acts accordingly. He is free for this intercourse with the divine providence.

But it is not a philosophy of history which gives him this freedom. Perhaps he has such a philosophy. Perhaps he is constructing one. And we repeat that there is no reason why he should not do so. But even at best such a philosophy cannot free him for this thankful and courageous recognition of the sway of providence. On the contrary, if he were under the delusion that in it he possessed the key to this knowledge, he could only be hampered. For it would then be a serious matter that it is only his own idea and invention or that of some other man, and that as such it may serve as a non-obligatory guide, but cannot give knowledge of the ways of God. If it fills and dominates his vision, it thus blinds him to God and makes him unfit for that intercourse with His providence.

[024] No, "thy word is a lamp unto my feet, and a light unto my path" (Ps. 119[105]). Our attempts to orientate ourselves in the dark, in the great movement of the masks of God which we call history, are necessary, right and good. But when it is a matter of receiving and having light in this darkness—and faith in God's providence does receive and have light in the darkness—we are forced back upon the Word of God, and this alone is to be received. To believe is to believe only in God and only God, we have maintained. But to believe in God in this twofold sense means concretely to believe in the Word of God and to believe the Word of God. This is the light which when and as we see it shines over history and causes us to see at various points in its course the sway of the Creator, disclosing the masks of God as such. It is not the case, then, that the man who believes in providence may easily or by means of any art read the book of history and see there the ways of providence. It is the case, however, that the Word of God in which he believes, and which he believes, can as such cause him to see something of God's rule, not His universal plan or total view, but God Himself at work at various points, and always and in every respect enough to give the man's faith in Him the character of a knowledge in which he may genuinely and rightly live by his faith. It is thus the case that when and as a man accepts the Word of God he does not have to interpret the cosmic process of himself, or according to the patterns given him by others, on the basis of his own assertions and judgments of right, value or taste, but that even while he does this he may also hear the infallible voice of his Lord, and cleave to it.

In faith in God's providence what is needed is the relationship to history of which we have an exemplary form in the Old Testament prophets. What makes them prophets is not that they can rightly perceive and publicly appraise past and present and future history, but that the hand of the Lord seizes them (cf. Is. 8[11]), that He says something to them which in relation to the thoughts of their contemporaries and even their own is always new and

---

[EN54] in the abstract

strange and unexpected and even unwanted, a "burden" laid upon them (Hab. 1¹), a fire kindled and burning in them (Jer. 20⁹), even a superabounding joy filling them (Jer. 15¹⁶). It is not that they had or acquired a particular insight into the things which happened, but that these things, far from happening by chance or according to an immanent law which man could and should divine, were done by the Lord God, who does nothing "but he revealeth his secret to his servants the prophets" (Amos 3⁷). Hence it is not from history or their own view of history but into history, apart from and even against their own view, that a very definite light is given to the prophets in the form of concretely directed and fashioned perceptions which are not only clear to themselves, but have to be shown by them to others, in individual assertions, in agreements and repudiations, in threats and promises, in particular decisions, and also in more or less connected and far-ranging historical pictures. Basically and structurally this prophetic relationship to history is also that of the belief in providence. It consists in the fact that the man who is apprehended and freed by the Word of God is not without light and therefore always sees light in the obscurity of world occurrence.

It is to be noted again that this is not the light in which all things are open to God. It is not the revelation and contemplation of *the* mystery, *the* history. But it is light, and as much light as God thinks necessary and salutary for the believer in his time and place, and will therefore give him.

It is to be noted further that in the knowledge of God's providence by faith there can never be any question of speculation or theory. The seeing of the ways of God can never be an end in itself. It can never be a matter of aesthetic contemplation. It is always a matter of the practical insights necessary and salutary for man at specific points. What man can receive through the Word of God in this respect is knowledge for life. It is daily bread, manna from heaven, which must be gathered and eaten but not kept. We cannot boast of having it, or become complacent. If it is not to be given in vain, we can only live with it, stretching out our hands for a further gift that we may always have it afresh.

It is to be noted further that in this knowledge even a practical principle is not given to man in the sense of a constant programme. The continuity and consistency of this knowledge rest with God who will give it to man by His Word. It arises for man only as he listens openly and attentively to what God will say to him in His Word, not as he reduces what is already said to inflexible rules. The relationship of the Old Testament prophets to the history of their time never took the form of a programme. Hence a vitally self-renewing knowledge of faith in this matter, as its object is the faithfulness and constancy of God, can never be rigid, or clearly enough distinguished from an obstinate clinging to insights already won, a sterile repetition of a position already adopted. That history necessarily repeats itself, and that pictures once seen must be regarded as necessary to-day, is the very last thing to be expected by the man who believes in the providence of God. Hence he will not allow even a sound view of the historical process to become a strait-jacket. Indeed, he will not allow even the best view, even and especially when he believes that at the time he did not adopt it out of human caprice but in obedience to the Word of God. It will not be his concern—and in this respect the different attitudes of Luther to such problems of his age as the Turkish War, the Peasants' War and the Jewish question are formally at least important models—to try to give his view and attitude a particular character or aspect by the rigid insistence upon a certain line. He will not be ashamed if it can be shown that he once thought or spoke otherwise. The man who believes in the providence of God is distinguished from the man who does not, but rests instead upon his own prudence, by the fact that he is not too proud to be a continual learner. If he is under the instruction of the Word of God he need have no fear that his way will not finally have and show far more line and character than the ways of those who so wish to be true to themselves that they cannot really be true to God.

[025]

It is to be noted further that it belongs to this knowledge of God's providence by faith that although it refers to the infallible Word of God it is a human and, as such, a fallible knowledge. Not everything which the serious believer seriously listening to the Word of God regards as such is in fact a divine disposing and directing in history, a hint and sign of providence. He might have misunderstood what God has really said to him. We surely have such a misunderstanding when Eusebius of Caesarea, the father of Church history, saw in the emperor Constantine a second Moses, and in his kingdom a kind of definitive revelation of the kingdom of God. That he did not take this from the Word of God but his own judgment may be seen from the fact that he could make nothing of the Apocalypse, which would surely have warned him in this respect, but wanted to see it demoted from the true Canon. A similar misunderstanding arose when the great J. A. Bengel, who was much too cocksure in his understanding of the Apocalypse, thought that he could fix on 1836 as the date of the defeat of the beast from the abyss. For the rest, Bengel had so clear a vision of his time and the then future that in spite of this blunder—or accepting the fact that there could be this admixture of error—we may adduce him as an outstanding example of the fact that, even though an only too human misunderstanding of the Word of God may disturb in detail the knowledge of God's providence by faith, it cannot prevent it in general (and therefore also in detail). We have to remember that there are fruitful as well as unfruitful misunderstandings of the Word of God. If the believer's understanding is false in one respect, it is perhaps so much the better in others. And in any case it is better to misunderstand the Word of God than not to understand it at all. We may well say that not only is it no *pudendum*[EN55], but it belongs to the very best in the Old Testament, to the character of Holy Scripture as human witness to the revelation of God, that in the history of its prophecy there should obviously be some clear historical errors and prophecies either unfulfilled or fulfilled in a very different sense from that of the prophets. The lesson to be drawn for the doctrine of providence from

[026] this side of the matter can consist only in the affirmation that since man is so capable of error in relation to God it must not rest on any of its achievements. It must be free to withdraw in all its detailed insights. It must be continually ready to receive new and better instruction, and to that extent to censure itself. In short, it must be willing as a movement of knowledge to take part in the great movement of reality which is its theme, the co-existence of the Creator with His creature in which the Creator constantly increases and the creature decreases, in which the Creator always precedes and the creature can only follow. Only, but always, as it takes part in this movement is it the faith for which man is given freedom in this matter.

It is to be noted finally that in the upshot the knowledge peculiar to the belief in providence can consist in its decisive content only in the knowledge of God Himself. It is a matter of God in His quality as the Lord of all lords and King of all kings, of His world government, and therefore of the concrete knowledge related to the course of great and small world-occurrence and filled out and shaped accordingly. It is not a matter of a dead knowledge of God's lordship over all things, to which there might correspond a blindness for the details. It is a matter of the living seeing of the living Lord in the details of history. Hence it is not a theoretical seeing but a practical, not a programmatic but a free, not an infallible but one which stands in need of correction. The unconditioned and constant element in this seeing will not consist, therefore, in something that man sees in the course of the world as such, but in what he sees in the course of the world of God Himself as its Lord and Ruler. The Word of God continually places the history of creaturely being in its light in order that God Himself, who speaks to man, may be the better known by him. God Himself is what is necessary and wholesome for man. God Himself is the goal and measure of human action in the world.

[EN55] embarrassment

God Himself is the free One in face of whom man cannot entrench himself in any programme. God Himself is the true One who speaks infallibly even when man is deceived as to what He has really said. That God Himself is known as Lord is the decisive difference between the belief in providence and every philosophy of history as stated in this second delimitation.

3. We now come to the third and most important delimitation. In its substance the Christian belief in providence is Christian faith, i.e., faith in Christ. The Word of God which it believes, in which it believes and which sets it in the light in which it may see the lordship of God in the history of creaturely being, is the one Word of God beside which there is no other—the Word which became flesh and is called Jesus Christ. And the history of creaturely being is—secretly but really—the history of the glory of God in the fact that it does not merely run alongside the history of Jesus Christ and therefore the history of the covenant of grace between God and man, but has its meaning in this, is conditioned and determined by it, serves it, and in its reflected light (and shadow) is the place, the sphere, the atmosphere and medium of its occurrence and revelation.

Hence the belief in providence is not a kind of forecourt, or common foundation, on which the belief of the Christian Church may meet with other conceptions of the relationship of what is called "God" with what is called "world." The lordship of God over world occurrence which is its theme is not a general form which might have a very different content. It is not a genus comprehending not only the lordship of the Father of Jesus Christ, the God of the election and covenant of grace, but also the sway of any other deities freely selected by religion or philosophy. In virtue of its relation to what God has done once for all in Jesus Christ, it is a happening *sui generis*[EN56]. [027]

In most religious and philosophical systems there is some conception of a relationship between a higher and lower principle, an absolute, infinite, unconditioned or heavenly being and an earthly, spirit and matter, nature and reason, and of the superiority and even dominion in this relationship of the first and higher element over the second. There are, of course, exceptions. We remember the Epicureans. We can also think of older and more recent forms of scepticism and agnosticism. And we reserve the right to ask whether in many (and perhaps strictly all) the so-called polytheistic religions the relationship between the two principles is not one of ambivalence, with no radical superiority of the one over the other. What is really meant by higher and lower? There can even be different opinions, though there ought not to be, as to the priority of the absolute over the relative, spirit over matter, reason over nature. But the relationship between Creator and creature with which we have to do in the Christian belief in providence stands outside this debate. The question whether there is in this relationship a Lord, and who this Lord is, is settled before it is asked. This alone shows us that the belief does not belong to the same category as religious and philosophical systems.

If we confine ourselves to the systems in which there seems to be a certain clarity in this respect, all kinds of pantheism drop away, because the superiority and dominion of one principle over the other as presupposed in them is from the very outset without centre or

---

[EN56] in its own category

25

form. To be sure, there is a lordship. There is a regnant power which permeates and determines all things and is described as that of Godhead. But we cannot distinguish and decide who or what is this regnant Godhead on the one side and the world controlled by it on the other. There is no confrontation. The controlling element and the controlled are identical, or so fully interfused that neither can take on a definite shape or character or have a distinct history, and there can certainly be no question of a history between the two. The Christian belief in providence has also to do with a relationship in which the controlling element confronts the other with penetrative and determinative superiority. But this superiority, the omnipotence of God, has a formed and distinctive centre in which the controlling element has its own life in face of the controlled, and the controlled, the creature, has also its own life, so that the two stand in genuine confrontation and the relationship between them can and must be a history. From this standpoint the difference of view cuts so deep that we cannot possibly bring the pantheistic unity of Godhead and world and the object of the Christian belief in providence under a single denominator.

But the sharp contrast between the Christian belief and what might be compared with it in polytheistic and pantheistic systems begins at a much earlier point. Even the elements and principles whose relationship is envisaged in these systems are not what the Christian belief means by Creator and creature. They are rather antitheses within what the Christian belief would call creature. The absolute, infinite, unconditioned, and even heaven, spirit and nature are not the Creator, the ruling God, with whom we have to do in the belief in providence, but more or less clearly the one and higher side of the creaturely world, confronted in the form of another and lower side by the relative, finite and conditioned, by the earth, matter, nature. Both of them, including the first and higher principle, are determinations of what the belief in providence does not regard as God, but the reality distinct from God and controlled by Him. It is thus no wonder that there is that ambivalence of the two principles in polytheistic systems, and that it is open to discussion whether the one or the other or both

[028]

or neither is really in control. Nor is it any wonder that in pantheistic systems there can be no question of any distinction and confrontation, of any encounter and history between them. The Christian belief is not involved in this debate as to priority, and it understands the relationship of the two principles as encounter and history, because its controlling principle, i.e., God as the Creator of heaven and earth, is above this antithesis, which for it is simply played out within what is for it the controlled principle. In virtue of this very different conception of the principles in question it cannot be compared with any of these views.

But it is only in appearance that it can be compared with views which seem to take quite seriously the concept of God as the Creator and Lord who is superior to the whole world and therefore to these antitheses within it. We refer to the semi-biblical religion of post-Christian Judaism and the paganised form of this religion, Islam. Here we have a Ruler of the world and His lordship over it. Here we have the will and work of a God with known physical and moral attributes, and a history between Him and His creation. Here, at least in Judaism, we have a history of salvation as the meaning and centre of universal history. But it is a history of salvation which has not reached its goal and strives towards it in endless approximation. And the fact that Judaism refuses to know anything of a history of salvation which has reached its goal means that it cannot penetrate beyond the knowledge of a supreme being furnished with those attributes, and beyond the confession of His omnicausality. Its God and Ruler of the world has necessarily a strangely obscure and hidden character. The devout Jew is never wholly clear as to His love or wrath, His grace or judgment. And His obscure character is projected into His government of the world, which the devout Jew follows, but only with anxious and hypercritical concern to justify it, and not with the childlike confidence of the clear presupposition that He the Lord will always be in the right. Where it is not known that God has already done the right in a fulfilled history of salvation, it is impossible to attain to

26

this presupposition in respect of His rule of the world. And in Islam this obscurity of God and His rule has been made a principle and therefore a caricature. That God rules, and the creature is wholly subject to Him, and can only serve Him in the dust to win a supreme creaturely felicity, is all that now remains of the unfulfilled Jewish thought of God and the belief in His rule. Is it any wonder that in both ancient and modern times there have been so many ways which have led back to pantheism and even polytheism, and at the end of which the idea of a history between God and man is inevitably lost?

The Christian belief in providence is given its content and form, and therefore its distinction from other views apparently similar, by the fact that the lordship of God over the world which is its object is not just any lordship, but the fatherly lordship of God. And this "fatherly" does not mean only "kind" and "friendly" and "loving." It means all this, yet not abstractly, but on a specific basis. Similar attributes of the supreme ruler or principle of the world are to be found elsewhere, but only in a way which is non-obligatory, contingent and problematical. In the language of the Christian belief in providence, "fatherly" means first of all, quite apart from any such predicates and as their solid foundation, that the God who sits in government is "the eternal Father of our Lord Jesus Christ." The Christian belief does not gaze into the void, into obscurity, into a far distance, height or depth, when it knows and confesses God as the Lord of the history of created being. It really knows this God, and therefore His rule. Under our second point we have established that it knows Him as it receives His Word. But His Word is not empty. It is not the reference to a supreme being which is supposed to have certain qualities. It is He Himself. But it is He Himself in a way in which He can be accepted by man. It is His person as a human person, His Word in the flesh, His eternal Son born in time as the Son of Mary, and crucified and raised for us. This "God with us" and "God for us" is God in eternity, the Son. And no other, but this God, is also "God over us," the eternal Father of this eternal Son. In the belief in providence it is a matter of "God over us," of God the Creator in His majesty, transcendence and lordship over His creature. But God the Creator is one God. The One who is for us as the Son is over us as the Father. As God has elected to be for us in His Son, He has elected Himself our Father and us His children. We are not in strange hands, nor are we strangers, when He is over us as our Creator and we are under Him as His children. We are His children for the sake of His Son and with Him (in whom He is so really for us that He becomes ona with us). And it is as such that we are creatures in His fatherly hand. This fatherly hand is the divine power which rules the world. We can know no divine power over us, nor is there any such power, which is not this fatherly hand. As and because it is this fatherly hand, it is kind and friendly and loving. It has these qualities as the grace with which the same God who elected Himself our Father in His Son is also over us as our Creator. He is over us in a way which corresponds to this election of grace, to this eternal "for us" in His Son. Even as our Creator He is not alien or ungracious, but gracious. He is gracious as a Father to His children. And in this connexion we have to remember that the

[029]

truth of this relationship is not to be found in what might take place between a human father and his children, but in what has taken place from all eternity, and then in time, between God the Father and the Son. He is our heavenly Father, in a way which surpasses all that we can see or think. We are thus warned in advance that we cannot make what we think we know as fatherly or any other kindness, friendliness and love the measure and criterion of His. It is a matter of the eternal fatherly fidelity which we can only try to see and grasp where it is revealed to us. "He that hath seen me hath seen the Father" (Jn. 14⁹). It is here that the Christian belief in providence sees the Father, and therefore God over us, and therefore the Lord of the world-process. It is here that the will which rules the history of created being is not concealed. It looks to the history of the covenant which is fulfilled in the mission, in the person and work of the incarnate Son, of the "God for us." And through and beyond this it looks to the divine election of grace. And it thus sees the Father, the "God over us," as it sees the Son. As it sees Him it hears the Word of God, and as it hears the Word of God it receives the light on God's rule in the world [030] beside which there is no other. The light which it receives and by which it lives will thus consist always in the fact that it may there perceive not only the will of an unknown Lord, not only the lines of an order and consistence, not only the stages of a process, but the demonstration of the Lord who is our Father for the sake of His Son, of the Lord of the covenant of grace, of the God of the eternal election of grace. In very general terms this is the specific and incomparable element in the Christian belief in providence.

For this reason, we cannot equate God with a principle whose superiority and lordship over all other principles must first be discussed. This may be true of spirit as compared with matter, of reason as compared with nature, etc., but it cannot be true when "God for us," the Son, has spoken, and in this "God for us" revealed "God over us," the Father. On this basis we cannot equate God any longer with a principle which in its unity with its opposite is formless and incapable of history. This may and must happen to the Godhead of pantheism, but it cannot do so to the "Father of Jesus Christ," for His rule is essentially encounter and history with the distinct reality of the creature to which He is gracious and with which He is not therefore identical. And on this basis we certainly cannot equate God with any of the principles which are themselves only elements of the reality created by God. For if God is the God of the covenant and election of grace, this decides His being in a freedom which can only be that of the Creator as compared with that of the creature. This God is in a freedom which cannot be proper to any principle. And as the God of the Christian belief is seen in the fulfilment of the covenant between Himself and man as this has taken place in Jesus Christ; as His will is not therefore an obscure and concealed but a clear and revealed will, it is obvious that He is also different from the God of Judaism and Islam.

All these differences may now be accepted as already elucidated, and this means that we are not only not obliged but forbidden to use a non-Christian concept of God, i.e., a concept which does not rest on a Christological basis.

But we have to take note of the astonishing fact that the older Protestant theology was guilty of an almost total failure even to ask concerning the Christian meaning and character of the doctrine of providence, let alone to assert it. Even in Calvin (*Instit.*, I, 16–18) we seek in vain for a single pointer in this direction. It would be excellent if we could accept the

assurance of W. Niesel (*Die Theologie Calvins*, 1938, 66f., E.T., 1956, 71f.) that Calvin understands the doctrine of providence wholly on the basis of the revelation of God in Jesus Christ,
and in it "praises the power and goodness of the triune God who has drawn near to us in
Jesus Christ." But unfortunately I have not found this assertion supported in the very slightest by the passages which Niesel quotes. That Calvin did occasionally think along these lines
is shown by the preface to his commentary on Genesis. He there explains that Christ is the
image in which God has shown us not merely His heart, namely, His love addressed to us in
Him, but also His hand and feet, namely, His external works in the sphere of creation. And
he there warns us that if we do not keep strictly to Christ we can only be betrayed into the
wildest hallucinations in respect of these external works of God (cf. *C.D.*, III, 1, p. 31). We
find a similar gleam of light in the statement (*De aet. Dei praed.*, 1552, *C.R.*, 8, 349): *ecclesia
propria est Dei officina, in qua suam providentiam exercet et praecipuum eiusdem providentiae
theatrum*[EN57]. But surely this thought should have been worked out in *Instit.*, I, 16–18, if it
was as important as Niesel says. Such ideas did not control his own exposition, nor were they
developed in the age which followed. We recall *Qu.* 26–28 of the *Heidelberg Catechism* with
their repeated underlining of the decisive concept of the fatherliness of God and their
express Christological explanation of this concept. And what important consequences it [031]
would have had if the dogmaticians had taken seriously what is written under *Qu.* 50 (with
references to Eph. 1[20f.], Col. 1[18] and Mt. 28[18]), namely that Christ has gone up to heaven to
show Himself there as the Head of the Christian Church "by whom the Father rules all
things"! But to the best of my knowledge these are isolated texts in the 16th and 17th centuries. The orthodox Lutheran and Reformed teachers are rather at one in teaching the divine
lordship over all occurrence both as a whole and in detail without attempting to say what is
the meaning and purpose of this lordship. They understand it as the act of a superior and
absolutely omniscient, omnipotent and omnioperative being whose nature and work do of
course display such moral qualities as wisdom, righteousness and goodness, etc. But this is
all. According to the agreed doctrine of orthodoxy, this empty shell is the object of the
Christian belief in providence. It does not seem to have occurred to whole generations of
Protestant theologians to ask what this lordship has to do with Jesus Christ, and the knowledge and confession of this lordship, and readiness to subject oneself to it, with faith in the
Gospel of Jesus Christ. How does man really come to trust in this lordship? Strangely
enough, the question is not raised even by Johann Cocceius and his disciples, who in their
concern for a biblical system make the covenant and its history the basic concept in theology. The formula that this ruling activity of God takes place *ad ipsius gloriam*[EN58] is sometimes met with in Reformed and Lutherans, but when we ask what is meant by the glory and
glorification of God we receive the mere shell of an answer (cf. A. Calov, *Syst.*, III, 1659,
p. 1142): *Omnia enim operatur, ut cuncta ipsi respondeant humiliter et voluntati eius obediant, vel id
praestent, ad quod facta sunt el quae iubentur a factore suo*[EN59]. What does this imply but the
absolute exercise of the absolute will of an absolute power in an absolutely subjected sphere
of power? The meaning, goal and purpose of this action are one with the action itself. In
other words, it is its own end. The *gloria* of God consists in the fact that He is so powerful in
relation to the creature; that He asserts Himself so thoroughly. And the question what this
controlling God actually wills of His creature can be left open. To be sure, there were many
who for the sake of fulness said that the God whose lordship is in question is naturally the

---

[EN57] the church is God's own workshop, in which he administers His providence and provides a
special exhibition of this same providence
[EN58] to His own glory
[EN59] For [God] directs all things, so that everything may respond humbly to Him and obey His will,
each thing executing that [purpose] for which it was made and what it has been commanded
by its maker

29

triune God: *Deus Pater, Filius et Spiritus Sanctus*EN60. But no one thought of deducing any consequences from the Christian definition of this subject in the description of its lordship. Even in the establishment of the knowledge of God's providence there was no thought of looking in the direction of the triune God, but the usual procedure was that of F. Turrettini (*Instit. Theol. el.*, 1679, VI, 1, 3f.), who simply argued as follows. To deny providence is to deny God Himself. It is thus a *primarium caput fidei et religionis*EN61. The voice of nature and the *consensus populorum*EN62 confirm its reality. Seneca and Cicero (and according to Turrettini even Aristotle) taught it. It results from the being of God as all-knowing, all-powerful and all-good. But it also results from the being of the creature as wholly dependent on its Creator and in need of His support. It results from the marvellous harmony and order of all things, which would be unthinkable without a supreme Director; from the existence and fulfilment of so many prophecies; from the fact of the preservation and renewal of the benefit of political orders; from the occurrence of extraordinary favours and judgments including human conscience. To be sure, A. Calov (*ib.*, p. 1132) in a corresponding list maintains under 8 that God's providence may be perceived *e miranda ecclesiae et fidelium conservatione*EN63. But under 9 he then says that it may be known *e conscientiae dictamine*EN64, and under 10 *ex interno testimonio animae*EN65. He obviously had no inkling that there might be a very special relationship between the government of the world and the Church, or that the Church might occupy in this matter the central position which Calvin once sought to ascribe to it. And confidently and self-evidently the *testimonium scripturae sacrae*EN66 was normally adduced in this list, usually at the beginning and often with the explanation that it is impossible to cite

[032] all the relevant passages: *tot enim fere sunt, quod sunt scripturae paginae, quando nihil frequentius, nihil clarius in verbo Dei inculcatur*EN67 (F. Turrettini, *ib.*, 1, 5), or even more strongly: *Tota scriptura nihil aliud est, quam pellucidum speculum, e quo, quocunque te vertas, promicat pervigil ille oculus providae directionis*EN68 (D. Hollaz, *Ex Theol. acroam.*, 1707, I, 6, 5). But what it means, and how it is connected with the theme of the Bible, that it is in fact so strong a witness to God's providence, is never discussed. Allusion is simply made to John 5^17, Acts 17^24f. and some of the more impressive Psalms and chapters of Job, these being set alongside the witness of reason and the *saniores Gentiles*EN69, and nothing materially new or decisive being seen in them. The total impression is that there was a naive belief that in this matter there could be agreement with all schools (except in detail, and apart from the Epicureans, Deists and Atheists). There was no perception of the fact that a concept of God was used, and a corresponding concept of providence developed, which in its essential features could be filled out in a way very far from Christian. There was no concern as to the possible consequences—the invasion of secularism so unsuspectingly prepared by adopting in the basic understanding of the relationship between God and the world the ground of a *theologia naturalis*EN70 and even *naturalissima*EN71. There was no attempt to ask whether the Keeper of

---

EN60 God the Father, the Son and the Holy Spirit

EN61 chief cornerstone of faith and religion

EN62 agreement of the peoples

EN63 from the miracles of the church and the preservation of believers

EN64 from the dictate of conscience

EN65 from the internal witness of the soul

EN66 testimony of Holy Scripture

EN67 for truly so many are the pages of Scripture that nothing is more frequently or more clearly stressed by the word of God

EN68 The whole of Scripture is nothing else than a bright mirror, in which, wherever you turn, the ever-watchful eye of [God's] prescient righteousness is evident

EN69 more sober heathen

EN70 natural theology

EN71 absolutely natural

Israel who neither slumbers nor sleeps (Ps. 121) is really identical with this directly visible all-wise, all-powerful and all-good being and his omnicausality, or whether what is said in the Sermon on the Mount about the needlessness of anxiety and the Father who causes His rain to fall on the just and the unjust really amounts to no more than what Seneca and Cicero could say in other words.

Unfortunately the connexion between the belief in providence and belief in Christ had not been worked out and demonstrated theologically by the Reformers themselves. Only occasionally and from afar, if at all, had they seen the problem of natural theology and the necessity of a radical application to all theology of their recognition of the free grace of God in Christ. In their case, to be sure, we almost always feel and detect, even though it is so seldom palpable theologically, that when they speak of the world dominion of God they are in fact speaking with Christian content and on the basis of the Gospel, not abstractly in terms of a neutral God of Jews, Turks, pagans and Christians. And this is what gives warmth and force to the matter in P. Gerhardt. But if in him there is an unmistakeable movement away from the Word of God to the experience of the Christian subject, this was to some extent a reaction against the dominant and self-evident abstraction with which the orthodoxy of his day followed another self-evident rut in these matters. This was the rut of a general theism which, apart from the mention of the *Deus triunus*[EN72], occasional quotations from the Bible and references to Church history, lacked any distinctive Christian content, being primarily concerned to distinguish itself from atheism, and limiting its consideration of the Gospel to the establishment and development of Christology and resultant doctrines. As if this were the real way to treat that *primarium caput fidei et religionis*[EN73]!

The truth is that in this matter the older, strict and true Protestant orthodoxy was blatantly "liberal" in its life and thinking long before there was an "enlightened " orthodoxy, or orthodox Enlightenment, or what is still called Liberalism and simply consists in liberation from the constraint of faith in Christ as the one Word of God not only in matters of providence but because at this point at every point, preference being given to a resolute attachment to the views which Jews, Turks, pagans and finally Christians can have in common concerning the existence and lordship of a supreme being. It was the older orthodoxy which made possible the question whether this was not everywhere legitimate and even necessary, and suggested only too plainly the answer to those who were inclined in this direction. At this point at least the references to the Trinity, the Church and passages of Scripture had no inner necessity for the orthodox. But if they were dispensable here, why not in other respects, and finally everywhere? The whole movement which followed was inevitable, and the subjectivism of the Pietists could not arrest but only further this necessary development. It also followed that this syncretistic belief in God and providence with no specifically biblical and Christian substance inevitably proved to be inadequate even in face of the Lisbon earthquake, let alone the external and internal catastrophies of the 19th and 20th centuries. The hour had to come, and has now come, when belief in history and its immanent demons could replace faith in God's providence, and the word "providence" could become a favourite one on the lips of Adolf Hitler. It was the older, genuine orthodoxy which first open the sluices to this flood. In face of this supposedly generally apprehensible doctrine of providence the Epicureans, Atheists and finally Nihilists have always been secretly and openly the stronger.

The result of this historical survey cannot be that we should dismiss as worthless what the older Protestant theology attempted and achieved in this sphere. It is fortunately the case in theology—and the true Christian belief in providence allows and requires us to count on

[033]

[EN72] triune God
[EN73] chief cornerstone of faith and religion

this fact—that even from very dangerous presuppositions (*hominum confusione Dei providentia*[EN74]) interesting, instructive and illuminating consequences can and usually do follow. For all the strange duality of their vision in this matter, the older orthodox were seriously trying to be Christians (as were many who went much further than they did). We cannot deny this from any superior seat of better knowledge. And if not, we cannot refuse to learn from them what can be learned in spite of their dangerous presupposition. Yet the fact remains that a better knowledge of providence is needed than that which they can give us. The Christian belief in God's providence is Christian and not general, and what Christian theology has to win and teach in this matter must be a Christian and not a general perception, not an extract from what Jews, Turks, pagans and Christians may believe in concert. The God of whose lordship we speak in this matter is the Father of Jesus Christ who as such is our Father. He is not another god, and must not be confused with another, with any of the principles on the basis of which attempts have been made to describe and explain the co-existence of a freely invented higher being with an opposed and subordinate principle quite apart from the Word of God in Jesus Christ. There is no place here for vague notions of higher and lower. If the doctrine of providence is a *primarium caput fidei*[EN75]—and the older orthodoxy was right in this—it is hard to see how there can be in it any question or application of a different ontics and noetics from that which obtains in the case of sin or reconciliation, of justification or baptism. The upshot of this historical review is that in respect of the paths taken by the older orthodoxy in detail we must always note carefully whether the dangerous presupposition proves fatal or not, i.e., whether we can follow their suggestions because they are usable when taken up on a different basis, or whether they will lead us astray and must therefore be ignored.

3. THE CHRISTIAN DOCTRINE OF PROVIDENCE

Our only remaining task in this introduction is briefly to describe what is meant by a doctrine of providence which is Christian, i.e., which corresponds to Christian faith and is therefore resolutely worked out from a Christian standpoint and with Christian material.

It is quite plain what God wills as the Lord of the being created by Him, and as the Lord of its history, namely, what is the meaning and purpose, the goal [034] and therefore the glory of His lordly action. It is not plain, however, because we have lifted the veil of this history and discovered its secret. It is not plain because we have perceived, planned or determined it of ourselves. It is plain because God Himself has revealed it to us in His Word. And He has revealed it in the simple way in which He has revealed Himself—and we must take this seriously—as the triune God who as the Father is over us and as the Son for us, and both in the unity in which as the Holy Spirit He creates our life as a life under Him and again for Him. He has revealed Himself as the One who in essence is free, sovereign and omnipotent grace. He is this so certainly as He is the triune God who, even before the creature was, addressed Himself in His eternal counsel to us men and created us in order that the fulfilment of this

---

[EN74] the providence of God amid the confusion of human beings
[EN75] chief cornerstone of faith

counsel should be the covenant between Himself and us. This is the eternal glory of God revealed in His Word. This, revealed again in His Word, is His glory as Creator. And this, revealed yet again in His Word, is His glory as Lord of the history of His creature. What God wills as He works "all in all" (1 Cor. 12⁶), and what He therefore works, is that His free grace should be radiant, and take form, and conquer and rule in the creaturely world. He wills and works what He has revealed as His will and work in Jesus Christ, His Son; what is revealed in Jesus Christ as His eternal will as the Father and also His eternal and life-giving will as the Holy Spirit. He wills and works this alone, with no reservations or secret suspicions that He might perhaps be doing something very different, willing and working a plan and purpose distinct from and quite independent of His glory, of His free and omnipotent grace. And He wills and works this wholly, in accordance with His sovereign will and almighty power to do it, so that there is no cause for anxiety lest something great or small should drop out of His will and work, or be able to disrupt it. If faith in providence is Christian faith, and therefore faith in Jesus Christ as the Word of God and therefore the self-revelation of God, there is for it no obscurity concerning the nature and will and work of the Lord of history, no ambiguity concerning His character and purpose, and no doubt as to His ability to see to His own glory in this history. This is the starting-point from which we must set out and to which we must continually return in this matter if we are not to go astray.

It is strange that the older theology never thought of deducing from the much quoted John 5¹⁷ that in the question as to the meaning and goal of the ἐργάζεσθαιEN76 of God the Father we should look simply, directly and fully at the ἐργάζεσθαιEN77 of the Son which is equated with it. It is strange that Colossians 1¹⁷ (τὰ πάντα ἐν αὐτῷ συνέστηκενEN78) was constantly adduced and yet the lesson was never learned from it that all things not only have their existence (v. 16) but also their consistence, their order and continued existence, their σύστημαEN79 (v. 17), in the Son of whom it is said in v. 14 that we have in Him our redemption, the forgiveness of sins, and in v. 15 that He is "the image of the invisible God, the firstborn of every creature." Quenstedt rightly observed concerning this passage: *totum Systema mundi dissolveretur, nisi per potentiam conservatricem Christi sustentaretur*EN80 (*Theol. did. pol.*, 1685, I, 13); but he did not draw the deduction from this insight. It is strange that there was not a more fruitful recollection of Hebrews 1³, where the Son of God is again indisputably described as "upholding all things by the word of his power," and immediately afterwards as the One who "when he had by himself purged our sins, sat down on the right hand of the Majesty on high." It is particularly puzzling in this case because in the second article of the creed this is given its full New Testament sweep and the *qui sedet ad dexteram Dei Patris omnipotentis*EN81 is fully accepted. This meant, and still means, that He sits at the place from which heaven and earth are ruled and all power has its origin and centre, not as a passive

[035]

EN76 working
EN77 working
EN78 by him all things consist
EN79 coherence
EN80 the whole System of the world would dissolve, unless it were sustained by the preserving power of Christ
EN81 who sits at the right hand of God the Father Almighty

spectator, but as the epitome of the wisdom, will and power of the Father, and with the Father as the source of the πνεῦμα ζωοποιοῦν EN82 without whom no creature can live and move. Yes, the Son of God, born of the Virgin Mary, crucified under Pontius Pilate, dead, buried and raised again, is seated at this point. Had it not been noted in Ps. 118^{16} that the right hand of the Lord "is exalted and doeth valiantly," or in Ps. 139^{10} that it holds man, or in Ps. 73^{23} that man for his part holds it, or in Ps. 18^{35} that it upholds, or in Ps. 44^3 that it brings Israel into its own land, or in Ps. 48^{10} that it is "full of righteousness"? What could have been more obvious, one might have thought, than to equate this ruling right hand of God with the One who according to the witness of the New Testament has His place at this right hand? Why did not Calvin and others work out that insight that the hands and feet of God, like His heart, are revealed in Christ and Him alone? And why did not this perception break through when it was read and sung in the best known of Luther's hymns?

> "Ask ye who is this same?
> Christ Jesus is His Name,
> The Lord Sabaoth's Son;
> He, and no other one,
> Shall conquer in the battle."

How could the subject of the universal lordship at issue in the doctrine of providence be left so indistinct, as if it were not known "who is this same"? How could it be left neutral, and necessarily subject to a different interpretation, as if it were another god than the One confessed in the second article of the creed, or as if side by side with the world dominion exercised by this right hand of God we had to reckon with another divine rule on the left hand which is perhaps to be regarded as the true sway of the Creator over and with His creature? All the astonishment which is legitimate at this point may be summed up in the question why it was not seen that, in the passage in Genesis 22$^{1-19}$ from which the *Deus providebit*EN83 was usually taken, the God who so wonderfully foresees and provides is not a mere supreme being but the God who, in this happening in which Abraham was to spare his son, acted as the Lord of the covenant in the fulfilment of which He Himself was finally not to spare His own Son. It was with a view to this goal of the history of the covenant of grace that Abraham was promised and given his successor Isaac, that he had then (as a prophecy of the One who was to come) to separate and bring him as an offering to God, but that he had not to die but live as a type of the One who was to come and give life through His real death, a substitute being found for him in the form of the ram. This divine *providere*EN84 belonged to this concrete context of the history of salvation. In view of this, ought not supreme importance to have been attached to the qualification of the presupposed concept of the subject?

[036]   If we take seriously the starting-point and concept of the subject given by the Word of God as His self-revelation, in its centre and substance we must have the following decisive understanding of the history played out under this lordship. It is the execution of the election of grace resolved and fulfilled by God from all eternity. It is thus the history of the covenant between God and man. It is the history in which God establishes His fellowship with man, and prepares and accomplishes its completion in His own self-giving to human nature and existence, to conduct it to its manifestation at the expiration of the last

---

EN82 life-giving spirit
EN83 God will provide
EN84 providing

time. As the creation of all the reality distinct from God took place on the basis of this purposed covenant and with a view to its execution, so the meaning of the continued existence of the creature, and therefore the purpose of its history, is that this covenant will and work of God begun in creation should have its course and reach its goal. There is no other meaning or purpose in history. For there is no other God, and in the will of this God there is no other purpose but the election of grace resolved and fulfilled by Him from all eternity. In the distinct reality created by Him, and even in the freedom of this action of the creature, all things always serve this purpose of its continued existence. They take place as they have a part in the history of this covenant. They take place for the sake of this history. They constitute an occurrence distinct from the activity of God. But they have no significance or value apart from God's covenant will and work or in independence of them. They do not have their purpose and goal in themselves or apart from the purpose and goal to which the covenant work of God hastens. They can only hasten with it in the one direction. As they come from God, from His election of grace and creation, they can go only where they are ordained to go by the very fact of their existence, serving this will and work of God, participating in it, executing what God has resolved in His free and omnipotent grace.

We should certainly not forget or erase the fact that the history of the covenant, and therefore the history which is the meaning of all creaturely occurrence, is within the totality of this creaturely occurrence a particular history selected for this purpose and determined and directed accordingly. It is an astonishingly thin line in a confusion of apparently much more powerful and conspicuous lines which seem to be independent and mutually contradictory, and especially to run quite contrary to the one narrow line of the history of the covenant. That world history in its totality is the history in which God executes His will of grace must thus be taken to mean that in its totality it belongs to this special history; that its lines can have no other starting-point or goal than the one divine will of grace; that they must converge on this one thin line and finally run in its direction. This is the theme of the doctrine of providence. It has to do with the history of the covenant, with the one thin line as such. Or rather, it has to do with it only to the extent that it for its part is undoubtedly one among the many other lines of general world-occurrence, and that these [037] many other lines of general world-occurrence have their ontic and noetic basis in the fact that the God from whom they come and to whom they return pursues on this one line the special work which the creature must serve on these other lines. The doctrine of providence must not level down the special history of the covenant, grace and salvation; it must not reduce it to the common denominator of a doctrine of general world occurrence. In so doing it would lose sight of the starting-point and therefore of its concept of the subject. And then it would no longer be speaking of the world dominion of God revealed in His Word. This God is the Father of Jesus Christ, the God of Abraham, Isaac and Jacob, the God of the prophets and apostles, the God who pursues His

special work on this special line of world-occurrence. The doctrine of providence presupposes that this special history is exalted above all other history. It
can and will understand all other occurrence only in its relation to this special
occurrence, namely, as an occurrence under the lordship of the One who
there pursues the work in which His will for the whole is revealed and operative. This is what gives it its proper theme.

It has to do with the history of the creature as such. The man to whom God
has addressed His eternal grace, and with whom He deals in His eternal grace
on the special line of this special history, is also quite simply His creature, and
indeed His creature within a creaturely cosmos, under heaven and on earth.
And as the history of the covenant, grace and salvation takes place; as Abraham and his descendants are called by God to be His people; as God in His Son
Himself becomes a man of this people, to be as such very God and very man
for all men; as the community comforted by the Holy Ghost proclaims the
name of its Lord and awaits His manifestation; as all this takes place, there is
simply enacted the history of the creature as such, the psycho-physical history
of man in time, and the history of the near and distant cosmos around him,
the whole titanic continuation of creaturely existence as such—a history of
apparently quite a different type, of what seems in part to be a more modest
and in part a more expansive content, the incommensurable drama of the
coming and going, the rising and falling of what is outside God. And the special occurrence in Israel, in Jesus Christ and in His community is not merely
embedded in this general occurrence, but so inextricably woven into it that
what takes place particularly in the one all bears the character of the other,
and can and must be understood from the standpoint of this general occurrence, as a part of the history of the creature. Abraham, and his descendants,
and the prophets and apostles, and even Christians as men called and
awakened to the consciousness, thankfulness, obligation and mission of
covenant-partnership with God, are all men in the cosmos and participants in
its history. For this reason their faith must be faith in providence, faith in the
God who even as their Creator, as the Lord of this general occurrence, is the
same as the One whom they may know by His summoning Word, or conversely
faith in the fact that the God who has called them by His Word is also their
Creator and the Lord of this general history. The doctrine of providence
relates to the fact that Christian faith is faith in the relationship thereby posited between the one occurrence and the other. It tells us how far information
is given us on this inner relationship by the Word of God.

To the extent that it does not deal with the history of the covenant as such,
but with the history of the creature ordered in relation to it, it has its own
theme. It is not obvious that the history of the creature takes place under the
lordship of God in such a way that it is ordered in relation to the history of the
covenant. This is open to question. If it is true, it is a matter of special knowledge, of a special content of the Word of God. But it might well be otherwise.
There might be two histories of the same divine origin and under the same

[038]

divine control, running parallel as two independent and unrelated sequences. The covenant is not creation, but its internal basis. And creation is not the covenant, but its external basis. It is not self-evident, but has to be seen particularly, that the covenant in virtue of its external basis and creation in virtue of its internal are also connected in their history, and in this too stand in a positive relationship to each other.

That there is a participation of man in the covenant, that there is a grace addressed and a salvation ascribed to him, might be related to his creaturely being only in the sense that the same God wills this who posited this being from the first as that of a creature under His protection and provision as Creator. Even then there might not be a positive relationship between his existence as a partner in the covenant, a recipient of God's grace and participant in His salvation, and his being as a creature of God. It might be established only at the end of the two histories and by way of a new creation. On the way from the beginning to the goal, in the course of his special history as the covenant-partner of God, man would then be able only to cling to the fact that the Lord of the covenant is also His Creator, and is therefore in some way the Lord and Guarantor of his creaturely being. But he could not count on the fact that his participation in God's covenant, grace and salvation definitely has and has had a direct significance even for his being as God's creature.

On the other side, the possibility might be formulated as follows. That man is God's creature, and has a history as such, might be related to his participation in God's covenant, salvation and grace to the extent that the God who has addressed this to him has also granted it to him to be his creature, and as such to have and fulfil his course under His protection and providence. It might be that this creaturely course of his under God's lordship has materially and properly nothing whatever to do with his history under the direction of [039] the same God as the Lord of the covenant of grace. A true and proper connexion between his creatureliness and his determination as God's covenant-partner might arise only on the basis of a new creation. On the way between his creation and this goal, man as a creature would be able to cling only to the identity of God and therefore the parallelism of his own being as a creature with his history in covenant with God, but not to a positive significance of his creaturely history for the other.

We have to make at this point a decision of great importance and far-reaching consequence.

If the matter were as assumed, and as unfortunately taught both explicitly and implicitly, then a passage like 1 Peter 5⁶: "Humble yourselves therefore under the mighty hand of God, that he may exalt you in due time: casting all your care upon him; for he careth for you," would have to be expounded as follows. Now that you must suffer persecution, you find yourselves as God's creatures under an absolutely superior and obviously grievous order and power. It is the order and power of God, the hand of your Creator, who is the "Lord of history." To be sure, you are Christians, but you have no option but to humble yourselves under the hand which so painfully overrules your creaturely existence, acknowledging that its sway is just, even though so strange and incomprehensible, because it is that of God. In another respect, in respect of the salvation addressed to you in Jesus Christ, God is not unknown to you. But in this respect, in relation to the present form of your creaturely existence, in relation to your being in world history, you must blindly trust that what He does is right. You may do so in view of the fact that the One before whom you can only humble yourselves now can and will exalt you in another hour of His own choosing. Therefore let your care in respect of creaturely existence be His. You can do this because you know Him well in that other respect, as the Lord of the covenant of grace. Indeed, it is because you know Him well in that other respect that you may trust Him blindly in this respect, although you do not know Him in this respect, as the One who rules over your creaturely existence, your external history, your living and dying.

A passage like Matthew 6[26f.] (about the birds which neither sow nor reap and yet are fed, and the lilies which neither toil nor spin and yet are more gloriously arrayed than Solomon) would then have to be regarded as a picture from this other order, the order of creaturely being and history; and the Christian could gather from it that even in this order to which he also belongs there is a divine lordship, protection and providence to which he may confidently commit himself in respect of food and clothing.

It will be seen that the expositions possible on the assumption of two parallel sequences are neither bad nor unhelpful. But on this presupposition how can we interpret Ephesians 1[11], where we are told that Christians are made heirs, being predestinated according to the prior decision (the $\pi\rho\acute{o}\theta\epsilon\sigma\iota s$) "of him who worketh all things after the counsel of his own will"? And what about Romans 8[28]: "We know that all things work together ($\sigma\upsilon\nu\epsilon\rho\gamma\epsilon\hat{\iota}$) for good to them that love God, to them who are called according to his prior decision" ($\kappa\alpha\tau\grave{a}$ $\pi\rho\acute{o}\theta\epsilon\sigma\iota\nu$)? If this is true, our whole assumption is obviously called in question. We have not to reckon with a parallelism of the two sequences, but a positive connexion between them. The particular decision of God concerning His elect and His government of all things, their love for God and their existence in the totality of things, are obviously not to be regarded apart but in conjunction, in material co-ordination. But if the One who has foreordained them heirs works all things, and if all things work together for good to those who love God, Christians can accept the occurrence of their creaturely history, certainly in faith alone, yet not in a blind faith, but in a faith which is objectively grounded, in a seeing faith, in the faith that there is here not merely a factual but a materially positive and inner connexion, so that even in their creaturely being they are wholly in the kingdom of Christ and not another kingdom.

[040]

It may thus be asked whether the foregoing exposition of 1 Peter 5[6f.] exhausts the meaning of the passage. If the mighty hand of God humbles Christians in respect of their creaturely existence, and if they really accept this humiliation in the hope of future exaltation, this is because this mighty hand is none other than the right hand of God where Christ is seated, and therefore in what comes upon them in some sense from without, as is constantly emphasised in the First Epistle of Peter, they are simply led by the divinely willed fashioning of their earthly life to the discipleship and fellowship of the suffering and dying Lord Jesus Christ. And if they may now cast all their care upon Him and know for certain that it is lifted from them and is no longer theirs, if in their sufferings they may live by that hope of future exaltation, this means that in their creaturely existence they may participate in the freedom and even the glory of the covenant-partnership with God given them in Christ. "Beloved, think it not strange concerning the fiery trial which is to try you, as though some strange thing happened unto you: but rejoice, inasmuch as ye are partakers of Christ's sufferings ; that when his glory shall be revealed, ye may be glad also with exceeding joy" (1 Pet. 4[12f.]). There are certainly two standpoints from which the being of man and God's dealings with him may be seen and understood. But it is not the case that these confront and continually contradict one another. The case is rather that the standpoint of creation history is lit up by that of salvation history. Is it not a fact that only on this assumption does the apostolic admonition amount to more than general edification in the sense of Stoicism and receive the stamp of distinctive and incontrovertible Christian truth and necessity?

It may be asked again whether we really have in Matthew 6²⁶ᶠ· no more than a picture of the divine order of creation held out to the disciples. Is this only a parable from which they may gather that like the birds and lilies they need not be anxious about their external preservation? That they need not be anxious is surely made clear to them in the fact that with the reference to the birds and lilies they are told that as the disciples of Jesus—much more than these—they live in the world of the heavenly Father who not merely as the Creator of all things, not merely as He has power over them and is responsible for their preservation as such, but as their heavenly Father knows that they need food and clothing and sees to it that they need not be anxious. Hence v. 33: "But seek ye first the kingdom of God and his righteousness; and all these things shall be added unto you." In "all these things," in their creaturely existence, their history, their needs and reversals, in this whole sphere of divine lordship, there is no question of a history taking place independently of the kingdom of God and their seeking it. The point is that in what takes place in the one we have a προστίθεσθαι^EN85. to what takes place in the other. That there really is this προστίθεσθαι^EN86, or συνεργεῖν^EN87 (Rom. 8²⁸), that the history of creaturely being is really ordered in relation to the history of the covenant, is the true theme of the Christian doctrine of providence as opposed to the assumption which we took as the starting-point of this excursus.

There is thus—and this is the not very obvious, but from the Christian centre true and clear point to be stated and developed in the doctrine of providence—a positive, material and inner connexion between the two series. The faithfulness of God, which is its supreme and proper theme, is indivisible. It is not first the faithfulness of the One who called Abraham, fulfilled the promise given to him and will finally manifest it in its fulfilment, and then again the faithfulness of the Creator who will not abandon His creature, but give it His support and continually direct its history. But the faithfulness of God is that He gives support and direction to the history of His creature in the fact that in this history He calls Abraham, and rules His people, and gives Himself in His Son, and will finally manifest Himself in this One as the Lord of the whole. The faithfulness of God is that He co-ordinates creaturely occurrence under His lordship with the occurrence of the covenant, grace and salvation, that He subordinates the former to the latter and makes it serve it, that He integrates it with the coming of His kingdom in which the whole of the reality distinct from Himself has its meaning and historical substance, that He causes it to co-operate in this happening.

[041]

The question arises whether in the whole witness of the Old and New Testaments to God's work and revelation any other meaning is given to creaturely being as such and its history than that of an integration and co-operation of this kind. Every page speaks, of course, of heaven and earth, natural and historical events, great and small historical contexts, peoples,

---

EN85 adding
EN86 adding
EN87 working together

kings and nations, rain and sunshine, health and sickness, wealth and poverty, joy and suffering, life and death. That man as the partner of God is also quite simply man in the cosmos, and the concrete meaning of this for him, are everywhere displayed and taken seriously, i.e., brought into relationship to God as the Lord of all. But this is never done in such a way that an independent significance and role are ascribed to him, or to God's rule over him. It is never done in such a way that a neutral and general world dominion of God becomes the theme of the biblical presentation, or even emerges from it. It is never done in such a way that we may suspect that in the history of creation as such we have to do with a sphere in which God is active according to a plan and law peculiar to it. On the contrary, the great and little things in this continually visible sphere are all taken seriously in the fact that they are seen and described as this integration and co-operation. They may and must all serve, not merely God in general and indefinitely, but God concretely willing and working in the history of the covenant and salvation. They all have their seriousness, their glory or shame, light or darkness, greatness or littleness, in the fact that they stand in this relationship. How can man in the cosmos, in his creatureliness and among other creatures, be at home or otherwise in creaturely history? How can he be justified or unjustified, blessed or cursed? How can he be exalted or abased as a creature, rewarded or punished, great or little? This is possible and necessary in the fact that here on earth under heaven, in natural and universal history with all the implications which it has for man at every stage and in every direction of its occurrence, God's covenant, grace and salvation are in action and His kingdom comes. As the Bible sees it, the occurrence of creaturely existence as such follows and corresponds to this occurrence. It receives from this occurrence its meaning and character. And as it stands in this relationship, it comes to man and for good or evil becomes his destiny. A free and secular creaturely occurrence, standing in a neutral relation to this other, is quite inconceivable in the context of biblical thought and perception.

[042] But our primary emphasis must now be upon the fact that this accompaniment of the history of the covenant of grace by that of creaturely being, this co-ordination, integration and co-operation of the latter, is the work of God. It is this no less than creation, and the establishment of the covenant in and with creation, and the history of the covenant. If in its continued existence the creature may serve the will of God in His covenant, grace and salvation, it does this in the individuality and particularity given it with its creation by God, in the freedom and activity corresponding to its particular nature. The creatures of the earth thus live their own lives. Man, too, lives his own life in accordance with the particular spirit which is the basis of human nature. All creation is made to exist in this relationship according to its own manner and freedom. But the fact that it actually does this is first and last the direct work of God. For neither generally nor in detail has God created a machine which works at once in harmony with His will and therefore with the history of the covenant of grace. To the relative freedom and autonomy in which the creature has begun and continues to exist in face of Him, there corresponds the perfect sovereignty in which God is present in its whole history and in which He Himself co-ordinates and brings it into a positive relationship with the history of the covenant of grace. As He is free in His dealings with the patriarchs and Moses, with judges, kings and prophets, and finally in His incarnate Son, and as He is gracious and omnipotent in His freedom, so He is in the dealings with and to

and through and in creation with which He accompanies this history at every step. The perfection of creation is not the power with which the latter sets and maintains itself in motion in this sense. The power in which it does this is the perfection of God, and concretely the perfection of His free and omnipotent grace, and even more concretely the perfection of the kingdom of Jesus Christ. Creation has its own perfection. We are told that God considered what He had made, "and behold, it was very good." But the goodness and even perfection of creation consists in the fact that God has made it serviceable for the rule of His free and omnipotent grace, for the exercise of the lordship of Jesus Christ. But this serviceability would be futile and concealed if there were no such rule and lordship, if it were not the living good-pleasure of God actually to use it. In other hands than His it cannot render the service for which it was ordained. There is needed the Master who has fashioned this instrument if its goodness and perfection are to be effective and revealed. This meets all the complaints of the creature against its supposed imperfection, which can be raised only by those who cannot control or see it in its perfection because it is not for them to use it. It also takes from creation all boasting or self-glory, because its glory can consist only in the fact that God has made and found it useful for Himself, and especially in the fact that He will and does use it in the service of the "kingdom of his dear Son" (Col. 1^{13}). It is not glorious in itself; it can become so only in the right hand of the living God. That He uses it in the service of this kingdom; that He co-ordinates and integrates it with His work in [043] this kingdom; that He causes it to co-operate in the history of this kingdom, this is the rule of His providence. In so doing God acts with a sovereignty which has its self-evident limit in His own being, in the unity and steadfastness of His will, in His own glory and mercy, in the immutability of His purpose. Accordingly it has its limit also in the nature of creation, in the goodness and perfection given it, in its serviceability to Him. But in what this consists is known only by God Himself as its Creator and Lord. We can perceive it, and therefore the limit of the sovereignty of God which it sets, only when we perceive the use which God wills to make and does make of it. The extent of this use is the extent of its nature, goodness and perfection, and the extent of His sovereignty over it. Since we do not know the totality of His rule, it is not for us to fix the limit of His sovereignty. It certainly cannot have its limit in what we know of it, or of creation.

From this character of providence as an actual and sovereign work of God there follows the fact that in its sway we have always to do with God Himself. We certainly have to do with Him in His relationship with His creatures, His presence in their presence, His working in their works, His freedom in their freedom. To that extent we have certainly to do with the creatures too, with their history, self-expressions, nature and perversion, immanent harmony and contradictions, riddles and revelations, indeed with the great drama of being and its impelling and imposing autonomous significance. We have already seen that on the thin line of the history of the covenant we have also to do with a part of the general history of the creature. If there were no revelation there; if it were not objectively real and subjectively true that God Himself is present, we might well think that this is only an act in that great drama of being. But what if on this thin line revelation takes place and awakens faith, because here God is present and active in the creaturely world in such a way that He makes Himself known and is actually known in the course of creaturely occurrence? A decision is then made not only for this particular history but for all the general sphere of creaturely occurrence, even for the innumerable and extended spheres in which God is concealed. This is that He is the Lord of this whole occurrence. But this means that the impression of an autonomous significance of this whole drama is broken and called in question. We can accord it only a relative autonomous significance. For it is finally clear, and generally and fundamentally so, that in creaturely occurrence we have to do not only with this as such, but properly and decisively with the doing of the will of God. The faith awakened at the one point by the revelation of God, being faith in God the Lord, is necessarily faith in His lordship even at points where there is [044] no such revelation, where to all appearances we have to do only with creaturely occurrence, where the orders and contingencies of nature, the works of caprice and the cleverness or folly, the goodness or badness of men seem to be the only reality. Nevertheless, God Himself is He who is freely and graciously and mightily present and active at these points too as the One who is prior to all creaturely occurrence, supreme over it and at work in it.

This Nevertheless is the problem of the belief in providence and the doctrine of providence. It can only be a Nevertheless. What man sees is simply the multiplicity and confusion of the lines of creaturely occurrence, which in itself and as such—for creation is not God—cannot be identified with the doing of the will of God, with the work of His freedom, grace and power. There can be no question of a transparency proper to this occurrence as such, or of an inherent ability of man to see through it. What man sees is simply creation in all the regularity and contingency of its own movement and development. If he did not begin with faith in God's providence, he might try to intepret this movement and development in different ways. But he certainly could not maintain and confess that God is the Lord who is prior to this occurrence, supreme over it and at work in it. The belief in providence maintains and confesses this with its Nevertheless. It has itself the character of a "foreseeing." In faith in God's particular revelation man sees God before he sees the general history of creation. And it is for this reason that as he sees the latter he sees God as the One who in concealment but supreme reality is before and over and in it as the Lord. Hence his Nevertheless is not blind. It is grounded in a supremely illuminating Therefore. And the man who ventures this Nevertheless, because he may so venture, is not ignoring reality. He does not imagine another reality. He does not think he sees through reality. On the contrary, he sees it as it is just because he encounters it with his Nevertheless, not believing in its apparently autonomous significance, but in the significance given it by the fact that in all its developments it stands under the lordship of God. He confronts world reality in all sobriety in the fact that he knows that in all its developments he has to do with God Himself, with His co-ordinating and integrating of creaturely occurrence with the history of His covenant, with the doing of His gracious and saving will, with His providing that all things must work together for good to them that love Him, and in all these things with God Himself, with the work of His right hand.

Is there a legitimate answer to the question of the concrete significance of this actual and sovereign work of God, and therefore of this co-ordinating and integrating of creaturely history with the history of His covenant of grace, to the question of the concrete significance of the co-operation of creation for good, and therefore in the doing of His gracious and saving will, as effected by God's disposing? If the answer is to be legitimate, it must be given at least with [045] great caution. It cannot in any circumstances maintain that in the history of the covenant of grace the creature can be a sovereign subject side by side with God. The fellowship of the creature with God actualised in the person of man is of course the goal of the covenant of grace, and again in the person of man it is God's partner in this covenant. But the creature does not establish, maintain or rule this covenant. Its history is the history of the divine acts and achievements, not those of the creature. In it, it is a matter of God's grace, and not of its own capacities and merits; of the salvation which God ascribes to and secures for it, and not of a salvation which it can attain of itself. If there is a co-ordination and integration of its history, of the history of the totality, to this particular history, and a consequent co-operation of the creature in this history, there can be no question of the created world either as a whole or in detail sharing with God in the establishing, maintaining and ruling of the covenant, in the dispensing of grace and in the sending out of salvation. There can be as little and even less question of this than of its sharing with Him in its own creation. Grace would not be grace if it were not free, but were conditioned by a reciprocal achievement on the part of the one to whom it is addressed. Nor would it be an eternal and true salvation if the creature for whom it is destined co-operated independently in its accomplishment and mediation. In the covenant of grace it is a matter of the reconciliation of the world with God, of the redemption of man, of the hushing of the sighing of all creation, of the revelation of the glory of God. What takes place in the covenant of grace does so wholly *for* man and not—even in part—*through* man. A *creatura mediatrix gratiarum*^{EN88} or even *corredemptrix*^{EN89} is a self-contradiction. One alone can be the subject of *gratia*^{EN90} and *redemptio*^{EN91} and none other beside and with Him—namely, God Himself.

---

^{EN88} creature as the mediator of grace
^{EN89} co-redeemer
^{EN90} grace
^{EN91} redemption

But something else has to be taken into account, and this is the theme of the Christian belief in providence. It is no accident that we cannot properly define it, but only indicate it in descriptions which are not really adequate in detail. While God alone is the ruling, determining and conditioning Subject in the history of the covenant of grace, He is undoubtedly not alone in this history, but has a partner in man, and to that extent in the cosmos. Again, as the history of the covenant is enacted, the creature is undoubtedly present as the subject of a separate history, nor is it present in vain as a passive spectator or mere object, but meaningfully. From the very outset the covenant had its external basis in creation. Similarly, the history of the covenant continually has its external basis in the existence and history of the creature. And it is a matter of the establishment and preservation of this external basis of the history of the covenant in the sway of the divine providence. How are we rightly to por-
[046] tray this "external basis" within the accepted limits of what is legitimate, not saying either too much on the one side or too little on the other?

If in the first instance we simply ask concerning the function in which the creature is this external basis of the history of the covenant, there primarily suggests itself the concept of service on which we have already touched. A servant is certainly present at the work of his lord, and has a meaningful part in it. The lord himself is exclusively the subject of this work and responsible for its planning, undertaking and fulfilling. At every point it must be his own work if it is to be good. But he must have time, space and opportunity for this work of his which none can lift from him and in which none can help him. And to create this according to his own direction and order he needs a servant wholly familiar with his work and engaged in it, yet restrained, avoiding any material interference and absolutely selfless. This servant, wholly involved in the work of his lord, but strictly from outside, and yet meaningfully involved in his particular function and indispensable in his own time and place, is the being and work of the creature in the relationship to God's action in the execution of His gracious counsel. But the metaphor is inadequate. For no human servant is at the same time the creature of his lord. Again, the value and glory of a human servant consist in deploying within his limits as much of his own initiative as possible in his participation in the work of his lord. Again, a human servant might ultimately serve another lord than the one he does. And finally, a wholly selfless purpose is too much to ask of the work of even the most loyal servant. The service of the history of creaturely being in relation to God's action in the history of the covenant of grace is to be understood, in contrast to this inadequate comparison, as a pure service in which the servant can have in view no purpose or advantage of his own, and cannot possibly transfer his service to another.

We shall now attempt a different comparison. The service of the creature is that of an instrument. We have said already that God uses it. An instrument is also present, and indeed meaningfully and indispensably, when it is used for a particular purpose. There can be no question of it being a subject. It knows nothing of the purpose for which it is used. And it cannot make the slightest use of itself. It is nothing if it is not picked up and used by the one who knows his purpose and the use of the instrument. But in these circumstances it is indispensable. And this is how things stand with the creature and its history. This metaphor speaks more clearly than the first of the freedom of God in relation to His creature. But it is no less obviously inadequate. The freedom of God in His dealings with the creature is very different from that of a human master in relation to his tool. For the latter is not also the creator of his tool, and the adaptation of the latter to the designed use can never be more than limited. The comparison is inadequate again because the creature is in God's   [047] hand not only with the passivity of an instrument but also with its own activity.

As God co-ordinates and integrates the history of the creature with that of His covenant of grace, so that it may co-operate in this history, the creature is not only a means but also an object of the divine action. As God works through creation, He works on it and for it. He makes of it what is in conformity with His good-pleasure. He shapes it according to His gracious will. From this standpoint it is tempting to describe it as the material of His action, as in the well-known comparison of the potter and the clay in Jeremiah 18[1f.] This comparison gives a general indication of the majesty of God and the insignificance of the creature. But it, too, fails to bring out the specific majesty of God which consists in the fact that He has not found but created the creature, and the specific insignificance of the creature, which is not alien matter in the hand of the living God but His own living possession.

Thus in answer to the question concerning the concrete purpose of created existence, or its co-ordination and integration with the history of the covenant of grace and co-operation in this history, we cannot give any true definition, but only some inadequate comparisons. In describing it as service, we have already said that it provides time, space and opportunity for the divine will and action in the covenant of grace.

In this connexion we may well recall the first creation story, in which creation is described almost as the building of a house or temple, man being finally introduced as the true inhabitant. It is also to be noted that the distinctive relationship between the work of the sixth day and the seventh as the day of God's rest points at once to the fact that the relationship of man with God or God with man which is the basis of the covenant in the midst of creation, is the goal for which the whole building is constructed, and that it is for the history of this covenant that time, space and opportunity are created with creation as such. Calvin perhaps had this in view when he described the totality of the cosmos and cosmic occurrence as the *theatrum gloriae Dei*[EN92].

There is one indispensable presupposition of the covenant of grace and the kingdom of Christ and its history even outside the free and gracious will of God. It consists in the fact that God is not alone but with the creature, so that

---

[EN92] theatre of God's glory

the latter has existence and continued existence alongside and outside Him. In order that God may work for and to and in it, it must be there in its distinct reality. But to its being, and therefore to God's dealings with it, there also belongs the fact that it has time, space and opportunity both to exist and to do so for God's glory. The psycho-physical life of man, and therefore the God who addresses Himself to this man in His grace, needs this. It must all be co-ordinated and integrated with the work of His grace and co-operate in it. It cannot in any degree help to effect this work. It cannot be its subject. It is genuinely an external and not an internal basis of this work, whether as *causa prima*[EN93] or *causa secunda*[EN94]. But it is indeed the external basis of this work. It is its *conditio sine qua non*[EN95]. This work of God, which is not an *opus ad intra*[EN96] like the inner acts of the trinitarian God but most definitely an *opus ad extra*[EN97], needs outside (*extra Deum*[EN98]) a theatre on which it can be enacted and unfolded. The created cosmos including man, or man within the created cosmos, is this theatre of the great acts of God in grace and salvation. With a view to this he is God's servant, instrument and material. But the theatre obviously cannot be the subject of the work enacted on it. It can only make it externally possible. This is done by the history of the creature as such. As it fulfils this purpose, it is indispensable. And the fact that it really serves this purpose is the meaning and problem of the doctrine of providence. This tells us that provision has been and is continually made for this theatre of the history of the covenant of grace, for time, space and opportunity for the divine work of grace and salvation. It tells us that this provision is made by God Himself. It speaks of the specific and as it were supplementary divine work of this provision. There will be time, space and opportunity for the history of the covenant of grace, for faith, knowledge, repentance, love and hope, until this history reaches its divinely appointed end. In great and little things alike all this will be continually furnished by the sustaining and overruling sway of God as the Lord of heaven and earth. This is the divine co-ordination and integration of cosmic history with the history of salvation. It is seen by the Christian faith in providence as follows. Even as God's creatures, and within the world of other creatures, caught up in the great drama of being, we are not in an empty or alien place. It is not God's fault if we do not feel at home in our creatureliness and in this creaturely world. This is a notion which can obtrude only if we suspend as it were our faith in God's providence and do not take seriously our membership of the kingdom of Christ. If we take this seriously, our eyes are open to the fact that the created world including our own exist-

[048]

[EN93] primary cause
[EN94] secondary cause
[EN95] necessary condition
[EN96] internal work
[EN97] external work
[EN98] outside of God

ence fulfils that purpose and constitutes that *theatrum gloriae Dei*[EN99]. It and we are present in order that God may have time, space and opportunity to pursue in the history of the covenant of grace the work which is the goal of His creative will and to hasten towards which He has made it His own most proper cause with the interposition of Himself in Jesus Christ. We are in the house of our Father, in a world ordered according to His fatherly purpose, as we are in the created cosmos, under heaven and on earth, and ourselves cosmic creatures. It cannot help us, or deliver us, or reconcile us with God, that we are at home in this sense. Our salvation and future glory do not have their source here. Yet it is not a matter of indifference, nor can we perceive it without joy and gratitude. The fact that we are given by God Himself the *conditio sine qua* [049] *non*[EN100], the time, space and opportunity without which we could not have a share in the kingdom of Christ, is co-ordinated and integrated with the divine work of grace and salvation. We certainly cannot and must not say that even the picture of the theatre and home is wholly adequate. It lacks the things which are plainly brought out concerning God's working through the creature by the pictures of the servant and instrument, and concerning the creature as the object of God's working by that of the material. But in the sense indicated it does at least indicate the way in which the teleology of the divine work is to be described.

But the question as to the concrete meaning of that co-ordination, integration and co-operation can be carried a step further, and may finally be put as follows. What recognisable character is proper to creaturely occurrence in relation to what it has to accompany under God's providence? What does it mean for an understanding of creaturely occurrence that it takes place in this co-ordination under the divine rule? We venture to answer, as we may well do in the light of 1 Corinthians 13[12], that creaturely occurrence acquires in this co-ordination the character of a mirror. The distinction and inter-connexion of the two historical sequences are both brought out in this comparison. The original, God's primary working, is the divinely ruled history of the covenant. The mirror has nothing to add to this. In it the history of the creature as such cannot play any role. The mirror can confront it only as a reflector. It cannot repeat it, or imitate its occurrence. It can only reflect it. And as it does so it reverses it, the right being shown as the left and *vice versa*. Yet the fact remains that it gives us a correspondence and likeness. The creature does not exist for nothing in this co-ordination. It does not have for nothing the same Lord in both cases. Its history under His lordship as Creator is indeed a different one from that of the covenant instituted and fulfilled by the same Lord. But its twofold history is comparable as creature is comparable with creature (for even the history of the covenant takes place in the creaturely sphere). Jesus Christ as very God and very man, the basis and fulfilment of the history of the

---

[EN] [99] theatre of God's glory
[EN100] necessary condition

covenant, is certainly not to be found again in general creaturely occurrence. This cannot then be more than a mirror and likeness. And everything thus takes place differently for all the similarities. Yet there are similarities. The contrast and connexion of heaven and earth, of the inconceivable and conceivable world, is not the same as that of God and man in Jesus Christ; but it is similar. The confrontation and fellowship of man and woman in marriage is not the same as that of Christ and His community; but it is similar. The antitheses of above and below, of light and dark, of beautiful and ugly, of becoming and perishing, of joy and sadness, which are obviously to be found in creaturely occurrence, are certainly not the same as the true antithesis of grace and sin, deliverance and destruction, life and death, in the history of the covenant; but they are at least similar. In the same way there is something of good and bad, right and wrong, spirit and the opposite, if not in cosmic history as a whole, at least in the history of man. How strange it is that there is still a people Israel, and that this people is so brightly spotlighted in our own day! Nor is there lacking the phenomenon of gods and their worship, of sacrifices, prayers and the like, of religious history. We must be careful not to identify the reflection with the original, the history of the creature with the true history of salvation. For reasons which have nothing to do with its creatureliness, the former is one long history of the very opposite of salvation, as emerges even more clearly in religious history, and in what is known as "Israel" in world history. But we cannot overlook or deny the fact that creaturely history is still similar in every respect to the history of salvation, as a reflection resembles the original. Creaturely history is not for nothing the theatre of the great acts of God, the Father's house. In virtue of its origin and in its whole structure its occurrence is calculated to reflect and illustrate and echo these acts of God. And this is what actually happens.

"The heavens declare the glory of God; and the firmament sheweth his handywork. Day unto day uttereth speech, and night unto night sheweth knowledge. There is no speech nor language; their voice is not heard. Yet their line is gone out through all the earth, and their words to the end of the world" (Ps. 19$^{1f.}$). What can be known of God is manifest ($\phi \alpha \nu \epsilon \rho \acute{o} \nu$) among men because God "hath shewed it unto them" ($\dot{\epsilon} \phi \alpha \nu \acute{\epsilon} \rho \omega \sigma \epsilon \nu$). His invisible being, namely, His eternal power and Godhead from the creation of the world, may well be understood as seen in His works ($\nu o o \acute{\nu} \mu \epsilon \nu \alpha$ $\kappa \alpha \theta o \rho \hat{\alpha} \tau \alpha \iota$, Rom. 1$^{19f.}$). But is this image really seen, this reflection recognised, this likeness understood? Are there the necessary seeing eyes to see it? The original must obviously be known to make this possible. But to know the original we need faith in God's Word and revelation to have a part in the history of the covenant, and then genuinely in creaturely history. If we are children of the Father, we certainly recognise His house in more and more likenesses. But we shall certainly not be guilty of the confusion of thinking that the house of the Father, what can be only a similitude, is the matter itself. We shall always see the likenesses as such. We shall always hear the echo as such. We shall therefore be at home even in creaturely occurrence. Is it not the case that the biblical view of cosmic occurrence, of natural and universal history, is one which, as opposed to every kind of dualism, is open and relaxed, and in the best sense attentive and grateful? It can and must be this, for its presupposition is that creaturely occurrence has its meaning and substance and centre solely but genuinely in the history of the covenant. The Bible regards creaturely

[050]

occurrence as the circumference of this centre. It sees it set in the light in view of this centre. This light is not extinguished by the fact that what takes place outside the history of salvation is a history of the very opposite. This light is still light even when it becomes so deceptive in the perverted eyes of men, even when it causes so much of that confusion, even when it usually summons them to so much natural theology (in complete misunderstanding of the truth which is to be joyfully but soberly recognised at this point).

In great and little things alike world-occurrence is a reflection and likeness. [051] We can and must say, of course, that this description, too, is not without its faults. It has something static about it. It gives rise to the impression that creaturely occurrence is an object which can simply be speculatively contemplated, whereas it, no less than the history of the covenant, is really an occurrence which comes upon man as such, and claims him totally, and leaves him no place for mere contemplation or idle experience. A mirror is indeed a futile implement which can be dispensed with if necessary. And when creaturely occurrence is called a mirror it may easily be forgotten that in it there take place service, work and action. Speculative thinkers are warned that they can find no entrance here; that this is only one aspect of the problem; that this aspect cannot be absolutised as such but can have significance only in respect of the character of creaturely occurrence in its relation to the divine activity of grace and salvation. And those who perhaps fear the rightly suspect *analogia entis*EN101 are reminded of the earlier descriptions in which it is quite clear that there can self-evidently be no question of anything but the *analogia fidei sive revelationis*EN102 even in this description of creaturely occurrence as a mirror and likeness.

As we sum up, we must try to be more precise. For not only this final venture but the whole discussion of the concrete meaning of the divine co-ordination and integration of creaturely history with that of the covenant of grace, or of the divinely occasioned co-operation of the creature in this matter, stands in need of more precise statement. We have spoken of the function of creaturely occurrence, and described it as that of a servant or instrument. We have spoken of its *telos*, and described it by calling the created world a theatre. We have spoken of its character, and finally described it as a mirror and likeness. These statements constitute a legitimate answer to the question of the meaning and purpose of this occurrence, and a permissible description of it as the external basis of the history of the covenant, so long as they are all taken together, the fragmentary nature of each of them being perceived and therefore none of them understood or asserted as though it were absolute. Each is merely an imperfect indication of what is here to be described, namely, the divine rule operative in creaturely occurrence. We are not to think, therefore, that what is to be described is really indicated or introduced in any one of these descriptions.

EN101 analogy of being
EN102 analogy of faith or relation

This condition, on which alone all that we have said here is valid, must finally be given an even stricter formulation. What we have said is legitimate only if we realise that it cannot be said of creaturely occurrence in itself and as such, but only of creaturely occurrence as it takes place under the sway of God's sovereign and actual providence. It cannot be said of qualities and determinations inherent to it, but only of qualities and determinations ascribed and imparted to it by God's action in the power of His omnipotent mercy. Creation in itself and as such never has the power, capacity or competence on the basis of the election of grace to be the servant and instrument of the God who acts in the covenant of grace and kingdom of Jesus Christ, to be the theatre of His action and therefore to afford it time, space and opportunity, to be for His children their Father's house and as such a mirror and likeness of His fatherly action. It has no power for this. How could it have? It was not with God when His counsel of grace took shape concerning it. It can know and fulfil the will of God only to the extent that in this counsel decision is made concerning its existence as such. But as creation it has no knowledge of the ways which God will take with it as it exists, and no control of the part which He will allot it. It can neither take, give nor keep the function, purpose and character in which God will and does use it in His dealings with it. We cannot say, therefore, that in itself and as such it possesses and has these qualities and determinations. It possesses and has them only as it receives them, as they are given it by God. We thus say too much if in the sense of an ontological definition we try to say that creation *is* God's servant and instrument, the theatre, mirror and likeness of His gracious and saving action. At this point any "is" can strictly relate only to moments in God's universal rule in which creation may become a servant and instrument, a theatre, mirror and likeness, by God's sovereign and actual will. It is all this as He takes it into His omnipotent and merciful hand in the execution of His plan, giving it these qualities and determinations. It is it in the event of the divinely accomplished co-ordination and integration, in the event of the co-operation for good, to which it is called, authorised and capacitated by Him. That it is created good and even very good by Him means only that it is prepared by Him to be grasped in this way. He has not prepared the creature in vain or for anything else. But as He speaks and commands, it is so (Ps. 33[9]). And it is so in the manner and form, in the function, with the *telos* and character, which it is to have ineluctably and with supreme objectivity, and therefore not merely in the sense of a human opinion, but with God's own truth. We must not abstract from this divine Speaker and Commander if we are to give a legitimate answer to this question of the concrete sense of creaturely occurrence. We must think always of God's living hand which continually lends creaturely occurrence this concrete sense. As the creature cannot anticipate its creation, or give itself existence and essence, so it cannot anticipate God's providence or its use in God's living hand, as though it already were what it must be in this use, or already had what it must have in it. It can only be ready for God, or more exactly for God's action in the

[052]

50

covenant of grace and kingdom of Christ. It can only wait for His omnipotent mercy, acquiring its function, *telos* and character, and becoming God's servant and action, the theatre of His action and mirror and likeness of His glory, in the event of His rule and dominion. We must see clearly that this rule of God's [053] providence over and in creation does not give up or break off, and has and leaves no gaps. It is not the case, then, that sometimes the creature does not acquire these qualities and determinations. The hand of God never rests. And it will never withdraw. Everything is always involved in its power and therefore in that receiving and becoming. For the faithfulness of God never ceases in the kingdom of His grace. There is no moment, place or situation in which His creature escapes Him or becomes indifferent, in which He has no further use for His creature or some part of it, or in which He forgets it. But we must be clear that it is God's faithfulness alone if creation in its totality is in fact always involved in this receiving and becoming, and may thus have this function, *telos* and character, and be this servant and instrument, this theatre, mirror and likeness. God does not owe it His love. He is under no obligation to co-ordinate and integrate it with His work in this way, and enable it to co-operate in His action. It has no glory of its own in this. It can only participate in His glory and glorify Him. What help would it be to have existence and essence by God's creation, and therefore to be made ready for His use, if He did not continually take it to Himself, and lend it this dignity and significance, and cause it to participate in His work, and give it the appropriate glory? What would it be without this active good-pleasure of its Creator? It can only receive, and receive grace for grace, and receive of His fulness (Jn. 1^{16}).

This is the insight without which there could be no legitimate answer to the question of the concrete sense of creaturely occurrence under God's providence, and of its participation in the doing of God's gracious and saving will. We shall conclude by mentioning some of the important deductions to be drawn from this insight.

1. We began this final discussion with the assertion that there can be no question of an independent co-operation of creation in the establishment, direction and fulfilment of the history of the covenant of grace, of a participation of creation in the procuring, attainment and mediation of the love of God which comes to it in this covenant. We made this assertion without giving any reason for it in this particular context. We can now give this specific reason. It takes the form of a conclusion *a minori ad maius*[EN103]. There is no question of an independence of creation in its co-ordination and integration with the divine work of grace, or in respect of its determination as a servant and instrument, a theatre, mirror and likeness of the kingdom of grace. The free love of God alone can give it this function, *telos* and character, and not its own goodness. But if this is so in this sphere, how much more is it the case when it is a matter of the preservation, reconciliation and redemption of the creature

---

[EN103] from the lesser to the greater

fallen into sin and hopelessly threatened in consequence! Since it has no glory, merit or claim of its own on the one side, since God has no obligations [054] towards it, since it is referred exclusively to the active good-pleasure of its Creator in this whole sphere, how could it possible add anything to God's work on the other with its own capacity and action? How could it possibly be *creatura corredemptrix*[EN104]?

2. Creaturely occurrence is the external basis of the history of the covenant. How far this is the case we have tried to show in our consideration of its concrete meaning. But after our last and more precise statement, we cannot overemphasise the fact that it is this external basis, and has therefore constitutive significance even for the occurrence of the history of the covenant, to the extent that it is enacted under God's providence, and this significance is not withdrawn from it, but continually given it by God. It thus has it, but only as it may receive it. Not even momentarily, therefore, can we think away God's free faithfulness towards it if we are to see this significance, and see it in its capacity as the external basis of the history of the covenant. God Himself and God alone continually sees to this external basis of the history of the covenant. He Himself and He alone makes creaturely occurrence His servant and instrument, the theatre, mirror and likeness of His action. It thus follows that we can recognise it as such only in faith in God and His free faithfulness. Hence there follows the simple but pregnant fact that in this respect we walk by faith and not by sight. We can never have this recognition if we look past the internal basis of the history of the covenant, namely, the divine election of grace revealed in Jesus Christ. This recognition can thus take place only in the act of hearing the Word of God, in the act of adoring His inconceivable goodness, in the act of gratitude and the corresponding willingness and readiness to do the will of God. It can be achieved only in the light and power of the Holy Ghost and by the man whom the Father draws to the Son and the Son to the Father. In relation to this recognition we do not find ourselves in a forecourt but in the very centre of the sanctuary. As the kingdom of Jesus Christ is revealed to men in Jesus Christ, so too is the sway of divine providence, the determination of creaturely occurrence, its function, *telos* and character. It is always a matter of recognition from within outwards, from the cross and resurrection of Jesus Christ to all other occurrence, from God's grace to the world of its addressees and recipients. The freedom of the divine providence by which all things are upheld and sustained and meaningful and right can be known only in the freedom of faith which has its origin where God Himself does the work for the sake of which He has created all things, and where He is revealed in this work.

3. This way can be traversed only in this direction. Not even subsequently can this sequence be reversed. We are confronted by the necessary impotence of all systems which radically or practically, primarily or subsequently, abstract

---

[EN104] a creature who is co-redeemer

from God's work of grace and the kingdom of Jesus Christ. In making this abstraction, they forfeit their inward and outward vision. They lack that which   [055] alone could justify their vaunting claims. Even without the freedom of faith, as those who are closed to the revelation of God, we could investigate in all kinds of ways the meaning of creaturely occurrence. But on what principle of exposition could we give an answer? If we do not know of a Creator, we do not know that in world-occurrence we have to do with a creaturely and therefore relative occurrence taking place in a definite connexion and definitely ruled in this connexion. We shall therefore posit absolutely one of its aspects, even perhaps that of its insolubility. But how then can we avoid ascribing to it an autonomous significance supposedly found in this aspect? How can we escape the unending debate whether this significance of the external world is to be found more in its historical aspects or more in its natural, more in its law-abiding or more in its contingent, more in its spiritual or more in its material, or in what combination of all of them? How can we justify ourselves in ascribing this particular significance to world-occurrence? World-occurrence as such does not speak unequivocally. If we hear it say this or that, how can we justify ourselves except on the basis of a significance with which we ourselves have already encountered it? From world-occurrence as such there are obviously only arbitrary and highly debatable ways to a world principle whose superiority, power and credibility can even remotely be compared with the world rule of God. And in that centre from which man in the freedom of faith and under the constraint of the Word of God can continually see afresh the ever new and living work of His hand, he stands quite alone, renouncing his own cleverness and responsibility, his own decision for this or that possibility, his own opinion. What is a world-view if it does not consist in the contemplation of a world-rule, and therefore of a reality which is superior to the world and all its contemplation and interpretation, and can effectively order and co-ordinate world-occurrence? But how can there be the contemplation of a world-rule if there can be no question of that of a world Ruler?

4. We have said that this sequence, and this way of considering it, cannot subsequently be reversed but must always be from within outwards. But this means that there can be a contemplation of the divine world-rule, and therefore of world-occurrence under this rule, and therefore a Christian view of things, only in the movement of faith itself from within outwards, and in the concrete realisation of its perception. We have said that this perception or recognition is possible only in the light and power of the Holy Ghost, in the freedom of faith in which the freedom of the divine providence is manifested. But on both sides this means that there cannot be a closed and static Christian system. What might be given this name can only be the insight of many or few individuals grounded in a concrete perception of God's work of grace and then expressed as such in an equally concrete perception of God's action in   [056] the creaturely sphere. This insight can never take the more solid form of a more permanent view, of theoretical notions of what constitutes God's work in

the creaturely sphere, of definitive assertions concerning the extent to which creaturely occurrence is God's servant, instrument, theatre, mirror and likeness. For the freedom of faith in which alone this insight is possible must always be given to man afresh as the gracious gift of the Holy Spirit. And when it is given afresh, it must always be a new freedom. The establishment of a fixed Christian view, of a lasting picture of the relationship between Creator and creature, would necessarily mean that in taking to-day the insight given him to-day man hardens himself against receiving a new and better one to-morrow. Having thought and spoken as a believer to-day, he would no longer do so to-morrow, but place himself on the same level as the unhappy inventors and champions of non-Christian systems. For what distinguishes him from them but the freedom of faith? What will distinguish him from them if he renounces the freedom of faith to-morrow? The knowledge received in enlightening and empowering by the Holy Ghost will never be closed but always open. Yet it is the objective side which is really decisive. As we have seen, we do not have to perceive immanent qualities and determinations of creaturely occurrence, but divine actions by which it is continually given afresh its function, *telos* and character. In the freedom of faith man follows the way and movement of the divine providence which is free in a very different sense. What God has done to-day, and revealed to man as His action, He will do again to-morrow, but He will perhaps do it quite differently, and reveal it to man in a very different form. That to-morrow as to-day He will give creaturely occurrence its function, *telos* and character is the faithfulness of God on which we can and should count, the constant element for which the believer will look even in respect of to-morrow. But what he cannot say is how God will do it. His world-view as his understanding of creaturely occurrence and the divine providence reigning in and over it will always be that which corresponds to the present measure of his faith and knowledge, to the insight given him by God to-day. It will certainly be a modest insight. Probably it will not usually concern itself with larger or total issues. It will be content to be a clear perception of individual points and questions making possible practical decisions for the next stretches of the way. It will probably consist less in the maintaining of principles and leading tendencies than in the discovery of a small series of promising standpoints. It will probably display many reservations and gaps. In this form it is less likely to acquire a form which will compel the believer sooner or later to become entangled in blatant self-contradictions. It will not become so easily the basis of a programme or party, or an object of debate. It will be an instrument to promote understanding with as many others as possible. But within these limits it will always be sure of itself and fruitful. If the matter is understood within these limits, we may well say that as the believer has faith in God's providence in world-occurrence he may live with a partial world-view which is provisional and modest but also binding. He will not, of course, believe in this partial world-view. But as he believes only in God the Lord, he will have enough light to make some such partial view of world-occurrence—the part which meets his

[057]

54

own requirements—indispensable. And he will be the more glad of it the more he is prepared to be continually led from this point. Man has always many new things to see even when he ostensibly made a serious beginning long ago, and has thus acquired no little genuine skill, in having open eyes for the ways of God in creaturely occurrence.

§ 49

GOD THE FATHER AS LORD OF HIS CREATURE

God fulfils His fatherly lordship over His creature by preserving, accompanying and ruling the whole course of its earthly existence. He does this as His mercy is revealed and active in the creaturely sphere in Jesus Christ, and the lordship of His Son is thus manifested to it.

1. THE DIVINE PRESERVING

Our present task is to unfold and clarify what takes place when God accomplishes what we define as His providential ordering and therefore His fatherly lordship over the creature.

We shall begin at once with the first affirmation that God fulfils His fatherly lordship over the creature by preserving it, that is, by upholding and sustaining its individual existence—the existence which He gave to it as the Creator and which is different from His own existence—and by giving to this existence its continuity. He does this—and on the basis laid down in § 48 we must give precedence to this statement—in His fatherly wisdom and power, as the Lord of the creature who is also the Lord of the covenant of grace. The power in which He sustains the creature is the mercy with which in His Son Jesus Christ He is revealed and active within creation and in creaturely form. And the purpose in which He sustains creation is the revelation of the lordship of His Son, for whose sake He has given to each creature its individual being. Therefore it is this specific power and purpose which makes divinely necessary and operative the preservation of the creature as such. The creature has to be preserved, and is in fact preserved, because this particular will of God has to be done, and is in fact done, both in heaven and on earth, because Jesus Christ is at the right hand of the Father and is our Advocate. It is He who represents our right to existence and the necessity of our existence, and of the existence of the whole creaturely world. It is He who is the divine basis of the preservation and continuance of that existence. For its preservation is for His sake. It is the outflowing, the presupposition and the consequence of the grace which God gave to the creature in His Son, and it takes place in order that in the creaturely world God may be glorified in and through His Son. It can be, and indeed it must be, because He is. This is what makes the preservation of the creature a divinely meaningful and a divinely effective work. Its wisdom and power consist in the fact that it has its basis in Jesus Christ the only beloved Son of God, and therefore in God Himself. It takes place as and because God the

56

Father is (in His Son) for the creature. For that reason and in that sense it is the work of His fatherly lordship and therefore the work of real, genuine, authentic and true lordship, a work which in its holy mercy is quite different from the self-seeking care of the owner for the preservation of his possession, and in its holy freedom quite different from the logical necessity with which a given B is maintained by a given A, a given effect by a given cause. It is the love of God which preserves the creature. This preserving is not, therefore, by chance. It is purposeful at the deepest possible level. It is not menaced by any external circumstances. It is a perfect act of lordship. Whatever we may say by way of definition and description, it must always be measured by the fact that we are dealing with this act of fatherly lordship, and therefore with an act of the eternal God.

We may aptly take as our starting point the Pauline ἐξ αὐτοῦ τὰ πάντα[EN1] (Rom. 11³⁶), which not only looks back to the act of creation but in so doing envisages the whole continuance of the universe as it derives from God, upon the basis of His effective preservation. Yet we must not interpret the phrase according to the sense which it originally bore in the non-Christian source from which Paul perhaps adapted it, but according to the sense in which Paul himself—baptising as it were an originally non-Christian expression—takes and uses it in this particular context, that is, in the thought of the mystery of the existence and history and future of Israel in relation to those who had hitherto been τὰ ἔθνη[EN2]. According to the similar passage in 1 Corinthians 8⁶ the αὐτός[EN3] from whom all things have their being is the εἷς θεὸς ὁ πατήρ[EN4]; and it is the same in the famous and relevant saying in the speech at Athens: ἐν αὐτῷ γὰρ ξῶμεν καὶ κινούμεθα καὶ ἐσμέν[EN5], a saying which is clearly of non-Christian derivation, but which, in relation to all the θεῖον[EN6] native to a world still hostile to Jesus Christ and needing the service of men's hands, either Paul or the author of Acts now uses in order to indicate the perfect rule of God over all creatures as fulfilled in the sending and raising again of Jesus Christ, and also the dependence of all creatures upon Him as the Sustainer of all things. In Hebrews 1³, where the reference is to the One who upholds all things by the Word of His power, it cannot be denied that it is the Son of God who does this. The God of whom it is said in Isaiah 40²⁶ that He "bringeth out the hosts of heaven by number: he calleth them all by names by the greatness of his might, for that he is strong in power; not one faileth"—that God is the God of Israel, a God who is basically different from all other gods or idols. And undoubtedly it is the same God of whom David so truly says in 1 Chronicles 29¹¹ᶠ: "For all that is in the heaven and in the earth is thine; thine is the kingdom, O Lord, and thou art exalted as head above all. Both riches and honour come of thee, and thou reignest over all; and in thine hand is power and might; and in thine hand it is to make great, and to give strength unto all." And more precisely in Nehemiah 9⁶ᶠ: "Thou preservest them all; and the host of heaven worshippeth thee. Thou art the Lord the God, who didst choose Abram, and broughtest him forth out of Ur of the Chaldees, and gavest him the name of Abraham." And we must not forget Psalm 104²⁷ᶠ: "These wait all upon thee; that thou mayest give them their meat in due season. That thou givest them they

---

[EN1] all things are from Him
[EN2] Gentiles
[EN3] He
[EN4] one God, the Father
[EN5] For in him we live, and move, and have our being
[EN6] divinity

gather: thou openest thy hand, they are filled with good. Thou hidest thy face, they are troubled; thou takest away their breath, they die, and return to their dust. Thou sendest forth thy spirit, they are created: and thou renewest the face of the earth." And similarly in Psalm 36[6f]: "Thou preservest man and beast. How excellent is thy loving-kindness, O God, therefore the children of men put their trust under the shadow of thy wings." And more precisely again in Psalm 73[23]: "Nevertheless I am continually with thee: thou hast holden me by my right hand. Thou shalt guide me with thy counsel, and afterwards receive me to glory." It is clear that these are not merely general thoughts concerning the dependence of the creature on the Creator and the care of the Creator for the creature—although they certainly are that, and have to be taken into account in the present context—but they are the concrete reflections of the great saving fact of the incredible and unmerited preservation of the people Israel, by which it is at once apparent and revealed who it is that maintains the existence of the creature as such, the creature Israel in its fields and its vineyards, and also with what goodness He does so. If we were to overlook the concrete reference of the Old as well as the New Testament, passages to the history of salvation—to the extent that this is possible in the case of some of them—we should rob them of their general meaning and relevance. It is only in appearance that they say something which can be and is in fact said in other spheres of religious history. They have their true significance and substance from the biblical context, whose explicit witness makes it unnecessary to look further afield in the case of almost all the passages here adduced.

[060]

By treating of God's providence primarily in terms of His divine preserving of the creature we are following the order of the older dogmatics. But on the basis already laid down we have already given to it a point which it does not have in the older dogmatics, for we differentiate between the God who sustains the creature and a mere supreme being, identifying that sustaining God with the God of the biblical revelation. It is significant that we should begin with the important recognition that the one God the Father is the One to whom all things owe and will always owe not merely their continuance but even the fact that they are there at all. The fact that God is for the creature, that in His own creaturely existence He becomes the pledge and guarantee of its creaturely existence, is the presupposition of the fact that He is also with and above the creature, and of all that as the Lord of the covenant of grace He wills to be towards it in the work and revelation of Jesus Christ. The recognition that of His free and unmerited goodness, and therefore with the highest degree of certainty, God and God alone guarantees the existence of the creature, its being and nature and the whole expression of its life—this belongs indeed to the very beginning of the doctrine of the divine providence.

The traditional concept of *conservatio*[EN7] contains the right idea. It speaks of preservation in being, of the maintaining of that which is, against the threat of dissolution. The *Leidener Synopsis* (1624, *Disp.* 11, 12) uses the expression *permansio*[EN8], by which it obviously means the abiding faithfulness of God towards the creature. Another expression occasionally used is *manutenentia*[EN9], which has all the richness of late Latin and yet is clear in content. With

---

[EN7] preserving
[EN8] persisting presence
[EN9] maintaining

respect to the commonly used *conservatio*[EN10] A. Heidan (*Corp. Theol. chr.*, 1686, 359) observes that it is not altogether a happy choice because it carries with it the idea of cooperation and therefore of a twofold *servatio*[EN11], whereas neither first nor last can there ever be any question of another *servator*[EN12] side by side with God. But perhaps a more relevant question is whether the word *con-servatio* should not be construed and taken with all seriousness in the sense that in the *servare*[EN13] which is here envisaged we may well have to do with a *servare* which is subordinate to another and true *servare*, that is, with the external and additional grace of the preservation of the creature which necessarily corresponds to the internal and genuine grace of redemption in Jesus Christ. In the 17th century no one thought of this explanation of the *cum*[EN14], but in so far as we have to explain it we can obviously do so only along these lines.

[061]

1. We will now consider in what sense we have to understand the statement that God preserves the creature. At first sight the answer seems to be quite simple. He arranges that it has its reality not only outside and beside Him in a moment which corresponds to His eternity (only to be snuffed out again), but also in a temporal sequence, so that it can have it again and again, thus enjoying a continuing existence. If God maintains the creature, then it is clear that there is no creaturely moment corresponding to His eternity. According to the first biblical record, did not the fashioning of the creature take place with the creation of time, and therefore within time? But the statement that God preserves the creature means much more than that He gave it time. When He created it. He might well have given it time in order not to preserve it indefinitely, but to set an early end to its being with the time which He created with it. But if He really sustains it, this means that He gives it more time, that He confirms it in its being in time. In the same way that He willed and gave it to the creature to become and to be, so He wills and gives it to the creature to be again and again, to continue to be. This is how he preserves it. And He preserves it as is fitting that He the Creator should preserve it, and that the creature should be preserved by Him. He preserves it eternally. He does not allow His creation to perish. He keeps faith with the creature. And yet He does not preserve it illimitably, but within the limits which correspond to its creaturely existence. The fact that He preserves is not exclusive but inclusive. Not merely creaturely individuals but the creaturely species and forms are all limited, as is indeed the creaturely world in its totality. Everything has its own time, and no more than that time. And the appointment of such a time shows that its being, and all created being as such, is a limited being. To no creature does it belong to be endless, omnipresent or enduring. The preservation which God grants to the creature is the preservation of its limited being. In its totality this preservation relates to a space which is limited, and in its eternity to a time which is limited. It will be understood that it is not for this reason partial, transitory or

---

[EN10] preserving
[EN11] service
[EN12] preserver
[EN13] serving
[EN14] with

imperfect. Indeed, for this very reason it is a complete and final and perfect preservation. For what could be more perfect than that God should give to the creature—to individuals, and species and forms, and the whole creaturely world—that which is proper to it, that to each one He should give that which is proper, that is, that which it is able to have of being, and of space and time for that being, according to its existence as posited by the wisdom and power of God, and that which it ought to have of being and space and time according to the righteousness and mercy of God? It is in this way and this way alone that in the biblical sense the divine preserving is a divine work and the preservation of the creature a divine favour.

[062]

For the creature to have its part in that history in which God displays His grace, and finally in the kingdom of Jesus Christ, it must continue to be there, and therefore it must be preserved. It must have a continuing existence in space and time; not of course an unlimited but a limited existence. Creaturely history can take place only amongst and on behalf of a plurality of many subjects which exist side by side with and in succession to each other. A creature which had an infinite existence would as such be excluded from the history of the covenant of grace which is the meaning of all creaturely occurrence. A preservation which consisted in extending the being of creation to infinity would certainly not be the work of God, who as the Preserver of the creature is also the Lord of the covenant of grace and of the history of the covenant. And it would certainly not be a benefit on the part of God. It is with a definite limitation that the Creator who is also the Lord of the covenant must preserve the creature, and it is with a definite limitation that the creature must be preserved by the Creator. And if it is asked whether a preservation which relates to a finite creature and is therefore itself finite can be a genuine and serious and full preservation, the answer is that its fulness is seen in the connexion in which it takes place. And this connexion is as follows. It is an eternal and divine, but also an external and additional preservation of being, which is complementary to that internal and proper preservation which is by participation in the kingdom of Jesus Christ, in whom there is given to the creature—to the individual, the species and forms, and the whole of creation—even within the limits of time and space the most genuine and serious and full preservation, namely, that which is ordained and promised in fellowship with the perfect and eternal being of God.

It is surprising that in their doctrine *De conservatione* the older dogmaticians did not feel more strongly the difficulty which lies in the fact that the divine preservation of the creature obviously has a limit even in relation to creation as a whole, let alone the individual or the forms or species; that everything as it now is will some day only have been. The problem was of course touched on occasionally and in part. *Creaturam ... libere conservat, quamdiu ipsi placet ... individua conservat in esse semper, dum sunt, non ad semper sive ut semper sint*[EN15], writes Quenstedt (*Theol. did. pol.*, 1685, I, 13, sect. 1, th. 14). And perhaps (P. van Mastricht *Theor.*

EN15 The creature ... He freely preserves so long as He wishes ... He preserves individuals in their being for the whole time that they exist, but not so that they should exist always or forever

1. The Divine Preserving

had in mind the eschatological problem of the end of the world when he defined the *conservatio*[EN16] as the action *qua persistere Deus res omnes facit, quamdiu sibi videtur*[EN17], or negatively as *Dei voluntas, qua res ad illud usque tempus et non ulterius existat*[EN18]. But we are not told to what extent this limitation of the *conservatio*[EN19] may not signify an imperfection of the divine act, a limitation and therefore a denial of the faithfulness of the Creator to the creature. They could portray quite impressively the mighty divine *sustentare*[EN20] of all things, but is it an act of the eternal and perfect God or is it not? And if it is, how can it have an end? Thomas Aquinas was occupied by this problem and the explanation which he gave is rather tortuous (*S. theol.* I, qu. 104, art. 4, ad. 2). There derives from one and the same sustaining God a *contrarium agens*[EN21] which prevents many although not all creatures (he is probably thinking of the immortal soul) from participating in the power of the divine preservation granted to them, and therefore from being preserved eternally. Although everything (both individually and collectively) has its time and some day will only have been, the sustaining love itself has no such limits and is therefore unceasing. As we have tried to show, this fact is reflected in the presupposition that the being of all things as preserved by God is correlated to the history of the divine covenant of grace. To recall *Conf. Aug.* VIII in this connexion : *Item docent, quod una sancta ecclesia perpetuo mansura sit*[EN22], is to see that there is no problem in the limitation of created being as such. And according to the *Heidelberg Catechism*, Qu. 54, in and with the knowledge "that out of the whole human race, from the beginning to the end of the world, the Son of God, by His Spirit and Word, gathers, defends and preserves for Himself unto everlasting life, a chosen communion in the unity of the true faith," we can have the direct and comforting assurance that "I am, and forever shall remain, a living member of the same."

[063]

Hence we may see that there is no contradiction between the death and end and passing of the individual and of creation as a whole, and its eternal preservation by God. For in its relationship to Jesus Christ, in its participation in the continuing history of His people from the beginning of the world to the end, each in its limited time and space can receive and enjoy its own perfectly satisfying participation in eternal life in fellowship with God. It does not have anything more than a finite preservation. Only in that finite preservation can it participate in the history of Jesus Christ and His people, and therefore in eternal life. But the older dogmatics could not deduce this line of thought from its presuppositions, and therefore it was unable to meet or even face the difficulty which confronted it at this point. Hence its praise of the faithfulness and constancy of God as the Preserver of all things, however sincerely meant, could not but fail to ring entirely true.

2. We enquire further concerning the order of the divine preserving of all things, and after full consideration we must reply that it takes place wholly and utterly as a free act of God, but in such a way that creation itself is the means by which it is preserved in being: the human body by the soul which directs it; the human soul by the body which serves it; the race as a whole and all the species of beasts and plants by natural propagation; the individual by his human and cosmic environment; and every creaturely thing by its environment and

---

[EN16] preserving
[EN17] by which God makes all things persist so long as it seems good to Him
[EN18] the will of God by which a thing exists for that length of time and no longer
[EN19] preserving
[EN20] sustaining
[EN21] contrary mode of acting
[EN22] And so they teach that the one holy church will remain forever

according to the particular order of that environment. God Himself sustains the creature, but He sustains it in the context in which He has created it and ordains that it should exist. That God preserves the creature means properly speaking that He preserves this context of its being and that He preserves it in this context. At this point we are confronted by an important formal distinction between the activity of God in His providence, and His activity as Creator on the one hand and as Lord of the covenant of grace on the other. In creation God acts directly, i.e., without the intervention of other things, for other things could enter in only as the product of His creative activity and not as the co-efficient of it—not even as a pure means. And the creative work of God has this in common with His work of grace—that when God calls Abraham, when He elects Israel, when He leads Israel through the Red Sea, when He awakens the prophets, when He causes Jesus Christ to be born of the Virgin and to die for the salvation of the world and to rise again from the dead to reveal that salvation, when in the whole course of these happenings He heaps up miracle on miracle, when He sanctifies water in baptism and bread and wine in the Lord's Supper, when He gathers and protects and sustains His Church, when the Holy Spirit calls a man by the Gospel, and sanctifies him and preserves him in a true faith, all these things take place within the created order with the very same immediacy as the act of creation itself, and creation is now as fully the object of His activity as it was then its product. But when it is a matter of the preservation of creation as such, when it is a matter of that which succeeds creation but precedes redemption, there is need of a free but obviously not of a direct or immediate activity on the part of God. In order to continue in being subsequent to creation and with a view to redemption, all that the creature needs is the preservation of the context of its being and its own preservation within that context, a context which was created by God in order that the individual might have its permanence and stability and continuity within the whole, and the whole within the individual, according to the will and ordination of God.

But again, if we are to see how necessary this matter is, we have to consider the significance acquired by creaturely existence within the divine covenant of grace. For there is more to be said than that within this covenant the creature can be only the object of the divine activity, nor is this the positive side of the matter. For in so far as the creature is the object of the divine activity and the recipient of the grace of God, it becomes *ipso facto*[EN23], not the means of this grace, for grace works directly or not at all, but its witness and herald and proclaimer. Thus even in the utter humility of its spiritual existence it acquires an active function within the history of the covenant. It has a mission to fulfil, or a commission to execute, a mission or commission to its fellow-creatures. Abraham becomes the father of Isaac and Jacob and therefore the forefather of Jesus Christ. Israel becomes a light of the Gentiles. The prophets are not

[064]

[EN23] for that very reason

prophets to themselves but to their people. Jesus Christ had to become man to represent as man all other men. The biblical miracles, and later baptism and the Lord's Supper, are signs of the work and revelation of God. The Church is either a missionary Church or it is no church at all. And Christians are either the messengers of God (with or without words) to both Jew and Gentile or else they are not Christians at all. Within the very covenant of grace in which, as in creation, we have to do wholly and utterly with the direct initiative and activity of God to the creature, there at once arises, and again wholly and utterly, a relationship of creature and fellow-creature, and creatures themselves are marked and singled out for the service of God towards other creatures. It is a purely spiritual relationship in which God Himself acts directly, and the creature can only point other creatures to that divine work and testify concerning it, but cannot in any way advance or mediate that work. And yet there can be no doubt that the relationship which we discern here is also a creaturely relationship. Even the covenant of grace both consists and is spiritually renewed and sustained in a creaturely nexus of this Kind. God acts directly in the great complex of the covenant history as it takes place in the creaturely world, beginning in Israel and continuing in the Church. He does not act by means of creation, but He certainly does not act apart from it. He acts towards it and within it. And the spiritual relationship of the creature in the covenant of grace is the dominant pattern or type of what God does when He preserves creation as such in being. God maintains its existence in a way which is not parallel but corresponds to the significance which it acquires in this covenant. He does this by maintaining the context of the being created by Him, and by maintaining all being created by Him within this context. The context, and itself within this context, is the means to the preservation of the creature. In the covenant of grace the creature is not the means but only the witness and sign, the liturgical assistant as it were to God, who is the only effective Minister. But when it is a question of its preservation here, with a view to what it is to become in the sphere of grace, here in the midst between creation and redemption the creature is a means both for God on the one hand and for itself on the other—always presupposing, of course, that God the Creator wills to use it as such. Its actual preservation is no less the free act of God because in this case He acts indirectly and not directly. Hence it is not really the creature which sustains the creature. It is not the context of the whole which guarantees the continuance of the individual, nor is it the individual which guarantees the continuity of the whole. And there can be no question of the creature being able even vicariously to do in its own strength that which God wills it to do. It is God alone who does everything according to His own free good-pleasure. But He does it by maintaining this relationship and therefore by maintaining the creature, by means of the creature. If we note the correlation between His work here and His work within the covenant of grace we shall be kept from the error of regarding either the creature or its nexus as the sustaining principle of creation. As we consider His work within the covenant we shall be constantly

[065]

[066] aware of the fact that His indirect work here in the nexus of being is no less His free decision than is His direct work there in that other and spiritual nexus. And even here in the nexus of being we shall not see anyone else at work save God Himself, not to mention the fact that we shall always distinguish sharply between the nexus of being which is the means and the One who uses this means.

When we say this, we are in some degree following Thomas Aquinas (*S. theol.*, I, *qu.* 104, *art.* 2) in his treatment of the question: *Utrum Deus immediate omnem creaturam conservet?*EN24 His answer is as follows: No, He does not preserve creation directly, but *Deus conservat res quasdam in esse mediantibus aliquibus causis.* EN25 The crucial objection which he has to meet is that if God is *immediate creator omnium* then of necessity He is *immediate* the *conservator*EN26 of all things. And his answer is as follows: *Deus immediate omnia creavit: sed in ipsa rerum creatione ordinem in rebus instituit, ut quaedam ab aliis dependerent, per quas secundario conservarentur in esse, praesupposita tamen principali conservation, quae est ab ipso (ad 1).* EN27. It will be seen that Thomas did not intend this *conservatio secundum ordinem*EN28 to apply to the whole of created reality, but only to a part, the other part being obviously reserved as the object of a *conservatio immediata.* EN29 In the context it is not definitely stated, but it is also not excluded, that by the part to which he was not referring (according to our reading) he meant that which belongs to the particular activity of the saving grace of God. At all events it was merely the caprice of a temporally conditioned natural philosophy which led Petrus van Mastricht (*loc. cit.*) to take a different path, specifying something very different, *quaedam immaterialia*EN30 (the heavens, the *materia prima*EN31, the elements), as the object of a direct divine preservation in contradistinction to the rest of creation.

It was R. A. Lipsius (*Lehrb. d. ev. prot. Dogm.*², 1879, 394f.) who on the other side pressed the concept of *conservatio mediata*EN32 to the absurd length of identifying the sustaining activity of God with the uniformity which rules in all things, and conversely of regarding the uniformity which we cannot yet perceive in its totality as the constant expression of the divine will of preservation. This is only typical of the total sacrifice which the Liberal theology of the 19th century felt that it must make to the spirit of the age—in the case of Lipsius perhaps to his Jena colleague Ernst Haeckel. But in making it he allowed two evident errors to creep in: 1. that we understand the nexus of being of all created things (what Thomas described as the *ordo*EN33 by which one thing is dependent on another) quite one-sidedly and therefore falsely if we understand it only from the standpoint of the uniform interconnexion of all being and events, for, as the (in this respect) far wiser older theology almost universally maintained, it has also the aspect of contingence in which all things must be considered according to their freedom; and 2. that even if we do understand the creaturely nexus of being more comprehensively, its identification with the divine preservation

---

EN24 Whether God preserves every creature directly
EN25 God preserves certain things in their being by means of other causes
EN26 direct creator of all things ... directly ... preserver
EN27 God created all things directly, but that act of creation He established an order among things, so that some depend on others, through which they are preserved in being - though God Himself remains the principal cause of their preservation
EN28 preserving according to order
EN29 direct preserving
EN30 certain immaterial objects
EN31 primal matter
EN32 mediated preservation
EN33 order

1. *The Divine Preserving*

involves a bland surrender of the concepts God and creation. For the identification of the divine preservation with the creaturely nexus means a flat denial of the fact that this nexus is not grounded upon or maintained by itself, but has over it an independent Lord and Sustainer. And it is a poor expedient when all that the religious understanding can do is to interpret as an act of divine preservation that which otherwise would have to be regarded merely as the foundation and preservation of the world by itself. To make a more cautious distinction and to interpret the ἐξ αὐτοῦ^{EN34} primarily as a sign of lordship above the τὰ πάντα^{EN35}, we do not need to overlook and deny the significance and power of the nexus which God created, of the *ordo*^{EN36} which has to be understood not only as a uniform process but also as a free movement, nor do we need to overlook and deny the constant, relative and immanent preservation of the creature by the creature. Augustine saw his way clearly at this point: *Sunt qui arbitrentur tantummodo mundum ipsum factum a Deo, cetera iam fieri ab ipso mundo sicut ille ordinavit et iussit, Deum ipsum autem nihil operari. Contra quos profertur illa sententia Domini: Pater meus usque modo operatur (Joh. 5¹⁷) ... sic ergo credamus, vel, si possumus etiam intelligamus, usque nunc operari Deum, ut, si conditis ad eo rebus operatic eius subtrahatur, intercidant*^{EN37}. He says this, and yet he does not fail to see that to all things, to angels and stars and winds and seas and the animal world and human history, God has lent the specific form on whose basis they have their own specific movement (*De Gen. ad lit.* 5, 20). He says this, and yet his view of the relation of God to the creature is as follows: *Implet Deus coelum et terram praesente potentia, non absente natura. Sic itaque administrat omnia, quae creavit, ut etiam ea proprios exercere et agere motus sinat.*^{EN38}. And J. Gerhard (who was also of Jena) reasons as follows: Nothing is more natural to man than to move of himself, *et tamen in Deo movemur*^{EN39} (Acts 17²⁸). Nothing is more natural for the sun than to rise day after day, and yet it is God who causes it to rise (Mt. 5⁴⁵). And this is how we have to understand Matthew 4⁴ ("Man doth not live by bread alone"): Even bread has no power to nourish in the sense that it could do so apart from the Word of God by which it was created and has its power to nourish, but in order to exercise this property it needs the continual influence (*influxus*) of the creative and sustaining Word of God. Similarly neither herbs and prepared medicines nor the physician who administers them can of themselves and as such heal a man, but only the hand of God present within them (*Loci,* 1610, VI, 6).

[067]

In short, even in the indirectness in which it is undoubtedly fulfilled, the preservation of the creature must still be regarded as an action of God as He freely disposes of the whole mediation of the creature, an action which is not conditioned by this mediation but on the contrary conditions it. In practice the older theology held fast to this truth, and when it referred to the "hand" or "Word" of God in this context, and quoted the text John 5¹⁷, it came very near to giving to this decisive insight a certainty which, if it had been present and active at a later date, would have made quite impossible any defection along the lines of R. A. Lipsius. In the light of the fatherly sovereignty of God in the kingdom of Jesus Christ, in

---

^{EN34} from Him
^{EN35} all things
^{EN36} order
^{EN37} There are those who think that although the world itself was made by God, still other things were made by the world itself as God ordained and commanded, yet with God Himself doing nothing. Against them this sentence of the Lord may be offered: "My Father works hitherto (Jn 5.17) ... Therefore we should believe this, and, if we can, we should also understand that because God still works now, if His work were to be withdrawn from the things founded by Him, they would be destroyed
^{EN38} God fills the heavens and the earth with his present power, but their own nature is not for that reason abolished. And so He directs everything which He has created in such a way as to allow them to exercise and pursue their own proper movements
^{EN39} and yet we move in God

which the meaning of creaturely existence is manifested in its office as a witness to fellow-creatures of the grace of God, the identification of this existence with God the Father, and of the sustaining power of this existence with the sustaining power of God, is basically excluded. But if we cease to look to this sovereignty, ignoring the correlation between the means of being and the spiritual nexus of creation, we may refrain from this identification, as did the older theology both unanimously and resolutely, but it is not basically excluded. In these circumstances the prohibition of the identification of the preserving of the Creator with that of the creature has no compelling force. It does not have the force of a conclusion *a maiori ad minus*[EN40]. And it is to this weakness of the "orthodox" position that we have here to draw attention in spite of our respect for all the faithfulness which it displayed in practice.

3. It has been rightly said that the *modus*[EN41] of the divine preservation is inconceivable. It is inconceivable because we can understand it only as an act of the free goodness of God. God does not owe it to the creature to preserve it, to give to it continuance, and to give to its continuance time. He did not owe it to the creature to create it. When He did create it, He might well have caused it to exist only in that moment and then not to exist any longer. His perfect will—and it would still have to be regarded as good—might well have been fulfilled towards the creature in that way. That He willed it otherwise, that He [068] has willed to preserve the creature thus far, and that He obviously wills to preserve it further, is an overflowing of His free love and therefore of His incomprehensibility. But since this overflowing does actually take place, we have to reckon with the fact that the preservation of the creature is in accordance with His good-pleasure and therefore with His holy being, for in God there is no caprice. God is, and is good, in such a way, and His goodness is inconceivable in the fact, that He wills to preserve the creature, to fulfil His will towards it in its permanence and continuity. And for this reason when we are face to face with the work of God there is always room for surprise and wonder and praise and thanksgiving. The election which God already made and executed when He created the creature was not a transitory, let alone a capricious election. It was God's eternal election, and it is confirmed to be such in the work of His eternal preservation of the creature. And this confirmation—at which we can never sufficiently marvel—is the modus of His preservation. God does not cease but continues to be to the creature the One who eternally elects, and who upon the basis of this election has already created it.

We cannot say that He continues to create it. That is unnecessary, for it has already been created, and created well. If He were to create it afresh with every moment of time, as has been suggested, this would not merely presuppose an imperfection in the original creation but it would also involve in some measure its continual dissolution and complete renewal, so that its continuing existence would consist in a permanent fluctuation between life and death and life, between being and non-being and being.

This view can have its attractions, for not only do we find something like it in the mystical

---

[EN40] from the greater to the lesser
[EN41] mode

teaching of all ages and countries, but also (it may be) in the thought expressed by Goethe in the poem entitled "One and All" (1821):

> "And to create anew that which is created.
> That it might not arm itself to immobility,
> This is the task of unending, living activity.
> And that which was not will now become
> Clear sun and coloured earth;
> But it can never rest.
> It must arise in creative action.
> First forming and then transforming itself;
> Only in appearance can it ever stand.
> The eternal moves forward in all things.
> For everything must dissolve into nothingness.
> If it is to continue in being."

In the poem entitled *"Testament"* (1828) Goethe with the wisdom of old age did of course place alongside this teaching a relative—but very relative!—*sed contra*[EN42]:

> "No being can dissolve into nothingness!
> The eternal moves forward in all things,
> Consider yourself blessed in being!
> Being is eternal: for laws
> Protect the living treasures
> By which the cosmos is adorned."

[069]

There can be no question that in these two poems, as a close analysis would show, he is not really contradicting himself, but, as is quite possible within his total conception of things, he is simply saying the same thing in two different ways. It was certainly not intentional when, in contradistinction to the corresponding line of the one poem, in the first line of the other he made a statement which is patent of a Christian interpretation. And the contention that in both poems he consciously foreshadowed poetically the law of the conservation of energy as discovered in the latter half of the 19th century (cf. E. v. d. Hellen, *Jub.-Ausg.* 2, 352) definitely overlooks what was for Goethe both that which preserves and also that which is preserved.

The understanding of divine preservation as a series of acts of creation, and the consequent notion of a divine constant in the flux of the being and non-being of creation, cannot possibly be right, for in such an idea the very thing upon which everything turns at this point in the Christian doctrine of preservation, the identity of the creature in its continuity, is wrapped in an unrecognisable obscurity if not completely destroyed. This is true even though it is a question of its continuity outwith identity, and not its non-continuity.

The "continuance in change" of which Goethe speaks was stated by him under this title in an older poem (c. 1800) which treats of the passing and transitoriness of all phenomena:

[EN42] on the contrary

> "Let the beginning and the end
> Come together in one!
> Let thyself flow past
> More swiftly than circumstances!
> Give thanks that the Muses' favour
> Promises thee the immortal:
> The content in thy bosom,
> And the form in thy spirit."

And similarly in the original words of the poem of 1817 entitled *"Daemon"* (according to his own commentary Goethe means by this the necessary, finite and unchangeable individuality of the person):

> "As on the day which lent thee to the world,
> The sun stood still at the greeting of the planets.
> Thou didst at once and constantly increase,
> According to the law by which thou didst begin,
> So must thou be, thou canst not escape thyself,
> Thus did the Sibyls and the prophets speak,
> And neither time nor force can ever mar
> The form already stamped in its living growth."

And similarly in the famous protest against Albrecht von Haller's distinction between the kernel and husk in nature:

> "Nature has neither kernel,
> Nor husk,
> It is all things all at once.
> Consider yourself first of all,
> Whether you are kernel or husk!"—

[070]   taken together with the closing words of Goethe's "Ultimatum"

> "Is not the kernel of the nature
> Of men in the heart?"

The decisive verse in the superficially contradictory "Testament" of 1828 is in complete agreement:

> "Enjoy in measure fulness and blessing;
> Reason is always present
> When life rejoices in life,
> For the past is constant,
> The future lives in advance—
> The instant is eternity."

Bernhard Groethuysen (cf. *Evang. Theologie*, 1948, 256) has given us a fine and pertinent restatement of Goethe's position. Man must not try to transcend himself if he is to be truly himself. What then? "I will constantly rediscover myself. I will be myself. There is only one life, the life of Goethe. There is nothing outside, everything is within. And everywhere you encounter yourself. You never escape yourself. You never escape your own life." There is no question of not being to-day the man I was yesterday. "I am to-day what I was yesterday and will be to-morrow. Looking back, I see myself, and I converse with the man I was. Are not he and I and the countless others which I once was all united in the same life? It was the life of childhood, and the life of old age, but both reach out to one another. The old man has not

68

destroyed the child. Look, it plays there still." Is it a terrible thought that there is no continuance, only change? On the contrary, "If I remained as I am, how could I be myself? Should I be alive at all if nothing changed either within or without?" This abiding element may in some sort be equated with the root of the soul which according to the teaching of the mystics is timelessly constant in its union with God even in the flux of phenomena. And in the last analysis may it not be that this view leads us to that of the moment in which the world created by God might have existed and not existed had God so willed? Supposing God only dreamed the creature? Or supposing a creature like God only dreamed its fellow-creatures—dreamed them in Goethe's sense, in what was for that god-like creature the most glorious and fruitful and constructive way? The company into which we are betrayed when we accept a *creatio continuaia*EN43 is no recommendation. Its charms must therefore be resisted. We must pay heed to the somewhat isolated objection which G. Thomasius (*Christi Person und Werk*, I, 1886, 146) once made to the application of this concept, that it destroys the limit laid down by Genesis 2^2 and Hebrews 4^4, and that consistently carried through it threatens to change into a mere appearance both the context of the creature and also the whole process of its existence. And it is a matter for surprise that a man like J. Cocceius (*S. theol.*, 1662, 28, 12 f.) did not perceive this, but like many others espoused the concept with some enthusiasm.

Leaving this view, we understand the *modus*EN44 of the divine preservation of the creature to be simply that God willed to be faithful to the eternal election of the creature which He made prior to creation and in which He ascribed to it its being and content and existence, and that even when the work of creation was finished He was faithful and will always be faithful to it. In relation to the creature He does not cease to acknowledge His obligation to that eternal election and to the act of creation grounded upon it. He does not repent of having associated with Himself the created cosmos, or of having associated Himself with that cosmos, of having made Himself co-existent with it, and to that extent [071] (that is, in that context) of having made Himself cosmic and human, as we read in the story of His Sabbath rest. He does not repent of having surrendered Himself to this attachment to the creature. The fact that He does not repent, that He wills to be and to remain to the creature that which in its creation He became and was, is His overflowing goodness in the preservation of the creature. We must reiterate that it is His free and unmerited goodness. Its basis is revealed only in the election of grace from which the election of the creature and therefore its preservation derives; and how should it not be revealed, in all its inconceivability, in that election, in Jesus Christ? It is therefore the majesty of God which is active in this His goodness. This is what makes His preserving effective. This is the guarantee that He who wills to preserve us can accomplish that which He wills, as an almighty God. And the almightiness of God is neither obscure nor capricious. There is no other majesty but that of His goodness. This is what makes His preserving reliable. It is the guarantee that He who alone can preserve us will in fact preserve us, as a trustworthy Father. If we describe the preservation of the creature as a divine act, a divine work which is done to it, a divine power which is given to it, we must be quite

---

EN43 continued creation
EN44 mode

clear that by this we mean simply that God continues to be to the creature this God, the God who on the basis of the election of grace elects it to its own specific being and existence. It is preserved in virtue of the fact that He is this God. In the fact that He is this God the act or work of preservation takes place.

Augustine spoke boldly but quite accurately of the *stabilis motus*[EN45] of this preservation (*De Gen. ad lit.* 5, 20). Anselm of Canterbury (*Monol.*, 13) described it as a *servatrix praesentia*[EN46]. And Thomas Aquinas expanded as follows: *conservatio rerun a Deo non est per aliquam novam actionem, sed per continuationem actionis qua dat esse; quae quidem actio est sine motu et tempore*[EN47]. (*S. theol.*, I, qu. 104, ad 4).

On this living and trustworthy basis in God Himself, it is decided, and continually decided, that the creature may have permanence and continuity. Without this living and trustworthy basis in God Himself, without the continuity in which God continually abides by His election, by His free but overflowing goodness, and finally, without the election of His grace which is the basis of His goodness, the creature could not and would not continue. But the living and trustworthy basis in God continues, and therefore the creature continues. Because of God it cannot not continue; it cannot perish.

Thomas Aquinas (*S. theol.*, I, qu. 104, art. 3–4) advanced the following consideration in relation to this aspect of the problem. The question is rightly put: *Utrum Deus possit aliquid in nihilum redigere?*[EN48] And we must answer in the affirmative: God had the power to do this. The preservation of the creature is just as much a matter of the free good-pleasure of God as its creation. Only if the existence and therefore the creation of the world were necessary for God (which they are not) could we answer the question in the negative. We cannot even appeal to the goodness of God, as though God were under some constraint either to or by that goodness to preserve the creature. For if the goodness of God is the basis of all things, it is so, not *ex necessitate naturae*[EN49], as though God had need of the created order, but *per liberam voluntatem*[EN50]. Hence the goodness of God could be withdrawn from the created order without in any way ceasing to be perfect goodness. The matter is quite different if we ask: *Utrum aliquid in nihilum redigatur?*[EN51] Put in this way, the question must be answered most definitely in the negative. God does in fact preserve all things, although he had the power not to do so. We see what Goethe might have meant (but did not) with his saying: "No being can dissolve into nothingness!" when Thomas explains briefly (*simpliciter*): *Quod nihil omnino in nihilum redigetur*[EN52]. And we must take note when after various other arguments we come to his final statement: *Redigere aliquid in nihilum non pertinet ad gratiae manifestationem, cum magis per hoc divina potentia et bonitas ostendatur, quod res in esse*

[072]

[EN45] steady motion
[EN46] preserving presence
[EN47] the preserving of things by God does not take place through any new action, but through the continuation of the action by which He gives being; and this is an action without motion or time
[EN48] Whether God is able to return any created thing to nothingness
[EN49] from a necessity of nature
[EN50] through free will
[EN51] Whether any created thing is returned to nothingness
[EN52] That nothing is in any respect returned to nothingness

1. *The Divine Preserving*

conservat[EN53]: which seems to suggest that the undeniable freedom which God has not to preserve the creature but to allow it to perish is not compromised by the revelation of the freedom which He has actualised as the freedom of His grace. As demonstrated in practice. His power and might are better attested in the fact that He does maintain things in being. In this context, this is the only occasion that Thomas mentions the point, and he makes striking use of it. It is perhaps of a piece with these presuppositions that he is so sure of the matter. He was far more sure of it than was F. Burmann after him (*Syn. Theol.*, 1678, 1, 43, 17), who only believed that perhaps there could not be any *annihilatio*[EN54] of anything that is—on the ground that God did not create any creature in vain—which is something that Burmann could not really know.

If we do not keep before us the living and trustworthy basis in God Himself, then either we cannot assert at all that His preservation of the creature is directly and eternally effective, that no being can perish, or else we can do so only in the form of a hazy surmise. It is the God who abides by His election of the creature, whose goodness overflows because it is in fact grounded in His election of grace, it is this God who sees to it that no creature can dissolve into nothingness. If the assertion is to be solidly grounded, it must relate to this God and it must be grounded in the work and revelation of this God. Related to any other god, or to a supreme being, it can never be made with certainty. And this means that to be made with certainty it must be a deduction from the primary assertion that for the sake of His Son God has elected the creature from all eternity, that in His Son he loves it eternally and that for the sake of His Son He will not allow it to perish. It must be an assertion grounded in the knowledge of the Father in the Son. Only in this form is it necessary or compelling. But in this form it is necessary and compelling. If the purpose of God in creation is the covenant of grace, then necessarily God gives to the creature an unshakeable continuity. We may go further and say that necessarily it cannot not have that continuity for the sake of God. And the necessary reminder that God is free to deprive it of that continuity then becomes an indispensable elucidation of the fact that His election of grace is an election of *grace*, His covenant of *grace* a covenant of grace, and that therefore any rights or claims which the creature might advance on the ground of its preservation are quite without foundation, are indeed completely excluded, as is the idea of an inward compulsion to which God in subjected in virtue of His Godhead, so that He has to preserve the creature. But taken seriously this reminder does not involve in any way a weakening or compromising but rather a constant deepening of the knowledge that, because the almighty God and trustworthy Father interceded for it with His own eternal being, the creature of God is indeed eternally hidden and kept and preserved in the whole temporal span of His eternal being. We have only to keep before us the living and trustworthy

[073]

[EN53] To return a created thing to nothingness is not appropriate to the display of grace, since the divine power and goodness are better demonstrated by the fact that created things are preserved in being

[EN54] annihilation

71

basis of this knowledge in God himself, the *manifestatio gratiae*[EN55], Jesus Christ, and we can have complete certainty in the matter. Without this ontic basis everything would, of course, be quite different. And without the noetic presupposition we should be dealing with something quite different—or at any rate what we have said could not be said with any certainty or on any very adequate basis.

It is true that the affirmation with which we began, that the *modus*[EN56] of the divine preservation is inconceivable, derives from F. Burmann (*h.c.* I, 43, 13), but again he establishes it somewhat inadequately: *cum operationes entis infiniti a natura finita plene percipi non possunt.*[EN57] This is not the Christian basis and therefore it is not the effective basis which we have to lay. It is not as *ens infinitum*[EN58] but in His grace that God is inconceivable, and He is so not to *natura finita*[EN59] but to the man who glorifies His grace. That is why the fact of man's preservation, and of the preservation of the whole creaturely world, is inconceivable. But to man and to that world grace brings with it the unexpected and undeserved and unmerited fact of the free movement of the free God. It brings with it that which can be recognised as fatherly goodness but cannot be apprehended as such, i.e., that which cannot be deduced from anything higher, but simply accepted with thankfulness as a fact.

4. We must now take expressly into account the fact that the creature for its part stands in need of preservation by God and therefore of His free goodness. Its creation rested upon the free resolve of God; it was God's free act. The creature was not from all eternity like God. There was a time when it was not. And God was not under any obligation to cause it to come into existence and to be. He created it "out of nothing," that is, by distinguishing that which He willed from that which He did not will, and by giving it existence on the basis of that distinction. To that divine distinction it owes the fact that it is. And to the same distinction it owes the fact that it can continue to be. By preserving the distinction God preserves the creature. It is a matter of its preservation, and we must now apply ourselves to the development of the concept *conservatio*[EN60] and say that it is a matter of its being maintained against overthrow by that which is not. That which is not is that which God as Creator did not elect or will, that which as Creator He passed over, that which according to the account in Genesis 1^2 He set behind him as chaos, not giving it existence or being. That which is not is that which is actual only in the negativity allotted to it by the divine decision, only in its exclusion from creation, only, if we may put it thus, at the left hand of God. But in this way it is truly actual and relevant and even

[074]

[EN55] display of grace
[EN56] mode
[EN57] since the operations of an infinite being cannot fully be perceived by a finite nature
[EN58] infinite being
[EN59] finite nature
[EN60] preserving

active after its own particular fashion. At this point we touch on a whole complex of problems which we shall have to face more specifically in the next section of this chapter. It is a question of the reality which we can adequately describe only by defining it as the possibility which God in His eternal decree rejected and therefore did not and does not will, which has and can have its actuality only under the almighty No of God, but does have and is actuality in that sense. To this sphere there belongs the devil, the father of lies. To this sphere, too, there belongs the world of demons, and sin and evil and death— not death as a natural limitation but eternal death, the enemy and annihilator of life. The power of God extends even over this sphere, for apart from His creative act it certainly would never have had or been this negative actuality. And from all eternity judgment has been pronounced and executed upon it by God. But creation in itself and as such does not have this power over it and cannot pronounce or execute judgment upon it. Creation in itself and as such is menaced by it, menaced by the chaos which to some extent borders it, couching at the door. It was not creation itself which distinguished itself from chaos. Nor can creation itself maintain this distinction. It cannot, therefore, guard itself against chaos. It ought not to do so. It is appointed to live, not by itself, but by the grace of God, and to triumph by that grace over all its enemies and over all the enemies of that grace. It stands always—we are still speaking of creation in itself and as such—in unavoidable and mortal peril of falling a victim to those enemies, of being swallowed up by them, of itself becoming chaos. It is not God. It is the reality which is distinct from God, elected, willed and actualised by Him, but differentiated from Him, and therefore not participating in His sovereignty or in the freedom of His election and decision. And as such, if God did not will to save and keep it, it might well, indeed it must, be overwhelmed by chaos and fall into nothingness.

Necessarily, then, it rests in what Genesis 1$^{3-9}$ describes as division, that is, the marking off and confirmation of light from darkness, of the waters above from the waters below, of the dry land from the sea, in a word, of the cosmos from chaos. Because the creature rests in this division, it is God who preserves it. Indeed, this passage might well be described as the biblical *locus classicus*[EN61] for the doctrine with which we are now occupied. But the story of the flood (Gen. 6–8) and the plagues of Egypt (Ex. 7–11) and many other biblical contexts show that it is not at all self-evident that the creature should be preserved from the danger which threatens it. It would indeed be given up to it without a struggle if God were to turn away His face from it. For good or evil it is referred to the fact that God does not do so.

The older theology undoubtedly tried to make this point with all possible force. Augustine, for example, rightly (*De Gen. ad lit.* 4, 12) thought that we must explain the ἐν αὐτῷ ἐσμέν[EN62] of Acts 17^{28} as signifying that we are in Him, not as though we were partakers of His essence, nor as though (according to John 5^{26}) we had life in ourselves, but *cum aliud sumus quam ipse, non ob aliud in illo sumus, nisi quia id operatur et hoc est opus eius, quo continet*

[075]

[EN61] classic reference
[EN62] in Him we have our being

73

omnia[EN63]. Similarly Thomas (*loc. cit.*, *art.* 1 c), in generalising an image applied by August-ine (*loc. cit.*, 8, 12) to the justification and sanctification of man, finely amplified it as follows. The whole of creation is related to the preservation of God as is the atmosphere to the sun which illumines it. The sun illumines it in virtue of its essence. The atmosphere becomes bright because it partakes, not of the nature of the sun, but of its illumining. If the illumin-ing were to cease, it would become dark. In the same way God alone is *ens per essentiam suam;*[EN64] the creature is only *ens participativum*[EN65]. It can have continuity only as God gives it. There is a corresponding note in the Reformed theology of the 17th century. If the crea-ture could maintain itself even for a single moment, this would mean that it is *a se* as God is, that it is eternal as God is, and therefore that it is a second God. But conversely, the fact that it is not this means that it cannot continue a single moment without God. Without God it would crumble away, just as a building whose main supports are removed must inevitably collapse. It needs the mighty hand of God to be able to continue (F. Burmann *loc. cit.*, 43, 8–10, 14). *Creaturae omnes, cum ex nihilo sint adeoque de nihilo participent ... indigae virtutis alienae quocunque momenta existunt*[EN66]. (H. Heidegger, *Corp. theol.*, 1700, quoted in *Heppe*[2], p. 208). And this *aliena virtus*[EN67] can only be that of God *quinetiam tanta ad rem conservandam quanta ad creandam virtus requiritur*[EN68] (Abr. Heidan, *Corp. theol. chr.*, 1686 I, 361).

All this is correctly perceived and logically inter-related, but are we left entirely free from the impression of a certain facility in this form of argumentation? And is it not of a piece that the very concept which ought to indicate that which menaces the creature and from which the creature can be preserved only by God, the concept of *nihil*[EN69] as opposed to *essentia*[EN70] and *esse*[EN71], is here understood and pressed only in a metaphysical and not a theological sense? By definition a relative being cannot continue without an absolute being—and notwithstanding the reservation in respect of the divine freedom it may be that by definition an absolute being guarantees the continuance of a relative. But it has still to be asked whether the reference is really to God's preserving as we have it in Gen. 1[2]. Does the creature's whole need consist in the fact that it is only *ens participativum* and therefore *participans de nihilo*[EN72] and therefore dependent upon the *sustentare*[EN73] of the *ens per essentiam suam*[EN74] to which it owed its own *essentia*[EN75] and *esse*[EN76]? We must not be unjust to Augustine and Thomas and our own older orthodox dogmaticians. In their expositions there is a certain agitation at this point which would hardly be commensurate with the prob-lem as they almost forcefully mastered it, if by the *nihil*[EN77] they had not instinctively at least envisaged something other than mere non-being in its formal antithesis to being. But they

---

[EN63] since we are other than He Himself, we are not "in Him" in any way, except in that He works in us with that work of His by which He contains all things
[EN64] a being who exists through its own power
[EN65] a being who exists by sharing in another's power
[EN66] All creatures, since that are from nothing, to that extent share in nothing ... and are in need of some external power for every moment that they exist
[EN67] external power
[EN68] since as much power is required to preserve a thing as to create it
[EN69] nothing
[EN70] essence
[EN71] existence
[EN72] sharing in nothing
[EN73] sustaining
[EN74] a being who exists through its own power
[EN75] essence
[EN76] existence
[EN77] nothing

never consciously raised the question of that something other, the true *nihil*[EN78], as it arises in this connexion. Certainly they never made any pronouncements concerning it.

Of all the older theologians known to me it occurred to only one, Anselm of Canterbury, to describe the preserving activity or being of God not only as *conservare, sustentare, communicare, influere esse*[EN79] and the like, but also at times (*Monol.*, 13 and 65, *De casu diab.*, 1) quite simply as *servare*[EN80], thus picturing it as a deliverance and indicating a preservation of the creature which has to be considered seriously from the theological standpoint. And Anselm then preceded (*De casu diab.*, 1) to connect the fall of the devil, who according to him as to the older theology in general was originally an angel, with an exclusion from this divine *servare*[EN81] which God did not owe to any of His creatures.

Why is it that the being of the creature is menaced by nothingness, menaced in such a way that it needs the divine preservation and sustaining and indeed [076] deliverance if it is not to fall victim to it and perish? Obviously it is menaced by something far more serious than mere non-being as opposed to being, although it is of course menaced by non-being too. But what makes non-being a menace, an enemy which is superior to created being, a threatened destroyer, is obviously not its mere character as non-being, but the fact that it is not elected and willed by God the Creator but rather rejected and excluded. It is that to which God said No when He said Yes to the creature. And that is chaos according to the biblical term and concept.

We have to do here with a concept which was lacking in the normative philosophy of the older Christian theologians. It was lacking because the outlook to which it corresponds was also lacking. And that outlook was lacking first and foremost because our present understanding of preservation and deliverance was necessarily unknown. If the older theology had filled out its admittedly not inapplicable concept of *nihil*[EN82] from this understanding instead of taking it over in the purely formal sense from the normative philosophy of the time, it would have attained at this point to the more significant and serious conclusions which were certainly within its reach but to which it did not in fact attain.

What God has eternally denied, what is not willed by Him, constitutes that which is not, that which is empty, which is necessarily nothing. But in all its singularity the non-existent which is characterised as such by God, the shadow which flees before God, possesses everywhere in the Bible its own ponderable reality. God knows this nothing as the opponent of the creature, as that which may and can seduce and destroy the creature. God knows that under the dominion of this nothing the creature must perish. It is always present—as it were on the frontier of the cosmos to which He has given being. It continually calls this cosmos in question. It has mounted an offensive against it. If only for a moment God were to turn away His face from the creature, the offensive would break loose with deadly power. In its relation to God chaos is always an

---

[EN78] nothing
[EN79] preserving, sustaining, communicating, or transmitting being
[EN80] serving
[EN81] serving
[EN82] nothing

absolutely subordinate factor, but it is always absolutely superior in its relation to the creature.

The tremendous danger, the most serious peril, which the non-existent involves for the creature may be seen already in the fact that the non-existent is so utterly opposed, that it is so completely hostile, that it is such an absolute denial of the essence and existence of the creature. It is the very fact that it stands on the frontier of the creature, that it is on the frontier and yet itself not a creature, which makes it so strange to it. And it is in virtue of this fact that it appears to be similar to and even like God, perhaps a second god. And yet it is still nothing. But again, its strangeness and its appearance of god-likeness are not without serious foundation. For in its absolute opposition and hostility to the creature, in its very non-creatureliness, in the nothingness in which it borders on the creature and is to some extent its neighbour, it is not present by its [077] own caprice, by a chance which is above both God and the creature and makes fools of them both, and therefore without God, but in a sense by means of God. Without God—in this case without His wrath and rejection and judgment—even nothing could not be present or of any power or consequence. It is present and of power and consequence because of the wrath of God. When in creation God pronounced His wise and omnipotent Yes He also pronounced His wise and omnipotent No. That is His wrath and rejection and judgment. He marked off the positive reality of the creature from that which He did not elect and will and therefore did not create. And to that which He denied He allotted the being of non-being, the existence of that which does not exist. God created light, approved it, divided it from darkness, and called it day, but the darkness He called night (Gen. 1^{3-5}). In the power—that is, the negative power—of this divine creating, approving, dividing and calling, there enters in with the creature that which in all these things is marked off from it, and it enters in with menacing power, the power of the denial of that which God has affirmed, as the non-being which does not exist, as that which is not created, as that which is so absolutely opposed and hostile to the creature, as that which is not, chaos. It is not an adversary to God, but only the shadow of His work which both arises and is at once dispelled by His wrath. But to the creature it is an adversary for which the creature as such is no match. To God it is no problem. But it is the radical problem which faces the creature. In face of God it has no power, but it has supreme power in face of the creature. As that which God has denied it has the tendency and power to negate the creature of God. It has the attractive force of a whirlpool—we are reminded of the power of a single minus placed before a bracket, which cannot be offset by any plus within the bracket—in whose eddyings the creature in itself and as such can only sink and perish. To set up of itself any effective opposition, to offer any real resistance, the creature would have to repeat the divine act of creating, approving, dividing and calling to which it owes its being and its distinctness from this sinister neighbour. It would need to maintain that distinctness and therefore that being. But the creature is not God, and therefore it is in no position to do this. And that which is denied and itself denies confronts it as something infinite. God elected and willed one thing. Therefore that which He did not elect and will, the non-existent, comprises the infinite range of all the possibilities which He passed over and with good reason did not actualise, the abyss in which the one thing which He did create must inevitably sink, the ocean by whose waves it must inevitably be overwhelmed, if He who created it did not also preserve and sustain it. If we could not count upon that, if there were no divine preserving and sustaining, then it would be the holy will of God first to utter a mighty Yes to a reality distinct from Himself, and then immediately to withdraw it by an even more mighty No, thus causing the light to perish [078] as He caused it to arise. We should then have to understand creation, not as the work of a will which is finally gracious even in its wrath, but as that of a will which is finally wrathful even in its grace, of a will in which God conceived and executed the idea of a non-divine or creaturely reality only immediately to withdraw it, thus remaining completely alone—for the non-existent has no autonomy over against Him—in the activity of His inner life as He was from all eternity, and just as glorious in His isolation. There are some conceptions of God, and there have been even within the sphere of Christianity, which approximate to this understanding. But the creature lives by and is dependent upon the fact that in practice this understanding is false, that the holy will of God was not and is not and will not ever be a will of wrath, that although His Yes to creaturely reality is accompanied by a No, He still causes it to be and to continue to be a Yes, not giving to that which He has denied the power to carry through the denial of that which He has affirmed. This is one point at which our conception of the creature's need of preservation by God must be quite different from that of the older theology. The non-existent is a more dangerous factor, its menacing of the creature is greater, and the creature's need of the divine support and preservation is more penetrating, than the older theology could ever reveal, confined as it was by the outlook and language of its metaphysical basis.

But now we must draw attention to another aspect of the matter which unfortunately the older theology did not present either forcefully or feebly, but completely overlooked. Our starting-point must be the proposition that the assurance that God does preserve the creature in spite and in the midst of this great and immeasurable danger is not at all a self-evident one, but one which requires a serious basis if it is to be convincing and credible. For why should the idea of a creation of wrath be a false one? We might put it in this way. God did at first will to preserve the creature even after creation, and He has done so for quite a time. But now He has had enough of us. Where formerly He exercised patience He now allows free rein to His wrath. He repents of having made the creature. He abandons it to the chaos towards which it always strove in spite of His patience. The creature is now threatened again by an *annihilatio*[EN83] beyond which God will be alone again and glorious in Himself. The question must surely have presented itself in many periods and situations in the past, and it surely calls for further consideration at the present juncture, whether there are any specific reasons why this should not be the case.

And the only valid answer is that it is not so because according to the work and revelation of God in Jesus Christ it is not at all the will of God to abandon the creature in its proximity to the non-existent, in its conflict with chaos; to

[079] withdraw to the secure height of His own remoteness from contradiction, and then (in consideration perhaps of its greater or lesser merit) to grant or not to grant it His assistance, preserving or not preserving it in its need. On the contrary, from all eternity—that is, in the eternal counsel of His grace as it is effective and revealed in Jesus Christ—His merciful will was to take up the cause of the creature against the non-existent, not from the safe height of a supreme world-governor, but in the closest possible proximity, with the greatest possible directness, i.e., Himself to become a creature. He placed Himself within the contradiction. He drew to Himself and bore away the whole enmity and problem and power of the non-existent. He tasted and suffered the whole onslaught of sin, the devil, death and hell, and in so doing He broke it, blunting its weapons and depriving it of all claim against the creature or superiority over it. He allowed Himself to be denied in order to remove the denial, thus completing the work of wrath but also the work of grace, uttering a complete No but also a complete Yes, and giving to the creature its freedom. This is the eternal will of God fulfilled and accomplished once and for all in time in Jesus Christ. And in the light of this will and work we have to regard the question of the *conservatio*[EN84] of the creature as one which has already been decided. It does not stand in the obscurity of a hidden will of God which may be fulfilled in one way or may be fulfilled in another. It stands in the light of a will which has already been accomplished and revealed, of a *servatio*[EN85] which has already been fulfilled. In this light the understanding of creation as a creation of the wrath of God can only disperse like a wisp of smoke, however seriously it may be presented. Certainly there is no other way of meeting the question whether it may not be so. But in this way it is completely met, for God does preserve the creature.

And in the light of this truth we can understand why and to what end He does so. The creature exists as the mercy of God operative in Jesus Christ is effective towards it, and in order that the glory of the beloved Son of God may be manifest in it. And this is why God preserves it. He does so because His representing of the creature is the beginning and centre and end of its exist-

---

[EN83] annihilation
[EN84] preserving
[EN85] serving

ence. He does so because it has been promised and given to it to come to terms not with the non-existent, not with chaos, not with its own denial, but with God's gracious intercession for it. He does so because its destiny is to participate in this work of salvation. And for this participation it must be able to be; it must have permanence and continuity. It must be preserved by God. God wills to be revealed and active in the created order. He wills to be glorified and honoured in this order because He frees it, because He deprives the non-existent of its power over it, because He prepares for this order freedom, the divine freedom which He Himself enjoys over that contradiction. God wills in this order a history, a history in which the share of freedom which it has already acquired—and for whom is it won if not for it?—will be attested and proclaimed and seized and apprehended: the share in His denial of the non-existent; the share in the sentence which He has pronounced upon it from all eternity; the share in the judgment which in His counsel He has executed upon chaos from all eternity; and above all, and positively, the share in His own eternal life, a life which is quite unthreatened because it is self-grounded and self-renewing. It is because God wills this history for this reason that He willed the creation and that He wills also the preservation of the creature. Because *servatio*[EN86], therefore *creatio*[EN87] and therefore *conservatio*[EN88]. For this history to take place the creature must have space and time and permanence. Because God wills the history He creates and gives it these things, and thus preserves the creature. At this point we can speak quite confidently of a necessary consequence and let go the restriction in favour of the divine freedom. The God who made use of His freedom to win for us salvation and liberation in Jesus Christ also wills and creates our preservation in the same freedom and for the same purpose of liberation. The *caveat* that had He so willed He might have acted otherwise is not only meaningless but most suspicious, for those who enter it may well have begun to turn their thoughts to another god than the One who in the work of Jesus Christ has revealed His whole heart and all the goodness of His Godhead. [080]

And it is in the light of this fact that we can now give a serious theological answer to the question of the creature's need of preservation by God. This need has a more urgent and indeed a more profound basis than the older theology would ever allow. It does not consist in the first instance in the powerlessness of the creature in face of the non-existent. It cannot then be described or understood in the first instance only as a weakness, privation, or imperfection of the creature. It has its root in the foreordination of the creature to participation in the divine covenant of grace. Because it has to be present in the divine work of deliverance and liberation, it can therefore be present—

[EN86] serving
[EN87] creation
[EN88] preserving

present as a creature—in all the immeasurable perils in which it cannot preserve or sustain itself. In the light of this foreordination it is not simply a limitation or humiliation to be present only in this way, and therefore in need. If its
destiny is to live of and by the grace of God, and if the fulfilment of this destiny
is the unfolding and revealing of the honour and dignity and glory which it
attains thereby, then what it attains, what is foreordained for it, is already
reflected in its existence and the limitation and need of this existence. The
fact that it is to partake of the *servatio*[EN89] is proclaimed already in the fact that
it needs the *conservatio*[EN90] of its existence, that it needs it so utterly and with so
complete a reference to the help and activity of God. For what else does this
mean but that even here, in respect of its very existence, it is referred to the
[081]   grace of God? Its very need carries within it the promise: the promise of the
honour and dignity and glory still to be unfolded and revealed; the promise of
its life in grace; the promise of the work of salvation in which God takes up its
cause against that which is not, and carries it to a successful issue. But if this is
the case, then to be present as only the creature can be present, in the divine
preservation, in total need, is strength as well as weakness, riches as well as
privation, perfection as well as imperfection, the highest exaltation as well as
shame and need, is something which not only has to be but ought to be.

And now we come to the last and decisive reason why this is so. Our need of
the divine preservation has to be so utter and complete because existence in
this need is the creaturely existence which corresponds to our participation in
the divine covenant of grace. In the fulfilment of this covenant God our Creator first gave up Himself to that need. He did not redeem us from outside,
from a safe distance, but from inside, by taking our place, by entering into our
resistance to that all-powerful negation of our being, by coming into the very
midst of our actual subjection and impotence in face of that negation. This is
how the covenant of grace was fulfilled. This is how our cause against nothingness and chaos was maintained in Jesus Christ and carried through to victory.
It is the first and chief greatness of the divine triumph, the honour and dignity
and glory of God, that He Himself fought and suffered and conquered, not in
the heights but in the depths where we are, in the midst of the immeasurable
perils in which the creature exists, thus being able really to act on behalf of the
creature, and actually doing so. The work of grace in which it is the purpose of
our existence to participate took place when the Creator Himself became a
creature in His Son, not counting it loss to expose Himself fully to the immeasurable perils of creaturely existence or to allow Himself to be totally denied or
to become wholly dependent upon free and undeserved and unmerited grace.
In this way He did for the creature that which the creature itself cannot do. He
repeated that creating, approving, dividing and calling, thus achieving for the
creature its impossible self-assertion and self-distinction in face of the power of

---

[EN89] serving
[EN90] preserving

chaos, in face of the denying of that which is eternally denied. If the creature exists only in these perils and therefore in this need, it exists at the very place where in Jesus Christ God Himself has existed and triumphed. In this respect, too, we have to reckon seriously with the situation. It is not a matter of caprice or chance. It is not something which has to be accepted and endured as an evil fate. It is the situation in which God Himself made, established and fulfilled His covenant with the creature; in which He vindicated His honour as the Creator by confronting and annihilating that which is not. The creature is not the Creator, nor can it do what the Creator can do. But in Jesus Christ the situation of the creature was also that of the Creator, and this means that it was [082] a hallowed situation, sanctified and pregnant with promise. At the point where we are powerless, He put forth His power on our behalf. At the point where we are defeated, deliverance was already effected. There is, therefore, no further reason to be ashamed of our situation, nor to bewail it, nor to complain against God for putting us in this and not in some other situation. By making the situation His own He ennobled it and made it a promise, justifying His creative Yes and No. Hence it is no empty assertion when we say that the future honour and dignity and glory of the creature is reflected in its need. In fact its need means that the creature discovers itself as such at the very place where in Jesus Christ God Himself entered in to save it. This very place has all the brightness of His presence. Therefore there can never be any question of the creature not taking its need seriously. There can never be any question concerning its immeasurable peril, its powerlessness, its being referred to God alone for preservation. There can never be any question of its secretly regarding itself as its own preserver. It is more than doubtful whether it could be kept from such a belief merely because by definition it cannot advance or make good that claim. But it is completely kept from it by the fact that at the very place where it might advance that claim its true Preserver has acted in person, accomplishing its salvation and at the same time assuring its preservation. And in so doing He has not so much destroyed that claim, the concealed or open titanism of the creature; He has simply rendered it superfluous. If it is saved, it is also preserved, and the anxiety or pride in which it might preserve itself is deprived of its object. And if it is saved there, its preservation is assured at the very place where the anxiety and pride could arise in which it might argue that it has to preserve itself. It is saved, and therefore it is assured of preservation even in its total need. And if this is the case, it cannot lack either the courage or the humility to admit its total need. Proof of its need is given in the very fact that it is assured of preservation. This is the second way in which the assertions of the older theology have to be deepened and enlarged.

The connexion between *servare*[EN91] and *conservare*[EN92], between saving grace in Jesus Christ and the gracious preservation of creaturely being by God the Father, emerges most

---

[EN91] serving
[EN92] preserving

clearly in the New Testament and especially the Pauline passages in which the verbs τηρεῖν, φρουρεῖν, φυλάσσειν, βεβαιοῦν, and στηρίζειν[EN93] are used to describe a specific activity of God or Christ in relation to Christians. An interesting side-light is also thrown upon our theme by the fact that of these five *conservare*[EN94] concepts at least φυλάσσειν, στηρίζειν, and above all τηρεῖν[EN95] are also used to describe a corresponding activity on the part of Christians, and therefore in the context of exhortations to them. We are reminded of what was said concerning the divine preservation of the creature by means of the creature itself. But the application of these concepts to the activity of God seems to be the more characteristic, and in the New Testament φρουρεῖν and βεβαιοῦν are used to describe this activity alone. This preserving, maintaining, guarding, assuring and strengthening is something which Christians have need of. According to some passages they already have these things. Thus in Jn 17[12]: "I kept them (ἐτήρουν) in thy name, and have kept them (ἐφύλαξα), and none of them is lost." Again, in 1 Peter 1[5] Christians are denned as those who are kept by faith (φρουρούμενοι), and in Jude 1 the readers are described as τετηρήμενοι κλητοί[EN96]. In 1 Jn 5[18] we have the present: "The begetting of God keepeth him (τηρεῖ), and that wicked one toucheth him not." More generally this divine activity is either proffered to them or requested on their behalf. Thus side by side with Jn 17[12] we find: "Holy Father, keep (τήρησον) through thine own name (Jn 17[11])," and: "I pray thee ... that thou shouldest keep them (τηρήσῃς) from the evil (Jn 17[15])." Again, the words which are put in the mouth of Jesus himself in Rev. 3[10] are in the form of a promise: "I will keep thee (τηρήσω) in the hour of temptation." An event, salvation in the death of Jesus Christ, is something which lies behind those to whom the words are said, but in its final and general revelation it is still before them. It is on the basis of this event that preservation is promised to them, and therefore the preservation corresponds to the basis. The assurance is given by Paul that God will keep (φρουρήσει) the hearts and minds of Christians through Jesus Christ (Phil. 4[7]). He prays for the stablishing (τὸ στηρίξαι) of their hearts that they may be unblameable in holiness (1 Thess. 3[13]). He desires that as they have received Christ Jesus the Lord they may walk in him, stablished (βεβαιούμενοι) in the faith (Col. 2[7]). He is confident that Christ will give them this confirmation (βεβαιώσει) unto the end (1 Cor. 1[8]). He exalts Christ as the faithful One who will stablish and keep them (στηρίξει καὶ φυλάξει) from evil (2 Thess. 3[3]). Conversely, he calls God the One who stablishes (βεβαιῶν) both himself and them in Christ (2 Cor. 1[21]). "The very God of peace sanctify you wholly ... and may your whole spirit and soul and body be preserved (τηρηθείη) blameless (ὁλόκληρον). Faithful is he that hath called you, who also will do it" (1 Thess. 5[23]). It is striking in how many of these passages this preservation is related to the final hope which still awaits Christians of their future deliverance with the return of Jesus Christ. This makes it plain that our concern is with the permanence or continuity of human, or better of Christian, existence—a matter which has become all the more pressing now that the last time has begun. The question is that of a specifically Christian existence, of the preservation of Christians in the name of God and in faith against temptation and the evil one. We are told this unequivocally in 2 Tim. 1[12]. Paul is persuaded that Christ "is able to keep that which I have committed unto him (τὴν παραθήκην μου φυλάξαι) against that day." But according to the New Testament view Christian existence implies a human and creaturely existence. When in the days of the Flood (2 Pet. 2[5]) God saved (ἐφύλαξεν) Noah and seven others the reference is not merely to the office of Noah as a preacher of righteousness but to Noah himself in his creaturely existence as the bearer of

---

[EN93] to keep, to protect, to guard, to confirm, and to strengthen
[EN94] preserving
[EN95] to guard, to strengthen, to keep
[EN96] preserved and called

1. *The Divine Preserving*

this office. According to these passages the hearts and spirits and souls and bodies of Christians are all to be preserved ("whole" in 1 Thess. 5^{23}) in Christ and in faith against the evil one. And this means that during the time allotted to them, and to the very goal and end of that time, their hearts etc., and they themselves, are literally preserved. In and with that which is committed to them their existence is preserved. In and with their spiritual life, in virtue of its origin and with a view to its destiny, their life is preserved in itself and as such. In so far as they live for Christ in faith, this $\pi\alpha\rho\alpha\theta\dot{\eta}\kappa\eta$ EN97 of Paul is not as it were clothed upon them like a foreign body. And on the other hand the fact that they live in time and in the cosmos cannot be abstracted from the higher and more decisive fact that they are in Christ and that they stand in faith. And the temptation or evil one frequently alluded to in these passages attacks and menaces not merely their Christian existence but in and with it—we are reminded of Paul's description of the thorn in the flesh in 2 Cor. 12^7—existence itself. Therefore if there is a preservation of Christian existence, the preservation of existence generally is fulfilled in and with it. Something of this implication appears in the saying: "Now [084] our Lord Jesus Christ himself, and God, even our Father ... stablish ($\sigma\tau\eta\rho\dot{\iota}\zeta\alpha\iota$) you in every good word and work" (2 Thess. 2^{17}). As long and in so far as they can exist as Christians in virtue of this divine preserving, maintaining, guarding, assuring and strengthening, they are generally preserved and maintained and guarded and assured and strengthened. It is from this standpoint that we should consider the absolute freedom, the complete absence of worry or anxiety, which was displayed by the men of the New Testament in face of all the problems of existence, whether spiritual or natural, psychological or physical. This freedom was not so hostile to the world and to life as it has often been represented (simply because the synecdoche, the implication of the creaturely in the Christian, the connexion between *servare* and *conservare*EN98, has not, or has not sufficiently, been taken into account). The very fact that the question of the *conservare*EN99 of an existence based upon the *servare*EN100 can arise at all in the living form in which we find it in these passages ought surely to have drawn attention to the further fact that the New Testament regarded the Christian as such, apart from the new birth, as a being existing in time and in the cosmos, and therefore in need, and also assured, of the divine preservation. And conversely, we may learn from this fact in what legitimate sense and with what reference we can speak at all of the divine preservation of a creature which lives in time and in the cosmos, referring back the divine *conservare*EN101 to the divine *servare*EN102 which is known by Christians and to that extent forms the basis of Christian existence.

And now we must add rather generally that all the Old Testament statements concerning Yahweh as the confidence and protection, the rock and fortress and refuge, both of Israel and also of the Israelite, have to be understood in the light of this relationship between *servatio*EN103 and *conservatio*EN104. As life itself shows, neither in prosperity nor in adversity is there any comfort or security either for the people or the individual except in the election, in the covenant, in the history of the covenant with its concrete experiences, and finally and decisively in Yahweh Himself as He who acts as Lord of the covenant. In the Old Testament Yahweh as the Founder and Preserver of the covenant, the faithfulness of His activity in the history of the covenant, the covenant itself as a spiritual reality (to use the language of the

---

EN 97 what has been entrusted
EN 98 serving and preserving
EN 99 preserving
EN100 serving
EN101 preserving
EN102 serving
EN103 serving
EN104 preserving

New Testament) is the one foundation upon which and by which Israel and the Israelite live according to their creaturely existence, and for the sake of which they are able to be in time and in the cosmos. This is the real basis of their preservation in being. And conversely, the meaning of their being is revealed in the works of grace and judgment performed by Yahweh as Lord of the covenant. Only with that reference back can their being be accepted and understood and valued, and truly magnified and extolled, as a divine benefit and favour.

We may conclude that as God preserves the creature, it may continue in being. Man may continue to be man. Individuals may continue as such. Natural and historical groupings may continue. Humanity itself may continue as the sum of the temporal and spatial totality of human creation on earth and under heaven and in relation to the whole conceivable and inconceivable cosmos. And finally, the known and unknown creatures of this cosmos may continue, following their own path in relation to man and in that autonomy over against him which to us is enshrouded in mystery. Not only did all these things become actual by the creative Word of God. They may continue to be actual because already that creative Word means Jesus Christ and therefore covenant and grace and mercy and goodness. They may continue to be because God [085] willed to fulfil and has already fulfilled this Word by Himself becoming a creature in his Son, by giving up Himself for the creature and its salvation, by Himself accomplishing this salvation. Because the creature is saved by Him, because it partakes of this salvation by Him, the creature is sustained and preserved by Him. It may continue to be because the Word of God is true and actual, because the grace of God is not merely an optional addition to its creaturely existence but the solid basis and wholly effective condition of this existence.

That the creature may continue to be in virtue of the divine preservation does not mean that either as an individual or in its totality it is a creature without any limits. It may continue to be as a creature within its limits. It may have its place in space, and its span in time. It may begin at one point and end at another. It may come, and stay, and go. It may comprehend the earth but not heaven. It may be free here, but bound there; open at this point, but closed at that. It may understand one thing, but not another; be capable of one thing, but not another; accomplish one thing but not another. That it may be in this way, within its limits, is not at all an imperfection, an evil necessity, an obscure fate. Were we in a position to compare and comprehend all the possibilities of all creatures, and the possibilities of the individual with those of the totality, we should be astonished at the magnificent breadth of these limits. And certainly it is not a curse but a blessing that there are these limits to humanity and creation, end that in some cases they are notoriously narrow limits, of which the brevity of human life is only a single if rather drastic example. The creature must not exist like the unhappy centre of a circle which has no periphery. It must exist in a genuine circle, its individual environment. It must not exist everywhere, but in a specific place. It must not exist endlessly, but in its own time. It must not comprehend or understand or be capable of or accomplish everything. It has freedom to experience and accomplish that which is proper to it, to do that which it can do, and to be satisfied. It is in this freedom that it is preserved by God. It is in this freedom that it comes directly from God and moves towards Him. It is in this freedom that it is ready to fulfil its destiny, i.e., by the grace of God to live by the grace of God. The fact that it is here and now, that it exists in one way and not another, is its opportunity; the one opportunity which does not recur; an opportunity which corresponds to the oneness of God and the uniqueness of the work of liberation which He accomplished in Jesus Christ. It is its own particular opportunity, the opportunity which is given specifically to it, the opportunity which is so definitely rich and pregnant with promise. As this opportunity is given to it, the creature is preserved by God for the kingdom of God. Having this opportunity, it is the object of the goodness of God. And by accepting it, by making a right use of it, [086] it magnifies the Creator: "I will sing unto the Lord as long as I live: I will sing praise to my God while I have my being" (Ps. 104^{33}; 146^2). And why not within these limits? Why not rightly within these limits? The creature will only stumble at a supposed imperfection or obscure fate when it magnifies God in its own strength, when it does not admit or accept these limits, when it loses itself in generalities or grasps concretely at another opportunity which is not its own. But where there is nothing to seek it will not find, and it cannot know that it is preserved by God. Of all creatures only man seems to have this impossible possibility of repudiating his preservation by God as a preservation within appointed limits. But he cannot alter the fact that like all creatures he is in fact preserved in this way, and rightly so, and to his own salvation.

That the creature may continue to be in virtue of the divine preservation means that it may itself be actual within its limits: actual, and therefore not a mere appearance engendered by some heavenly or hellish power; itself actual, and therefore not an emanation from the being of God and certainly not from non-being. God preserves the creature in the reality which is distinct from His own. It is relative to and dependent upon His reality, but in its relativity and dependence autonomous towards it, existing because it owes its existence to Him, as a subject with which He can have dealings and which can have dealings with Him. In this way it is adequate to its determination for existence in the divine covenant of grace. As it did not proceed out of chaos, but was marked off from chaos by God the Creator, so according to the will and on the basis of the saving act of God its Saviour it cannot and should not and must not be overwhelmed by chaos and perish. And as it did not proceed from God's own being, but was freely created by God, so it cannot return to God, nor can it or should it in any way forfeit or surrender its autonomy in face of Him. God is to be all in all (1 Cor. 15^{28}), but this does not really mean that the "all" will no longer be, that God will be alone again. It means rather that in the final revelation of His ways He will be seen by the creature to have attained His ultimate goal in all things with the creature, the creature not ceasing to be distinct from Himself. In all its forms pantheism is a conception which does violence and injustice not only to God but also to the creature. The creature itself may be actual within its limits. For this it is indebted to the divine preservation. And we saw that this preservation is direct in the sense that God gives it to the creature to preserve itself within the context in which it exists. The fine saying in Proverbs 8[31], which tells us of the wisdom of God which was daily His delight and rejoiced before Him, rejoicing in the habitable parts of the earth, and having its delights with the sons of men, is far truer in its mythological form than much that has been said in apparent exaltation of the sole efficacy of God but really in disparagement of the creature and therefore of its Creator. That the creature may not only be, but may continue to be what it is, running its course within the limits marked off for it; that God does not begrudge it this, or deprive it of it; that there is a delighting or sport in which first the Creator and then the creature has a part: this is the grand free mystery of the divine preservation. Not merely the creaturely worlds of the sidereal kingdom, and amongst them the tiny planet which is the vast dwelling-place of man, may tread the path appointed for them, but also the small and the very smallest things which are around and far below us. And so "man goeth forth unto his work and to his labour until the evening" (Ps. 104[23]); to which it belongs that he can use his senses and understanding to perceive that two and two make four, and to write poetry, and to think, and to make music, and to eat and drink, and to be filled with joy and often with sorrow, and to love and sometimes to hate, and to be young and to grow old, and all within his own experience and activity, affirming it not as half a man but as a whole man, with head uplifted, and the heart free and the conscience at rest: "O Lord, how manifold are thy works" (Ps. 104[24]). It is only the heathen gods who envy man. The true God, who is unconditionally the Lord, allows him to be the thing for which He created him. He is far too highly exalted either to take it amiss or to prevent it. Does not the divine wisdom have its true delight in the children of men? This is a bold assertion, and one which calls for closer analysis and more profound meditation. But there can be no doubt that with an autonomous reality God does give to man, and not only to man but in different ways to all His creatures, the freedom of individual action. There can be no doubt that as the One who is the Giver of this gift He is the One who preserves them.

That the creature may continue to be in virtue of the divine preservation means finally that—itself actual and active within its limits—it may continue before Him eternally. We have already seen what is meant by the phrase "within its limits." It does not only mean a limitation to its own particular place. It means also a limitation of its possibilities and capacities, of its development and operation. Above all, it means a limitation of its existence in itself and as such. There are myriads of creatures which have been, and only have been. There are myriads more which are and continue to be, but which one day will only have been. And the time will come when the created world as a whole will only have been. In the final act of salvation history, i.e., in the revelation of Jesus Christ as the Foundation and Deliverer and Head of the whole of creation, the history of creation will also reach its goal and end. It will not need to progress any further, it will have fulfilled its purpose. Everything that happened in the course of that history will then take place together as a recapitulation of all individual events. It will be made definitive as the temporal end of the creature beyond which it cannot exist any more. Its life will then be over, its movement and development completed, its notes sounded, its colours revealed, its thinking thought, its words said, its deeds done, its contacts and relationships with other creatures and their mutual interaction closed, the possibilities granted to it exploited and exhausted. And in all this it will somehow have a part in that which Jesus Christ has been and done as its Foundation and Deliverer and Head. It will not need any continuance of temporal existence. And since the creature itself will not be there, time which is the form of its existence will not be there. Yet this does not mean that its preservation by God is terminated. It is a preservation within appointed limits; the preservation of its being in its limited place, with its limited possibilities, and in its limited temporal duration. But inasmuch as it is a divine activity and attitude, the *motus stabilis*EN105 of the divine being; inasmuch as the faithfulness of God is an eternal faithfulness, this preservation is an eternal preservation. It does not end with the ending of the existence of the creature, just as it did not begin with that existence and is not limited by its limitations. In the eternal counsel of God it was applied and assured to the creature before creation itself. Similarly it is still applied and assured to it even when the creature has completed its appointed course, even when it does not exist any longer. It lays hold of the creature as it were in and with its limitations; even in and with the limitations of its temporal duration. This is how God willed and created the creature. This is how He preserves it in time as in all its other limitations. And this limited creature—limited in time, but only in time—He loved and preserved from destruction by Himself becoming man in His Son, by constituting Himself in the Son its Foundation and Deliverer and Head. He took to Himself that transitory speck of dust in order that in that restricted and mean and insignificant setting He might give to the covenant of grace its history. And He gave to that transitory speck temporal duration as the setting of that history. Its limitations do not involve its destruction because God preserves it in those limitations. How could the limitations of temporal duration involve its destruction, as though God could not or would not preserve it even in that limitation, or as though God did not guarantee eternal preservation by Himself becoming a creature, by Himself entering that limitation?

Eternal preservation does not mean a continuation of the existence of the creature. To what end and for what purpose could it continue to be when already it has had and fulfilled its course, when in that course it has already accomplished its purpose and in the revelation of Jesus Christ attained its end, when the cover under which it had real life and activity in temporal duration

[088]

EN105 steady motion

87

[089]   has been removed, when the fire of judgment without which it cannot depart at this uncovering of its existence has already passed over it? What need has it of more time and duration, of more reality and activity, when in the limits marked off for it God has akeady given to it all things, namely, Himself, in the person of His Son, when its end was to be manifested as the recipient of that gift?

The eternal preservation of the creature of God means negatively that its destruction is excluded no less by its beginning in the creation of God than by its end in the revelation of Jesus Christ, and therefore by its very limitations. It was not in vain that God gave to it time and duration, and in time and duration reality and activity. He gave them to it as to the transitory speck of dust which it is, but He gave them in reality and not in appearance. And that which was no appearance He will not allow to become appearance even when it is over. If it did become appearance, this would mean that the non-existent had triumphed over the creature of God, that by giving such power to the non-existent God had finally revoked His own work, and that He had finally retracted that Yes and given Himself to isolation. But the love of God for the creature was far too costly, in Jesus Christ God gave to the creature far too high a dignity, and God bound Himself to the creature far too seriously and unreservedly, for Him to be able to repent and to desire to be in isolation and apart from the creature. By means of that which He did on behalf of the creature when He Himself became creature, He has in fact broken the power of the non-existent against the creature, destroying it and removing the threat of it. Where, then, is the power which can force the creature to become appearance and not reality? It can only be the power of God Himself. But God—the God who acted and revealed Himself in Jesus Christ—will not make exercise of His power to that end.

The eternal preservation of the creature means positively—and this is the final point—that it can continue eternally before Him. God is the One who was, and is, and is to come. With Him the past is future, and both past and future are present. There was nothing that He could not perceive and know of all that began to be, and was, and was preserved by Him. Nothing could escape Him, or perish. Everything was open and present to Him: everything in its own time and within its own limits; but everything open and present to Him. Similarly, everything that is, as well as everything that was, is open and present to Him, within its own limits. And everything that will be, as well as everything that was and is, will be open and present to Him, within its own limits. And one day—to speak in temporal terms—when the totality of everything that was and is and will be will only have been, then in the totality of its temporal duration it will still be open and present to Him, and therefore preserved: eternally pre-
[090]   served; revealed in all its greatness and littleness; judged according to its rightness or wrongness, its value or lack of value; but revealed in its participation in the love which He Himself has directed towards it. Therefore nothing will escape Him: no aspect of the great game of creation; no moment of human

life; no thinking thought; no word spoken; no secret or insignificant enterprise or deed or omission with all its interaction and effects; no suffering or joy; no sincerity or lie; no secret event in heaven or too well-known event on earth; no ray of sunlight; no note which has ever sounded; no colour which has ever been revealed, possibly in the darkness of oceanic depths where the eye of man has never perceived it; no wing-beat of the day-fly in far-flung epochs of geological time. Everything will be present to Him exactly as it was or is or will be, in all its reality, in the whole temporal course of its activity, in its strength or weakness, in its majesty or meanness. He will not allow anything to perish, but will hold it in the hollow of His hand as He has always done, and does, and will do. He will not be alone in eternity, but with the creature. He will allow it to partake of His own eternal life. And in this way the creature will continue to be, in its limitation, even in its limited temporal duration. And how could it not be when it is open and present to Him even at its end, even as that which has only been? This is how it will persist. In all the unrest of its being in time it will be enfolded by the rest of God, and in Him it will itself be at rest, just as even now in all its unrest it is hidden and can be at rest in the rest of God. This is the eternal preservation of God. It is not a second preservation side by side with or at the back of the temporal. It is the secret of the temporal. It is a secret of the temporal which is already present in the fulness of truth, which is already in force. And yet it has still to be present in the fulness of truth; it has still to come into force; it has still to be revealed in all its clarity. As we read in Psalm 136 (repeated twenty-six times): "For his mercy endureth for ever."

2. THE DIVINE ACCOMPANYING

The proposition that God preserves the creature describes only one aspect of His fatherly lordship. We shall now describe a second aspect with the proposition that He accompanies the creature. This concept refers to the lordship of God in relation to the free and autonomous activity of the creature. Already in order fully to describe the divine preserving of the creature we had to take into account the fact that its preservation as actuality necessarily includes its preservation in activity. As God gives to it duration, it persists. Going through a series of changes and movements it is what it can be according to its own nature and potentialities. Its being is its activity. It is the object of the [091] *operatio*EN106 of God in creation and preservation, and as such it is caught up in an *operatio* of its own: in the limited efficacy which God has created and maintained for it; in its own finite activity which is different from the activity of God, just as its actuality is different from the actuality of God.

But in this autonomy of the creature in its own activity we see in a new light the activity of God in providence, in the exercise of His fatherly lordship over

---

EN106 activity

the creature. Quite obviously the concept of preservation is not of itself adequate to describe this lordship. The fact that the divine lordship extends beyond the creation of the creature means also and primarily that He maintains it in its own actuality, that He gives it space and opportunity for its own work, for its own being in action, for its own autonomous activity. How could He really preserve it if He grudged it that, if either He did not concede it at all, or conceded it only in appearance? But again, He would not be acting as the true Lord if He gave it in the same way as a father might hand over to his son an interest-bearing property to be used and applied according to his own good-pleasure, if He let it go its own way in its autonomous activity, if He left it entirely to its own devices. The fatherly providence of God involves far more than that God preserves the creature and gives it its own autonomous activity. He does do this, of course. As the older dogmatics put it, this is the "first act" of the divine providence. We have never to lose sight of this act for a single moment. We have not to say anything which might compromise it, or cross it, or destroy its force. But this can only be the first thing. And now we have to describe a second with the proposition that God accompanies the creature.

> At this point I am following the formulation of J. Coccieus: *nutus voluntatis in Deo ... comitatur operationem creaturae*EN107 (*S. theol.*, 1662, 28, 25). The concept is a very general one and for that reason most hazardous. It might suggest a being who acts with weakness, or indifference, or indeed passively, or with only a partial interest, side by side with another. But if we remember and consider that the subject is God, *nutus voluntatis in Deo*EN108, we shall easily avoid any false notions suggested by the predicate "accompanies." And Coccieus was careful to safeguard himself at once in this direction. When the subject and object are both taken seriously, the predicate being understood in the light of the subject and the subject interpreted in the sense of the predicate, then the general proposition that God accompanies has the advantage that it does at least suggest with an initial exactness, and under the three crucial headings, that which we have now to consider as the second aspect of the divine providence.

God accompanies the creature, and therefore (1) He certainly does not preserve it merely to abandon it to its own activity once He has set in motion. Every moment of its activity and existence the creature has need of a momentary preservation. And the fact that God does preserve the creature means [092] already that He goes with it. And He does so not merely as the One who preserves it but in all His activity as the living and holy and mericiful God, in an activity which is not exhausted by His preservation of the creature, in all the richness of His divine being, in all the definitiveness of His will and counsel towards the creature in its own activity. Thus the activity of the creature takes place in its co-existence with God, in the presence of God, His *praesentia actuosa.* EN109 It is therefore accompanied and surrounded by God's own activity. Let us at once lift the matter above the level of a merely formal consider-

---

EN107 the assent of the will in God ... is accompanied by the activity of the creature
EN108 the assent of the will in God
EN109 active presence

ation. Alongside the act of the creature there is always the act of the divine wisdom and omnipotence. The history of the covenant of grace accompanies the act of the creature from first to last. When by divine preservation the first creature came to exist in activity, God had already acted, offering His grace, making His mercy in Jesus Christ operative and effective to the creature, revealing the majesty of His beloved Son. Where or when could the creature accomplish or perform even the slightest act without this also taking place, without God being with it in this act of lordship? It is in view of the enactment of His own gracious will that God preserves it. But there is more to it than that. For when the creature is at work and active on the basis of its preservation, the gracious will of God is executed in that which borders upon it, in its environment, in the nexus of being in which it has its duration. Whatever that may or may not mean, it is not alone on the way, but as it goes it is accompanied by God, by the God who is this Lord. It is accompanied by the divine wisdom and omnipotence in their specific form as fatherliness. It is accompanied by its Lord in the attitude and purpose towards it which are characterised by His fatherly will. Its own activity stands under the controlling sign of the activity of this companion. Since God is God, He is the one who inevitably and inescapably accompanies the creature, no matter what may be the attitude which the creature adopts towards Him.

God accompanies the creature. This means (2) that He affirms and approves and recognises and respects the autonomous actuality and therefore the autonomous activity of the creature as such. He does not play the part of a tyrant towards it. He no more wills to act alone than as the Creator He willed to be alone or as the Sustainer of the creature He affirms that He does not will to continue alone. Alongside Him there is a place for the creature. Alongside His activity there is a place for that of the creature. We even dare and indeed have to make the dangerous assertion that He co-operates with the creature, meaning that as He Himself works He allows the creature to work. Just as He Himself is active in His freedom, the creature can also be active in its freedom. God Himself can guarantee this to the creature. It is His creature. And even the freedom in which it can work is His gift. And since He Himself accompanies it as the Lord in the use which it makes of that freedom, it is provided that His own freedom will not only not be hampered but will actually prevail by it. The [093] concept "accompany" is a particularly good one because it includes the freedom which God has granted and allowed to the creature. God Himself is not alone on the way. But at this point the decisive consideration must be the material one that the God who accompanies the creature is the Lord of the covenant of grace. If God had willed to act alone, or by means of non-autonomous agents or instruments, there would have been no need to institute a covenant, and the fulfilment of His will in creation need not have taken the form of a covenant-history. Again, grace would no longer be grace if its exercise consisted only in the elimination or suppression as an autonomous subject of the one to whom it was extended. The gracious God acts not only *towards* the creature but also—however we explain it in detail—*with* the creature. His lordship is not despotism. If it were, could it ever have attained its goal by God Himself becoming a creature in His Son, and in that way by His free act of obedience and suffering effecting the liberation of the creature? If over against Him the act of the creature were autonomous only in appearance, the Lord of the covenant of grace would not be God the Creator, the true and living God. It is not in the might of an autocrat but in the power of fatherly majesty that God Himself, the living God, accompanies the creature, doing all things, and yet not doing them without the creature, but working with the creature.

God accompanies the creature. This means of course (3) that He goes with it as the Lord. God is not any kind of companion. Nor is it a matter for jesting that He goes with the creature and co-operates with it. God is the Creator and Sustainer of the creature. It is not of itself that it can exist and work side by side with Him; it is always the work of God and the gift of God. The creature does not belong and is not subject to Him like a puppet or a tool or dead matter—that would certainly not be the lordship of the living God—but in the autonomy in which it was created, in the activity which God made possible for it and permitted to it. And this is how God really overrules the creature, in a way which is congruous to and worthy of Him. God rules in and over a world of freedom. And this is how He rules genuinely and unconditionally. This is how He rules with the absoluteness which is possible only for the Creator ruling over the creature. This is how it is provided that His will is done on earth as it is in heaven, that nothing may or can take place as the action of the creature which is not in a very definite sense His own action. No compulsion is exercised towards the creature. No necessity is worked out in relation to it. It is better not to speak at all, or to do so only infrequently, of the dependence of the creature—although sometimes the expression is perhaps unavoidable—because the word "dependence " almost necessarily suggests a mechanical relationship. But the free God is always a step in advance of the free creature.

[094] The free creature does go of itself, but it can and does only go the same way as the free God. It goes its own way, but in fact it always finds itself in a very definite sense on God's way. And if we are to understand, then at this third and decisive point we must again think of the form in which God is almighty, genuinely and supremely almighty, in Jesus Christ and in the covenant of grace. And what is it that is done here? What is it that we experience here of God's dealings with the creature? Manifestly this, that He loves the creature, that He genuinely recognises and affirms it for what it is in itself and what it does by itself, that He does not annihilate it but for the first time reveals its true nature. But He loves the creature—and here already we have the actualisation of His majesty towards it—quite freely and without any question at all of merit or achievement on its part. And He loves it—and here we see the culmination of His majesty—in such a way that He gives himself to it. He loves it in accepting solidarity with it. Has it anything which He did not give it? Is there anything

which it did not derive from Him? Can it or does it do anything which He does not do with it, which is anything more than a magnifying of His inconceivable goodness and the presence of His grace? And how can the divine lordship be more complete than that? How can it be more secure and exclusive than that?—even although and by the very fact that here can be no question of compulsion, or of a mere dependence of the creature on God; even although and by the very fact that all that happens between God and man takes place quite freely, in the freedom of the spirit. Our experience of God's dealings with the creature at the point where He opens His heart as the Creator and reveals His will and plan, and therefore Himself, and the creature too in its relationship with Him, is that He Himself is the true and genuine Lord and King and Law-giver and the sole Ruler of the creature by His own Holy Spirit, who does not strike down but raises up, who does not bind but looses, who does not kill but makes alive. The preceding of the Creator and following of the creature would be inconceivable, and the lordship and obedience could and would indeed be constantly questioned, were it not that at this point— where their claim and power are highest—they are seen in action: the fatherly lordship of the Creator; the childlike obedience of the creature; and the Spirit in whom both take place together. At this point there is actualised in its original form the fact that the activity of the creature along the way on which God accompanies it and it can accompany God is simply a confirming of the divine activity. At this point, where we do not see any law but only grace, the fact of God's accompanying can and must be understood as the law of the whole divine co-existence with the creature, as the law of the activity of the divine providence.

In order to describe this divine accompanying the older dogmatics coined the concept of *concursus*[EN110].

What particular moment in the concept of the divine providence they had in mind may [095] best be seen if we take note of the passages of Scripture to which reference was customarily made. Especially we must recall the second application of the statement in Rom. 11^{36}: δι’ αὐτοῦ τὰ πάντα[EN111]. Surely P. van Mastricht (*Theor. Pract. Theol.*, 1698, III, 10, 1) was basically correct in his exegesis of this expression when he believed that the διά did not define God as the *causa instrumentalis*[EN112] but indicated the *ipsa operatio*[EN113] of Father, Son and Holy Spirit as it takes place in the work of providence. Reference was also made to Ac. 17^{27}: "Though he be not far from every one of us"; to 1 Cor. 12^{6}, where God is described as ἐνεργῶν τὰ πάντα ἐν πᾶσιν[EN114]; to Phil. 2^{13}, where it is stated expressly of God that He is ὁ ἐνεργῶν ἐν ὑμῖν καὶ τὸ θέλειν καὶ τὸ ἐνεργεῖν ὑπὲρ τῆς εὐδοκίας[EN115]; to Mt. 10^{29}, where the disciples are told that without the will of the Father not a single sparrow can fall to the ground; to Ps. 127^{1}: "Except the Lord build the house, they labour in vain that build it:

EN110 accompanying
EN111 all things are through Him
EN112 instrumental cause
EN113 proper activity
EN114 working all in all
EN115 working in you both to will and to do of his good pleasure

except the Lord keep the city, the watchman waketh but in vain"; to the particularly impressive saying in Is. 26^{12}: "Thou also hast wrought all our works in us"; to Jer. 10^{23}: "O Lord, I know that the way of man is not in himself: it is not in man that walketh to direct his steps"; to the words of Joseph in Gen. 45^8: "So now it was not you that sent me hither, but God: and he hath made me a father to Pharaoh, and lord of all his house"; to Prov. 16^{33}: "The lot is cast into the lap; but the whole disposing thereof is of the lord"; to Prov. 21^1: "The king's heart is in the hand of the Lord, as the rivers of water: he turneth it whithersoever he will" (on which Abr. Heidan commented: *Quid magis independent quam cor regis? At illud ita est in manu Dei, ut rivi aquarum*^{EN116}, *Corp. Theol.*, 1686 1, p. 363); to 1 Sam. 10^{26}: "And there went with him a band of men, whose hearts God had touched" (on which Heidan says: *Quomodo adduxit? Nunquid corporalibus vinculis alligavit? Intus egit, corda tenuit, corda movit, eosque voluntatibus eorum, quas ipse in illis operates est, duxit*^{EN117}.); to Prov. 16^1: "The preparedness of the heart in man, and the answer of the tongue, is from the Lord"; to Prov. 16^9: "A man's heart deviseth his way, but the Lord directeth his steps"; to Prov. 19^{21}: "There are many devices in a man's heart; nevertheless the counsel of the Lord, that shall stand." Summary reference was also made to the great theodicy at the end of the book of Job, in which Chapter 38 adduces all the works of nature, Chapter 39 more specifically the remarkable life-stories of the wild goat, the wild ass, the wild ox, the horse, the hawk and the eagle, and Chapters 40 and 41 those of the rhinoceros and the crocodile—in these cases heightened and depicted with mythical splendour—all of them as direct testimonies to that same overruling of God which is none the less real because it is concealed from man.

The problem raised by these passages is indeed a genuine one, and that is why we have addressed ourselves to it in this sub-section. And the fact that in more than one of the passages express mention is made of the way trodden by both God and man and of their mutual relationship upon that way is a confirmation that generally at least we were on the right track when we selected the concept of accompanying. It is in accordance with the biblical view if we understand the action of God as Lord of the creature as a living relation to the action in which the creature—in whom it is accompanied, differentiated and overruled by that of God—is also involved. For the *concursus*^{EN118} doctrine of the older dogmatics, and therefore for us too, the problem is to present this relation clearly in all the individuality in which it is revealed in Scripture. And so far as this is possible at all, the problem is also to mark it off from all the misleading conceptions which might creep in at this point. We might well conceive of the antithesis as the antithesis between an intrinsically unmoved and passive God and a moved order of creation. Or we might conceive of it as the antithesis between a living, active and working God and an order of creation which is moved by Him from without, and therefore passively and without any activity on its own account. Again, we might conceive of a divine action which consists in the invention, establishing and initiating of a *perpetuum mobile*^{EN119} which would have its own limit on the limit of creaturely action, which would make creaturely action possible, and then hand over the control to it, leaving it to run its own course. And finally we might conceive of an identity between the divine and creaturely action, of the undifferentiated existence of a God-world, which in all its elements and movements might be interpreted equally well as divine or not divine, with a constant amphibole of concepts. The older theologians were right when from the scriptural passages they at least made the deduction that according to the Christian knowledge of the Old and New Testa-

[096]

---

^{EN116} What is more unconstrained than a king's heart? But even it is in the hand of God, as the rivers of water

^{EN117} How did He draw them? Did He bind them with physical chains? He moved them within, he grasped their hearts, and He led them by their wills, which He set in motion within them

^{EN118} accompanying

^{EN119} machine capable of perpetual motion

ment attestation of the divine work and revelation all these possibilities have to be negated. And it was in an attempt to do justice to the problem of a co-existence and antithesis of the divine and creaturely action which should correspond with the testimony of Scripture that they worked out their doctrine of the *concursus*[EN120].

At this point it is as well to correct a false representation which appears amongst other places in R. A. Lipsius (*op. cit.*, p. 397f.) and the *Lehrbuch der. ev. Dogmatik* of Nitzsch-Stephan (1912, 421). According to this account the doctrine of the *concursus*[EN121] was peculiar to Lutheran dogmatics, the Reformed school holding to the view that God alone is active, and regarding the creature merely as his tool, thus excluding all idea of co-operation apart from an insignificant application amongst some of the younger representatives of the tradition. But even with the Lutherans the question of the *concursus*[EN122] as a third problem between that of the *conservatio*[EN123] on the one hand and that of the *gubernatio*[EN124] on the other was raised as an independent issue only by Quenstedt, Hollaz and Baier, and under the heading *De providentia* J. Gerhard treated only *De conservatione* and *De gubernatione*. It is remarkable that even A. Calov kept to the same outward form, dealing with the *concursus*[EN125] only in relation to two questions of detail. On the other hand, it was not only the Lutherans who in this matter took up what was a problem and formulation of the Scholastics, and especially Thomas Aquinas. Nor is it the case that only a few of the younger Reformed dogmaticians adopted the Lutheran approach to the question. For already in J. Wolleb (*Comp. chr. Theol.*, 1626, I, 6, *can.* 5) we find the decisive affirmation whose wording recalls a famous dictum of Thomas: *Providentia Dei causas secundas non tollit, sed ponit*[EN126], and Wolleb also speaks expressly (*can.* 9) of the *praecursus, concursus et succursus divinae virtutis*[EN127]. Again, in the *Leidener Synopsis* (1624, *Disp.* 11, 11) it is stated expressly not only of acts of the human will but of the factual contingent action of all created things that the *operatio*[EN128] of the divine providence not only does not destroy but rather confirms them in their autonomy: *Non corrumpit naturam sed perficit; non tollit sed tuetur*[EN129]. And again in the same context (11, 13) we find the extremely clear and comprehensive definition of the *concursus*[EN130]: God so co-operates with His creatures *ut actions sua immediate in actionem creaturae influat, et una et eadem actio a prima et secunda causa dicatur proficisci, quatenus unum opus seu ἀποτέλεσμα hinc existit*[EN131]. And in all the later Reformed dogmaticians the closest attention and the greatest possible care is given to this issue: certainly not less than in the case of their Lutheran contemporaries. The palpable error may perhaps be traced back to Alexander Schweizer's *Glaubenslehre der ev.-ref. Kirche*, from which the 19th century rather rashly assumed that it could give instruction in the older Reformed theology. In this work (Vol. I, 1844, 320) we read the following: "The Reformed view does not recognise any effective potencies side by

---

EN120 accompanying
EN121 accompanying
EN122 accompanying
EN123 preserving
EN124 ruling
EN125 accompanying
EN126 The providence of God does not abolish secondary causes but establishes them
EN127 God's power of preceding, accompanying and succeeding
EN128 activity
EN129 It does not destroy nature but perfects it; it does not abolish but upholds
EN130 accompanying
EN131 that by His action He immediately sets in motion the creature's action, so that it may be said that one and the same action is initiated by the primary and secondary cause, insofar as one work or result flows from it

side with or outside or independent of God. Hence *praecursus, concursus* and *succursus*[EN132] are all properly excluded." For such a conclusion Schweizer could appeal only to some of the more extreme utterances of Zwingli, and it is not shown to be representative of even one, let alone *the* Reformed standpoint. Indeed, it is no more than an element in his own quite modern systematisation, and one which we can only reject as a denial of the divine preservation of the creature. For what sort of a creature would that be which was divinely preserved and therefore existed without any real potency of its own? Surely there are no grounds for ever believing the legend that this was a normative tenet of Reformed theology.

[097]

As *particula veri*[EN133] of the legend there is only the fact that in the development of the doctrine of the *concursus*[EN134] the Lutherans had a special interest in the second point mentioned in our introduction, the relative autonomy of creaturely activity, in the light of which they interpreted the concept of the divine *concursus*[EN135] more along the lines of a *succursus*[EN136], whereas the interest of the Reformed school was rather in the point raised by us under the third heading, the absolute priority of the divine over the human activity, an interest which decidedly led them to interpret the *concursus*[EN137] more along the lines of a *praecursus*[EN138]. In putting the emphasis where they did the Reformed theologians had the advantage that all the biblical passages commonly alleged have the same emphasis, speaking of the *maior Dei gloria*[EN139]. This is a fact which we must bear in mind. But what the Reformed thinkers wanted to emphasis, in stricter accordance with Holy Scripture, can only be brought out when the *minor gloria creaturae*[EN140] asserted by the Lutherans is also taken into account, as implicitly affirmed in the same Scriptures—we have only to think of Job 38–41. Certainly there can be no question of any antithesis between the two, and we cannot see that we are in any way compelled to choose between them.

It is clear that according to the sharpness or carelessness with which the two parties expressed themselves distinctions and contradictions could easily arise, and even a split in confessional theology. And it is understandable enough that this is what actually did take place. But what is more important is to establish the fact that on both sides the problem was at any rate perceived and therefore tackled. Whether or not they succeeded in their efforts to deal with it, whether or not they were able to bring out effectively this difficult union of opposites, we cannot deny that in their own way the Lutheran dogmaticians did try to establish the absolute majesty and primacy of God no less than the Reformed, nor can we deny that in their own way the Reformed dogmaticians did aim to set forth the autonomy of creaturely activity no less definitely than the Lutheran. As always in the difference between Lutheran and Reformed it is a question of academic antitheses. In many cases these antitheses are of such a kind that to-day we can pass them by as out-moded. But in many others— and this is one of them—they are of a kind still to call for decision. It is not a matter of indifference whether in the last analysis the *gloria Dei*[EN141] is more important to us than the *gloria creaturae*[EN142], or *vice versa*. But what we have here is a shade of emphasis within the

---

[EN132] preceding, accompanying and succeeding
[EN133] grain of truth
[EN134] accompanying
[EN135] accompanying
[EN136] succeeding
[EN137] accompanying
[EN138] preceding
[EN139] greater glory of God
[EN140] lesser glory of the creature
[EN141] glory of God
[EN142] glory of the creature

same confession and not an irreconcilable contradiction. Therefore here, too, the antithesis is only academic.

There is, however, a fundamental question which we have to ask and answer in respect of the achievements of both wings of the older Evangelical theology.

F. Turrettini (*Instit. Theol.*, 1679, VI, 5, 1) commenced his exposition of this doctrine with the profound sigh: *Quaestio de concursu Dei est ex difficillimis, quae in theologia occurrunt*[EN143]. Certainly it is not at all easy to give either to oneself or to others a reasoned account of the fact or extent of the divine co-operation with the creature. Already we have seen that within Protestantism itself two not irreconcileable but at any rate quite different interests were asserted. Again, both Lutheran and Reformed theologians had to mark off themselves from the Romanists on the one side. One clumsy movement, especially in the development of the Lutheran emphasis, might have had the most serious consequences in the form of a fresh outbreak of synergism in the doctrine of grace. And in this connexion it had also to be considered that there were two wings in the Romanist theology of the time: the Thomists, who in Romanism sought after their own fashion to represent the *maior gloria Dei*[EN144] so dear to the Reformed branch of Protestantism, with the result that the Thomists could be appealed to quite freely as *testes veritatis*[EN145]; and the Jesuits, for whom as for the Lutherans the *minor gloria creaturae*[EN146] was the main point of interest. And on the other side the Lutheran and Reformed theologians had to make common cause against the monism and [098] determinism of modern philosophy as determined partly by the Renaissance and partly by the exact natural sciences then in process of development. And behind that philosophy as a relative limit there might well be discerned the more dangerous monism and fatalism of Islam, which at that time practical politics brought forcibly to the notice of Christendom. And if the Lutherans had leanings towards the Romanist side, the Reformed had undoubtedly a similar tendency in this direction. But since, as we have seen, the Lutherans and the Reformed represented the same cause in spite of all the differences between them they had to be on guard no less on the one side than on the other.

Face to face with the difficulty both schools, the Reformed no less than the Lutheran, made a formal borrowing at this point from a philosophy and theology which had been re-discovered and re-asserted at the end of the 16th and the beginning of the 17th centuries—the philosophy of Aristotle and the theology of Aquinas. The borrowing consisted in the adoption and introduction of a specific terminology to describe the two partners whose activities are understood and represented in the doctrine of the *concursus*[EN147] in terms of a co-operation, the activity of God on the one side and that of the creature on the other. The concept which was adopted and introduced was that of "cause." For it was by developing the dialectic of this concept that they both effected the differentiation of themselves on the one side and the other, and also decided the difference which already existed at this point within the Evangelical faith itself. This, then, is the controlling concept for the form assumed by Evangelical dogmatics in this and in all kindred topics.

As the starting-point for our consideration of the problem we will take the comprehensive formulation of the doctrine of the *concursus*[EN148] given by H. Heidegger (quoted from *Heppe²*, p. 200): *Concursus s. cooperatio est operatio illa Dei, qua is cum causis secundis utpote ab eo sicut in esse ita etiam in operari dependentibus immediate ita cooperatur, ut et ad operandum illas*

[EN143] The question of the divine accompanying is one of the most difficult that arises in theology
[EN144] greater glory of God
[EN145] witnesses to the truth
[EN146] lesser glory of the creature
[EN147] accompanying
[EN148] accompanying

excitet s. promoveat et una cum iisdem modo primae causae conveniente et naturae causarum secundarum accomodato operatur. [EN149].

Now we cannot deny that even from the standpoint of the subject itself the concept *causa*[EN150] could and necessarily did both advance and commend itself. It was indeed the whole problem of *causa*[EN151] which had formed the topic for discussion even in the 16th century, and this not only in the doctrine of providence of Zwingli and Calvin but also in Luther's *De servo arbitrio.*

It is ostensibly a question of the relation between the divine activity and the creaturely. But activity means *causare*[EN152]. Activity is movement or action which has as its aim or object a specific effect. To act means to bring about an effect. The subject of such *causare*[EN153] is a *causa*[EN154], in English, a "cause," something without which another and second thing either would not be at all, or would not be at this particular point or in this particular way. A *causa*[EN155] is something by which another thing is directly posited, or conditioned, or perhaps only partly conditioned, that is, by which it is to some extent and in some sense redirected and therefore altered. Now if we are speaking of the activity, and therefore the *causare*[EN156], of God and the creature, then wittingly and willingly or not, we are describing and thinking of both of them in terms of *causa*[EN157]. And at once we have to begin our manipulation of the dialectic of the concept, and it was in this process that the older dogmaticians found inspiration and guidance in Aristotle and Thomas. For quite obviously God is a *causa*[EN158] in one sense, and the creature in quite another.

The peculiarity of God as a *causa*[EN159] consists primarily and supremely in the fact that since He is the source of all *causae*[EN160], the basis and starting-point of the whole causal series, there is no *causa*[EN161] which is either before or above him, but He is his own **[099]** *causa*[EN162]: *causa sui*[EN163]. But it also consists in the fact that since everything which is distinct from him is caused by Him, is His effect, all *causae*[EN164] outside Him and their *causare*[EN165] are not merely partly but absolutely conditioned by Him—indeed they are not merely conditioned but in the first instance posited by Him, seeing that they are created. All other *causae*[EN166] can only affirm and attest Him as the one *causa*[EN167]. All other *causare*[EN168]

[EN149] Accompanying or co-operating is that activity of God in which He co-operates with secondary causes, inasmuch as they are immediately dependent on him for their activity as for their being, so that he incites or moves them to activity, working with them through a mode of accommodation that connects the primary cause to the nature of the secondary causes

[EN150] cause

[EN151] cause

[EN152] causing

[EN153] causing

[EN154] cause

[EN155] cause

[EN156] causing

[EN157] cause

[EN158] cause

[EN159] cause

[EN160] causes

[EN161] cause

[EN162] cause

[EN163] the self-caused cause

[EN164] causes

[EN165] causing

[EN166] causes

[EN167] cause

[EN168] causing

can only affirm and attest His *causare*[EN169] as the true and genuine *causare*[EN170]. As the *causa pure causans*[EN171] He is the *causa causarum*[EN172]. It was in this sense that He was known to the older theology as the *causa prima*[EN173], the *causa princeps*[EN174], the controlling cause which governs all other *causae*[EN175] and their *causare*[EN176].

The creature is also *causa*[EN177]. But the peculiarity of the creature as *causa*[EN178] consists primarily in the fact that as *causa*[EN179] it is posited absolutely by God. Without God it would not be at all, and it would not be *causa*[EN180]. Its *causare*[EN181] can only be a participation in the divine *causare*[EN182], from which it is materially distinguished by the fact that it can consist only in a conditioning or partial conditioning but never in a positing. But again, its peculiarity consists in the fact that not only does it condition other things but it is itself conditioned or partly conditioned by other divine operations and therefore by other *causae*[EN183]. Not only does it work under God but it also works in connexion with a creaturely series of causes in which it is itself something which is effected by other creatures. As *causa causans*[EN184] it is therefore *causa causata*[EN185] in this twofold sense. And that is why it is called *causa secunda*[EN186], a *causa*[EN187] of the second order, of the order to which the whole reality of heaven and earth which is distinct from God belongs, or *causa particularis*[EN188], one cause amongst many others, and as such a cause which has only a limited share in the full force of the concept *causa*[EN189].

This was the conceptual basis on which the older Evangelical dogmatics understood the *concursus Dei*[EN190] within the overruling of providence. As *causa prima*[EN191], or *princeps*[EN192], God co-operates with the operation of *causae secundae*, or *particulares*[EN193]. The divine *causare*[EN194] takes place in and with their *causare*[EN195]. And this means that their operations are also His operations, and in view of the difference in dignity between the two orders they are first and decisively His operations. Now if the problem defined by us as that of the accompanying of the creature by the Creator, of the activity of the creature by that of the Creator, is seen to be a genuine problem in the light of Holy Scripture, there would appear to be no

---

[EN169] causing
[EN170] causing
[EN171] absolutely active cause
[EN172] cause of all causes
[EN173] first cause
[EN174] chief cause
[EN175] causes
[EN176] causing
[EN177] cause
[EN178] cause
[EN179] cause
[EN180] cause
[EN181] causing
[EN182] causing
[EN183] causes
[EN184] active cause
[EN185] cause that has itself been caused
[EN186] secondary cause
[EN187] cause
[EN188] particular cause
[EN189] cause
[EN190] divine accompanying
[EN191] primary cause
[EN192] chief cause
[EN193] secondary or particular causes
[EN194] causing
[EN195] causing

fault in the introduction of this terminology. Every terminology is a possible source of error. From this truth not even terminologies based upon the vocabulary of the Bible are absolutely exempt. The term *causa*[EN196] does not derive from the Bible, but this does not mean that its introduction into the language of theology is a mistake. The term may well be useful in the developing and applying of the message of the Bible. It could be a particularly useful weapon in the controversies in which the theologians of the 17th century were involved. And it has to be shown—if it can be shown—how the use of some such concept can be avoided if we are to deal radically with the question of the activity of God and that of the creature in their relationship the one to the other. When we talk at all of the divine working, do we not necessarily say *causare*[EN197] in that primary sense? Do we not necessarily speak of the original working which is not merely a conditioning but a positing? And again, when we speak of the working of the creature of God, do we not necessarily say *causare*[EN198] in the secondary sense? Do we not speak of the derived and dependent working which is posited and caused by God, and also caused and partially caused by another working which is itself caused? It is indisputable that to talk in this way can lead to error, for the terminology is not so unequivocal that it cannot become the instrument of false theological conceptions or asseverations. But whether or not it does lead to error depends upon the use to which it is put. It depends upon whether the dynamic and teleology of its use are determined by and continue to be determined by the fact that when it is introduced into theology its task is to help to an understanding and exposition of the message of the Bible, or whether its use gives

[100]   rise to a dynamic and exposition which are foreign to the message of the Bible and under the pressure of which there emerge theological conceptions and asseverations which are foreign and even completely antithetical to that message. But the fact that the terminology is pressed into service does not of itself mean that error necessarily arises.

Historically, then, it is not at all the case that in the older Evangelical theology positive error derived merely from the introduction of the term *causa*[EN199]. If we consider the conceptions and asseverations of the older Lutheran and Reformed dogmaticians, we shall find on both sides dangerous approximations to the forbidden frontiers. In the Lutherans we shall often catch notes which have a remarkably Romanist and even Jesuit sound, and in the Reformed we shall catch notes which have a remarkably Stoic, or contemporary monistic, or even slightly Turkish sound. But on neither side is this due to the fact that they made use of the term *causa*[EN200]. It is due rather to the fact that quite apart from the application of this concept they did not always show the same sureness of touch in this matter as they tried to build up the form and content of their doctrine upon the message of the Bible. Apart from such vacillations we have to allow that the doctrine which they expounded is as a whole formally correct and even serviceable and normative. The experiment in Aristotle and Thomas did not in fact turn out quite so badly as a careful observer might at first have expected. And we have also to allow that by the remarkable *concursus*[EN201] which they not merely discussed but without realising it attained, they were able to shed a light which without this *concursus*[EN202] (of the Bible and Aristotle!) they might not have been able to do. Apart from any other considerations, it is utterly monstrous that E. Troeltsch (*Glaubenslehre*, 1925, 254) should have had the audacity, without any good reason, to dismiss as "completely worthless" the efforts made by the older theology in this matter.

[EN196] cause
[EN197] causing
[EN198] causing
[EN199] cause
[EN200] cause
[EN201] accompanying
[EN202] accompanying

2. *The Divine Accompanying*

Two points have constantly to be borne in mind. Formally, the orthodox presentation is correct even in and in spite of and indeed by means of the new terminology introduced at that time. But materially, the same cannot be said concerning it. For it missed completely the relationship between creation and the covenant of grace. In its whole doctrine of providence it spoke abstractly not only of the general control of God over and with the creature, but of the control of a general and in some sense neutral and featureless God, an Absolute. It spoke abstractly of a neutral and featureless creature. It separated between world history and salvation history. And the result was that when the dogmaticians came to speak of the *causare*[EN203] of the *causa prima*[EN204] and the *causae secundae*[EN205], neither in the one case nor in the other had it any specifically Christian content. There is indeed a form of co-operation as they described it, and the older theologians gave a fine and correct and instructive picture of that form. But it lacked the content without whose express indication even the form which is finely and correctly and instructively pictured may well be the form of a content which is completely different. It lacked the Christian content without whose express indication that well-developed abstraction may well be informed by a dynamic and teleology which have nothing whatever to do with the exposition of the message of the Bible. And this brings us to the second point. In the older orthodoxy, the doctrine of *concursus* in the form determined by the term *causa*[EN206] lacked any definite safeguards against the mischief which might result simply because it was expressed in that form. The enemies which it was its business to repel, the enemy of synergism on the one hand and monism on the other, of the Papacy on the one hand and the Turk on the other, could also make use of exactly the same form. They could not be repelled merely by the use of that form. When the Evangelicals were seen to be looking to Thomas, it might easily have been a cause of triumph and a source of hope not only in Rome itself but also in countless other states which openly or secretly were seeking a uniform doctrine. The antithesis and conjunction of *causa prima*[EN207] and *causae secundae*[EN208], wherever the emphasis was laid, might easily have been interpreted   [101] as the conjunction in antithesis of systems which had nothing whatever to do with the message of the Bible but were rather opposed to it. This mischief never did result in the older Evangelical theology. But this theology was not so proof against it that it could not result later, and even make a strange appeal to this theology. And seeing that it did result later, we must regret that it was not prevented in time.

We have to ask, therefore, on what conditions the concept can legitimately be applied to this doctrine.

We may begin by mentioning certain preliminary conditions, and we shall then show that the fulfilment of all of them is dependent upon the fulfilment of one decisive condition with which we shall deal in conclusion.

1. If it is to be applied legitimately, the term *causa*[EN209] must not be regarded as the equivalent of that of a cause which is effective automatically. If we had no choice but to think of *causa*[EN210] or cause as the term is applied in modern science, or rather natural philosophy, with all its talk about causality, causal nexus, causal law, causal necessity and the like, then clearly it is a concept which we could not apply either to God or to the creature of God, but could only reject. That was how A. Ritschl understood the term, and in consequence he

---

[EN203] causing
[EN204] primary cause
[EN205] secondary causes
[EN206] cause
[EN207] primary cause
[EN208] secondary causes
[EN209] cause
[EN210] cause

conceded that the whole doctrine of the *concursus*[EN211] has to be dismissed, as though it stood or fell with this particular understanding of cause. As he saw it, the idea of God cannot be squared with the scientific explanation of nature, and therefore we should be doing violence to God if "under the concept cause we compared Him with natural causes which can be understood by observation" (*Unterr. in d. chr. Rel.*, 1875, § 15). We cannot charge either Thomas or our own orthodox dogmaticians with being guilty of any such comparison. The *causa prima*[EN212] as they envisaged it cannot easily be identified with a natural cause which can be understood by observation. They did not even explain their *causae secundae*[EN213] altogether within the limits of the modern idea of necessity. According to their understanding of the creature, even within the uniform course of events peculiar to the *ordo naturae*[EN214] there was still a secure place for natural contingency and the freedom of the human will, for miracle and the suspension of law, quite outside that *ordo*[EN215]. Even within creaturely history there was still a secure place for the history of the covenant and the Church. These were genuine conceptions of *causae*[EN216] and *causare*[EN217] which were not overlaid by the concept of automatically effective causes. Naturally the divine and human operations do have a mechanical component to the extent that in their mutual relation they have the element of necessity. In this respect there are some equivocal statements on the Reformed side, especially in Zwingli and Calvin, and occasionally in the 17th century. But the element of necessity is not to be explained by a foreign concept of mechanical. The mechanical aspect of the relation must be viewed and understood in its peculiar distinctness from what is usually understood by the term mechanical. All that is needed at this point is to perceive and affirm in principle the freedom which the older theology did enjoy and exercise in practice in their concept both of God and also of the creature. But to do this it is necessary to have a basis which we do not find in the older writers.

2. If the term *causa*[EN218] is to be applied legitimately, care must be taken lest the idea should creep in that in God and the creature we have to do with two "things." The German word for cause, *Ur-sache*, might easily suggest this. A "thing" or "object" (*Sache*) is something which in part at least is perceptible and accessible to man. If we have to do with a "thing" then this means that even if only defectively we believe that we are capable of examining, recognising, analysing and defining, in short of "realising" it, and in some degree we know how to control it. But neither God nor the creature is a *causa*[EN219] in this sense. When we turn to Thomas and our own orthodox fathers we have to ask seriously whether on their definition God and the creature as primary and secondary *causa*[EN220] could not easily become something very like "things." For at this point we are confronted by the mortal danger which faces all theology. All theology is a meditation about God and the creature. But since it meditates and speaks *about* them they are always in danger of becoming things. The human thinker and speaker is in constant danger of forgetting the inconceivable mystery of their existence and being, their presence and operation, and of imagining that he can think and speak about them directly, as though both they themselves and also their relationship to each other were somehow below him. Now when the Aristotelian dialectic of

[102]

EN211 accompanying
EN212 primary cause
EN213 secondary causes
EN214 order of nature
EN215 order
EN216 causes
EN217 causing
EN218 cause
EN219 cause
EN220 cause

2. The Divine Accompanying

the causal concept was applied to the operations of God and the creature, did it not to some extent involve thinking and speaking about them in that way? The causal concept, like the concept of being, is certainly an invitation to error at this point. And if the concept is used, this invitation must be resisted at all costs. Rather remarkably, a true theological realism consists primarily in a constant awareness of the fact that neither God nor the creature is a "thing," that on the contrary, to those who really want to think and speak about them, to theologians—if they are not to thresh empty straw—they must always be *self*-revealed. If the purest and strictest orthodoxy once relaxes this awareness, then immediately it becomes a dead orthodoxy. And that is what we must not allow to happen at this point. But a particular basis will be needed if our awareness is to be awakened and kept awake in this matter. Our forefathers knew the basis, but they did not make any use of it. Hence it is hardly surprising that there are good reasons for thinking that they did not have the awareness in sufficient measure.

3. If the term *causa*[EN221] is to be applied legitimately, it must be clearly understood that it is not a master-concept to which both God and the creature are subject, nor is it a common denominator to which they may both be reduced. *Causa*[EN222] is not a genus, of which the divine and creaturely *causa*[EN223] can then be described as species. When we speak about the being of God and that of the creature, we are not dealing with two species of the one genus being. When we speak about the divine nature and the human nature of Christ, we are not dealing with two species of the one genus nature. And so, too, in this case. To put it rather differently, it must be clearly understood that when the word *causa*[EN224] is applied to God on the one side and the creature on the other, the concept does not describe the activity but the active subjects, and it does not signify subjects which are not merely not alike, or not similar, but subjects which in their absolute antithesis cannot even be compared.

It is true, of course, that although there is no identity of the divine and creaturely operation or *causare*, there is a similarity, a correspondence, a comparableness, an analogy. In theology we can and should speak about similarity and therefore analogy when we find likeness and unlikeness between two quantities: a certain likeness which is compromised by a great unlikeness; or a certain unlikeness which is always relativised and qualified by a certain existent likeness. The great unlikeness of the work of God in face of that of the creature consists in the fact that as the work of the Creator in the preservation and overruling of the creature the work of God takes the form of an absolute positing, a form which can never be proper to the work of the creature. But at the same time the divine work in relation to the creature also has the form of a conditioning, determining and altering of that which already exists. And inasmuch as the conditioning of another also belongs to creaturely activity, there is a certain similarity between the divine and the creaturely work. In view of this likeness and unlikeness, unlikeness and likeness, we can and should speak of a similarity, a comparableness, and therefore an analogy between the divine activity and the human. We have to speak of an *analogia operationis*[EN225], just as elsewhere we can speak of an *analogia relationis*[EN226].

But the concept *causa*[EN227] does not merely describe activities, but acting subjects. And between the two subjects as such there is neither likeness nor similarity, but utter unlikeness.

[EN221] cause
[EN222] cause
[EN223] cause
[EN224] cause
[EN225] analogy of operation
[EN226] analogy of relation
[EN227] cause

[103] We cannot deduce from the fact that both subjects are *causa*[EN228] the farther fact that they both fall under the one master-concept *causa*[EN229]; that they may both be reduced to that one common denominator; that they are both species belonging to the one genus. On the contrary, they cannot even be compared.

Indeed, it would be a mistake to try to compare them simply because they are both *causa*[EN230]. In the same way it would be a mistake to argue as follows. The Creator exists and has being no less than the creature. Therefore although the being of the Creator and that of the creature are unlike, in some respects they are like and therefore similar. There is therefore an *analogia entis*[EN231] between God and the creature. To that extent there is a master-concept, a common denominator, a genus (being) which comprises both God and the creature. And it would be a really serious mistake if we were to adopt this argument. Jesus Christ has a divine nature and a human. Therefore, although the two natures are unlike, they are also alike and similar. There is therefore an *analogia naturae*[EN232] between God and man. And to that extent we can speak of a master-concept, a common denominator, a genus (nature) which comprises both God and man. This is the type of mistake which we have to avoid at this point. This is the deduction which we have to recognise as false and therefore illegitimate.

The divine and creaturely subjects are not like or similar, but unlike. They are unlike because their basis and constitution as subjects are quite different and therefore absolutely unlike, that is, there is not even the slightest similarity between them. The divine *causa*[EN233], as distinct from the creaturely, is self-grounded, self-positing, self-conditioning and self-causing. It causes itself—and it is the Christian knowledge of God which gives us the decisive word on the matter—in the triune life which God enjoys as Father, Son and Holy Spirit and in which He has His divine basis from eternity to eternity. This is how God is a subject. And this is how He is a *causa*[EN234]. And for this reason there is not a single point at which the creaturely subject can be like Him. For the creaturely *causa*[EN235] is not grounded in itself but absolutely from outside and therefore not at all within itself. It owes the fact that it is a *causa*[EN236], and is capable of *causare*[EN237], not to itself but first of all to God, who created it and as the Creator still posits and conditions it, and then to the other *causae*[EN238] of its own order, without whose conditioning or partial conditioning it would not exist. This is how the creature is a subject. And this is how it is a *causa*[EN239]. What likeness is there then between the creature and the Creator who in His unity and triunity posits Himself without any outside assistance at all?

It is quite indispensable to a true doctrine of the divine accompanying that the absolute unlikeness of the two *causae causantes*[EN240] should be brought into sharp relief, with the consequent rejection of any idea of an *analogia causae*[EN241]. For otherwise there can never be any certainty that we are speaking of two distinct subjects, God and the creature, when we

---

[EN228] cause
[EN229] cause
[EN230] cause
[EN231] analogy of being
[EN232] analogy of nature
[EN233] cause
[EN234] cause
[EN235] cause
[EN236] cause
[EN237] causing
[EN238] causes
[EN239] cause
[EN240] active causes
[EN241] analogy of causation

deal with that twofold *causare*[EN242] which is our present subject. In respect of other essences we can easily take two quantities and range them under a single master-concept, a common denominator or a genus, thus comparing them the one with the other. But we cannot do this with God and the creature. If we tried to do so, the twofold activity whose relationship we should be discussing would not be the activity of these two subjects.

To return to the doctrine of the *concursus*[EN243] as it is presented in the older Evangelical dogmatics, it is from this standpoint that we have to judge whether and to what extent the characterisation of the two causes as *prima*, or *princeps*, and *secunda*, or *particularis*[EN244], can really do justice to the absolute unlikeness of the two *causae causantes*[EN245]. It is clear that in the philosophy of Aristotle and the theology of Thomas, from which they took the character-isation, this absolute unlikeness was not safeguarded. Indeed, it is more likely that in these two cases, in which the analogy of being was also envisaged, no such unlikeness between God and the creature was even intended by the characterisation, but at the back of it there was the idea of an *analogia causae*[EN246] which would involve a complete denial of the unlikeness of the two subjects. But if this was so, then necessarily they would come under a single master-concept, they would form part of a single genus, they would be reducible to a single common denominator. And we could only conclude that we are not really dealing with God and the creature and their mutual co-operation. Now it cannot be denied that we should be far happier if the older dogmaticians had clarified this aspect of the matter when they adopted and introduced that particular terminology. They might have done so quite success-fully if in view of the unsatisfactory usage of the sources they had dropped altogether the predicates *prima*[EN247] or *princeps*[EN248], and *secunda*[EN249] or *particularis*[EN250], and spoken sim-ply of *causa divina*[EN251] or *creatrix*[EN252] and *causa non divina*[EN253] or *creata*[EN254], in the same way as they spoke of *natura divina*[EN255] and *natura humana*[EN256] in their Christology. This material instead of purely formal description would have expressed the unlikeness of the two subjects and safeguarded their peculiarity as God on the one hand and creature on the other. They could also have made the clarification successfully if they had taken over the predicates but radically reinterpreted them in a way quite different from the sources: *prima*[EN257] or *princeps*[EN258] with express reference to the doctrine of the Trinity and in the sense of *divina*[EN259] or *creatrix*[EN260]; and *secunda*[EN261] or *particularis*[EN262] just as expressly as

[104]

[EN242] causing
[EN243] accompanying
[EN244] primary or principle and secondary or particular
[EN245] active causes
[EN246] analogy of causation
[EN247] primary
[EN248] chief
[EN249] secondary
[EN250] particular
[EN251] divine cause
[EN252] creating cause
[EN253] non-divine cause
[EN254] created cause
[EN255] divine nature
[EN256] human nature
[EN257] primary
[EN258] chief
[EN259] divine
[EN260] creating
[EN261] secondary
[EN262] particular

non divina[EN263] or *creata*[EN264]. But since the older theologians did not make the clarification either the one way or the other, it is an open question whether with the terminology they did not also take over the uncertainty who or what is really intended by the two causes, and whether they are really speaking about God and the creature. We for our part cannot dispense with the clarification. Without this safeguard, without a clear perception of the absolute unlikeness of the two *causae*[EN265] in question, we cannot accept as legitimate an application of the causal concept in the present context. But once again we must add that we still need the particular basis which we do not find in the older theologians if we really want to attain absolute clarity on the point.

4. The third condition is the most important so far mentioned, and if it is fulfilled the fourth will also be fulfilled. We do not need to speak of it, therefore, except very briefly. When the causal concept is introduced, it should not be with either the intention or the consequence that theology should be turned into philosophy at this point, projecting a kind of total scheme of things. If it is clear (1) that in its application both to God and the creature the concept *causa*[EN266] must be kept quite free from the encumbrance of mechanical ideas, (2) that it ought not to have the result of making God and the creature two "things," two known and controllable quantities, and (3), and above all, that it must not be interpreted in such a way that the incomparableness of God and the creature is compromised, then from the negative standpoint at any rate the autonomy of the theological thesis here propounded should be quite secure in face of a philosophical conception which apparently approximates to it. But even this negative safeguard was lacking in the older theology. And it is noticeable that the Scripture proofs certainly adduced in this theology do not have any real bearing upon the statement of the problem. They remain in the background behind the discussion proper, and there is an almost grotesque attempt to make it clear that in virtue of these proofs the being who is later discussed as *causa princeps*[EN267] is necessarily the God of Job and Paul, and that all the Old and New Testament statements about man as he goes his own way and therefore God's way (not to speak of Behemoth and Leviathan) can quite comfortably be included in the concept of *causae particulares*[EN268], thus completely losing their original form. It is true that in the δἰ αὐτοῦ[EN269] (Rom. 11³⁶) P. van Mastricht perceived the *operatio*[EN270] of the triune God, that is, the God of the biblical revelation, but this interesting exegesis was peculiar to himself and was not followed by any of the others. Yet it is absolutely essential that there should be this safeguard against defection into purely philosophical thinking. For when theology is guilty of such a defection it is wilfully entangling its tenets in the contradictions and uncertainties of problems which are alien to it, it runs the risk of speaking about what are really two quite different quantities when it uses the titles God and the creature, and the encumbrance with another and alien task necessarily means that its own work suffers. And this is something which we cannot allow to happen at this point.

[105]

5. But this safeguard, and all the negative safeguards so far mentioned, can be recognised as necessary and therefore valid only if we set against them the positive pre-condition which must be fulfilled in this matter. As the doctrine of the *concursus*[EN271], and indeed the whole doctrine of providence, is expounded, there must be a clear connexion between the first

---

[EN263] non-divine
[EN264] created
[EN265] causes
[EN266] cause
[EN267] chief cause
[EN268] particular causes
[EN269] through Him
[EN270] activity
[EN271] accompanying

article of the creed and the second. If the causal concept is to be applied legitimately, its content and interpretation must be determined by the fact that what it describes is the operation of the Father of Jesus Christ in relation to that of the creature. Basically, the doctrine of the *concursus*[EN272] must be as follows. God, the only true God, so loved the world in His election of grace that in fulfilment of the covenant of grace instituted at the creation He willed to become a creature, and did in fact become a creature, in order to be its Saviour. And this same God accepts the creature even apart from the history of the covenant and its fulfilment. He takes it to Himself as such and in general in such sort that He co-operates with it, preceding, accompanying and following all its being and activity, so that all the activity of the creature is primarily and simultaneously and subsequently His own activity, and therefore a part of the actualisation of His own will revealed and triumphant in Jesus Christ.

Who and what is this *causa prima*[EN273] which confronts us here as the solemn companion of the *causae secundae*[EN274]? Certainly we cannot speak yet of the God. who became flesh in Jesus Christ, identifying Himself in this way with a *causa secunda*[EN275] and effecting eternal salvation. But we can speak of the God who in the execution of His election of grace and the fulfilment of His covenant of grace willed and effected this inconceivable benefit, of the God who was already the Father of mercy and the God of all comfort (2 Cor. 1³), of the God who thereby accomplished this eternal deliverance. In the very purpose and intention and in the execution of the will thereby revealed and effected, He was already the Creator of the creature, and He is also its Sustainer, and the One who co-operates with it in its own work—always and everywhere. As *causa prima*[EN276] He precedes and accompanies and follows the *causae secundae*[EN277]. Therefore His *causare*[EN278] consists, and consists only, in the fact that He bends their activity to the execution of His own will which is His will of grace, subordinating their operations to the specific operation which constitutes the history of the covenant of grace. In all things and in all their particular operations this is the first and final achievement. And it is because of this that His *causare*[EN279] is almighty and all-powerful, the true and original *causare*[EN280] above which there is no other. It is because of this that the One who is *causans*[EN281] at this point is the *causa causarum*[EN282], the *causa sui*[EN283], the *causa princeps*[EN284], in relation to which all other causes can be only *causae particulares*[EN285]. He is *causa*[EN286] in the sense specified and qualified by the power of His grace. And it is in this form and for this reason that He is *causa prima*[EN287].

And who and what is the *causa secunda*[EN288] which confronts us here as that which is sovereignly accompanied by the *causa prima*[EN289]? Certainly it is not yet the new creation which is

---

[EN272] accompanying
[EN273] primary cause
[EN274] secondary causes
[EN275] secondary cause
[EN276] primary cause
[EN277] secondary causes
[EN278] causing
[EN279] causing
[EN280] causing
[EN281] causing
[EN282] cause of all causes
[EN283] self-caused cause
[EN284] chief cause
[EN285] particular causes
[EN286] cause
[EN287] primary cause
[EN288] secondary cause
[EN289] primary cause

taken up into unity with the Creator in Jesus Christ. Certainly it is not yet the creation which as the Church and people of Jesus Christ, in the knowledge and faith of Him and in His discipleship, already has a part in the eternal deliverance which was accomplished by Him. But already it is the creation which in some degree approximates to this new creation, which by its very existence is posited and sanctified with it under the promise, which already is ordained to be the object and recipient of the divine mercy. There is no creature which does [106] not owe its existence as such and as *causa*[EN290], which does not owe its opportunities and operations, to the Creator and Sustainer whose will was from all eternity the election of His grace, and whose will is already accomplished in the deliverance which was effected in Jesus Christ. As *causa secunda*[EN291] it is accompanied by the *causa prima*[EN292] and preceded and followed by it. Therefore its own *causare*[EN293] can take place only under the determination and limitation appointed by it. Its own operations can have a place only as they are subordinated to the divine operations which constitute the history of the covenant of grace. They can therefore be only the indirect divine operations of grace. Seeing that all things with their own particular activity must serve the activity of grace, their activity is a subordinate one even in its autonomy. The operation of *causae particulares*[EN294] is under the direction of the *causa princeps*[EN295]. They have to be thought of as *causae secundae*[EN296] in the true sense i.e., *secundae*[EN297] not in relation to some higher power, but to the grace of God and the almighty operation of that grace.

This is the positive condition under which the introduction of the causal concept into the doctrine of the *concursus*[EN298] may be regarded as theologically possible and incontestable. If this condition is fulfilled the proofs from Scripture adduced by the older dogmaticians lose the air of fortuitousness which clings to them in their writings. We see the biblical centre which makes the matter a genuine problem of theology. Interpreted in the light of this centre the causal concept is certainly not exposed to the dangers against which we have been considering a defence. And in the light of this interpretation of the causal concept the defence itself is meaningful, compelling and effective.

In these circumstances the concept *causa*[EN299] has (1) on both sides a content in virtue of which it certainly embraces natural events and the uniformity of their processes, and yet cannot be identified with the narrow concept of a mechanical natural cause which effects and is effected automatically. For what can there be in common between Jesus Christ and a despot? What can there be in common between the fulfilment of His gracious will in heaven and on earth, the strictness with which His activity of grace precedes, accompanies and follows the activity of the creature, and an absolute compulsion? What can there be in common between the activity of the creature under the conditioning and within the limitation of this governance, and an automatic process?

The concept *causa*[EN300] has also (2) a content in virtue of which it certainly cannot be identified either on the one side or the other with a "thing." If the *causa prima*[EN301] is the

---

[EN290] cause
[EN291] secondary cause
[EN292] primary cause
[EN293] causing
[EN294] particular causes
[EN295] chief cause
[EN296] secondary causes
[EN297] secondary
[EN298] accompanying
[EN299] cause
[EN300] cause
[EN301] primary cause

mercy of God, and the *causa secunda*[EN302] is its object and recipient, then it follows that neither the one nor the other can ever be controlled by the one who meditates or speaks concerning them. For what is there here that we can "realise"? We stand before the mystery of grace both on the one side and on the other. It is clear that the *causa prima*[EN303] can be known only in prayer, and the *causa secunda*[EN304] in gratitude, or else not at all. No thinker or speaker can ever be above these things, but only under them. If in a dead orthodoxy he is over something, then *ipso facto*[EN305] it is not either the *causa prima*[EN306] or the *causa secunda*[EN307] in this sense.

The concept *causa*[EN308] has (3) a content in virtue of which the two things signified by it cannot possibly be compared. If we keep before us the archetype of divine-human co-operation, the co-operation of the holy God and sinful man in the covenant of grace; if we have regard to the antithesis which in Jesus Christ became an antithesis in unity, we shall refrain from drawing any parallels or comparisons, we shall be delivered from the evil desire to find a master-concept, a common denominator, a genus, a synthesis, in which God and the creature can be brought together, and we shall be kept from the pleasure of finding analogies between the two subjects. In fact the two subjects are together and they work together, but this fact can be understood only as the gracious mystery of an encounter in which that which is quite inconceivable and unexpected and undeserved has actually come to pass.

And self-evidently, the causal concept has (4) no content in virtue of which it ceases to be [107] part of the Christian confession and theological knowledge and becomes part of a philosophical scheme of things. For when the two subjects are so very different, but so closely inter-related, clearly it is only by revelation and in faith that the *causa princeps*[EN309] and the *causa particularis*[EN310] can be known both in and for themselves and in the *concursus*[EN311] of their two-fold *causare*[EN312].

These, then, are the five conditions under which we can approve the use of the causal concept which was so significant in the *concursus*[EN313] teaching of the older dogmatics. The fulfilling of the first four of these conditions depends upon the fulfilling of the fifth. And of the fifth the older dogmatics unfortunately did not make any mention. No wonder, then, that they were not secure even in respect of the first four. It is true that the experiment with Aristotle and Thomas did not turn out so badly as it might have done. But this merely goes to show that even the history of doctrine *hominum confusione Dei providentia regitur*[EN314]. It is, therefore, a living example of that which we are here concerned to maintain. But this fact does not absolve us from the task of developing the interpretation of the causal concept in which alone the form of the proposition as we have made it cannot be disputed.

We now turn to the material side of the question and our answer to it. But first we make the methodological observation that even here we have to do

---

[EN302] secondary cause
[EN303] primary cause
[EN304] secondary cause
[EN305] for that very reason
[EN306] primary cause
[EN307] secondary cause
[EN308] cause
[EN309] chief cause
[EN310] particular cause
[EN311] accompanying
[EN312] causing
[EN313] accompanying
[EN314] The providence of God rules amid the confusion of human beings

only with the operation of God. It is the question of His operation from the standpoint of a co-operation with that of the creature, but it is still a question of His operation, of His accompanying of the creature even in its own operation. And this means that we cannot consider propositions concerning the creature as such, but only concerning God the Creator in His relationship with the creature.

When God works, His operation is almighty in relation to that of the creature. It is an operation which is absolutely above the power of the creature. The majesty in which He accompanies the activity of the creature and co-operates with it is quite unconditional both in general and in particular. And the majesty of the operation of God consists in the fact that it is the operation of His eternal love. We describe it very badly if we simply ascribe to it formally a much greater potency than that of the creature. It is the relation of purely creaturely potencies that we have to measure and understand quantitatively, not that of the divine potency to the creaturely. And we also describe it very badly if we count its potency relative to the creature as part of the general relationship of infinity to one. We could not describe even the relation of heaven and earth in that way. And in any case it would give us only an immanent contrast without touching the real antithesis between God and the creature, and their mutual inter-connexion. The divine potency, and therefore the divine working in relation to that of the creature, is above that of the creature because God is eternal love. The love of God is primary. The creature can only be loved by God, and then at best love Him in return. The love of God is essential. As Father, Son and Holy Ghost, God is love in and of Himself, and in the overflowing of this love He loves the creature. But the creature can only [108] accept this love, and be content to try to respond to it. The love of God is eternal. God loves even as the Creator of time. But at best the creature can love God, and does love Him, only in the time allotted to it. And all this means distance in the relation between God and the creature—and not only distance, but the pre-eminence of God over it, the relation of his absolute power to the lowly power of the creature. Hence the almightiness in which God accompanies and co-operates with the creature consists in this absolute distinction of the two potencies. And the difference in the potencies at work carries with it an irreversibility in the order of precedence and dignity of the divine and human activities. It is hardly possible to see any necessary irreversibility in the order of precedence of the greater and the less, or infinity and one. The greater needs the less, and infinity one, no less than the reverse. But the order of precedence of the eternal love of God and the creature as the object of this love is absolutely irreversible, for God does not need the creature, but the creature has absolute need of God.

This means that we can never look too high when we think of the Father of Jesus Christ who accompanies the creature as *causa prima*[EN315]. The power of

---

[EN315] primary cause

natural phenomena, or historical forces, or even ideas, may have something shatteringly great about it. And so too, in the proper context, can that which we mean by natural necessity. And so too can that which in many languages and forms has been described as destiny, fate, *ananke*, or *kismet*. But we do not look high enough if we expect to find the greatness of God in the greatness of experiences and perceptions and concepts of this sort. There is no irreversibility in the relation of these high quantities to the other quantities ostensibly ranged so utterly beneath them. We cannot question their superiority. Not in any form or to any degree can we defy or oppose their preeminence. But we can at least explain their superiority as a relative superiority. It is a superiority which is not grounded in a qualitative distinction. God alone is genuinely and ultimately and absolutely superior in relation to all the reality which is distinct from Himself. God alone is unequivocally *causa prima*[EN316], and He is so because He is eternal love, and His activity is eternally to love. This is why His activity is greater than all these other activities, of which the same cannot be said. This is why He Himself is holy as contrasted with all the beings with whom He co-operates. This is why He is to be feared by all those whose ways and works He accompanies. He is the Lord of all lords and the King of all kings. He is the One who dwells in a light which is inaccessible to all those who go and work with Him. Can there be any question which they have more reason to fear as they themselves are active according to the measure of their creaturely being—the depth of the abyss of nothingness which is always ready to engulf them and to frustrate all their striving on the one hand, or the height of God on the other, of the God who upholds them, and without whose upholding   [109] they would immediately be lost, and the futility of their striving would immediately be confirmed? It is because God is love, and no creature can continue for a moment if it refuses this love, that God is the only One who is really to be feared.

We have not made any secret of the way in which we know that the divine activity accompanies that of the creature with so great a superiority. We have understood this supremacy as the supremacy of God's eternal love. We have not deduced it from any human conception of God. We have sought it rather in the holiness which is at the heart of all divine activity. We have listened to the Word of grace in which God has Himself revealed Himself in Jesus Christ. We have learned and perceived who and what God is, and how He works, according to His own Word. It is there in that Word that we have seen the height from which He works. It is there that we have seen the irreversibility in the order of precedence of His own activity and all other activity. It is there that we have seen the qualitative distinction of His power as contrasted with all other powers, and its absolute superiority over them. It is there that we have seen Him as eternal love. And what we have received there, we possess with a decisive and final certainty. That is why we cannot treat of the perception and

---

[EN316] primary cause

111

understanding of the superiority of the divine work in the same way as we can of a human opinion, or as indeed we must of even the most serious of human suggestions. In other words, we are not in any position to treat of this perception and understanding as though they were open to discussion. Naturally, our own comprehension and exposition and formulation of them are always open to discussion. By its very nature the matter is one which demands constantly a better formulation. But as it does so, it remains outside and above the sphere in which it can itself be called in question. It is a matter which questions us. Our relation to it can consist only in our rendering an account *to* it rather than *of* it.

It is because it is eternal love that the power of the divine operation is superior to all other powers, and the knowledge of it is not open to discussion. But if this is the case, then in relation to all other operations or activities we must think of the divine activity as first and foremost a free activity—free in the sense that it is a work which God does not owe either to Himself or to the creature. God does not will to work without the creature but with it. And He holds to this and does it. He does it with an inward necessity. And this involves an unbreakable order in the work of the creature, for in that the creature exists God exists with it in the supremacy of His own work. Because God wills to preserve it in its reality, and because this reality is change, God accompanies it in this change. This law of the creaturely world, that God is present and active in all that occurs within it, is more fixed than any natural law or mathematical axiom. But the necessity with which God does hold to this and do it is the

[110] necessity of His love. And love is free or it is not love. Therefore when God accompanies the creature He gives Himself. In so doing He is not the prisoner either of Himself or of the creature. He still acts according to His goodpleasure. When the love of God overflows in the creating, the preserving, and now the accompanying of the creature, this means that it is revealed in its freedom. And it is in this freedom that it is necessary to God.

It is excellent to see how in H. Heidegger a knowledge which is Christian in origin and character—although it is not of course recognised to be such—can still break through the limitations of Aristotelian conceptuality in which a freedom of this kind cannot be ascribed to God: *Causae primae convenit, ut ad extra independenter et libere operetur. Proin concursus est libera Dei operatio, quam adhibere vel non adhibere possit*[EN317]. By His own eternal decree (and only so) God has bound himself actually to fulfil this *operatio*[EN318], constituting His co-operation with the creature a *firma et adamantina lex*[EN319] (quoted from *Heppe*[2], 210). Even as He gives Himself to this relationship to the creature, God is still its Lord.

For this reason the presence and co-operation of God cannot be thought of as a predicate or exponent of creaturely occurrence. The proposition that

---

[EN317] It is appropriate that the primary cause should be free and independent with respect to its external operation. Accordingly, the divine accompanying is a free activity of God, which He is able to undertake or refrain from undertaking

[EN318] activity

[EN319] fixed and unyielding law

God is immanent in this occurrence is a true one in the sense that in face of it He does make this and not another use of His freedom, that He gives Himself to it as a Companion, that in His supremacy—the supremacy of His love—He on His side co-operates with all creaturely activity. It is true in so far as it speaks of the fidelity with which God is true to His own resolve and therefore to the creature. But since this first proposition is true only in this very precise sense, the further proposition that all occurrence is immanent in God is necessarily false. When we speak of God in nature, or God in history, we cannot mean that in some degree it belongs to nature and history, as one of their properties, that God should be at work in them. They have no claim upon God for that. They on their side have no power to co-operate with God. It can only turn out that they do so in fact to the extent that God takes the initiative towards them, He Himself co-operating with them and giving them on their side the opportunity—beyond any capacity of their own—to co-operate with Him. By the grace of God the events of nature and history are authorised and qualified to co-operate with him. In itself and as such their activity is their own. It is limited as they are limited, and it cannot go outside those limits. And when God with His activity associates Himself with them, this does not mean that nature and history become God. Even when the events of nature and history are in every respect the work of God, the same is not true of nature and history as such. It is rather that God Himself accompanies those events, co-operating in them, introducing them and revealing them as His own work. Hence it follows that the work of God in the working of the creature, and His revelation in the revealing of the creature, can never be ascribed to the creature, but only and always to God Himself. That which works is His co-operating love. That which speaks is His co-operating Word. And for that working and speaking the creature on its side has no capacity. It is not, then, the creature which works in God's working, but God Himself who works on and in His own working. God alone is and remains eternal love. The creature can only be loved by Him, or at the very best love Him in return. The freedom of God cannot be violated. An awareness of the supremacy of God over all the power of the creature, of the qualitative distinction between divine and creaturely potency, of the irreversibility of the order of precedence in divine and creaturely activity, must be brought into play and relentlessly kept in play at this juncture. [111]

It is quite impossible to build upon the doctrine of the *concursus*EN320, the perception that God accompanies all creaturely occurrence, a scheme of things in which the world as such is also divine, nature as such is the nature-God, history as such is the history of God, and man as such is the God-man. Such a view can only be a magical one. The godhead or divinity to which it refers can only be a plurality of demons, or a single arch-demon. This is a possible point of entry for all the dangerous heresies which have first endangered the knowledge of the divine providence and then Christian knowledge as a whole. In one connexion or another we are given the (within its limits) quite legitimate impression of the power of creaturely activity. It may be the activity of nature, perhaps an isolated phenomenon or a great

---

EN320 accompanying

113

natural process. It may be the activity of men as they are caught up and swept forward in a specific movement. It may be the activity of the human spirit in one or other of its different forms. We are so mastered and carried away by the impression that we think it impossible to conceive of anything more majestic or significant, more solemn or overpowering: *quo majus cogitari non potest!*[EN321] And we think it necessary to attribute this *causare*[EN322] to a *causa*[EN323] of a similar character, to a first and final subject, personal perhaps or impersonal, but in either case incomparable. We think that we are driven back to an A and O. We participate in the revelation which it brings, subjecting ourselves to its dominion, and receiving from it comfort and direction. And this—we deduce quite logically—is the power in all events. It is this which is before and after and above and with all things and all events. It is this with and by and to which man must live. It is this which he must love and praise—this goodness, it may be this utility, perhaps this beauty, perhaps quite simply this greatness, this force, this extreme and potency of creaturely occurrence. And it is to this that the trembling finger points, and the eye is rooted and turns, and the ear bends and the whole heart strains—this demon or arch-demon by which man has been overpowered and to which he has made surrender: "They changed the truth of God into a lie, and worshipped and served the creature rather than the Creator" (Rom. 1^{25}). That is what may happen when the perception of the almightiness of God as contrasted with all the power of the creature is not so safeguarded that it cannot possibly be disputed. Secretly or openly, a powerful creaturely *causa*[EN324] is exalted to the divine dignity and function, and under this one sign and at this one crucial point the doctrine of the providence of God becomes the doctrine of the divinity of the cosmos. And it is not impossible that this type of secularised doctrine of providence may for a time be accompanied by what is in the narrower sense a religious doctrine of salvation and redemption, in which on one or another view or interpretation there may even be a place for Jesus Christ. The first half of the 19th century had its Schiller and Goethe, its Fichte and Schelling and Hegel, but taken as a whole it was not immediately or in any exclusive sense

[112] hostile either to the Church or to Christianity. And when the building of the National-Socialist temple first began, it was commonly believed that at least in the forecourt there would be a Christian, a German-Christian chapel, and that in that chapel there would be a place and a use for the Bible, and for Jesus and Paul and Luther. But this type of alliance does not usually last long. A decision is required, for we cannot really serve two masters. On the one hand, the Christian chapel, assuming that it does not disappear altogether, will quickly become the cult-centre of the god who is really believed to be the world-ruler. On the other, it will come to be seen, or it will be remembered, that Jesus Christ will not allow Himself to be relegated to the place of a redeemer side by side with whom there may be a world-ruler of quite a different stamp, whether ideal or aesthetic or technical or political. Jesus Christ Himself occupies the position of World-ruler, and side by side with Him there is no room for another—and as this is seen or remembered there will grow up a centre of resistance even within that chapel. But quite apart from this Christian decision, and quite apart from the fact that Christians may or may not resist, such heresies and the demons which achieve power by means of them usually have their day, and then when their course is run their dominion passes. In our own age we have lived to see the temple-building of a newly resuscitated slavery. Its façade is radical Marxism. It seems in this case that a Christian chapel has been provisionally omitted. It would be to the honour of the Gospel if it could remain so. But what is certain is that this error, too, will have its day, and then go the same

---

[EN321] than which nothing greater can be conceived
[EN322] causing
[EN323] cause
[EN324] cause

way as it came. It is only unfortunate that in spite of all our previous experiences the hydra-heads continue to spring up, and one error seems so rapidly to be dissolved by another which is apparently contrary to it, and yet no less deadly. For example, the idolising of the spirit in the first half of the 19th century was followed by that of matter in the second, and both by the strange absolutising of human existence in the first half of the 20th. The only thorough and comprehensive and radical safeguard is in the Christian decision. If the supremacy of the activity of God is not secured first, the creaturely forces are too strong for such impressions not to be made and such errors not to arise. But the supremacy of the activity of God is secured only when the irreversibility of its relationship to all other forces is secured, and this is secured where its qualitative distinction from those forces is secured, and this in turn is secured only when it is secured that it is the power of eternal love. But it is only in the knowledge of the work and revelation of God in Jesus Christ that all this can be perceived to be secure, and perceived in such a way that categorical decisions can and must be taken in the light of it—decisions which will give us a thorough-going and comprehensive and radical safeguard against all the quidproquos possible or conceivable at this point.

A first thing which we have to say concerning the freedom of God is that God applies His activity only on the basis of His own good-pleasure. The *concursus*[EN325], or divine operation in relation to the creature, is an act of sovereignty the honour of which is God's honour. There can be no question either of transferring this honour to the creature or of sharing it between God and the creature.

But now we must go on to say that it is God's own will which is done in this act of sovereignty. And this will is not limited by the "givenness" or determination of the creature, nor is it conditioned by any act of the creature. On the contrary, it is the will which conditions these acts. The concept of *concursus*[EN326] is itself irreversible. God "concurs" with the creature, but the creature does not "concur" with God. That is, the activity of the creature does [113] not impose any conditions upon the activity of God. As against that, the "concurrence " of God with the creature, being His own and absolutely supreme, means that the activity of God conditions absolutely the activity of the creature. As God co-operates with the activity of the creature, His own activity precedes, accompanies and follows that activity, and nothing can be done except the will of God.

It is here that we see clearly how necessary it is to explain the doctrine of divine providence from the biblical and Christian standpoint, that is, to consider the rule of God over and with the creature in the light of His rule in the covenant of grace, and of His work and revelation in Jesus Christ.

Let us suppose for a moment that we found it quite impossible to perceive or understand from this biblical centre that which we have already said generally concerning the sovereignty of the will and work of God in relation to the creature. In that case "God" would be a purely formal concept, denoting a supreme being endowed with absolute, unconditioned and irresistible power;

[EN325] accompanying
[EN326] accompanying

the "will of God" would be a purely formal concept denoting the unconditioned and incontrovertible purpose of this supreme being; and the "work of
God" would denote the unconditioned and irresistible execution of this purpose over against and in and on the activity of the creature. It is obvious in
what an impasse we should then find ourselves. We could think of God's rule
over and with and in the creature only as that of a sovereign caprice, in the
hands of which the creature would appear to act, but in fact would only be
acted upon, and this in pursuance of a purpose which is utterly obscure. The
demand for belief in God would then be a demand for the recognition and
willing acceptance by man of the unconditioned work of the unconditioned
will of this unconditionally supreme being, and his willing submission to it
without any real perception of what it is that he must approve, or of the extent
to which there can be any question of a real willingness on his part. And what
will our reaction be when we find ourselves in such a position?

It may be that we will cease to reflect upon the goodness or nongoodness of
the lordship imposed upon us, or our own willingness or unwillingness in face
of it, and simply decide upon submission to superior force, or resignation. But
if we do this, how far are we really obedient to God? That is, how far is this a
genuine faith, involving a perception of the will of God and a real submission
to it? Is not this what the Stoics are taught to do in face of an all-powerful
destiny, or the Moslems in face of the inscrutable will of Allah? How can a
consciously blind decision of this character be a genuine decision of the Christian obedience of faith?

[114] But who knows, may it not be that we will take up the opposite attitude of
complaint, protest and rejection in face of this dominion imposed upon us?
We will perhaps describe this dominion as the dominion of caprice, and the
God who rules with this absolute sovereignty a tyrant. And in this opposition
we will either despair or conclude that we are absolved from all further responsibility and justified in frivolity. And we will argue that God is responsible
either for our despair or our frivolity. We will not presume to deny His
supreme and unconditioned and irresistible disposing, but openly or secretly
we will hate and despise it. And it will not be long before we refuse to this all-
dominating force the name of God, rejecting a God who is the author of the
inescapable process of events, and speaking instead of destiny or nature or the
like. And under this title we will finally conclude with this force a separate
peace of exhaustion, thus returning to the first path. Clearly, this second possibility has nothing whatever to do with the Christian obedience of faith.

But is it really any wonder that we vacillate between those two possibilities
when we learn of the will and work of God only in this formal way? Where
there is only this formal instruction, is not the demand for belief in Almighty
God too great? Does not this kind of instruction almost necessarily drive us to
one or other of those forms of unbelief? But there is still a third possibility. It
may be that we will simply deny that the divine will is so sovereign in execution,
or its operation so unconditioned and irresistible, as has so far been assumed.

2. *The Divine Accompanying*

May it not be after all that the concept *concursus*^{EN327} is in some degree reversible? May it not be that there is as it were a conditioning and determining and to that extent a limiting of the activity of God by the activity of the creature? May it not be that although God did in fact know of this activity from all eternity, so that in this sense at least it is still under His dominion, yet this divine foreknowledge is not an omnipotent operation, but a proportionate liberty is granted to the activity of the creature, and the work of God is fulfilled with a regard to that of the creature which means in effect an accommodation to it? Obviously, this line of retreat is open. It has been taken with innumerable variations. And we have to admit that in that impasse, if we are not to give way to resignation or to go over to complaint and protest, if we are not to fall victim to either despair or frivolity, the path is attractive and readily accessible. It removes the unbearable tension of the assertion that God is all in all. The demand for belief in God becomes a possible one because in effect it resolves itself into the twofold invitation, to believe in the divine will and work as it is limited by the creature, and to believe in a creaturely will and work which limit the Creator. This demand is obviously supportable, for after all, what is there to believe? At a pinch, such a relationship could be imagined quite apart from God. But even in that form, does it really give us God when it offers us a supreme being whose will is not sovereignly executed in all the activity of the creature, whose eternal knowledge is not his will and work but only the knowledge of a helpless or disinterested spectator, whose activity is "concurred" in and conditioned by that of the creature? And does it really give us the creature of God when it offers us a creature which can "concur" in the activity of God, conditioning and influencing this activity and forcing its accommodation to its own creaturely activity? And if we subject ourselves to the will of God on this presupposition, is it really the Christian obedience of faith? Is it subjection at all? Is it obedience? And what has it to do with faith? Is it not another form of unbelief, and perhaps the worst form of all, seeing that it removes this serious demand? But to be fair we must admit that if the first two possibilities fall to the ground because of their manifest impiety, what is there but this third possibility with its secret impiety—always assuming, of course, that we have only that formal knowledge of God and of the will and work of God.

[115]

It is here that from the historical standpoint we come to what might be called the tragedy of the Reformed doctrine of providence and more particularly of the divine *concursus*^{EN328}.

The great advantage of this doctrine is that it did venture, and even carried to its logical conclusion, the proposition which alone corresponds to the true relation between God and the creature: that it is absolutely the will of God alone which is executed in all creaturely activity and creaturely occurrence. It did genuinely think of the *concursus divinus*^{EN329} as irreversible. It did not take into account any possible concurring of the creature in the will

---

^{EN327} accompanying
^{EN328} accompanying
^{EN329} divine accompanying

117

and work of God. It conceived of this will and work as unconditioned and unlimited and irresistible. It accepted and emphasised the demand implicit in this confession. We can see this in Calvin (*Instit.* I, 16–18) no less logically if not so provocatively as in Zwingli's *De providentia*, and in the Reformed orthodox theologians of the 16th and 17th centuries no less logically than in Calvin. Indeed, the concepts and terminology taken over from Scholasticism were applied by them in such a way as to push this aspect of the matter to its logical conclusion. We must be quite clear in our minds that it is this conception which stands at the back of *Questions* 26–28 of the *Heidelberg Catechism*, and that we cannot expound the *Catechism* literally if this conception is denied.

If only the Christian sense of it, as it appears in the *Heidelberg Catechism*, had been more clearly perceived, or better, more radically developed! But this was not the case either with Zwingli or Calvin, or the later Reformed dogmaticians. They ventured the proposition and carried it to its logical conclusion, and for this we must applaud them when we consider the way in which it has been weakened and watered down in the later history of the doctrine right up to the present time. But they ventured it—and this we can and must describe as their tragic fault—only on the same presupposition of purely formal concepts of God and His will and work as that of their opponents. Naturally, they maintained and protested that the will and work of God is holy and just and good. But they could never explain or say how it is that those qualities can be ascribed to it, or how far men can reasonably and justifiably be demanded to believe in the God who works all in all, or to what extent submission to the will and work of God is the obedience of faith necessarily required of the Christian. They were in fact pointing us to the dark when they spoke about the decree of God fulfilled in creaturely events. In their general discussion of the relation between God and the creature they could not and would not take into account the content of this decree. They pointed to the supremacy of God which excludes any possible conditioning by the creature, but they could not characterise this supremacy.

[116] The result was that in practice at any rate they could not exclude the possibility of an interpretation of the Christian obedience of faith in terms of a Stoic or Islamic resignation. And a further result was that in practice they did not cease to foment the murmuring of the clay against the potter (Rom. 9[20f.]), the revolt against a capricious sovereign rule, and the despair or frivolity which is the inevitable consequence of this revolt. But the chief result was that those who held back from the first two possibilities were provoked to take the line of retreat—a retreat to the mediaeval synergism which the Reformation had victoriously left behind with its doctrine of grace and justification, and which the Reformed divines were seeking to overthrow in this very matter. The Romanist propaganda of the Counter-Reformation must have taken malicious pleasure in what appeared from a distance to be the quite absurd picture of a Calvinistic God who rendered illusory any individual activity on the part of the creature. So this was the evil consequence of the mistake which the Reformers had first committed in the sphere of grace and justification! And at this point there rang out the challenge—which the fathers of the Council of Trent thought that they had heard, but now in respect of the whole field of theology—to put forward more prudently than with the later Scotists, with a proportionate regard for the contest of Augustine with Pelagius, and a clever mobilising of the new Humanistic interest, but all the more consciously and determinedly and tenaciously, the solution according to which the sole dominion of God has its own conditioning in the work of the creature, and must not transgress this limit. In the same way Lutheranism—which after the death of Luther had quickly abandoned the *De servo arbitrio* and committed itself to the mediating theology of the older Melanchthon—necessarily took serious offence at the over-logical Reformed doctrine of God and providence, some Lutherans even going so far as to accuse and convict all Calvinists of apostasy to Islam, and protesting that they themselves had more fellowship with Rome than with a Geneva which

maintained such a doctrine of the *concursus divinus*[EN330]. Again, even within Calvinism itself it was inevitable that there should be many reactions towards synergism under Renaissance influences. The most famous of these was the movement of Jacob Arminius and his friends, which was defeated only with great effort and at great cost at the Synod of Dort. The final upshot was that the school of Saumur at the end of the 17th century, and the later orthodoxy of the Enlightenment, relapsed into a fairly crude semi-Pelagianism of a pietist-rationalist type.

We may bewail the many-sided declension from the older Reformed conception, but we cannot overlook the fact that, in so far as it meant a demand for faith which, constituted as it then was, it could not possibly meet, it was itself the cause of this declension. The concept was a correct one, but from the very outset it lacked the foundation which would have made it credible, distinguishing it from a questionable philosophoumenon. It is no less true, of course, that the synergistic constructions opposed to it by the Romanists, Lutherans, Arminians, and later the Moderns, could not be distinguished from a mere philosophoumenon, but all of them lay sick in the same ward, playing with the same empty concepts without any reference to the biblical centre. But although their conception was correct in itself, the Reformed fathers were in no better case than the others. On the contrary, their opponents had the advantage that in their statements they did seem to take more account of the demands of ordinary reason and practical piety than did the sinister heralds of an even more sinister deity. For this was what the Reformed divines appeared to be. Indeed, this is what they were—shockingly enough—and all because of their inability to apply fruitfully to this field the proper centre of all Reformed knowledge, the doctrine of grace and justification. It is certainly no accident that, notwithstanding the zeal with which it was defended throughout the 17th century, the doctrine which they did not fruitfully apply quietly became so much dead capital, so that when a great inventory was made at the beginning of the 18th century, it was in evitably discovered that for a long time it had only been valueless paper with no possible purchasing power in the age which was then dawning. [117]

And it was little consolation that against all the expectations of the Reformed Church there arose a great theologian, of a stature approaching that of Zwingli and Calvin, namely, F. E. D. Schleiermacher, who apparently, but unfortunately only apparently, exalted against all forms of synergism the great conception of the sole dominion of God and the absolute dependence of the creature. For what Schleiermacher discovered was as little influenced by the Reformation doctrine of grace and justification (which he never understood) as was the doctrine of providence held by Zwingli, Calvin and their Reformed successors, who had certainly understood it, but did not know how to apply it. What Schleiermacher discovered was a kind of compromise, a philosophical doctrine of the sole supremacy of God which rested upon the dialectic of nature and spirit, and within which there was of course a specific and indeed a central place for the religious possibility as such. Hence the historical religions could be rated very highly, and especially the religion founded by Jesus of Nazareth. And in the same way Schleiermacher could speak quite cleverly of the self-evident nature of the Evangelical Church in its Reformed dress. But in no sense did he succeed better than the older Reformed divines in giving a sounder or deeper basis to the Reformed conception of the *concursus divinus*[EN331], or in rendering the conception more credible, although it is one with which he must have had some sympathy as an expression of the absolute dependence of the finite on the infinite, of the individual on the totality. On the contrary, we have to admit that the way in which he championed the conception exposed it to all the suspicions which have surrounded it from the very outset, even to that of Spinozism, or more generally of a

---

[EN330] divine accompanying
[EN331] divine accompanying

pantheistic-naturalistic monism. The result was that it was pushed more and more into the shadows, and this time seriously, in the eyes of all right-thinking men. In this respect Reformed theology reaped what it had sown as early as the 16th century with its failure to think out the basis of its doctrine of providence from a serious Christian standpoint.

To understand the *concursus divinus*[EN332], the divine accompanying of creaturely activity, in a Christian sense as the sovereign act in which the will of God is unconditionally and irresistibly fulfilled in the activity of the creature, we have not to begin with empty concepts but with concepts which are already filled out with Christian meaning.

When we say "God" we have to understand the One who as Father, Son, and Holy Ghost is eternal love, and has life in Himself; the One who as such is the self-existent One, the Almighty high above all creatures, the *causa causarum*[EN333].

When we say "the will of God" we have to understand His fatherly good-will, His decree of grace in Jesus Christ, the mercy in which from all eternity He undertook to save the creature, and to give it eternal life in the fellowship with Himself; the will which as such is His kingly will, disposing unconditionally and irresistibly of the existence and activity of the creature.

And when we say "the work of God" we have to understand His execution in history of the covenant of grace upon the basis of the decree of grace, with its fulfilment in the sacrifice of His Son and its confirmation in the work of the Holy Spirit awakening to faith and obedience: the work which as such is His work of power in the whole created sphere, above and in and before and with and after all creaturely activity; the work in virtue of which all creaturely activity is completely under His control and subject to Him. And in all these things what is needed is a radical re-thinking of the whole matter. First we have to drop the ordinary but harmful conception of cause, operation and effect. Then, when we know who God is and what He wills and how He works, we have to take it up again, but giving to it a new force and application in which we do not look back to what are at root godless notions of causality.

[118]

If we will take this course, we can avoid the impasse into which we are inevitably led by those empty concepts. We can also avoid the extremely unpleasant choice between the three false possibilities by which we are otherwise inescapably confronted. If this is the meaning of the sovereign and almighty rule of God, if it has this aspect, the only aspect which is really commensurate with it, then it cannot be described as obscure or capricious, nor can the creaturely activity which occurs under the divine lordship be thought of merely as an effect. The overruling love of the triune God is light and not darkness. And although the rule of this love confronts the creature as supreme in fact, and externally inscrutable in detail, in itself, and known to be the rule of God, it is still light and not darkness. Again, the world-rule of the fatherly good-will of

---

[EN332] divine accompanying
[EN333] cause of all causes

God, if it is known to be such, does not bear any relationship to caprice. And since its activity is the activity of grace, its almightiness does not in any sense destroy the free activity of the creature. On the contrary, we have to think of the majesty and absoluteness and irresistibility of the divine activity as the confirmation and continually renewed basis of the singularity of the creature to whom God is gracious, and of its worth, and independent activity. It is only empty concepts of God and His will and work which will give rise to perverted notions of this type. They are excluded by concepts which are filled out with a Christian meaning. And if we take this seriously, then it means that the demand for faith in God, and in the dominion of God, is also meaningful. We can learn in the Word of God who and what this invisible and inconceivable God is who rules over all things, and what it is that this God wills and does. And with all the inscrutability of the form of creaturely occurrence, we can take this knowledge to our hearts. And as believers in the Word of God and witnesses to the work of the Spirit we certainly lose any desire to discuss whether in face of the unconditional supremacy of God there can be such a thing as a human willingness to believe. We are now in a position to say to all the errors to which we are inevitably led in that impasse: No, No, and again No. No, for in the decision of faith we are worlds removed from the apathetic surrender to the inevitable, which may work out either for joy or sorrow, but is always fatal, because it is fatalistic. We are worlds removed from such a surrender, because at the crucial point of decision we are not blind, but see. And No, for we cannot for a single moment continue to repudiate the almighty lordship of God, [119] and certainly we cannot allow ourselves to slip into despair or frivolity. For what sense is there either in a weak capitulation or in the futile defiance of despair or frivolity when it is the fatherly good-will of God which is the power over all things. And No again, for least of all can we take that line of retreat; least of all will it occur to us to make of the God who is all in all a God who is only much in much, regarding His sovereignty and omnipotence as limited, His activity as conditioned, concurred in or partly conditioned by the creature, and therefore the divine *concursus*[EN334] as reversible. If we hold fast to God's decree of grace in Jesus Christ, and to His activity of grace in the history of the covenant, we can never dream of setting the creature over against God as a kind of second party to the contract, knowing as we do that the creature has no freedom but that which is grounded on the unconditioned and irresistible freedom and supremacy of God, having no power to concur but only to corroborate and understand and glorify. If we take absolutely seriously the meaning and character of the divine lordship, we are in a position to take with equal seriousness recognition of it as such.

The activity of God precedes, *praecurrit*, that of the creature. As we vindicate and follow the older Reformed theology we must take this proposition first.

[EN334] accompanying

§ 49. *God the Father as Lord of His Creature*

What concerns us is the activity of the merciful God. It is the Father of Jesus Christ whose almighty will and work precede all other will and work—His eternal love. God precedes with His own will and work all other will and work because His decree of grace in Jesus Christ has already preceded the creation of all things and therefore the being and activity of the creature. He precedes it in the same way as His eternity—not any eternity but the eternity of His love, His eternal being as Father, Son and Holy Ghost—precedes all time and all being in time. Always and everywhere when the creature works, God is there as the One who has already loved it, who has already undertaken to save and glorify it, who in this sense and to this end has already worked even before the creature itself began to work, even before the conditions, and pre-conditions, and pre-pre-conditions of its working were laid down. "My Father worketh hitherto, and I work" (Jn. 5¹⁷). God created the conditions and pre-conditions and pre-pre-conditions of all creaturely working. God gave them to the creature. All the preliminaries of creaturely activity were the effect of God's activity, of His friendly activity in the sense and to the end revealed and active in Jesus Christ, and in the history of the covenant of grace, of His activity as it was determined and controlled by His saving will. From the very first the purpose of God was to save and glorify the creature. All the works which are causes of this or that creaturely activity are the works of His mercy. Already in the sphere from which this or that creature comes to do this or that work He is the sovereign Lord of the creature, not limited by any contradiction or opposition, but sovereign in the definite sense. And it is from this sphere that God accompanies the creature and controls its activity.

[120]

*Concursus Dei praevius est, quo ... causa secundam ... ad agendum praedeterminat adeoque creaturae actum non tempore sed ordine, dignitate, et praecellentia praecedit*EN335 (H. Heidegger quoted from *Heppe²*, 210). We accept this formulation generally, although understanding by *ordo, dignitas* and *praecellentia*EN336 the fatherly wisdom of God. But we must not overlook the extent to which the *concursus Dei*EN337 must precede the *actio*EN338 of the *causa secunda*EN339 even in time as well: certainly not in time only; but in time as well to the extent that the creaturely conditions normative for the operation of the *causa secunda*EN340 are also in time, and even in their temporality are the effects of His eternal divine activity. *Aeternitate et tempore, ordine namque dignitate et praecellentia gratiae praecedit*EN341—this is how Heidegger's statement ought to run. And the correction is important because it means that the predetermining activity of God cannot be given a Kantian sense as the *a priori*EN342 of reason as

---

EN335 The divine accompanying is prior, in the sense that ... it foreordains secondary causes to act in a particular way, so as to precede the act of the creature not in time, but in order, dignity and pre-eminence
EN336 order, dignity and pre-eminence
EN337 divine accompanying
EN338 action
EN339 secondary cause
EN340 secondary cause
EN341 It has precedence in eternity and in time, in accordance with the order, dignity, and pre-eminence of grace
EN342 unconditional presupposition

opposed to an empirical event. On this view the opposition and connexion between divine and creaturely activity would be immanent within the world. Our understanding is a safeguard against any such transformation. It is quite impossible to demand that the work of the Father of Jesus Christ should be expounded as an *a priori*^{EN343} of reason. But any such view is precluded by the fact that the eternally preceding activity of God does not exclude but includes a temporal preceding.

What concerns us is a preceding activity and not merely a preceding knowledge of the merciful God. It is not merely that God foresees a certain work of the creature in virtue of His eternal knowledge of all things, and then awaits the accomplishment of it, leaving the creature the choice between this or that possibility of action, and then in its execution granting the indispensable assistance of His own almighty operation.

At this point the older Lutherans attempted artifices of which we can say only that they are equally suspect and unnecessary. According to their account the *concursus divinus*^{EN344} in a sense only begins with the creaturely action. *Non antecedit sed fit cum actio ipsa producitur: concurrit, coagit, cooperatur*^{EN345}. That the creature chooses this or that movement is its own doing, not God's. What is of God in it is simply the *vis operandi*^{EN346} in the execution of the movement chosen (A. Calov, *Syst. theol.*, 1655f., III, *art.* 6, 2, *qu.* 1). In opposing the Calvinist view of the *concursus*^{EN347}, and therefore the predetermination of creaturely activity, the intention was to avoid fatalism, and especially the dreaded conclusion: *Deus auctor et mali*^{EN348}. But it was done at the price of making God a strangely passive spectator and assistant of the creature, excluding the divine activity at the decisive point where the creaturely activity is itself decision—a truly fateful secularisation of creaturely freedom for which the honour paid to the divine activity in wider spheres was no adequate compensation. And in any case we cannot escape fatalism and the *Deus auctor et mali*^{EN349} simply by denying the *praedeterminatio*^{EN350} but accepting the *praevisio*^{EN351}, ascribing the will to the creature, but the execution of it to God. In theology as elsewhere it is an ill-advised policy to try to avoid much-dreaded dangers by half-measures.

The foreknowledge of God is a movement of His omnipotence. It has therefore to be distinguished in concept although not separated in fact from the totality of His preceding will and work. What God knows He wills, and what He wills He does. Not only does He know all in all but He also works all in all, and He does so as the eternal God. If we are clear in our minds that what concerns us is the knowledge and the will and the work of the Father of Jesus Christ, this proposition is not a dangerous one, let alone one which we need to suppress, but a necessary and indisputable one. The activity of God cannot, then, be

[121]

---

^{EN343} unconditional presupposition
^{EN344} divine accompanying
^{EN345} It does not precede but takes place at the same time that the creaturely action itself does: it accompanies, joins, and is united with it
^{EN346} power of acting
^{EN347} accompanying
^{EN348} God is also the source of evil
^{EN349} God is also the source of evil
^{EN350} foreordination
^{EN351} foreknowledge

split into two distinct parts: on the one hand His restraint and inactivity in face of the creaturely freedom of decision; and on the other His giving to the creature the physical capacity to carry out the decision reached by it. On the contrary, the one God effects both the will and its accomplishment, the decision and its execution. Again, if we are only clear in our minds with whose and what kind of activity to do, we need have no anxieties with regard to the affirmation. In the Christian doctrine of providence the dreaded conclusion that on this view God can and must be thought of as the author of evil can be avoided by other means than by the partial—and this means the total—repudiation of its decisive content, i.e., that the sceptre and dominion are in the hands of God.

When we think of the *concursus divinus*[EN352] as the divine foreordination (*praedeterminatio*) of creaturely activity, this means that the divine activity has to be differentiated from all other forms of ordination or determination which may underlie creaturely activity, and that in its difference from such forms it has to be given precedence over them. Undoubtedly we can and must consider all specific creaturely actions in their conditioned and conditioning relationship with other actions, and ultimately with the totality of creaturely activity. No creature appears to act except as it is surrounded and impelled and conditioned, in a word accompanied, by the total activity of all creatures. And this total activity, too, appears to accompany it in such a way that it also precedes it. To that extent there seems to be some similarity between this total activity and the work of God. It is a conjecture which necessarily gives rise to reverence and awe by its utter vastness and incomprehensibility that whenever I move my little finger I am perhaps determined by all the activity which has taken place up to the moment of my doing so, and that of all the creatures and their movements which have been, not one could fail which was necessary to lead up to that movement. Yet it is still the case that the totality of creaturely activity which accompanies and precedes my movement, and the determination of that action, however rigorous it may be, is not at all the same as the divine foreordination. The sceptre is not in the hands of even the totality of created things in heaven and on earth. It is in the hands of the One who is before creation. And no matter how comprehensive the activity of creation may be, it is not the same as His activity. And it is not the same as His because its determinative power is wholly and utterly at the disposal of His power, of the divine foreordination. Just as human nature does not become the divine even in their union in Jesus Christ, so creaturely activity does not become the divine simply because God conjoins the divine with it. Even the total creaturely activity of heaven and earth is not the true and proper preceding of individual creaturely actions. As compared with the true and proper preceding of God and the work of God, the totality of creaturely activity takes place on a level of its own, and that a lower level. And the inter-relationship on this level is reversible. The individual activity no less than the totality of creaturely activity is wholly and

[122]

[EN352] divine accompanying

utterly at the disposal of the divine foreordination. We can think of the individual activity as the final link in a causal series, and therefore as conditioned by the totality of preceding activity. But if the series is regarded as final, we can also think of the totality of activity as pre-conditioned by the final link, and therefore determined by that individual activity in which it attains its end and goal. Supposing that everything that happened did so only that it might culminate in that movement of my finger? And might not that be an elevating thought too? But the relation between the divine and creaturely activity cannot be reversed as the relation between the individual activity and the totality of creaturely activity can be reversed. And this is what distinguishes the divine activity from the totality of creaturely activity, no matter how highly we may rate the totality in relation to the individual, or how greatly superior it may actually be.

If the individual activity does take place under a creaturely ordination, i.e., on the presupposition of the totality of all previous creaturely occurrence, the totality of activity which determines the individual is not an autonomous causal nexus but one which is itself accompanied and dominated and controlled by the divine activity. It is not absolute but relative. It does not subsist of itself but its ordering and cohesion are the work of God. It is not closed but open. Not merely in its creation and beginning, but at every point in its history it is open to the divine activity which does not rend and destroy it but continually gives it the form which it has to have according to the divine goodpleasure. Hence it has no autonomous or absolute power over individual creaturely occurrence, but only the limited and qualified power which is given to it by the superior power of the preceding divine activity. Similarly it has no native wisdom of its own. There is no cosmic reason, no world-soul, by whose principles or intuitions the activity of the creature has its ordination. It has wisdom and reason only in the sense and to the extent that the preceding operation of God enables it to be a witness to the divine wisdom and reason. Our next task will be to consider two different conceptions of the causal nexus which precedes the activity of the individual creature, and in the light of these we will make our own meaning more precise.

Materially, we can conceive of this nexus as the sum-total of all moving forces [123] in the cosmos. If we do, the total force may be thought of as infinite or finite, inexhaustible or at some point exhaustible, according to the individual metaphysical standpoint, and quite irrespective of what the nature of this force is supposed to be. But we do not have to accept responsibility either for this conception or for the detailed way in which it is worked out, for it has no positive significance either in the Bible or in theology. Let us grant, then, that before and in all individual creaturely activity there does operate the active force of creaturely being as a whole and in general, and that the activity of the individual creature has to be understood as a participation in this total force. But if we grant this, then the divine activity which is the foreordination of all creaturely activity cannot possibly be equated with the activity of this total force. The idea of such a force may be useful as a comprehensive concept to describe the life which is given to the creaturely world by God and which indwells it as His gift. But we must remember that even this total force is still the gift of God. It is not the giver. Its operation is not the divine operation. It operates independently only as God allows it to do so, and where and how He wills to co-operate with it. It is not the case that the creature participates in the power of God and is preceded by the overruling divine activity, in virtue of the participation of its own activity in this total force. On the contrary, it is in virtue of its participation in the power of God, and its preceding by the overruling divine activity which co-operates with it, that its individual activity participates in the total force of the creaturely order. For the activity of God is not exhausted by its preserving of this total force for the creaturely world as such, confirming it in its possession and making possible the exercise of it. Naturally, it does do this. But this does not mean that it then as it were withdraws, to be vicariously represented by the activity of this total force, and only indirectly to precede and overrule individual creaturely activity. It does, of course, do this. But it also overrules and ordains this activity directly. It is true that the total force is preserved and confirmed by the divine working, and its operation made possible by it. But this does not constitute it an autonomous subject which mediates as such between the activity of God and that of the individual creature. Rather, it is itself an instrument in the hands of God. Both in individual activity and in relation to the activity of the individual creature it operates conformably to the divine foreordination of that individual activity.

But it is not necessary or legitimate to deduce any specific event finally or properly or seriously from a cosmic force of this kind. To do this is heathenism, even if the total force is differentiated from God; even if it is in some sort regarded as the delegate of God; even if provision is made to bring this event into a direct relationship with the activity of God as well. As is now known, there is no heathenism which does not make provision for a chief or supreme God superior to all the gods who in practice are honoured and worshipped and served. But obviously the interesting and the finally and properly and seriously significant relationship is necessarily the practical one to the delegate of God and not the theoretical one to God Himself. What determines the outlook, the imagination, the conscience, the heart, and ultimately the decisions or non-decisions of the human onlooker is not the conception of God, but that of the *élan vital*[EN353] in all things, that of the inbreathing and outbreathing *universum*[EN354], that of the total nexus of nature or history, or perhaps a concrete conception like that of the influences of sidereal events upon those of this world, or of a real or fancied power of spirit or spirits, or of certain physical or psychical or social structures. And in such circumstances is it not inevitable that God should become an "old Lord," to whom regard must occasionally be had, but who is not normally considered because all genuine and practical consideration is claimed by the contemplation of the principles of power which in any case operate between God and individual occurrence? And this is heathenism and nonsense precisely because the operation of this cosmic power, however we may conceive the power or its operation, cannot possibly take place except under the foreor-

[124]

EN353 vital force
EN354 whole

dination of the divine operation, being released and directed and formed and aimed according to the good-pleasure of God, and not enjoying in any sense the plenary powers of a divine delegate. Therefore those who contemplate and participate in the individual event have to do only indirectly with the total force of creation, but directly and therefore practically and vitally with a consideration, not of this force, but of God Himself. Hence the imagination and conscience and heart and ultimately the decisions are in fact claimed by this consideration, and they cannot be claimed by any other conception except subsequently and under the control of this prior consideration of God.

There is a precise and accurate statement of the matter in H. Heidegger: *Cooperatio illa Dei immediata est, non quod solus nulla adhibita causa secunda operetur, sed quia inter actionem Dei et inter effectum non intercedit efficacia creaturae, quae propius attingat effectum quam Deus. Non enim Deus creaturae duntaxat facultatem et virtutem agendi ita tribuit et conservat, ut creatura interim proxime et immediate, Deus mediante sola virtute, quam creaturae dedit et conservat, actionem edat aut effectum producat—sed ob rationem illam dependentiae creaturae omnem actionem et effectum creaturae immediate attingit*[EN355]. δἰ αὐτοῦ τὰ πάντα[EN356] (Rom. 11³⁶) means: *omnia immediata et proxima eius ut primae causae virtute facta*[EN357] (quoted from *Heppe²*, 210).

But formally, we can also think of the creaturely nexus which precedes individual creaturely occurrence as the sum and substance of the norms to which all creaturely occurrence is subject according to the judgment of human experience and the capacity of human thought. Once again, theology cannot accept responsibility for this conception or its individual features. But hypothetically—and even Christians will not cease to do it—we can reckon with the fact that there are such things as the so-called unbreakable and unbroken external physical laws, i.e., laws which in human experience are so regular as not to admit of any exception, and also the intellectual laws which conform to them, mathematically comprehended perhaps in a higher logicality to form a system of objective laws of being and motion in which room may well be found for a kind of moral law of nature as the norm of historical occurrence. In biblical thinking this idea plays absolutely no part at all, and in this it may be compared with the conception of a total force. But does this mean that there is [125] any reason not to reckon with it as a hypothesis? We can still accept norms of this kind, and perhaps a sum and substance of all these norms. We can still presuppose and expect that every individual occurrence will take place within the framework of these norms and therefore as a process predetermined by law. It may still be the case that

---

[EN355] The co-operation of God is immediate, not because He acts alone without the contribution of any secondary cause, but because between the action of God and its effect no creaturely efficacy intervenes which produces the effect more immediately than God. For God does not simply surrender the power and capacity to act to the creature and allow the creature bring forth an action an action or produce an effect directly and immediately, with God acting by a mediate power alone, which He has given and reserved to the creature - but on account of the dependency of the creature He is immediately occupied with every creaturely action and effect

[EN356] all things are through Him

[EN357] all things are in direct and immediate relation to Him, since they are effected by the power of the primary cause

"According to great, eternal,
Brazen laws,
We must all
Fulfil the circle
Of our destiny."   (Goethe 1783)

But even conceding that that is the case we still cannot equate the practical validity and actuality of those laws with the divine activity which foreordains creaturely occurrence. We can perhaps make this clearer in the following way.

Let us begin with the absolutely maximal assumption possible with a view to such an equation, that to the exclusion of all doubt or exception we have a knowledge not only of individual laws but of *the* law of all creaturely occurrence, the law which embraces the whole creaturely nexus and comprehends every event within that nexus; and that we have a knowledge of this law with the same certainty as we have the knowledge of God by the Word of God, and with such clarity that we know what it is that we say when we maintain that this law involves the foreordination of this or that individual creaturely activity. Now assuming that that is the case, we have to ask what is the exact significance of the term "foreordained." Obviously it means that the individual activity, supposing it takes place at all, must always do so within the limits of the order and form imposed by this law. But even on this maximal assumption it would not be a foreordination whether or not this activity should take place at all, and if so, where and when. An effective law is a valid law, and no more; valid, that is to say, in respect of the order and form of a particular event. No law, not even that which is absolutely valid and therefore absolutely effective in that sense, has as such the power to cause even the most trivial of creaturely events actually to take place. Even a law which embraces and comprehends all creaturely occurrence cannot do that. Even the existence of such a law, if we were in any position to appeal to it, could only reveal itself in the form of a prior decision concerning the order and form of an actual event. Even on this maximal assumption we should have to look elsewhere for provision that the event should actually take place—granting that when it did, it did so in the order and form foreseen by this law. Therefore even on this maximal assumption the concept of a law of this kind presupposes that the nexus formed and to be [126] formed, ordered and to be ordered in accordance with it, is effected and actual from some other source. The reality of such a law foreordains only in respect of the order and form of creaturely activity, but the object of the divine activity is creaturely activity in itself and as such. Therefore even on this maximal assumption the two cannot be equated.

The antithesis between the divine activity and what is denoted by the concept law is all the sharper when we take our original pre-supposition and relate it more closely to the actual facts of the case. For then we shall make the far more modest assumption that to the exclusion of all doubts and exceptions we have a knowledge not of *the* law of all creaturely occurrence, but of certain laws which are normative for particular fields of creaturely occurrence, and that we have a knowledge of them with such clarity that we can responsibly maintain that the foreordination of this or that individual activity consists in the actuality of these particular laws. But if we reckon only with certain laws or a few such laws—and obviously we shall be nearer the truth if we do—then this means that even the given foreordination of the order and form of a specific event is restricted to the particular spheres of creaturely occurrence for which these laws are normative, while around these spheres there is a large area where they are not normative and where they cannot predetermine even the order and form of occurrence. Thus the concept of divine operation is further distinguished from that of this kind of law by the fact that no such limitation is imposed upon the divine operation in its sphere, but it embraces and comprehends, not merely a particular creaturely nexus, but every nexus, and all creaturely activity as a single nexus. Naturally, with this more modest concept of law the first antithesis still stands in all its rigour. However valid or effective a law may be in its own sphere, it cannot foreordain more than the order and form of an event which is already presupposed in that sphere, and certainly it cannot foreordain the event itself.

But we still have formulated the maximal and more modest conceptions of law far too favourably for the sake of a comparison or even an equation with the activity of God. For we have supposed that either the one all-comprehensive law or the individual laws of creaturely activity can be known with an absolute certainty which excludes all doubts and exceptions, and with such clarity that we can responsibly describe the law or laws as in their own sphere at least the formal foreordination of a particular event. But in fact we are going much too far if we seriously suppose that there is any such knowledge. What we know as the law or laws of creaturely activity are noetic assertions for whose ontic content we have no guarantee which can justify us in raising them to such a height or ascribing to them the same qualities as the divine activity. At very best they are assertions which necessarily impress themselves upon us on the basis of the scrupulously tested fulness of our experience or in a conscientious realisation of the possibilities of our thought. It is we [127] ourselves who discover and guarantee them. They are great and brazen laws in virtue of the exactness, the completeness, the logical consequence of our human knowledge by which they are discovered and guaranteed; in virtue of the high measure of noetic clarity and certainty which we think it permissible and obligatory to ascribe to them, and of the high degree of reliability which we impute to them. Seeing that they are great and brazen in this sense there is no reason not to regard them as practically valid and therefore effective in all occurrence. But there is also no reason to pass them off as "eternal" or to compare or equate them with the law or laws of God. There is no reason to do it even in the restricted sense which is the only possible sense—as though they were the foreordination of at least the order and form of all actual occurrence in their own sphere. No law is known to us with the certainty with which God is known to us by His Word, or with such clarity that even in relation to its own sphere we can responsibly pass it off as at least the formal foreordination of all actual occurrence within that sphere. No high measure of noetic certainty or clarity can give to laws known to us, i.e., discovered and guaranteed by us, the character of ontic laws, the character in virtue of which we necessarily perceive in them the laws of God, and therefore in effect the real foreordination of creaturely occurrence at any rate from the formal standpoint.

But the laws known to us are obvious attempts within the framework of our own experience of creaturely occurrence, and the possibilities and necessities of our own thought, to establish and attest the fact that there are such ontic laws, and a foreordained order and form of all creaturely occurrence. The laws known to us are well-grounded hypotheses on the basis of which we can go forward prepared in some measure for further experience and thought and equipped for further reliable knowledge, with the certain expectation that all further events which confront us will at any rate take place within this or that order or form. Concerning the actuality of the laws known to us we will already think rather more modestly because we will be aware that they cannot in any case originate or effect the event itself and as such, that even presupposing their validity they must still be referred to the fact that the event takes place at all only on the basis of a completely different operation. And we will also leave the laws known to us open to the revision of content and formulation which may become necessary as a result of our encounter and their confrontation with new and actual occurrence. These laws are as it were arrows pointing in the direction of real order and form, i.e., of the order and form which are objectively immanent in and proper to actual occurrence itself. But for this reason they can never become absolute dogmas, nor assume the character of ontic law, and therefore of a foreordination even of the order and form of any given event. We take account of the laws to which the causal nexus of crea-turely existence is subject in respect of its order and form. We believe that we can perceive and describe and define at least some of these laws. And to this extent we acknowledge and proclaim—not from the standpoint of the Cre-ator, but from that of the creature—that there is a necessary order and form in the nexus by which all individual existence is conditioned. It is not chance which rules but constancy, not caprice but faithfulness. All occurrence, inas-much as it takes place at all, takes place within the framework of a definite rule.

[128]

But we will acknowledge this the more seriously and proclaim it the more effectively, the more scrupulously we cease trying to equate even one of the laws known to us, even the law which we perceive with what we imagine to be the greatest clarity and certainty, with the order and form or constancy and faithfulness which rule in that causal nexus, with the rule to which all occur-rence within it is subject. Only as we cease doing that do we give evidence that in the laws perceived and described and formulated by us we are aiming at real law; at the ordering and forming which takes place in the occurrence itself and not simply in our experience and thinking, which is not merely an ordering and forming but also an effecting and calling forth of the actual occurrence itself. It is remarkable enough that the less we believe that the laws known to us have anything at all to do with the real foreordination of creaturely occurrence, the more they really have to do with it, the more clearly they testify by their own particular, that is, noetic, clarity and certainty that there are indeed valid laws, that in the causal nexus in which each individual activity has its place and by which it is conditioned there does rule a unitary and—we can now legitimately use the description of Goethe and say—an "eternal" law, which no occurrence can escape, in accordance with which we must all fulfil the circle of our destiny, and not merely must but can, for this law is not simply one of order and form, but as such it is also *the* law, the positing of existence, life, activity itself. It is the foreordination of God.

The divine foreordination is not subject to the limitations to which our concepts of law are subject. It does not relate merely to order and form. Nor does it relate only to specific spheres. Nor has it only a noetic character. Freely and correctly understood and handled, our own limited concepts of law can be to us witnesses of the divine foreordination. They still attest it involuntarily even when they are not freely and correctly understood and handled. But there can be no question of interpreting the divine foreordination in terms of our concepts of law, as though the divine foreordination of creaturely occurrence were only what on the basis of those concepts we thought we could expect in view of the order and form of the occurrence. There can be no question of thinking that the foreordination of God, and therefore His working and forming and ordering, are limited by what we can perceive and describe and define [129] as the order and form and rule of creaturely occurrence.

Hence it follows that we cannot interpose an autonomously controlling subject between God and the individual creaturely event under the name of any law known to us. It also follows that we cannot hypostatise the concept of law, as though in our dealings with it we really had to do with the ruling representative and vice-gerent of God. It is also not the case that we are only indirectly before God, but directly before all kinds of operative laws of nature, spirit and life. The very reverse is the case. We have to do directly with God, and only indirectly with the laws, so far as they are known to us. It is God Himself, in fact, who is the law of all occurrence. What we see to be law can only remind us of this law, and therefore of Him. Foreordaining all creaturely activity by His will and work, He also orders and forms that activity. This forming and ordering is unbroken and unbreakable. It is the very essence of constancy and continuity. But even this forming and ordering is not identical with the laws known to us, but with the free disposing and directing of His own good-pleasure. Naturally there can be no question of His contravening or overturning any real or ontic law of creaturely occurrence. This would mean that He was not at unity with Himself in His will and work. But we must allow that He can ruthlessly ignore the laws known to us, that is, our own perception of the ontic laws of creaturely occurrence. Even then God does not act as a god of disorder, but as the God of His own order, who precedes creaturely occurrence even in the fact that He is not bound by our human concepts of order, however great may be the noetic clarity and certainty which we believe them to possess. Of course, it cannot be that He precedes creaturely occurrence in such a way that there is no possibility of a subsequent understanding of His action in the sphere and orbit of the concepts of order which we know. It cannot be that we are able to understand His foreordaining work only as a work *supra et contra naturam*[EN358]. And yet it could be so. There is no reason for irritation if our concepts of order prove inadequate to an understanding of God's order and form. There is no reason for surprise when—especially in the attestation of covenant-history, and the more so as we approach the centre of this history—mention is made of miracles, and the impossibility of a purely "historical" consideration, i.e., of one constructed upon our concepts of order, is revealed. The more definitely the coming of the Son of God is announced in the Old Testament, and the more directly His revelation is attested in the New, the more natural it appears to unprejudiced reason that mention has to be made of events which can be understood only as an activity *supra et contra naturam*[EN359], as an ordering and forming which is beyond the stage of development so far reached by our concepts. And the final revelation of the Son of God at the end of all times will be an event of the same kind. The creation of heaven and earth at the beginning of all times was an event of this kind. We must be quite clear in our minds that what is revealed in these events is not a *miraculous* exception but the *rule* of divine activity, the free good-will of God Himself, i.e., the law at which we are aiming with our concept of law. And we must also be quite clear in our minds that with all our concepts of law we can never do more than aim at this law.

[130]

To sum up, the divine foreordination of creaturely occurrence always and everywhere takes place before and above all the other foreordinations and determinations which may fall to be considered side by side with or apart from it. It is not conditioned or limited by the self-determination of the creature. Nor is it supplanted or replaced by those predeterminations of creaturely occurrence which seem to derive from the idea of an effective total force, or effective laws of the cosmos. It includes all such determinations. It does not destroy but relativises them. It is the only true foreordination or predestination. It is the only one which works directly. It is the only one which works unconditionally and irresistibly.

If we hold fast to our starting-point it becomes meaningful to say that what we speak of is the activity of the merciful God, who to His own glory and the salvation of the creature has turned to the creature in eternal love. *Per se*[EN360]

[EN358] above and against nature
[EN359] above and against nature
[EN360] in itself

the foreordaining activity of this God is not a constraining or humiliating or weakening of the creature. Such a postulate is possible only in relation to the activity of a God who is omnipotence, a supreme cause, and no more. But of this God we cannot merely postulate the very opposite, but can definitely expect and confess it. The God who Himself became a creature in Jesus Christ, the God who places the creature so absolutely at His own disposal only that He may place Himself absolutely at the disposal of the creature—this God is not exalted in the suppression of the creature. He does not find His triumph in the creature's lack of freedom or power as compared with His own unconditional and irresistible lordship. He does not work alone when He works all in all. In His kingdom there are no co-gerents, representatives or vice-gerents. The least thing no less than the greatest derives directly from Himself. But the least thing no less than the greatest has its own sphere of action. And all things can attain their own rights, and exist in freedom. And what better provision could be made for this freedom than that the freedom of God—of *this* God—is unconditional and irresistible in relation to it, that it is radically denied every other freedom but the one genuine freedom which God gives it in His grace? In Him, and not somewhere near Him, we live and move and have our being— and not on the basis of our self-determination, or of the determination of a field of force within which, or a system of norms under which, we may happen to find ourselves. The only free God, who is the Father of Jesus Christ, is the Creator and basis of all freedom worthy of the name. But how absurd and sinister, how unworthy of the name, would be a freedom consisting in the fact   [131] that the creature is wholly or in part independent of this God, that it has to look to a field of force or a system of norms instead of to Him!

If we hold fast to our starting-point, however, it is clear that this knowledge of the unconditional and irresistible nature of the divine lordship is not only meaningful but necessary. As long as the concept *causa prima*[EN361] is not filled out in a Christian manner, we can think in many different ways, according to the inclination and ability of the predominant theological metaphysician, concerning the relationship between the *causa prima*[EN362] and the autonomy of the *causae secundae*[EN363], and between these and the intermediate concepts of cosmic force and cosmic law. We can understand predetermination either rigidly or loosely, either directly or indirectly, as Calvinists, or Catholics, or Lutherans, or Arminians. And the matter can never be decided. A decision is possible, and in one definite direction, only when we know and remember that it is the Father of Jesus Christ who is the Lord over all things, and keep continually before us the majesty and omnipotence and the constancy and faithfulness of this Lord. For this God does not let go the creature; He does not allow it to fall, not for a single moment or in any respect. This God does not

---

EN361 primary cause
EN362 primary cause
EN363 secondary causes

allow Himself to be mocked or trifled with. This God has taken into His own hands the relationship between Himself and the creature, and He has no time for representatives or vice-gerents. This God is directly present to the creature always and in all places by the Holy Spirit. This God cannot stand towards the creature in the broken relationship envisaged in Calvinist and Catholic and Lutheran and Arminian teaching. The operation of this God is as sovereign as Calvinist teaching describes it. In the strictest sense it is predestinating. If only the older Calvinist teaching had made it clear that what concerns us is the predestinating activity of this God! Unless this is made clear we cannot confidently prefer that teaching. But once it is made clear, we can do so without hesitation.

We can now turn to the second essential proposition, a proposition which is central by its very nature and which has given its name to the whole doctrine in the older dogmatics, namely, that the divine activity accompanies that of the creature: *concurrit*[EN364].

The difference between the *concurrit* and the *praecurrit*[EN365] which we have just considered is self-evidently only a difference of concept and not of content. What we speak of is the activity of Him who was and is and is to come, who precedes and accompanies and follows all actual concurrence. But the fulness of the divine activity must be revealed in the light of its relationship with creaturely activity. We are not dealing with another or second activity of God side by side with His predetermining activity. There is one indivisible operation. And the conclusions which we have reached when considering its aspect as [132] foreordination are still valid and need only to be reconsidered and reaffirmed under a different aspect. For the predestinating activity of God itself takes on the character of an accompanying of the creature—an accompanying in the first and most evident sense that it goes hand in hand with it. As the creature works in time, the eternal God works simultaneously in all the supremacy and sovereignty of His working. The *concursus divinus*[EN366] is a *concursus simultaneus*[EN367].

In the light of what has gone before, the first thing that we have to say on this point is that it is God who effects creaturely occurrence, that is, He is the living basis of its occurrence as such, and the living basis of its order and form. Both the fact that it happens and the way in which it happens derive from Him; they are decreed and brought to pass by Him. The divine foreordination now comes into force. He could not lose the creature, nor could it escape Him, for the sovereign almighty God, which was and is, is the living God now at very moment of the occurrence of the individual event, not as an idea which hovers over it, nor as a bored spectator, but as the One who acts as Lord, as the One who is true to His own will and sets it in action. The creature does not have any

---

[EN364] it accompanies
[EN365] it precedes
[EN366] divine accompanying
[EN367] simultaneous accompanying

kind of companion. God is with it. And the Emmanuel, whose point and meaning are of course revealed only in the history of the covenant of grace, can never be taken too seriously in the understanding of the general rule of the divine providence. The fact that God is with us, even with us creatures as such, means that He is so as the sovereign and almighty Lord. It means that His activity determines our activity even to its most intimate depths, even to its most direct origins. It means that always and in all circumstances our activity is under His decision. It means that He rules over us as He foreordained before us: and all with the certainty that He does not take any repose or rest, that He does not pause or cease, that there are no lacunae in the fulfilment of the decree of salvation and grace without which heaven and earth would not be, and in the execution of which they were created; all with the same certainty as that all things and events must serve the one final purpose.

The conclusion to be drawn from this first insight is that we have to understand the activity of God and that of the creature as a single action. And already we have indicated the limits of the concept "accompanying." If God the Lord accompanies the creature, this certainly does not mean—with a single exception—that the Creator becomes a creature, let alone the reverse—for even in the case of the exception we cannot say that the creature became the Creator. If God the Lord accompanies the creature, what it does mean is that He is so present in the activity of the creature, and present with such sovereignty and almighty power, that His own action takes place in and with and over the activity of the creature. It is He Himself who does what Moses and David do. It is He, Yahweh, who thunders out of Sion when the prophet speaks. It is He who judges when the Assyrians capture Samaria and the Babylonians Jerusalem. It is He who speaks to the Church when Paul composes his Epistles. [133] And according to the testimony of both Old and New Testament Scriptures there is no difference here between salvation history and world history in general. It is He who does what heaven and earth and the sun and rain and lightning and thunder do. In the rule of God we do not have to do first with a creaturely action and then—somewhere above or behind, but quite distinct from it, like a hidden meaning and content—with an operation of God Himself. To describe the *concursus divinus*[EN368] we cannot use the mathematical picture of two parallel lines. But creaturely events take place as God Himself acts. As He Himself enters the creaturely sphere—and He does not cease to do this, but does it in the slightest movement of a leaf in the wind—His will is accomplished directly and His decisions are made and fulfilled in all creaturely occurrence both great and small. He would not be God at all if He were not the living God, if there were a single point where He was absent or inactive, or only partly active, or restricted in His action. The earth is His and all that therein is (and the heavens as well), and this is something which continues to be true in the directest possible way.

[EN368] divine accompanying

In this sense, and with an appeal to Is. 26^{12}, the doctrine of the concursus was already held by Thomas Aquinas: *Sic intelligendum est Deum operari in rebus, quod tamen ipsae res propriam habent operationem*^{EN369} (*S. theol.*, I, qu. 105, art. 5 c). In relation to it he asked and answered the following questions: Does not this involve an unnecessary duplication? Would not the activity of God be sufficient alone? Is not that of the creature superfluous (*vid.* 1). To these he replied: The activity of God is indeed sufficient as *primum agens*^{EN370}, but this does not make superfluous the activity of *agentia secunda*^{EN371} as such (*ad.* 1). Again, can the same activity be carried out by two agents at the same time (*vid.* 2)? To this he replied: It would be impossible if the two agents belonged to the same order, but not when the one *primum agens*^{EN372} and the other *secundum agens est*^{EN373} (*ad.* 2). The conclusiveness of both answers clearly depends upon whether the distinction between the *primum* and *secundum agens* is of such a kind that the two subjects cannot be compared, but belong to two different, two totally different orders, and confront each other in a necessary relation of superiority and subordination. It is only then that the activity of the former can accompany that of the latter. It is only then that there is a legitimate place for the latter side by side with the former. But are there two subjects which stand in this relation, and between which this kind of *concursus*^{EN374} is possible? Thomas defined his *primum agens*^{EN375} and *agentia secunda*^{EN376} as though there were. But is definition enough? It would obviously have been better to refer to the relation between Creator and creature revealed in the Word of God, the relation between the Creator who is gracious and the creature which receives His grace. It is here that we see both the incomparableness and the interconnexion. It is here that the *concursus*, the simultaneous activity of God and the creature, is not merely possible but necessary. But this was not the path chosen by Thomas, and that is why his arguments are not redeemed from an ultimate lack of certainty.

In relation to the identity of the divine and creaturely action, A. Quenstedt (*Theol. did. pol.*, 1685, I, 13, *sect.* 2, *qu.* 3, *ekth.* 13) expressed himself in the following unimpeachable terms: *Non est reipsa alia actio influxus Dei, alia operatio creaturae, sed una et indivisibilis actio, utrumque respiciens et ab utroque pendens, a Deo ut causa universali, a creatura ut causa particulari*^{EN377}. And

[134] it is quite refreshing when he goes on to compare the relationship in this action with that of writing, which is done wholly by the hand and wholly by the pen, and not partly by the one and partly by the other. If we overlook the defects which cling to this as to all illustrations, the comparison necessarily teaches us that as in the one action of writing the hand guides and the pen is guided, so the divine activity overrules in its conjunction with the creaturely, and on the part of the creaturely there can only be submission. It was far from the intention of a Lutheran like Quenstedt to make this point, yet strangely enough this is how he expounds the parable: *Ita concursus Dei non est prior actione creaturae propria prioritate causalitatis, cum in re sit omnino eadem actio, adeoque totum effectum producit Deus sicut et causa secunda, quod fit per*

EN369 Thus it is necessary to understand that when God acts in created things, creatures still maintain their own distinctive mode of activity

EN370 primary agent

EN371 secondary agency

EN372 primary agent

EN373 is a secondary agent

EN374 accompanying

EN375 primary agent

EN376 secondary agency

EN377 It is not the case that God's influence on the creature is one action and the activity of the creature another; rather, creaturely action is one and indivisible, attending to and depending on both causes: on God as the universal cause and on the creature as particular cause

2. The Divine Accompanying

actionem Dei exteriorem, quae intime in actione creaturae includitur, immo una eademque est cum illa[EN378]. In the comparison of the hand and the pen what interested Quenstedt was the unity and not the obvious difference in unity of the action of the two agents. What interested him was the fact that the hand and the pen work together, and not the irreversible peculiarity of the way in which they co-operate in the one action. There is a real danger at this point. An interest in the legitimate assertion that the *concursus Dei*[EN379] and creaturely activity have to be understood as a single action can very well take the form of a mere emphasising of the fact that God accompanies creaturely occurrence with such sovereign power that the occurrence as such is quite simply and directly the execution of His will and therefore identical with His own action. This could easily be said in a straightforward exposition of the parable. But Quenstedt's interest—and it is not easy to see the theological justification for it—is directed to the *una eademque actio*[EN380] as such. God and the creature (unlike the hand and the pen) apparently share equally in this action without any *prioritas causalitatis*[EN381] on the side of God. Hence we can describe it only as an external action of God which is secretly enclosed or included in that of the creature. The danger here is the danger of reversibility; the possibility of understanding the *divine concursus* with the creature as also a creaturely *concursus*[EN382] with God. But this kind of reversibility is absolutely forbidden if we are not to fall into wild speculation about God and the world. We must always be clear who is and who is not the Lord in this nexus and therefore in this one action. It is God who has called forth this action of the creature, and in and with this action He Himself is at work in sovereign power. And inasmuch as He is at work in and with it, He determines the action. However strong our emphasis upon the unity of the action, to affirm the reverse would be patent blasphemy. For this reason we cannot deny the *prioritas causalitatis*[EN383]. Strictly speaking, the one-ness of the action (like the one-ness of the two natures in Jesus Christ) can be maintained and perceived and understood only in the light of the operation of the divine subject. We cannot, therefore, deduce from it abstract propositions about an action of the creature which takes place in conjunction with the action of God and encloses the divine action within it. We cannot gather from it the abstract theory of a secret operation of God within the general occurrence of nature and history. Otherwise we shall suddenly find ourselves—and this was the danger in the Lutheran understanding of the *concursus*[EN384], a danger which had threatened already in Lutheran Christology and Lutheran eucharistic teaching—in the midst of the Hegelian dialectic, in which there can be all kinds of reversals between the higher and the lower, *prius* and *posterius*[EN385], God and the creature. In considering the one-ness of the action we have always to give the glory to God and not in the same way to the creature. But this is what Quenstedt's exposition denies. And since Lutheran theology was working with a concept of God which did not safeguard it against this type of reversal, that is what makes it highly suspect.

[EN378] So the divine accompanying is not prior to the creature's own action in terms of causal priority, since in the event they are completely the same action, to the extent that God and the secondary cause each produce the whole effect, since it happens through the external action of God, which is enclosed in the inmost part of the creature's action, and is indeed one and the same with it

[EN379] divine accompanying

[EN380] one and the same action

[EN381] causal priority

[EN382] accompanying

[EN383] causal priority

[EN384] accompanying

[EN385] prior and subsequent

[135]　But the time has now come when we must consider what we mean when in this matter of God's operation, and therefore in the exercise of His sovereignty and omnipotence, His pre-eminence over the activity of the creature, we speak about the fulfilment of His will in creaturely occurrence. How does God call forth the activity of the creature? How does He control it? How is it that He is so completely the master of it, and so disposes concerning it, that we can say that it is the fulfilment of His will and therefore His own activity?

The reminder and warning which J. Cocceius (*S. Theol.*, 1662, 28, 22) inserted at this juncture must not pass unheeded: that the How? of the relation between God and the creature escapes our understanding no less than the How? of creation. This is something which is known only to God, for He alone knows His own power and resources. Job 28[20f.] may be recalled in this connexion: "Whence then cometh wisdom, and where is the place of understanding? Seeing it is hid from the eyes of all living, and kept close from the fowls of the air. Destruction and death say. We have heard the fame thereof with our ears. God understandeth the way thereof, and he knoweth the place thereof." What more can we say except to repeat the words of Eccles. 3[11]: "God hath made everything beautiful in his time," and satisfy ourselves with Ps. 139[1] that God knows all our thoughts and ways, in which we have to confess that we have no conception of the divine doing and knowing, and no concepts to describe them. But Cocceius himself then continues that we have a duty to declare all that is open and manifest in this matter, to the glory of God.

To the glory of God, we have at any rate to declare as open and manifest the fact that in the operation of God as a co-operation with that of the creature we have to do with the mystery of grace in the confrontation and encounter of two subjects who cannot be compared and do not fall under any one master-concept. And that means that from the standpoint of the creature what takes place in the divine operation is always inconceivable, unexpected and unmerited. It is not merely that the divine Subject is quite unlike the creaturely, but also that the divine operation is itself quite unlike the creaturely, being not simply a conditioning and determining of what already exists but a pure and free and absolute positing and therefore a conditioning and determining in a way which is impossible for creaturely activity. Hence the divine work is not merely done after a higher and superior fashion, but within a completely different order. And the fact that there is still a connexion between them, a positive and indeed an intimate and direct connexion; the fact that the divine activity is fulfilled in and with and over the creaturely, and that the creaturely is itself the fulfilment of the divine will—this is the high truth and the high mystery of grace which we have now to bear in mind.

And if we do bear it in mind there is no room for those conceptions of God's operation which are no more than the ascribing to it of a higher potency as compared with the lower potency of that of the creature. It is not merely that God works with a higher or absolute force on beings whose force is less, so that they have no option but to yield and submit to the pressure of His power and accommodate themselves to it. For that is how stronger creatures work on

other and weaker creatures. But the work of God on the creature is far more [136]
than comparatively a stronger or superlatively the strongest work.

Again, there is no place for conceptions in which the divine operation is related to the creaturely in the way that an actual is to a potential, as for example, a motor to the mechanism associated with it, which has the power to propel but in practice can do so only when it is caused to do so by the action of the motor. For creatures can act in this way on other creatures which are capable of action but do not act. But the work of God on the creature is far more than an action which stirs up the creature itself to action.

Finally there is no place for conceptions in which the operation of God produces that of the creature in the way that a first and general action gives rise to a series of actions and thus brings about a united activity, like a locomotive setting in motion the carriage immediately next to it, and by means of this carriage all the carriages and therefore the whole train. For creatures can also act upon each other in this way. But the work of God on the creature is far more than the first of a series of actions which sets in motion the whole series, and in and with it each individual action.

It now becomes clear how essential it was, when we considered the introduction of the causal concept into the discussion, to safeguard ourselves against all mechanical interpretations of the divine *causare*[EN386]. In all the conceptions mentioned the divine operation is obviously thought of as mechanical. But to that extent we remain only in the sphere of the creaturely. We conceive, but what we conceive is not the divine operation, for whose peculiar nature there is no parallel in the creaturely sphere.

But of course we shall fall into the opposite error if we try to represent the divine operation in terms of the imparting of a quality or quantity of the divine essence or operation to the creature and its activity, as a kind of infusion of divine love or divine power or divine life into the essence of the creature. The difference in order between the working of God in, with and over the creature, and the working of the creature under God's lordship, cannot be envisaged as one which has been resolved or removed. It is still in force even when God stoops down to the creature and the creature is raised up to this close proximity with Himself. It is the secret of grace that God does this, and the creature experiences it. But it is also the secret of grace that even when He does it He alone is God, that He alone has and retains the divine essence, that the essence of the creature is not affected or altered. By His unconditioned and irresistible lordship He does not subtract anything from the creature or add anything to it, but He allows it to be just what it is in its creaturely essence. Even in the union of the divine activity and creaturely occurrence there remains a genuine antithesis which is not obscured or resolved either by admixture or transference, either by divine influence or infusion. There is still a genuine encounter, [137]
and therefore a genuine meeting, of two beings which are quite different in type and order.

[EN386] causing

Our older divines were careful to safeguard themselves quite definitely at this point: the *concursus*[EN387] is not a *virtus Dei in creaturas transiens*[EN388] (B. Pictet, quoted from *Heppe*[2], p. 209). But they used the (in this context) ambiguous expression *influxus* far too readily and freely not to give occasion for this kind of error. In this respect caution must also be exercised in relation to the intrinsically attractive power-terminology of the 18th century, in which especially the South German theology deriving from J. A. Bengel and developed mainly by F. C. Oetinger and later J. T. Beck (but we must also mention the Bremen divine G. Mencken) came to speak about the reality, substantiality and dynamic of the activity of God in creaturely activity. But from this it is only a step and we are suspiciously close to gnostic and gnosticising doctrines of emanations and infusions. Again, it is only a step and we are involved in dangerous affinities to the Roman Catholic conception of the impartation of grace. This theology was not formed only from the Bible, as it claimed. It was also drawing on a contemporary theosophical movement which is characteristic of the whole period 1750–1850 but has not even the remotest connexions with the Bible. On quite different grounds did not J. G. Herder and Franz Baader and finally Schelling make use of a very similar terminology to leap over all the barriers which stand between God and the creature? To speak strongly on this point, we have not to speak too strongly. We must not weaken the reality, substantiality and dynamic of the activity of God in, with and over that of the creature by removing the barrier of creaturehood and ascribing to the creature properties and capacities which can belong as such only to the Creator. It is not by way of a higher naturalism (which can so easily revert to a lower) that we shall do justice to the mystery of this divine activity, and with it to the participation in the divine activity allotted to the creature.

Having safeguarded ourselves on both sides, we are now in a position to go forward to something more positive. But before doing so, let us draw yet a third line of demarcation. Like the divine essence, the divine activity is single, united and therefore unitary, but it is also manifold, and therefore not uniform, monotonous and undifferentiated. It does not owe its manifoldness to that of the creature while in itself it is without form or colour, a formal act of power lacking any specific character or content, like a sunbeam, perhaps, which shines in all its colours only in the rain, or perhaps like the heat of a single radiator which melts or dries up or kindles according to the character of the objects reached, or it may be like a master-key which will open a hundred locks. The divine activity is indeed one and the same in all things, but it is not one and the same in the sense of eternal recurrence, or as the only constant pole in the flux of phenomena. It is not something which is enriched; it is something which is already rich in and of itself. The divine *concursus*[EN389] is not simply as manifold as the *causae secundae*[EN390]. From the very first and prior to the existence of these *causae*[EN391], it is more manifold than they are. It is the operation of the Creator of all things, who knows not only the things themselves but all the potentialities intended for them, who is also free to give

---

[EN387] accompanying
[EN388] power of God transferred to creatures
[EN389] accompanying
[EN390] secondary causes
[EN391] causes

them new potentialities, i.e., those hitherto concealed both from the things [138] themselves and from those who observe them. It is the operation of One whose power over the creature is so complete because it is differentiated, because it can find and re-determine each one according to its particular nature, because it can use it in its particular place, because in controlling it, it gives to each one that which is proper to it, that which God Himself has ordained should be proper to it. God is not a pedant. He is not like a schoolmaster who gives the same lesson to the whole class, or an officer who moves his whole squadron in the same direction, or a bureaucrat who once an outlook or principle is embedded in his own little head rules his whole department in accordance with it. But, if the term may be allowed, God is a genuine aristocrat who can achieve a highly personal rule without any fear for His own authority or for the unity of His plan. The events in which He co-operates with His creatures, and His and their activity are a single occurrence, are not therefore so many "cases" in the one rule, but individual events which have their own importance and have to be considered in and for themselves, but which He Himself holds together as a single whole in the one objective form and structure: He Himself who in the very fulness of His individual works is always the same in being and purpose.

We must not be led astray at this point by a false conception of the simplicity of the divine essence. This simplicity has not to be explained as the simplicity of the absolute as compared with the relative, or of the general as compared with the particular, or of the digit 1 as compared with its multiplications and divisions, or of the concept as compared with its perception. It is the simplicity of the God who is eternally rich in His threefold being: "May God in His eternal riches always give us in our lives a cheerful heart and noble serenity." It is simplicity as opposed to divisibility and separability, as opposed to inward disloyalty and inconstancy, as opposed to all forms of self-contradiction. But it is the simplicity of the One who in Himself as Father, Son, and Holy Ghost is love, who in Himself does not merely exist but co-exists, who in Himself has space and dimension, who in Himself has life (Jn. 5[26]). It is the simplicity of the One who in His own being is not nowhere but everywhere, not never but always; of the One who is therefore omnipresent before and above and after all space, and eternal before and above and after all time: who at one and the same time is distant and near, yesterday, to-day and to-morrow. It is this God, who is not poor in Himself but rich, who works together with the creature. He does not do it uniformly or monotonously or without differentiation, for He is not uniform or monotonous or undifferentiated in Himself. If He were to do it in this way He would be doing violence to His own nature; He would not be God.

In the light of this fact we can understand the unconditioned and irresistible nature of the divine activity. All the theologoumena in which these characteristics are imprisoned and exposed to dispute, as though the creature were playing its own game over against God, have as their presupposition one or other of these false conceptions of the simplicity of God, the idolatrous notion of a god who in himself is uniform, monotonous and undifferentiated, who is not really living, omnipresent and eternal. The result is that the operation of God can be understood only as a neutral operation which encounters something alien and therefore limited in the manifoldness of creaturely activity, which in becoming manifold necessarily adjusts and orientates itself according to creatures and their activity, which in determining

[139]   and conditioning them is itself determined and conditioned by them, and is not therefore an omnipotent operation. The god of all synergistic systems is always the absolute, the general, the digit 1, the concept. And it is clear that the operation of this god and that of the creature (the relative, the particular, the multiplied or divided part, the perception) have necessarily to be thought of as reciprocal. But this god is not God. Between this god and the creature all kinds of reversals are possible, and the devious dialectical mind of man has constantly made them. This in itself is proof enough that when we conceive of this god our thought is still moving in the creaturely sphere and any notions we have of the divine operation are radically false. As against that the God who is eternally rich in Himself is not imprisoned in His own simplicity, but the differentiated nature of the world created by Him derives from Himself even as the one. He cannot encounter any limits in the creaturely sphere which can and must compel Him to conform, differentiating, and adjusting and orientating Himself according to the activity of the creature, and therefore allowing Himself to be determined and conditioned by it. He is absolutely sovereign in relation to all the different possibilities of the creature, for there is not one of them which was not preceded by His own long before the creature ever laid hold of its own possibilities, long before it ever existed or was free to lay hold of any possibilities. This can be done only in the sphere of the divine freedom. And this means that the reign of God is indeed unconditioned and irresistible.

We can now proceed to answer positively the question of the How? of the divine operation.

From all that has been said it might appear that the conditions which such an answer must fulfil are almost insuperably difficult. The positive answer must not describe the relation between God and the creature in terms of the relation between creature and creature. It must be quite free from mechanistic influences. Again, it must not compromise the character of the relation between God and the creature as a genuine encounter. It must avoid any idea of emanations of infusions of the divine essence. Again, it must not overlook the richness of the being of God or the manifold nature of His work. It must not be an answer merely in terms of a principle. From first to last it must do justice to the inconceivability of the being and work of God. It must speak quite definitely of the divine mystery. But it certainly cannot take the form merely of an *ignoramus*[EN392], for is not the question thrust upon us by the very fact that the divine work is continuously in the world as event, demanding to be known and recognised? The difficulty with which we are faced appears to be an insuperable one, and it would be so, and would remain so, if we had to consider whether we could give an answer, and if so what, merely within the framework of a general philosophy of God and the world. For then we should have no option but to fall back, on very poor grounds and certainly with a very bad conscience, on one of the conceptions which we have definitely excluded. Otherwise we could only admit that a positive answer is impossible. And when we weigh up the different possibilities of this or that general philosophy, everything points to the fact that the best of them simply omit or reject or ignore the

---

[EN392] we do not know

whole problem. But then we have to ask again whether the matter can rest at [140] that, and at once there is the lurking danger of a relapse into one or other of the conceptions already excluded.

Unless I am mistaken, in the older Evangelical theology this problem of the How? was first formulated, and the answer at any rate indicated, by Cocceius and his disciples, that is, at the time when the necessity of a biblical basis even for theological method was again being considered. Previously, and for some time after in circles where the necessity was not recognised, the various divines had always acted as though they knew exactly what they were talking about when they referred to the divine *causare, operari, efficere*[EN393] etc. This could only mean that they were leaving the question open, with the result that they were all the more defenceless against the temptation to make a casual and unregulated use of the various quite unsuitable conceptions, speaking of the operation of God in mechanical or emanationist terms, or in complete forgetfulness of the richness of the divine being, and always in constant violation of the divine mystery, with all the unfortunate consequences which were bound to result, and did in fact result, on every hand.

In theology we must always be suspicious when questions are left open and problems evaded, for in practice it means that they are linked with certain necessary answers which because they are casual and unregulated may well be completely false. It is in those situations where we can proceed only by surreptitiously leaving questions unanswered that we easily find ourselves in deep waters in our theological thinking and utterance. And to a large extent that is what happened to the older Evangelical theology on this particular issue.

Within the framework of a general philosophy, whatever it may be, the one factor upon which everything depends is the unknown one of this operation of God in and with the creature as it actually takes place, continually becoming event, and demanding to be known and recognised. To know this factor it is not enough merely to be an eye- or ear-witness of the general occurrence of nature or history. It is not enough merely to contemplate this occurrence and then for some reason to decide that we have to describe and understand it as the operation of God, of a being who is endowed with supreme power and wisdom and certain other maximal qualities. For even if, when we do this, we bring this occurrence under the highest concept accessible, without too much serious exertion, to the mind of man, this does not mean at all that we have known them and recognised them as the work of God. This is possible only when the true God, the Creator and Lord above all the creaturely world, who foreordains and sovereignly determines its activity even in His conjunction with it, and who is not accessible to human conceptuality, when this God makes Himself known, and in so doing is known and recognised by man. The true God and His activity can never be perceived within the framework of a general philosophy. Otherwise it would not be a general philosophy. It would not be looking first of all to cosmic occurrence in general, and then bringing what it sees and hears there under a highest concept as its presuppositions allow. It would have to look first at the true God and His activity—in a specific occurrence. And in the light of this it would then consider cosmic occurrence

---

[EN393] causing, working, effecting

[141] in general, understanding it in its conjunction with the divine operation. But since it does not do this, since it cannot do it without destroying itself, without abandoning its claim to be a general philosophy, the operation of God as it actually takes place can never be to it a known but only an unknown factor. Always supposing that its nature allows, it believes, it presupposes, i.e., it has decided to conjecture, and it now maintains, that its own conceptual image is the true God, and therefore that the cosmic occurrence in whose light it has evolved this image is His operation. But how does it know that? Where and how does it perceive it? How can it recognise it? And how can even the problem of the How? of this operation arise in any serious sense, let alone the possibility of a serious and worthy answer? Theoretically it may have the wisdom, if not to see, at least to suspect the brokenness of all the broken answers which crowd in upon us, and therefore to refrain from returning any such answer. But what alternative remains except to evade the problem, thus admitting that it does not really know what it is talking about when it speaks about the operation of God. But when for some reason it still tries to do so, without knowing what it is that it is doing, is it not necessarily reduced to foolishness? Can it possibly avoid in practice a casual and unregulated harking back to one or other of those broken answers? Can it possibly avoid a form of extremely hazardous borrowing?

But Christian theology can and must differ from a general philosophy of God and the world in the fact that to Christian theology the factor upon which everything depends, the activity of God which becomes event, is not an unknown but a known factor, and known in such a way that it demands a knowledge and an acknowledgment of the How? If Christian theology sticks to its own last, not launching out into problems for whose origin it cannot accept responsibility, it will concern itself with seeing and hearing the work of the true God which precedes any consideration of cosmic occurrence as such. It has to do with the God who foreordains all cosmic occurrence, who joins Himself to it only that He may determine it with full sovereignty, who is not accessible to any human conceptually, but who has made Himself known, and in so doing can now be known and recognised. As its very name suggests, Christian theology has to do with Jesus Christ, with the history of the covenant of grace as it leads up to Him and has its source in Him, and therefore with the almighty operation of God governing all cosmic occurrence as it is revealed at this point. It does not first consider the creature and its activity in general, then work out a concept of the supreme being, then confer upon this being the name of God, and then conclude that there may perhaps be an activity of God in and above the activity of the creature. On the contrary, it first knows the activity of God in a particular cosmic action in which God has made Himself known. It perceives that the One who acts at this point and in this way is the

[142] supreme being. And in the light of that perception it sees that this God is at work in and over the activity of creation as a whole. It does not rest upon conjecture but upon knowledge. It is not an assertion but a confession of the

divine operation. It knows about this operation. And that means that the problem of the How? is raised for it in such a way that its reaction cannot possibly be one of omission or evasion. It is raised in such a way that it not merely suspects but necessarily perceives the brokenness of those broken answers. It is raised in such a way that those broken answers are excluded once and for all, and cannot play any further part in the discussion. The problem of the How? of the divine operation is raised in such a way that it is confronted with the answer to this problem as it is given in the event of the divine operation itself. Its one necessary concern must be to find the description which can do justice in our thought and utterance to what we see and hear of the divine operation.

And now we can and must give the simple positive answer that the operation of God is His utterance to all creatures of the Word of God which has all the force and wisdom and goodness of His Holy Spirit. Or, to put it in another way, the operation of God is His moving of all creatures by the force and wisdom and goodness which are His Holy Spirit, the Spirit of His Word. The divine operation is, therefore, a fatherly operation.

This is the answer already given to us when by the revelation of God we are summoned and empowered to believe in Him, and in believing in Him to know His operation, in the actuality of His operation in the covenant of grace, in and through Jesus Christ. This is how God works in the specific event which forms the centre and meaning and goal of all creaturely occurrence: objectively, proceeding from God by His Word; and subjectively, moving towards man by His Holy Spirit. For everything which happens there, no matter how great or small, does so in the relation of claim and response, of speaking and hearing, of command and obedience, which both objectively and subjectively God Himself has instituted and ordained and in which He Himself is in both cases the One who acts, in the one case as Word and in the other as Spirit. Every time that God shows forth His power to the men of His choosing, and through them to others, every time, then, that He acts, He does so in the following way: His Word goes forth to these men, to be received by them in the power of His Spirit; His Spirit is given to these men, to receive His Word of power.

The question facing us is simply this: Are we to understand the general activity of God in and over the creature in the light of this true centre and meaning and aim of all creaturely occurrence, or are we required or authorised in respect of this general operation either to seek some other concept, or perhaps to claim that we cannot know anything at all about the *modus*^{EN394} of the divine activity? To this question we must give the simple answer that we are free only to accept the first alternative, that the second is neither required nor authorised because, if it is God Himself who teaches us always and everywhere about Himself, there is no point at which we can break free from that instruction and seek a different answer from that which He Himself has given, or fail

[143]

---

^{EN394} mode

to recognise that answer as all-comprehensive and final. For the God who in Jesus Christ is active by His Word and Spirit reveals Himself as the One beside whom there is no other being or operation. And He Himself is the One who is and works only in the one way, who works always and everywhere as there revealed, and who does so even when He does not encounter us directly as in the history of the covenant of grace, in Jesus Christ, but is rather concealed and hidden. As we believe in Him and confess Him at this point, so we believe in Him and confess Him at all points—as the One who is always active in and with and over His creatures by His Word and Spirit. The fact that this is true always and everywhere allows and indeed compels us to think of all His activity as fatherly. It if were not true, or if we would have it to be true only in some other way, we should have to ask ourselves whether to speak about the fatherly providence of God is not mere sentimentality without any basis in fact. The fact that the Lord of the world is our Father stands or falls with the fact that even in the world His activity is the activity of His Word and Spirit.

Unless I am mistaken, it is the merit of the school of Cocceius to have introduced the concept *iussio*[EN395] into the discussion of the *concursus*[EN396]. So F. Burmann: *Actio (Dei) hic concipienda est, qualis in creatione et conservatione, nimirum iussio aeterna, unica et simplicissima voluntatis Dei*[EN397] (*Syn. Theol.*, 1678, I, 43, 25). Indeed, it was already clear from the plain text of Gen. 1, quite apart from the particular activity of God in the covenant of grace, that God created heaven and earth by His Word. Why then should we suddenly arrive at a different conclusion, or at no conclusion at all, in respect of His activity in, with and over the creature? The language of the Bible, and especially of the Old Testament, necessarily gives us pause. What is the biblical understanding of this How?, of the technics of the divine sovereignty over the creature? Is it not obvious that in the Old Testament the creature—especially individual man, but also universal history and its events, and finally all natural occurrence—is set in train by a divine address, word, call, command or order? The Word of God and creaturely occurrence seem to form an indissoluble unity. Everything that happens can be traced back to a Word of God. Therefore "the Lord God will do nothing, but he revealeth his secret unto his servants the prophets" (Am. 3⁷). And conversely: "The word that I shall speak shall come to pass .... I will say the word, and will perform it, saith the Lord God" (Ez. 12²⁵, cf. 37¹⁴). "I the Lord have brought down the high tree, have exalted the low tree, and have made the dry tree to flourish. I the Lord have spoken it and have done it" (Ex. 17²⁴). He called his Son, the people of Israel, out of Egypt (Hos. 11¹). He calls the kingdoms of the north to the siege of Jerusalem (Jer. 1¹⁵). And again, "he saith to Jerusalem, Thou shalt be inhabited; and to the cities of Judah, Ye shall be built, and to the deep, Be dry" (Is. 44²⁶ᶠ·). He calls Cyrus, the bird of prey from the north (Is. 46¹¹, 48¹⁵). He appoints him His shepherd (Is. 44²⁸). And He also commanded Shimei to curse David (2 Sam. 16¹⁰). He calls the generations one after another (Is. 41⁴). When He turns man to destruction He says, "Come again, ye children of men" (Ps. 90³). He speaks, and it means the pulling down and building up of whole peoples (Jer. 18⁷ᶠ·). He calls for a sword upon all the inhabitants of the earth (Jer. 25²⁹). But He also summons the heaven and the earth to action (Ps. 50¹⁻⁶). He brings out the host of heaven by number, calls them all by names, (Is. 40²⁶.) He commands

[144]

[EN395] command
[EN396] accompanying
[EN397] This action of God's in creation and in preservation must without question be conceived as the eternal, single and utterly simple command of God's will

the snow and the rain (Job 37^6), the gad-fly (Ps. 105^{31}) and the great fish of the prophet (Jon. 2^{11}). He calls for the corn (Ez. 36^{29}). He sends out His Word, and the ice melts (Ps. 147^{18}). And when the grass withers and the flower fades, it is because His Spirit blows upon it (Is. 40^7). This is how God works by His Word. And it is to be regretted that while the disciples of Cocceius saw this quite clearly they merely indicated the thesis and did not maintain it more strongly.

Nor is it the fatherliness alone but also the divinity of this operation which depends upon the fact that it is an operation in the Word and therefore by the Spirit, in the Spirit and therefore by the Word. If we perceive this and say it, then we stand within the Christian and Trinitarian conception of God, and we are on firm ground. To have a good conscience, we can only be silent in relation to the operation of a supreme being, as of all dumb idols, for we really know nothing about it. But we do justice to the operation of the one true God when we describe it as Word and Spirit, because when we do so we again pronounce the holy name of God; because as we are invited and enabled to speak by God Himself, we speak concerning Himself, His active person. The mystery of His operation is also safeguarded when we think of it as Word and Spirit. For it is only in the divine inscrutability that it can be revealed to us how in His covenant of grace God calls, illumines, justifies and sanctifies man by His Word and Spirit, and it is in this inscrutability that we believe and recognise the whole activity of God as the activity of the Word and Spirit of God. And if this is so, it is also meaningful to speak about the eternity, omnipresence and omnipotence of the divine operation, for as predicates of this Subject the concepts lose the emptiness and coldness which inevitably characterise them as the predicates merely of a supreme being. They acquire life and light. The Word of God is omnipotent, and His Holy Spirit is eternal and omnipresent. Again, on this presupposition we can gladly and unhesitatingly ascribe to the divine work the honour which is due to it. It is an unconditioned and irresistible work. And the flight into synergism becomes unnecessary, for if the supremacy of this work is the supremacy of the Word and Spirit it does not prejudice the autonomy, the freedom, the responsibility, the individual being and life and activity of the creature, or the genuineness of its own activity, but confirms and indeed establishes them. The One who rules by His Word and Spirit recognises the creature which He rules as a true other, just as He Himself as a Ruler of this type remains a true Other. He takes His creature seriously; He respects it by acting towards it so incomparably as a Ruler of this type, and in so doing He Himself continues to be respected.

We can therefore conclude our exposition of the *concursus simul taneus*[EN398], [145] the sovereign and overruling accompanying of the creature by the divine operation, with the proposition that even under this divine lordship the rights and honour and dignity and freedom of the creature are not suppressed and extinguished but vindicated and revealed.

[EN398] simultaneous accompanying

From the standpoint of historical theology we come here to the specific concern of the Lutheran (and in Roman Catholic theology the Jesuit) doctrine of providence. But to do justice to it, it is quite unnecessary to make the movement which under Jesuit inspiration the Lutherans themselves made: the dissolving of the divine *praedeterminatio*[EN399] into a mere *praevisio*[EN400].

Now it is true that the *concursus simultaneus*[EN401] takes place on the presupposition of the divine predetermination of creaturely activity and therefore of the unconditioned and irresistible lordship of the divine activity over the creaturely. But this does not mean that only God is really active. The idea that God alone effects all things to the exclusion of all *virtus creata*[EN402] had already been rejected by Thomas Aquinas (*S. Theol.*, I, qu. 105, art. 5 c) on the very good ground that it would mean that the Creator had not given to the creature any *virtus agendi*[EN403] at all—which would be contrary to His own *virtus agentis*[EN404] as Creator. Therefore the Lutherans were certainly quite right to emphasise the fact that the divine activity in *concursus*[EN405] with that of the creature cannot mean an abrogation of that of the creature or of its manifold individuality. So Quenstedt (*Theol. did. pol.*, 1685, I, 13, sect. 2, ekth. 12): *Neque enim immutat Deus naturas agentium aut eorum agendi rationem et ordinem, sed agentia naturalia sinit agere naturaliter, libera libere*[EN406]. But our suspicions are naturally aroused when he continues with a quotation from the Spanish Jesuit Francis Tolet (*sex pontificum concionator*[EN407], as he admiringly calls him): *Concurrit Deus cum causis secundis iuxta ipsarum naturam, cum liberis libere, cum necessariis neccssario, cum debilibus debiliter, cum fortibus fortiter, pro sua suavissima dispositione universali operando*[EN408]. And our suspicions are confirmed when Quenstedt himself explains: *Concurrit Deus cum causis secundis iuxta uniuscuiusque indigentiam et exigentiam h. e. quando, quoties et quomodo causa illa concursum illum postulat pro conditione naturae suae* .... *Naturis rerum agentium sese accomodat et cum illis* ... *concurrit descendendo ad singula iuxta uniuscuiusque capacitatem et indigentiam*[EN409]. Well may we ask what the author of the *De servo arbitrio* would have had to say about a Lutheranism of this kind. And we can also ask quite pertinently what would become of the rights and dignity of the creature if the lordship of the Creator in and with and over its activity consisted only in meeting and satisfying the particular needs and requirements of the creature (almost as though on request!).

The older Reformed divines, while they avoided this more Jesuitical than Evangelical overemphasis, unanimously accepted the proposition formulated by J. Wolleb: *providentia Dei*

[EN399] foreordination
[EN400] foreknowledge
[EN401] simultaneous accompanying
[EN402] created power
[EN403] power of acting
[EN404] agential power
[EN405] accompanying
[EN406] For God does not alter the natures of agents or form and structure of their action, but He lets natural agents act naturally and free agents freely
[EN407] a pundit to six popes
[EN408] God accompanies secondary causes according to their natures: freely with the free, necessarily with the necessary, feebly with the feeble, powerfully with the strong, working in accordance with His supremely gentle and universal management
[EN409] God accompanies secondary causes according to the need and claim of each; that is, when, how often and in whatever manner that cause requires that accompaniment for the maintenance of its nature .... He accommodates Himself to the natures of created agents and accompanies them ... condescending to individual creatures in accordance with the capacity and need of each one

2. The Divine Accompanying

causas secundas non tollit sed ponit[EN410]. We find exactly the same view in the definition given by the *Leiden Synopsis: pro ratione naturae uniuscuiusque ad agendum movet et applicat creaturis concursum suum*[EN411]. The Calvinists did not question the particularity of the activity of each creature, the contingency of natural occurrence, or even the freedom of the human will. Certainly they never doubted the spontaneity of human action, as they are frequently accused of doing. If Calvin himself (*Instit.*, I, 16, 2) occasionally described the function of at any rate unconscious creatures as that of instruments which are merely used, the later divines expressly corrected the thought, stating with much greater precision that we are not to believe *causas secundas simpliciter et in se mera Dei instrumenta esse, adeoque passive non etiam active se habere, quasi Deus cum causis secundis agat sicut artifex cum instrumentis suis, quae non aliter agunt, quam quatenus a principali agenti moventur …. Causae secundae proprie et insita virtute operantur*[EN412]. God does work *effective*[EN413] in and with them, as *causa prima*[EN414] and the   [146] Lord of their power to act, but He does not work *subjective, inclusive* or *exclusive*, passing over their activity as though the power which He had given them were an empty power (H. Heidegger, quoted from *Heppe*², 210). The point at issue between the Lutheran and Reformed divines was not whether but how to state the autonomy and particularity of creaturely activity in its difference from the relationship with the divine. What separated the Reformed from the Lutherans was that they would not concede any *libertas voluntatis in creatura, quae non sit ex participatione libertatis summae increatae, quae sit causa prima propria atque intima omnis creatae libertatis omniumque liberarum actionum*[EN415] (*Leiden Synopsis*, 1624, *Disp.* 11, 10). It was because they did not wish their position to be compromised by the *suavissima dispositio universalis*[EN416] of Jesuit invention that they rightly resisted the Lutherans on the point. But it is much more important to assert that they agreed with them both in a definite repudiation of the idea of the sole efficacy of God and in a positive concern to safeguard the freedom of creaturely activity. The ethical indifference and quietism which would have resulted had things been otherwise were never characteristics of the older Calvinism in its historical form. But we may ask: What was the historical result of that strange "disposition" by which God is not strictly speaking the Lord but only the omnipotent Supporter and Helper of creaturely activity? Was it not the peculiarly Lutheran conception of the autonomy of all events, and the corresponding tendency to a secular ethics whose application God could ultimately assist only with a pious blessing, but certainly not as the Lord? This much at least is certain, that a pre-deterministic understanding of the *concursus simultaneus*[EN417] obviously gave to Calvinism all the greater cause to reckon seriously with creaturely occurrence as a whole, and especially with human spontaneity and activity—in direct responsibility, of course, to the commandment of God Himself.

[EN410] the providence of God does not abolish secondary causes but establishes them
[EN411] He initiates and applies His accompanying to creatures so that each one acts according to its own nature
[EN412] that secondary causes are simply and in themselves mere instruments of God, to the extent of their having their existence passively and not also actively, as though God acted with secondary causes like a craftsman with his tools, which do not move except insofar as they are moved by the principal agent …. Secondary causes work through their own proper and intrinsic power
[EN413] effectively
[EN414] primary cause
[EN415] freedom of the will in the creature that is not a matter of participation in the supreme and uncreated freedom which is the primary, proper and most intimate cause and of all created freedom and of all free actions
[EN416] the most charming and universal disposition
[EN417] simultaneous accompanying

The unconditioned and irresistible lordship of God means not only that the freedom of creaturely activity is neither jeopardised nor suppressed, but rather that it is confirmed in all its particularity and variety.

Tantum abest, ut operatio divinae providentiae destruat libertatem voluntatis creatae, ut haec absque illa prorsus consistere nequeat[EN418]. (*Leid. Syn.*, 1624, *Disp.* 11 11).

The basic condition for a perception and understanding of this proposition is not intellectual but spiritual, that of overcoming and removing the fear-complex which suggests that God is a kind of stranger or alien or even enemy to the creature; that it is the better for the freedom and claim and honour and dignity of the creature the more it can call its own a sphere marked off from God and guaranteed against Him, and the worse for it if this sphere is restricted, and worst of all if it is completely taken away; that it may be and necessarily is a legitimate interest to defend the claim of the creature in face of an unjustified and dangerous claim on the part of God. To put it in the older terminology, the *causa secunda*[EN419] is not secure unless it can play the role of *causa prima*[EN420] in a secret corner of its own. But let us suppose for a moment that there is absolutely no foundation at all for this complex. God is the Father—not the father of a father-complex but the Father of Jesus Christ and

[147]   therefore our beloved Father. It is thus the better for the creature the more fully it stands under the lordship of God, and the worse for it the more that reservations and restrictions are placed upon this lordship. The rights of the creature are most radically known and acknowledged—indeed they are only really known and acknowledged—when the rights of God over against it are fully and unreservedly acknowledged. It is good for the *causa secunda*[EN421] simply to be a *causa secunda* and no more. But if this is the case, then how simple it is not merely to ask the question but to answer it. And is it not a remarkable testimony to the hardness of the human heart and the unrepentant nature of man that even Christendom, and even the specialists of Christendom, the strange breed which we call theologians, and the Evangelicals as well as the Catholics amongst these theologians, have been so little free from this complex that they have always thought it necessary to see and make new difficulties in the matter? What is the value of all our thought and talk about Christ and His resurrection, about grace, about the glory of our regeneration and the new creation, about the majesty of the Word of God, about the Church as a divine institution, about the causative and cognitive power of the sacraments, if in face of the simple demand to acknowledge God as the One who does all in all we are suddenly gripped by anxiety, as though perhaps we were ascribing too much to God and too little to the creature, as though perhaps we were

---

[EN418] So far is the operation of divine providence from destroying the freedom of the created will that apart from it this freedom is absolutely incapable of existing

[EN419] secondary cause

[EN420] primary cause

[EN421] secondary cause

encroaching too far on the particularity and autonomy of creaturely activity and especially on human freedom and responsibility? As if there could be any sense in sheltering from such a demand under the safe cover of a crude or subtle synergism! What sorry lip-servants we are! And there is a reason for it. For in the very depths of the Church, in the very depths of the Christian conscience and Christian theology, our fear of God is in fact far stronger than the love with which we are able to love God. This phenomenon makes it devastatingly plain that if in the proper place theology and Christian preaching has to speak about sin and demons and chaos generally, it would do well not to study the subject remotely but in its own conduct, in the characteristic fear of God and fear for the creature in which we Christians barricade ourselves against the truth which we confess with our lips, with the result that we can see that truth only over a barricade—there is a real *circulus vitiosus*[EN422] in the matter—and therefore confess it only with our lips and without any genuine conviction. If our Christian perception and confession does not free us to love God more than we fear Him, then it is obvious that we shall necessarily fear Him more than we love Him. At root, this is the only relevant form of human sin. And this is the one and only reason why it is so hard to grasp that the freedom of creaturely activity is confirmed by the unconditioned and irresistible lordship of God. And a reason of this kind cannot be disputed away by theological arguments. If we fear God and fear for ourselves, then we do fear. And since we all of us have the habit of fear of God, this habit will not go out of us except by prayer and fasting. All that we can say is that when and to the extent that it does really go out, the theological arguments which follow will acquire force and validity.   [148]

The God who is the true God and on the seat of power is the One who reveals Himself to Abraham and Moses, who speaks to and through the prophets, who has made Himself the God of the people Israel and the Lord of its history, who has become man in Jesus Christ and the Head of a congregation of men, who is active in all these ways with sovereign power, unconditionally and irresistibly, and yet with mercy and forbearance, who has dealings with men after the manner of a man. Man himself in his doing and non-doing, in his thinking and acting, in his greatness and insignificance, in his own nature and its limitations, was and is the object and end of God's work. But as man he also was and is the means, or instrument, or organ of this work. The history of the divine covenant and glory and salvation is also the history of man—not merely of human passion, but of every conceivable form of human action. If we consider the prophets and apostles, who can mark off the boundary where the freedom of God ceases and the freedom of the creature begins? Is there any humanity more free or autonomous or proud than that of the men after God's own heart who according to their own confession experienced the divine activity towards them without any will or response at all on their own part?

[EN422] vicious circle

Is it not the case that such men—not to speak of Jesus Christ their pattern—were activated by this experience in a way which we cannot explain by any other liberation than that which brought them so absolutely under the lordship of God? And this is the God who rules the world, who rules unconditionally and irresistibly in all occurrence. It is He who is at work in all the great or small things which can happen to man, dealing with him not as a stock or stone but as a man, as a being who can know and will, as a free being, with an appeal to his responsibility, He Himself being the One who makes him responsible. And it is He who is at work in all other happenings, allowing the creature to act according to its own nature and limits, which are of course known only to Him, and given by Him. The very fact that this God rules as Creator means that in their own way, and at their own time and place, all things are allowed to be, and live, and work, and occupy their own sphere, and exercise their own effect upon their environment, and fulfil the circle of their own destiny. That He is the Master in all things does not alter the fact that each is allowed to develop in its own activity. On the contrary, the rule and disposition of God consists in the very fact that each may and can do that. And whenever and wherever it does so, it has to thank the divine rule and disposition for it. It could never do it at all unless from first to last it was allowed to do so by the divine rule and disposition. Far from being a threat to its freedom, this is the [149] very reason why at its own time and place, in its own existence and form of existence, it can reveal its highest possible spontaneity, i.e., magnify the Lord who has made it what it is and permits it to work as such.

Once it is established who the God is to whom we refer in this matter, then we have to say, secondly, that just as the activity of God over against that of the creature (which He makes His own in virtue of His mastery over it) remains His own, so too it is provided that the activity of the creature over against that of God remains the creature's own. It would be a twofold misunderstanding of the grace of God to try to suppose that the overruling will of God involves a kind of absorption and assimilation of creaturely activity into the divine, and therefore a disintegration and destruction of the creaturely in favour of the divine. To do this would be to forget that the activity of God is the activity of His continually free grace, an activity from above downwards, a condescension in which God is beyond comparison, in which He does not cease to be the true God, in which there cannot then be any question of the suppression of the variety, and therefore of the autonomy and particularity, of creaturely activity in face of His own. And it would also be to forget that, since the activity of God is indeed an activity of His grace, it does not aim at the destruction and suppression of the creature but its affirmation, deliverance and glorification. The contemplation of the true God preserves us from all theories of emanation and infusion. It is our safeguard against pantheism and monism. And it is also our assurance against the fear that little and ultimately nothing will be left for the nature and activity and freedom and responsibility of the creature. For it is not only that not nothing and not too little is left, but that everything is left.

And why say: It is left, as though the creature were subjected to a kind of assault in face of which it has to console itself more or less with the fact that this or that is left to it? The very fact that there is still a gap between the activity of God and that of the creature—it is overcome by God's lordship below as well as above, but being overcome only by God it is still there—means that what is proper to the creature, to the being below, to that which is distinct from God, is not removed from it but assigned and granted to it. Just as God Himself is respected by reason of His unconditioned and irresistible activity, the activity of His grace, so He respects as such the creature to whom He is gracious. That creature cannot ask for itself anything better than to be ruled absolutely by the divine activity of grace. If this activity were to cease or pause, if God were to reveal to the creature a sphere in which it would be something other than the object of His grace, then there would be every reason to fear for its freedom and rights and honour and dignity. And if anyone thinks it necessary to diminish the sovereignty of the activity of God or to set a limit to His omnipotence, let him consider well what he is doing. For if that is the direction in which his thoughts and utterances run, then he is contending for the greatest possible [150] evil that could ever befall the creature as such.

And now thirdly, and finally, we must recall all that we have already said concerning the *modus*EN423 of the divine operation. To emphasise again the decisive point, it is an activity of the God who is eternally rich, and it is His activity by His Word and Spirit. And in saying this we are simply describing two different aspects of one and the same thing. The eternal riches of God are the riches of His trinitarian life as Father, Son, and Holy Spirit. And for this reason His operation by Word and Spirit is the demonstration of a life which is eternally rich. From both angles we arrive at the same result. If God works by His Word and Spirit there is no reason whatever why the activity of the creature should be destroyed or suppressed by His omnipotent operation. On the contrary, it is necessarily the case that the omnipotent operation of God not merely leaves the activity of the creature free, but continually makes it free. Where the Word and Spirit are at work unconditionally and irresistibly, the effect of their operation is not bondage but freedom. We could almost put it in this way, that the bondage which results from the operation of the Word and Spirit is itself true freedom. What room is there for anxiety in face of the omnipotence of the Word and the omnipotence of the Spirit? How can we ever think of reservations of this omnipotence? What kind of concept of freedom would that be which had the result of an attempted safeguarding of the creature against the threat of this bondage? But again, if God works as the One who is eternally rich in Himself, there is no reason to be afraid that the variety of creaturely activity will as it were be ironed out by His activity, and that we ourselves will have to guarantee with the wisdom of a *suavissima dispositio*EN424

EN423 mode
EN424 the most charming disposition

that everything in our little cosmos can maintain its own place and individuality: as though the plenitude of all the possibilities either given or about to be given, i.e., still to be revealed, were not already contained in the omnipotent divine operation in itself and as such; as though the variety of the creature and its activity were not guaranteed continually by the activity of God, beside whose riches all the variety of our cosmos is the veriest poverty. Surely it betrays an appalling ignorance of the Word and Spirit of God, and therefore of the true and triune God, or it betrays perhaps a forgetfulness of all that we ever knew, if we are afraid of this God and afraid for the creature at this point.

These, then, are the theological arguments which we have to put forward. But I repeat that we stand here at a place where the theological arguments can have force and validity only as the habit, the bad Christian habit, of a fear-complex in face of God is in process of expulsion. In adhering so decidedly to the older doctrine of the Reformed Church and theology in our own conclusions in this matter, we have dared to count upon the fact that even yet this bad
[151]   habit can be—not reformed, but expelled. It is a risk to count upon that expulsion. But unless we take the risk, it is difficult to see how we can say anything meaningful about this subject.

We conclude the sub-section as a whole with the third proposition that the activity of God follows that of the creature, *succurrit* (*sc. ad effectum*[EN425]). What we have to say on this point really merges into the theme which must be developed in the next sub-section on the divine directing of creaturely being (*De gubernatione*). We can, therefore, be brief.

Again it is our first duty to assert that we make this third distinction only to help the conceptual development, that is, to make it plain that the one operation of God in relation to that of the creature has this dimension as well, that it covers the whole range of creaturely activity. In its totality, the conception of God accompanying the creature on its own path includes not merely His preceding and accompanying it as the Lord, but also His following it, again as the Lord. And this "following" as well as the "preceding" must be related to the eternal being of God as well as to his temporal action. God is eternal. It is as the eternal God that He acts in time. And this means that He acts not merely before the work of the creature as this work occurs within the limits of its own time, not merely contemporaneously with it, but also after this work is concluded, and therefore after the time allotted to it has come to an end. God was, and was at work, even when the creature had not commenced its work. God is, and is at work, in the accomplishment of this work. God will be, and will still be at work in relation to this work, when the creature and its work have already attained their goal.

The goal of all activity is an effect, that is, an alteration in the active subject, and to some extent of its environment, which is either purposed in the particular action, or at any rate produced, or brought about, or in some way caused by

---

[EN425] succeeds (namely, with respect to outcome)

it. Now if we were dealing only with the activity of the creature we should have to say that once the creaturely subject—admittedly under the influence of many earlier actions of its own and also of many actions of other creaturely subjects which preceded its own activity—has performed this or that action, once the change produced by its action is complete, a fact has been established, a fact which may be changed again by the future activity of the same subject or of others, but which is still a fact, which has been caused and is therefore present as an effect in a way which corresponds exactly with the desire, capacity, and actual execution of the particular subject. What it has done it has done, what has happened has happened, in the form and compass and with the meaning and range foreseen by the particular subject, and according to its conscious or unconscious purposes and possibilities, and to the extent of its actual execution. "What I have written I have written." As we make our beds, so we must lie on them. What a man sows, that he must reap. What comes to pass, is—is in a way which corresponds with that by whom or   [152] which it came to be, and with how it came to be. No matter what may happen in the future, this change has already been made, and is irrevocable and unalterable. The decision reached has produced a situation whose factuality, and nature, and limits, cannot be disturbed. The effect is there, just as it was bound to be as a result of the activity of the particular creaturely subject.

This is how we should have to conceive of the end of creaturely activity, and therefore of the situation obtaining at this end, if we had to do only with the activity of the creature, and did not have to reckon first and last with the activity of God accompanying the activity of the creature. But God accompanies the activity of the creature as its Creator and Lord. And this means that even the effects of this activity, even the changes brought about by it, are still subject to His disposing and control. There is no withdrawal on the part of God. God does not retire when the creature has attained its end and goal, when the effect was there as it is meant to be and could be and actually was according to that activity. God's arm remains outstretched even when that of the creature has been allowed to fall. God outruns the creature, and His activity follows the activity of the creature, in the sense that He acts as the Lord even of the effects of creaturely activity. The end of the temporal act is like its beginning. The act could only begin with God, and it can only end with God. And in the one case as in the other "with God" means in the service of His omnipotent operation.

Therefore the forward as well as backward context of the activity of each creature is not merely that of its relation to similar activities which either were before or will be after it, and under the effects of which its own operation takes place, and upon which it exercises a reciprocal effect. Certainly it does stand in this context, but it does so only with God. For it was the omnipotent operation of God that the preceding of other creatures and the effects of that preceding helped to bring about here and now the particular activity of the particular

155

creature. And it will again be the omnipotent operation of God that the particular activity produced helps to bring about the later activity of other creatures. From the very first the individual activity of the creature—and the same is true of the preceding activity of other creatures—stands under the dominion of God. But for the moment we are stressing the other side of the matter—that the effect produced by it stands under the same dominion. The activity can end only as it began. It can attain its goal only in the source to which it owes its will, capacity, and execution.

But if this is the case, then the effect produced by the particular creature, the change which it effects either in its own circumstances or in those of its creaturely environment, is not its own. The moment it is produced, the effect [153] which I produce is no longer mine. I did produce it, and the fact of it is irrevocable, for I did not produce it apart from God, but with God, and under the lordship of His *praecursus*[EN426] and *concursus*[EN427]. But just because the effect is brought into being under the divine lordship, it does not belong to the creature to appoint or fix the form and compass or the meaning and range of this effect, no matter how ineluctably the effect follows from the most personal being or activity of the creature. Nor does it belong to those other creatures who experience that effect to appoint or fix its character, no matter how deeply they are affected by it or how thoroughly they make it their own.

The word which I utter now is absolutely my own. And having uttered it, I have really uttered it. I have given rise to a specific fact which cannot be recalled. But for all that, I cannot hasten after my word, and arrange that as my word it will be received and understood and repeated in the way that I myself intended. It remains the word which I uttered, but as a word which has been uttered it acquires its own history quite independently of anything that I contributed to it. I have no further power over the fact to which I gave rise. And again, when someone has heard my word, he has really heard it. But it is not in his own power to give that word the content and meaning and power in which it will become to him a relevant and enlightening and convincing word. Just as I cannot hasten after it, he cannot hasten towards it. It is the word which he has heard, but as such it has its own history independently of him. It is for him a fact, but it is a fact over which he has no power.

In its independence of the creaturely subject, and of all similar subjects, the effect produced by the creature has its own history. The change brought about in the creaturely sphere when it becomes an event has its own freedom. This history and this freedom are the freedom of God and of the rule of God. God Himself decided concerning my word even before I uttered it. He decides concerning it at the very moment when I utter it. And He will decide concerning it, what it is and what it means, after I have uttered it. He decides concerning my word as an actual effect, a divine effect which undoubtedly is my effect

---

EN426 preceeding
EN427 accompanying

as well, an effect which has become a fact for my creaturely environment, my hearers. He decides concerning the form and compass and meaning and range of this fact, concerning the content and meaning and power of the word which I have spoken as a creature and my fellow-creatures have received as such. This is the assistance, the help, the succour which God causes to be given to creaturely activity. It was not in vain that He preceded it with the decision of His will. It is not in vain that He accompanies it as Lord and Ruler. And now He follows this activity where the operation of the creature itself cannot go, to the result of its activity which is beyond the reach of the creature. It is He who arranges its effect. As an event, as something which is beyond the reach of the creature, the effect of the creature is in the hands of God. It is under the [154] judgment of God. It is quite literally at the disposal of God. It is wholly sub-ordinated to the context of His wider purpose. It is, therefore, in good hands.

   It is this positive aspect which we have to emphasise. The fact that as effect everything is merely what it can be and is for the creature and similar creatures in virtue of the active creaturely subject is only a provisional aspect of occur-rence. And it is only a provisional aspect that in relation to its own effects the creature cannot do more than adopt an attitude of resignation, simply stating that they are this or that, that they have this or that character, and that they came about in this or that way. Just as its activity derived from a higher source than its own planning and determining, and took place under a higher lord-ship and ordaining than its own nature and requirements, so its effects are in higher hands than its own, which at the end and goal of its activity could hardly prevent it from falling. What actually happened is something which God decided and ordained. And since it is God who does it, there is no place for resignation when we consider the effects of the creature, but only for con-fidence and assurance and hope. For the fact that God does it means that for every effect produced by the creature, whatever it may be, there is in the final and best sense of the word a meaningful and good and right application, that not one of these effects is lost, and that no activity of the creature is in vain. It is these effects of the activity of all the creatures of God as willed, produced, assessed and co-ordinated by God which together, in the forward and back-ward context, constitute the expression of His rule and government of the world. In their obvious independence of any creaturely contribution, in the definitive character which appears to be peculiar to them, these effects all serve the divine over-lordship. Their true independence and definitiveness are not proper to them in their relation to the active subjects and their envir-onment, but in the plan and in the process of fulfilling the will of God. Seeing that they belong to this order—and how can it be otherwise when the activity which produced them also belongs to this order?—it is the freedom of God which we have to respect and to love and to honour within them. That it has to be loved and honoured results from the fact that He who is Lord and Master in this respect, too, is not a God who is unknown to us, but the God who is our Father in Jesus Christ, the eternal Father of all His creatures.

3. THE DIVINE RULING

[155]

We come now to the third aspect of the fatherly lordship of God over all His creatures, and one that is decisive for the whole doctrine of the divine providence. The fact of His overruling as such is the fact that in the majesty of His mercy He continually preserves us in being and continually accompanies us with His presence. But this fact itself is one which calls for explanation. The power of God over all things is not a blind power. He does not rule merely for the sake of ruling. He rules as a Father. His ruling is the ruling of His definite and conscious will. Behind it there is meaning and purpose, plan and intention. God has an aim for the creature when He preserves and accompanies it. His preservation and accompanying are as such a guiding, a leading, a ruling, an active determining of the being and activity of all the reality which is distinct from Himself. He directs it to the thing which in accordance with His good-pleasure and resolve, and on the basis of its creation, it has to do and to be in the course of its history in time; to the *telos* which has to be attained in this history. It is He Himself who has set for it this *telos*, and it is He who as Ruler guides it towards this *telos*.

De gubernatione was the title under which the older theology arranged this third discussion within the general framework of the doctrine of providence. And in their definitions of the concept they referred to an *ordinare, moderari, derigere, perducere (in fines et in finem)* [EN428] which embraces all created beings, all their powers, and all their ventures and achievements, their whole existence both in totality and as individuals.

Their main concern—and it must also be ours—was to develop an insight already expressed in the Old Testament when Yahweh is described as King. In the later books of the Old Testament He is "the king of the whole earth" (Ps. 47[8]); "the king of all peoples" (Jer. 10[7], Ps. 47[9] and cf. Rev. 15[3]); "the king of heaven" (Dan. 4[34]). He is "king over the whole world" (Ps. 47[3]) and also "king over all the gods"—that is why He can be called in the New Testament "the great king" (Mt. 5[35]), "the blessed and only $\delta υνάστης$ [EN429], the king of kings and lord of lords" (1 Tim. 6[15]), "the king of the ages" (1 Tim. 1[17]). But in itself the concept of the kingship of God is older than its universal form. And did it first arise only under the so-called monarchy? For if so, how could the institution of a human king over Israel (1 Sam. 8[7], 10[19], 12[19]) be described so sharply as a wrong against God which at best He could only tolerate? Already in Ex. 15[18], at the end of the Song of the Red Sea, we read: "The Lord is king for ever and ever"; and in Num. 23[21], in the second song of Balaam: "He hath not beheld iniquity in Jacob, neither hath he seen perverseness in Israel: the Lord his God is with him, and the shout of a king is among them"; and again in Deut. 33[4f.], in the blessing of Moses: "His inheritance is the congregation of Jacob, and he was king in Jeshurun." What the older form of the concept signified is that only Yahweh, and Yahweh in all His peculiar love and power and readiness to help, is the King of Israel, a King who at best cannot be

---

[EN428] ordering, managing, directing, guiding (with respect to to individual and collective ends)
[EN429] potentate

3. The Divine Ruling

more than represented by a human king, and even then not without danger. And when in Is. 43^{15} Yahweh calls Himself "your Holy One, the creator of Israel, your King," we see that the older understanding did not completely disappear even in the later and universalist. The God who is high above all peoples is also the God of Israel who is great in Sion (Ps. 99^2). And it is as Judge of the whole world that Yahweh is King in Mount Sion and Jerusalem (Is. 24^{23}). The verse in the call of Isaiah has sometimes been described as the earliest example of the fuller understanding (Is. 6^5). It contains the distinctive name of God: The King, the Lord of Hosts, which is later taken up by Jeremiah (46^{18}, 48^{15}, 51^{57}) and Zechariah (14^{16}). This title perhaps indicates the way in which the later and universalist extension arose. For clearly the later universalism was an extension of which the idea was capable and which it required even before it was actually made. The concept is a dynamic one, in keeping with the historical nature of the Old Testament concept of God, and this is proved by the fact that in some sense it swings between two poles, the one at which the enthronement of Yahweh is thought of as still to come, or in the process of coming, or only just come, and the other at which His kingly rule seems to have been long established, and already in full sway. It is this Old Testament idea of the divine kingship which challenges and directs us to expound the divine ruling.

[156]

But in the New Testament the Old Testament idea assumed a far more radical form from which we cannot abstract it in the present context. For in the New Testament we find that the idea of the divine kingship was united with another idea which is certainly present in the Old Testament, but independently and without any attempt at reconciliation. This is the idea of the Saviour-King who is awaited at the end of the age, the Son of Man, the Messiah of the House of David; and He, too, is a figure who to some extent moves from a particularist Israelitish significance to a world-historical and universalist. It is under the concept $\beta \alpha \sigma \iota \lambda \epsilon i \alpha$ [EN430] (cf. the article by K. L. Schmidt in G. Kittel I, 579 f.) that the union is effected in the New Testament. The word $\beta \alpha \sigma \iota \lambda \epsilon i \alpha$ ($\tau \hat{\omega} \nu$ $o \hat{\upsilon} \rho \alpha \nu \hat{\omega} \nu$, $\tau o \hat{\upsilon}$ $\theta \epsilon o \hat{\upsilon}$, $\tau o \hat{\upsilon}$ $\pi \alpha \tau \rho \acute{o} \varsigma$, $\tau o \hat{\upsilon}$ $X \rho \iota \sigma \tau o \hat{\upsilon}$) [EN431] denotes at one and the same time both the dignity and power, the majestic actuality of the divine being and essence and action, which is absolutely supreme over all men and all human ordinances and indeed the whole cosmic structure and process, which breaks through and reveals itself from above, as absolute miracle—and also the concrete, once-for-all actuality of the Son of Man and Son of David, the Messiah and Saviour of the world, *Christus ipse* [EN432] (Marcion) manifested as $\alpha \hat{\upsilon} \tau o \beta \alpha \sigma \iota \lambda \epsilon i \alpha$ [EN433] (Origen). But the New Testament concept of God, actualised now in the accomplished incarnation and epiphany of the Word, is also historically dynamic, and for the first time truly so. At this point too, then, we meet with the same tension as we find in the Old Testament conception of kingship. The $\beta \alpha \sigma \iota \lambda \epsilon i \alpha$ is here, and yet it is not here; it is revealed, yet also hidden; it is present, but always future; it is at hand, indeed in the very midst, yet it is constantly expected, being still, and this time seriously, the object of the petition: Thy kingdom come. In the task before us we must always bear in mind this New Testament development of the conception of the divine kingship.

But in this respect, in spite of all its fidelity to the Bible, the older theology deviated widely from the concept of God as found in the Old and New Testaments, and it paid the inevitable penalty in the striking insipidity of its exposition. According to the Christian sense of the concept *gubernatio* [EN434] the God who rules is not merely a supreme *gubernator*, a

---

[EN430] kingdom
[EN431] kingdom (of heaven, of God, of the Father, of Christ)
[EN432] Christ Himself
[EN433] the kingdom-in-Himself
[EN434] ruling

gouverneur[EN435] who accidentally finds himself in the place of authority and is respected because of this authority. He is βασιλεύς [EN436] and His lordship is βασιλεία. And this means that His position and function and authority and claims and decrees and measures are not merely sovereign, but in their sovereignty they are also right. They are grounded not only in His person, but in the office which is inseparable from His person. They are determined not only by His will, but by the regal content of His will. In the true sense He is the King of the people elected and called by Him, and for their sake He is the King of the universe elected and created by Him. He has associated Himself with this people and cosmos, even accepting likeness and solidarity with it. He has entered into this relationship with a purpose. And it is in this purpose, or as the older divines had it, on the basis of this *propositum*[EN437], that He rules. It is this purpose which makes His sovereignty right, which characterises Him as the One whose office it is to be sovereign, which constitutes the very definite content of His will. For this is no casual purpose, but the purpose of His heart, which corresponds exactly to His being as Father, Son and Holy Ghost, and is therefore the source of all lightness and worth and reality. In this purpose He enjoys and exercises supreme power. And where He does so—and there is nowhere where He does not—this purpose is the meaning of that power. That power is royal power. God does not merely control. He rules, rules as a King rules, rules as He alone, the true King, rules and can rule. And it is because He rules in history, because in Jesus Christ, in the divine-human αὐτοβασιλεία [EN438], He rules in history, and therefore in time, and therefore in the movement from yesterday to to-morrow, that according to the remarkable testimony of the Old and New Testaments His rule or government is always a completed fact from which we derive and which can be known to us, and yet also an imminent event towards which we are only moving and which is still concealed from us.

[157]

This is the first lesson that we have to learn at this point from the biblical conception of God the King and of His kingdom.

When we make the simple but meaningful and momentous statement that God rules, we must understand it primarily to mean that God alone rules. He alone as Creator has the right and power and freedom and wisdom necessary to rule. It is a question of ruling over the reality which is distinct from Him and yet posited by Him, posited by Him and yet distinct from Him. It is a question of ruling over His own creature, and therefore over His possession in the highest sense of the term. And as such, this ruling can be only His work. No one else has any legitimate claim to rule His creature. To no one else is it so closely bound that it has to obey him. No one else perceives and understands and knows it in such a way as to be able to rule over it in any meaningful sense. The rule of another would be an alien rule: usurped, incompetent, weak; the bungling of an amateur. Open or secret opposition to any such rule would be possible, imminent, and probably successful. Certainly it would be legitimate and necessary. And even if the rule succeeded, the final upshot of it would be anarchy and destruction. No one can represent God in this task: no other god, for God is the only God, and there is none beside Him, and even if there were, no matter who or what it might be, not being the Creator, it would not be

---

[EN435] ruler
[EN436] king
[EN437] resolution
[EN438] the kingdom-in-Himself

eligible or competent for this task, or in any way adapted to it; and no creature, for there is no creature, not even the highest of all, which is qualified to take up this office and function in relation to its fellow-creatures; and not the sum total of created reality, for it would not be created reality if it did not need to be ruled, or if it could satisfy this need itself. God Himself is irreplaceably and unexchangeably the Subject of this rule. There are, of course, in and under His rule celestial and terrestrial powers and agents and officers which exercise a limited and provisional rule. But there are no autonomous powers, no powers independent of Him, no powers which are not in some way instituted or authorised by Him and controlled by Him. There is no collateral rule side by side with His, and no counter-rule opposed to it. He alone can rule, and ought to rule, and wills to rule; and He alone does so.

We may now take up the third obvious application of the words in Rom. 11^{36}: *Εἰς αὐτόν τὰ πάντα* EN439. *Εἰς αὐτόν* because *ἐξ αὐτοῦ*, because *δι᾽ αὐτοῦ* EN440, because He alone is [158] the Lord who preserves all things and accompanies all things. But *εἰς αὐτόν* means (P. Van Mastricht) *ad finem suum* EN441. The goal towards which everything moves in its own history is the goal which God alone has fixed and appointed for it. During the course of this history lesser and provisional goals are sought and attained. But there are no autonomous or definitive collateral goals which can be finally sought and attained side by side with or apart from the goal which God Himself has appointed. If there were such goals, they could only be the counter-dominion which had at some time and in some way been set up and established. But the kingdom of God is the only true kingdom. In the attainment of its own collateral ends such a counter-dominion could exist only in the form of a revolt against that only reality—an outstanding revolt, it may be, but at bottom, foredoomed to failure. Any revolt against that reality is as such foredoomed to collapse and failure. And this means that the goal of such a revolt can never be an autonomous, definitive, absolute goal side by side with the divine rule. There cannot be an *εἰς αὐτούς* EN442 or *εἰς αὐτά* EN443 side by side with the *εἰς αὐτόν*. There is no real collateral or counter-government which can limit or compromise the rule of God. We shall have to give separate consideration to the problem of chaos, which is the problem of sin, evil, the devil and demons in their relationship to the divine providence. In this sphere it does seem, of course, as though something like an autonomous collateral government, or counter-government, is at work, limiting and compromising the sole rule of God. But we must already oppose any such idea. Whatever we may have to say concerning this peculiar sphere in its peculiar relationship to the created universe and the government of this universe by God the Creator, one thing we definitely cannot say is that the rule of God meets with competition in this sphere. No matter how seriously we have to take this particular factor, we cannot in any circumstances ascribe to it the dignity of a second creator and ruler of the universe. We do not take it seriously by conceding more to it than the peculiar being of a potent appearance. We can say at once, then, that even the potent existence and reality of this particular factor does not in any way alter the fact that God alone rules. And it certainly does not mean that there are or can be other ends for the cosmos which God has created side by side with those which God has ordained for it. We can properly consider that

---

EN439 all things are to him
EN440 to him because of him because through him
EN441 to the end determined by Him
EN442 to them
EN443 to that

hostile appearance only when we have first made this decision, this conscious prejudgment in face of it. Those who cannot make such a prejudgment in face of chaos as such have already become its victims, as is seen in the fact that in this respect they necessarily limit and deny the divine providence. But if it is denied at one point—and a point so decisive—the providence of God is no longer His providence. We can only confess and maintain this providence when we take as our startingpoint the quite definite and conscious prejudgment that God alone rules. And this means an end of chaos and all its sinister powers.

But the phrase "God alone," although at first sight it might appear to be a rather formal definition, provides us at once with a first and general filling out of the content of the idea of God's ruling. For literally, the fact that God alone rules includes the further fact that He Himself is the only goal which He has appointed for the creature and towards which He directs it. Proceeding from God and accompanied by God, the creature must also return to God. It must; for this is its greatness and dignity and hope. The movement towards God is the meaning of its history. Basically there is nothing greater or richer or finer that we can say concerning its goal, and therefore concerning the goal and intention, the plan and purpose of the divine government, than that God [159] Himself is the goal. For the exclusiveness with which God Himself leads all things to this goal has its justification and glory in the fact that the goal is no more and no less than Himself: Himself as the One who confirms and unfolds and expresses and reveals His wisdom and goodness towards the creature; but Himself in all these things. For all the things which might presumably be called the goal side by side with or apart from Him, all the benefits which He assigns to the creature and which are therefore the end of His government, are simply an expression of Himself in the form of His own attitude and movement towards His possession. He Himself is the benefit of all the benefits which He has intended for the creature, and which He makes, therefore, the end of His overruling of creaturely history. It is not, therefore, because He is jealous of competitors—for how can He be jealous when there are no competitors?—but because of His loving zeal for the creature that He retains to Himself the control of all things and will not and cannot share it with another. There is no other who could have his glory as world-ruler by himself being at the same time and as such the true and supreme and only benefit which can give meaning to world-history. The glory of God is the salvation and glorification of the creature. That is how and why God is the true and great King, and His kingdom an unlimited and unconditioned kingdom.

In this respect we may well describe as the most gifted definition of the *gubernatio*[EN444] that of J. Cocceius (*S. theol.*, 1662, 28, 38). He will not allow that the divine operation has any other goal but God Himself, and he explains it quite simply as the *actio Dei, in qua sapientiam suam in suis operibus demonstrat, sive manifestet misericordiam et clementiam, sive iudicium, sive dominium et potestaiem*[EN445]. Others such as Calov and Quenstedt—and in substance they

---

[EN444] ruling
[EN445] the action of God in which he demonstrates His wisdom in His works, or otherwise manifests mercy and pity, or judgement, or dominion and power

were right—referred to the glory of God on the one hand and the salvation of man on the other: *ad universi huius bonum*[EN446], Quenstedt added. More nicely, the goal of God's overruling will might within this basic definition be identified as the will to reveal His wisdom, i.e., to declare and make manifest the true and original and eternal meaning of His own life, or, to put it in another way, to declare and make manifest His own being in a Word—and that *in suis operibus*[EN447], in the works of creation, which in some sense form, therefore, the consonants and vowels of this Word and thus serve the revelation of Himself. It is only with this purpose, for the sake of this self-revelation, that He rules the creature. And in this way He acts both as a King—to His own glory—and also as a Father, to the supreme good of creation and the salvation of man. The fact that He reveals His wisdom, and therefore Himself, includes all other benefits.

We can now understand rather better what might be called the absolute majesty of the divine rule. Because He rules alone, and because He Himself is the goal to which He directs creaturely history, He is uplifted both above the necessity which rules and is revealed in this history, and also above its real and obvious contingency, above the continuities and discontinuities, above the various uniformities and the various freedoms of world-occurrence: and not merely above the necessity which is known to us, but also above the necessity which is concealed from us or only suspected by us; not merely above the con- [160] tingency which is known to us, but also above that which is concealed from us or only suspected by us. It belongs to the divine ruling of creaturely occurrence that it can be known or conjectured only under this twofold and antithetical aspect: that every generalisation is challenged by the individual factor which will not harmonise with or allow itself to be negated by the general; and that every individual factor is challenged by the great generalisations which compromise its individuality. It belongs to the world-rule of God that this is the case, and this is one of the most cogent reasons why we can believe in this rule but cannot see it. What we can see is only necessity and contingence, continuity and discontinuity, law and freedom, which exist side by side with each other and in opposition to each other. That is why God laughs at all our attempts to see His rule with the eye of our human reason, let alone at our efforts to take the throne and play the part of world-ruler ourselves. This divine laughter rings out over the folly of all our crude or refined human imperialisms, and they will inevitably come to grief on this laughter. One day it will be granted to us to see what now we cannot see—that beyond the antithesis God is the true King and World-ruler, the Lord of all things and everything, the Lord of the general and also of the particular. But we ourselves are not beyond the antithesis. Only God is that, and He always was and always will be. God controls it. God uses it. God avails Himself of it. Perhaps we may risk the illustration that the general and the particular, or however else we describe the antithesis, are as it were the two basic sounds by which God wills to manifest His wisdom, to declare His Word and therefore Himself, in the works of creation. Not only

---

[EN446] to the good of this universe
[EN447] in His works

does He rule over the antithesis. He also rules in it and by it. For it is in and by the antithesis, in the distinction and relatedness, the contradiction and co-existence of the general and the particular, of necessity and freedom—it is in and by all this that there arises creaturely history in time as opposed to a timeless existing. But in and by this antithesis there also arises the ruling of God from His own divine place, from the throne established over this antithesis.

God Himself is not one of the necessities which the cosmic process reveals. Nor is He the sum and substance of them. God's rule is not as it were identical with the logic with which natural events are seen to occur according to the norm of what we call natural laws, although no doubt it is present in and by this logic. Nor is it in the least identical with the logic with which we think of ourselves as morally bound by certain laws, and perhaps by the one all-inclusive, or at any rate formalised law of custom or habit, although obviously it does take this form. Nor is it identical with the logic of world-historical, political or economic developments and relationships, although there certainly are such things, and God's overruling is certainly present in and by them. A clear [161] perception of necessity in world-occurrence does not mean that God has to be explained or approached as though He were so tied to this necessity that He is virtually its prisoner. God rules in and by this necessity, but He also goes His own way through it. He is also Father and King in the contingency and discontinuities and above all the freedom of world-occurrence. This way of God cannot be calculated or foreseen. There will constantly be new surprises even for the wise. God is always doing something new and disclosing something new. He is the God of miracles.

But it is also not the case that God is found only in the extraordinary, in the exceptional, in the unexpected climaxes and nadirs of world-occurrence. The rule of God is not at all identical with a series of events which can be explained only as contingent, individual, unique and thus discontinuous. The marvels of natural phenomena, the inscrutabilities of physico-psychic individuality, the border-line cases of moral conduct and action, the freedom which defies all expectation or prevision in the wider or narrower coherences of history—all these are obviously the work of His rule. And naturally, whatever our view of things may be, we must admit that He can perform true and genuine miracles. But a clear perception of the fact that creaturely history has this aspect and the rule of God this undoubted character, a clear refusal to rationalise or civilise or domesticate the divine control, must not lead us to think of God as subject to a higher power on this side too, as though He were merely the God of the exception, the incident, the individual case; as though He were merely the God of a magical conception of things, the archetype and ideal of every form of irrationalism and surrealism, of daemonic striving and bohemianism. No: God honours law as well as freedom. He loves the law-abiding bourgeois as well as the nomad. And it would be an inversion, a new form of spiritual Philistinism, if we were to wish it otherwise. Those who for the sake of their own spirits preferred a God of disorder to a God of peace were not true prophets (1 Cor. 14$^{32f.}$). Even in the form of the divine activity represented by the prophet He is still a God of peace and not of disorder. And so the victories of common sense, with their rules and inevitabilities and generalisations, are also a part of the revelation of His wisdom, and therefore of Himself. To this revelation there belongs the wonderful revelation which is particularly dear to His Holy Spirit that two and two make four and not five. To this revelation there belongs supreme law, and therefore the necessary application of sound common sense. In short, if God rules in and by freedom, He goes His own way through it, and He rules no less in the necessities and continuities, in the static nature of creaturely occurrence. We cannot identify with the divine dynamic, or substitute for it, that which we ourselves think to be dynamic as opposed to static.

If we are to understand the true character of the divine rule—and if we have already apprehended that He alone rules, and that He Himself is the only meaning and purpose of this rule—then everything turns upon the fact that we must not make deductions from His transcendence over both these aspects of world-occurrence. A deviation either to the right hand or to the left will inevitably lead to the worship of a god which has nothing whatever to do with the true God who is Father and King, that is to say, of an idol. [162]

We must compliment the older Evangelical dogmaticians on the fact that they saw this problem, and tried to steer a middle course between this Scylla and Charybdis. Their doctrine of *gubernatio*^{EN448} was aimed specifically against the two ancient systems of Stoicism on the one hand and Epicureanism on the other, both of which had come to life again as a result of the Renaissance. On the one hand they opposed the Stoic doctrine of fate, and on the other the Epicurean doctrine of chance. It is of a piece with the varying interests of the Reformed and Lutheran schools that the Lutherans broke the more expressly and sharply with the doctrine of fate, and the Reformed with that of chance. But basically the same two enemies were engaged quite decisively on both fronts. There is, therefore, no real point in concerning ourselves with the foreshortenings of perspective with which the Lutherans and Reformed viewed each other, leading the Lutherans to accuse and ridicule the Reformed as Stoics and the Reformed to accuse and ridicule the Lutherans as Epicureans.

But it is instructive to note how the older Calvinists did preserve the doctrine of *fatum*^{EN449} on what was ostensibly, and often actually, their weaker side, in their opposition to a belief in destiny. Even at a first glance it is still suspicious that this school did not *a limine*^{EN450} and absolutely repudiate the concept *fatum*^{EN451}. But they could rightly appeal to Augustine. In *De civ. Dei*, V, 1, 8, 9, Augustine said that in order not to foster false ideas he preferred not to use the word *fatum*^{EN452} to describe the *connexio seriesque causarum*^{EN453} which is ruled by the divine will and power and in which everything occurs. But he also agreed that the use of the

---

^{EN448} ruling
^{EN449} fate
^{EN450} from the outset
^{EN451} fate
^{EN452} fate
^{EN453} structure and sequence of causes

word should not be prohibited. *Fatum*[EN454] derives from *fari*[EN455], and its original meaning is simply *dictum*[EN456]. We may recall Ps. 62[2f.] in this connexion: *Semel locutus est Deus ...* [EN457]. This *semel locutus*[EN458] is the legitimate sense of the concept *fatum*[EN459]. It means: *Immobiliter h. e. incommutabiliter est locutus, sicut novit incommutabiliter omnia quae futura sunt et quae ipsae facturus est*[EN460]. On the ground of this opinion of the father, and in his sense, many of the older Reformed divines were confident, in spite of Lutheran suspicion, that they could rightly speak of a *fatum Christianum*[EN461]. Burmann (*Syn. Theol.*, 1671, I, 44, 29) defined it as the *rerum et causarum a divino decreto dependens ordo et series*[EN462]. He definitely opposed it to the *fatum mathematicum*[EN463], astrological predestination; the *fatum naturale seu physicum*[EN464], the compulsion of sublunary natural causal sequences; and the *fatum Stoicum*[EN465], the depriving of creatures and of God Himself of any contingency or freedom by an all-controlling necessity. H. Heidegger (*Heppe*[2], 206f.) draws a particularly clear and distinct line of demarcation between the Christian view of the divine world governance and the inadmissible sense of the concept *fatum*[EN466]. He makes five points. 1. The divine governance, which is an eternal and free resolve, is located in God Himself, but fate in the inadmissible sense always resides in things, in the series of causes and effects. 2. The divine world-governance is the action of God as *agens liberrimum*[EN467]; therefore far from constraining, things and their order can only follow it. It is therefore unconditionally free to dispose of them *vel praeter, vel supra, vel contra naturam*[EN468]. But fate in the wrong sense confines God to the prison-house of the Parces, not allowing Him to act at all outside the *ordo causarum*[EN469]. 3. Faith in the divine governance distinguishes between the eternal (divine) and the temporal (immanent) necessity of world-occurrence, but belief in fate confounds the two. 4. Within the framework of the divine governance and in the light of a perception of it there is a place both for contingency in general and for a freedom of the human will in particular, but fate and the belief in it involve a mechanisation and destruction of the two. 5. The world-governance of God extends even to the sphere of sin, yet not in such a way as to make God the author of it. But the rule of fate inevitably means that sin is one of the necessities posited by God side by side with others. We have to admit that this Calvinistic demarcation against Stoicism was as clear and exhaustive as possible, and it certainly did not give occasion for any justifiable objections on the other side.

[163]

Similarly it is instructive to note how the Lutherans for their part opposed the Epicurean doctrine of chance. If we wished to be malicious it would be possible, in view of their particular doctrine of the divine *concursus*[EN470], to rank them with the Epicureans just as they

---

[EN454] fate
[EN455] to speak
[EN456] statement
[EN457] God once spoke
[EN458] having once spoken
[EN459] fate
[EN460] He spoke unchangeably, that is, ineffably, just as He knows ineffably everything which will be and those things which He is going to do
[EN461] Christian fate
[EN462] the order and sequence of events and causes depending on the divine decree
[EN463] mathematical fate
[EN464] natural or physical fate
[EN465] Stoic idea of fate
[EN466] fate
[EN467] absolutely free agent
[EN468] either outside of, or beyond, or against nature
[EN469] order of causes
[EN470] accompanying

ranked Calvinists with the Stoics. But in reality they represented the absolute directing of all occurrence by the providence of God just as emphatically as in the light of their particular understanding of providence the Calvinists maintained both natural contingency and human freedom. For instance, when A. Calov (*Syst.*, III, 1659, 6¹, *qu.* 1) discusses the question *Utrum mundus casu vel fortuna, in vero providentia divina regatur?*[EN471], he replies that we can speak of luck or chance only *respectu nostri*[EN472], and in consideration of *causae secundae*, but not *respectu Dei*[EN473]. In other words, we can speak of them only relatively and not absolutely. For providence we can never substitute chance, or the goddess *fortuna*[EN474], which can be represented only as blind, inconsequent, capricious and oscillating, the benefactress of the undeserving. The Epicureans say that it would disrupt the blessedness of the gods and be a weariness to them if they had to concern themselves with the governance of the world. But for God (and here Calov opposes the Epicurean and Neo-Platonist philosophy of Ammonius, Plotinus—and Augustine) the work of world-governance does not carry with it any distaste, or burden, or weariness. The essence of God is always the same, whether He works or not. *Novit ipse quiescens agere et agens quiescere*[EN475] (Augustine, *De civ. Dei*, XII, 17). The Epicureans say that to rule the universe and its excesses would in some sense defile God. But does not the sun shine on filth without itself being defiled? How much less can God be defiled! They then point to the obvious imperfections and anomalies which are found in the world-process. But in respect of these we have to say with Augustine (*De Gen. ad lit. imperf.*, 7) that as there are pauses in a song or musical composition, as there are shades in a picture, so contrasts belong to the perfect beauty of the cosmic whole. And often is it not because of our own limited nature that we do not see how the things which we regard as ἄτακτα καὶ ἀνόμαλα[EN476] are really, *si providentiam Dei spectes*, ἀνάλογα καὶ εὔτακτα[EN477]? Does not the wisdom and goodness and power of God—and here the Lutheran is dangerously near to the Calvinistic heresy!—consist in the fact that God is able to bring forth good out of evil? It is alleged in favour of a doctrine of chance that in the actual course of events things often turn out badly for the good and well for the evil. But according to Scripture God does well to the good when by means of hard experiences He summons them to a knowledge of their sin, to trust in Himself, and to prayer, thus proving their faith, whereas in His longsuffering He either calls the wicked to repentance or in the words of Jer. 12³ keeps them as fatted beasts for the day of slaughter. The final objection is this: Can the existence of evil be brought into line with the world-governance of God? Does it not rather point to the existence of something very like chance? To this Calov replies that for the sake of its freedom God did not make it absolutely impossible for the *creatura intellectualis*[EN478] to sin. His governance, therefore, can take the form of *permissio*[EN479]. And once again we have to remember that, as the story of Joseph shows, even sin can be made to result in the salvation of men. Of the Lutheran, too, we have to admit that within his limits he did vigorously maintain his position on what was for him a very dangerous front.

We have not seen either party on its stronger side. The Reformed were naturally at their strongest when they had to defend their position against the doctrine of chance, the Lutherans against the doctrine of fate. But by listening to what they had to say on what was propor- [164]

[EN471] Whether the world is governed under genuine divine providence by chance or luck
[EN472] with respect to our perception
[EN473] with respect to God
[EN474] luck
[EN475] He knows both how to act while resting and to rest while acting
[EN476] disordered and random
[EN477] if seen from the perspective of God's providence, proportionate and well-ordered
[EN478] rational creature
[EN479] permission

tionately the weaker side, we have been able to grasp the main point at issue. For both sides saw that it was a question of the transcendence of God over every immanent necessity or contingency, generalisation or particularisation—and therefore over fate and chance. And what both parties knew that they had to avoid at all costs was a compromising of the divine world-governance by identifying it with a cosmic principle either on the one side or the other.

It must be granted that on neither side do the arguments lead us to the necessary end: not because most of what is said, and perhaps all of it, is not quite true in itself; but because neither side saw on what basis and therefore with what specific emphasis it had to be said. The proof of all proofs, the height from which the argument really proceeds, is never revealed. And the result is that there remains an impression of flatness, and even of uncertainty. Have the arguments really proved what they set out to prove? However, it is still a fact that our Evangelical fathers did see and tackle the real problem at this point, and it is our present concern to draw attention to this fact.

We have now contended that God alone rules, that He Himself is the goal of His ruling, and that He rules in transcendence over the cosmic antithesis of freedom and necessity. We must now turn to the concept of divine ruling itself. Having clarified the presuppositions we can take as our starting-point the statement that God rules creaturely occurrence by ordering it. In this context the concept order does not have the passive sense of the permanent structure of a thing, its qualities and circumstances, but the active sense of a continuing operation by which an occurrence in time takes place in accordance with a definite plan, and is determined and formed and directed through constantly changing situations and stages. In this sense rule means order. The rule of God is the operation of God over and with the temporal history of that reality which is distinct from God; the operation by which He arranges the course of that history, maintains and executes His own will within it, and directs it wholly and utterly in accordance with that will. The rule of God is the order of God in this active sense. His ordering of all temporal occurrence.

In this connexion the older, especially the Reformed, dogmaticians liked to use the concept of the eternal divine *propositum*[EN480]. We have not to think of this one-sidedly as signifying a fixed divine plan which precedes the creation of the world and therefore all temporal occurrence, finding its subsequent fulfilment in this occurrence. Not one-sidedly: for certainly we must say that everything which occurs in the temporal course of that history is ordered and determined and overruled by God. P. van Mastricht (*Theor. pract. Theol.*, 1699, III, 10, 12) is quite right when he speaks of an already existing *ordo rectus, immobilis, et indissolubilis*[EN481], which no creature can escape. But this does not mean that in all His activity God is not in the fullest sense Himself. It does not mean that He is not the living God. It does not mean that He ceases to will, to decide, to plan, and therefore constantly to order. The plan of God is, and consists, and is divine, in the fact that He actually carries it out, that by His power His decision continually becomes an event. This is its essence and content. The divine activity in time is identical with His willing, so that the divine willing is not somewhere behind this activity but has to be perceived and adored within it, and the activity cannot be a

---

[EN480] resolution
[EN481] an order that is solid, fixed, and indestructible

later fulfilment of His willing, nor can it be under stood as such. It is in the temporal activity [165] of ordering that the divine order is realised, and it is because God causes it to be realised in time that it is eternal. And since in the order willed and executed by Him it is a matter of an eternal *propositum*^{EN482}, this *propositum*^{EN483} has the nature and force of a self-realising *proponendum*^{EN484}, so that we can never represent God as the prisoner of His own design, but He enters in and is known as the absolutely free Lord in the execution of His own design. M. F. Wendelin's definition of the *gubernatio*^{EN485} (*Chr. Theol.*, 1634, 1, 6, 11) is therefore illuminating. It is the *ordinatio, qua Deus ... omnia in ordinem redigit, fines certos et bonas constituendo et media ad fines disponendo et disposita regendo*^{EN486}. The definition is illuminating because in the concept *ordo* it quite rightly reveals the presupposed decision and plan of God as such, but at once connects it with that of the *ordinatio*^{EN487}, the living divine *constituere, disponere, regere*^{EN488}, thus giving it its full dignity and power. It cannot be otherwise if we are not to make temporal history completely empty, removing the living God, fundamentally denying His actual and sovereign and therefore free activity, and making a dead idol of the eternal *propositum*^{EN489}. We have here an exact parallel to what we said earlier about the unity of the divine *praecursus*^{EN490} and *concursus*^{EN491}.

If God orders world-occurrence, then this includes at once the general fact that He controls creaturely activity. This does not mean that He suspends it as such, substituting for it His own activity. That would not be to order it, but to suspend and destroy it. It would result in the undoing, or at any rate the ignoring of His creation. God has created and He preserves the creature, and in so doing He gives to it a sphere in which to work. And the work of the creature is the object of His divine ordering. The fact that He controls it means that He is the Lord of the creature even while it has its own activity. He controls its independent activity as such. He uses it for His own ends. And in so doing He does not encroach too much upon it. He does not do violence to the character and dignity which it has as the reality which is distinct from Him. On the contrary, as the reality posited and existing by Him, this reality is different and autonomous, and it is therefore maintained by Him and given a sphere in which to work. Its character and dignity, its individuality as a creature, are safeguarded in the mere fact that He confirms His relation to it and its relation to Him. He could not pay it any higher honour, nor treat it more seriously, than by acknowledging in face of His own lordship as Creator the fact that He makes the activity of the creature the means of His own activity, that He gives to the creature a part in His own operation. This is the depth of His mercy. This is the greatness of the glory which He intends for it and lavishes upon it. We can and

---

^{EN482} resolution
^{EN483} resolution
^{EN484} proposition
^{EN485} ruling
^{EN486} the determination by which God ... puts all things in order, establishing definite and good ends, arranging means to those ends, and governing those arrangements
^{EN487} determination
^{EN488} establishing, arranging, governing
^{EN489} resolution
^{EN490} preceding
^{EN491} accompanying

must accept the fact, without demur or resentment, that God does actually control creaturely activity. This activity is always the individual and free activity of the creature. The fact that according to its own nature and its place in the context of the existence of fellow-creatures the creature works under law and necessity is a separate issue. Its activity is still free, contingent and autonomous. But God controls the activity in its freedom no less than its necessity. The control of God is transcendent. Between the sovereignty of God and the freedom of the creature there is no contradiction. The freedom of its activity does not exclude but includes the fact that it is controlled by God. It is God who limited it by law and necessity and it is God who created it free. And it is also God who in preserving it gave to it a sphere in which to exercise its freedom. And it is also God who in accompanying it through time is the Lord of the use which it is able to make of its freedom. It does use this freedom. It is active at every moment. But in every moment it uses this freedom on the basis of the particular divine permission to do so. It works always within the framework and the limits of this permission. There can be no question of a compulsion laid upon it. But also there can be no question of an activity apart from this divine permission. In this permission the creaturely freedom encounters the divine freedom from which it derives and in which it finds its natural and self-understood limit. And this limit is at the very place where its creaturely conditioning by law and necessity also has its limit. Freedom apart from this limit would not be creaturely freedom but the freedom of a second god. To claim this kind of freedom would be sin and death for the creature. Hence we have to think of the activity of the creature as an activity which is limited by the permission constantly given to it by God, being directed by a series of permissive acts and therefore controlled by God. If it is not to sin, and in so far as it does not do so, in so far as it does not cease to affirm its own nature even when it does, the creature does not do anything but that which God wills, i.e., it does not do anything but that which God causes it to do even in its freedom by constantly giving to it this permission.

It is even more evident that this is the case, and that it cannot be otherwise, when we remember that all creaturely activity aims at a certain effect. This aiming at an effect is as such a matter of the free striving and willing of the creature, directed of course by God even in its freedom. It is in this striving and willing that the creature is active. But its activity as such is not effecting, and its striving and willing is not attaining and achieving. The end attained and the goal achieved and the bringing about of the effect desired—all these lie quite beyond the striving and willing and working of the creature. It may be that the effect does come and crown the endeavour. But it may be that it does not, or that if it does it has a different form and bearing from that which corresponds with its striving and willing and working. Whether the effect comes, and if so how it comes, is a completely new factor in relation to the activity. This is true whether we consider it from the standpoint of necessity or from that of freedom. And if it is God who controls creaturely occurrence and not fate or

[166]

chance, then we have to say quite baldly that the decisive moment, the very meaning of creaturely activity, its effect, and the goal or end in which it culminates, are all the gift and dispensation of God. The activity can exist at all only on the basis of the divine preservation of the creature. It is constantly [167] formed and directed by the permission given to it by God. And in the same way it is God who decides where and how it will actually culminate, what will be its upshot, as the saying goes. And this is true both when the culmination and effect correspond more or less to the creaturely activity and also when either by its non-existence or its different form and bearing it is a complete surprise in relation to it. In every case the result of the creature's activity is something new, something from God. This is not altered in the least by the fact that it is the result of the creature's activity, and that there is therefore a connexion between the activity and the effect, between the freedom of the acting creature and the ends actually attained by it. At the end of its working the creature itself will always be the same as at the beginning. It will, therefore, be confronted by its own effect. It will reap what it has sown. It will answer for what it has said and done. But what this is, what harvest comes up from the seed, what happens as the goal of its striving and willing and the result of its working, whether it is non-existent or existent, whether it is what was striven after and willed or something quite different, whether it is good or bad, salvation or perdition—this is not the creature's concern. It is decided, decreed and directed by God. Both in general and in particular God Himself fixes for the creature its goals, that is, the goals that it will actually attain. In one way or another it will ultimately realise the divine decree.

This, then, is the divine order of world-occurrence; the controlling of creaturely activity in its execution and also in its results. Since this control is universal, and embraces and concerns all creaturely activity and its effects, it is actually an ordering of everything that happens. If fate were the controller of occurrence it could not and would not guarantee this order; nor certainly would chance. If these are forces at all, they are blind and meaningless, and simply control. But while all ordering is undoubtedly a controlling, not all controlling is necessarily an ordering. God controls, but in so doing He orders. Hence we see that in so far as God determines all creaturely activity and its effects, it is settled that the individual actions which go to make up world history are at least co-ordinated actions, co-ordinated, that is, by His all-embracing ordination.

But if we are to understand the divine rule as the ordering of world-occurrence, we shall have to go much deeper than this. In determining creaturely activity and its effects, God directs it to a common goal, that is, Himself. But this does not mean that particular creatures and individuals and natural and historical groupings and relationships are prevented by Him from existing in their particularity and for particular ends. Nor does it mean that the particularity of their activity and effects, and the endless variety of happenings which go to make up world history as a whole, will later be ironed out and

[168]   destroyed in favour of an all-comprehensive and unified plan. The Ruler of
world history is also the Creator who has given this particularity to the various
creatures and creaturely groupings. And in preserving them, He gives them
room for their particular activity. It is this particular activity which He directs
by His constantly renewed permission. There are also particular effects which
He sets as individual goals that they are allowed to attain. He Himself as the
Lord is so rich that by His lordship He does not need to do violence to any
creature in its particularity—He is far too free not to be able to accept and
joyfully to affirm it in its particularity—and yet at the same time He can direct
all creatures to the one goal, and subordinate all other goals to this one. He
has a unified plan which is in the process of execution, and there is no creature which this plan does not embrace, and which does not in its own place
and its own way help forward this plan. But in its own place and its own way.
This unified plan has nothing whatever to do with a levelling down and flatten-
ing out of individuals and individual groupings. On the contrary, God's
propositum[EN492] and *proponendum*[EN493] relates to individual and their individual
features as such, and it is realised in their purely individual aims. God can
affirm these aims. To each of them He gives its own glory, its lasting worth, its
definite value. And He does so by allowing them to serve this common aim,
and therefore Himself. In so doing, He does not take anything from the creature. He gives everything to it, just as He does not take anything from it but
gives everything to it by directing its free activity and furthering its individual
aims. For what would creatures be without this common aim, without the subordination of their individual aims to this one, without this orientation
towards God? What would they be in all the particularity of their activity and its
effects? God preserves them from the wretchedness of a pointless existence in
and for themselves, from the mutual contradiction and opposition from which
they could not keep themselves, from which in the last resort they obviously
could not be kept by the dominion of fate or chance. The totality of world-
occurrence, and within it all individual happenings, and all individual creatures as the subjects of these happenings, are preserved by Him from the
descent into chaos into which they would at once slide if He were to abandon
these creatures and their activity and effects to mere individualism, if together
with their many aims as given and posited by Him He did not also direct them
to a single goal. In so doing He answers the question: Why does He will to
control all creaturely activity and its effects, and to what extent is this control
really an ordering? The answer is that God controls all things because in and
with and by and for all things He wills and actually accomplishes one thing—
His own glory as Creator, and in it the justification, deliverance, salvation, and
ultimately the glorification of the creature as it realises its particular existence
as a means of glorifying the Creator. He gives it this office by subordinating its

---

[EN492] resolution
[EN493] act of resolve

particular ends to this common end, by allowing it even in the particularity of [169] its activity and effects to have a place in the fulfilment of His own plan.

At this point a further consideration arises. If God directs the individual to Himself as the common goal, this does not mean only that He preserves it from individualism or from the opposition of other individuals. Nor does it mean only that He preserves the totality from chaos. It must also have the positive meaning that a subordination of all creatures to God, the ordination which is thereby effected is also a co-ordination of the creatures one with another, i.e., the creation of a mutual relationship between the individual creatures and creaturely groupings. If they are not abandoned to individualism in their activities and effects towards God, neither can they be in their relationships one with another. We must again emphasise that the fact of this relationship does not encroach upon the individual meaning and right of even the most lowly of creatures. God harmonises and co-ordinates the creatures one with another, but this does not mean that the individual creature has no meaning nor right to exist except as a non-autonomous atom, a mere cog in a machine, a functionary in a collective action, and ultimately and supremely in the one collective action of world-occurrence as a whole. The rule and dispensation and authority of God refer to the individual creature as such. And if we ask what is the practical significance of this direct relation of God to each individual creature, the answer is that, as it shares with its fellowcreatures a common aim, so in its activity and in the effects of this activity it is brought into an active, and passive, and on both sides a positive relationship with them, a relationship of giving and receiving. Not merely in its relation to God, but also in its relation to its environment, it is not isolated and left to its own devices, it is not referred back to itself or responsible to itself. In directly accepting it, in dealing with it directly as the Lord, in making use of it, God incorporates it into the history of creation as a whole. He assigns it a place and status in this history. He gives it continuity and protection and light both from right and left, from near and far, from above and below. He allots it specific functions in which it has to serve Him, i.e., to serve its fellow-creatures, mediating to them continuity and protection and light. This is how the creature can exist by and to its fellow-creatures. It belongs to the glory of God and its own salvation that it can exist in this way. It could not experience the justification and deliverance of its existence in particularity by subordination to God if it did not also know this co-ordination. And it could not resist the latter without resisting the former, without forfeiting its particular meaning and right, and the individual worth of its activity and effects. But as no creature can truly or fully withstand this subordination to God, no creature can truly or fully withstand this co-ordination with its fellow-creatures. That which occurs as an individual action also occurs with this horizontal relationship from and to others. And [170] this co-ordination of creatures is God's ruling. It cannot be understood of itself, and it is not fulfilled of itself. Like the attaining of the effects of individual creaturely actions, it has continually to take place. It is quite certain that neither fate nor chance can guarantee that this will happen. It is God Himself who does it. It is He who arranges that His creatures can praise Him together, and therefore truly as individuals. It is He who arranges this *nexus rerum et actionum*[EN494], and therefore creation itself, both in its individual parts and also in its totality, and in either case for His own glory. And in doing this, He rules and orders all world-occurrence.

Before we turn to the true substance and centre of the doctrine of the divine world-governance, certain distinctions and elucidations must be made which are forced upon us by a study of the history of the doctrine.

We have referred to the subordination of all creaturely occurrence to the one goal posited by God, which is itself God, and also to the mutual co-ordination of its individual moments and actions as thereby conditioned. Now it is clear that both these concepts involve a thoroughgoing relativisation of all creaturely occurrence. If God gives it His own end and ends, then this means that the occurrence has a significance outside itself. It is not moving in circles, but moving towards a destiny which is posited and given from without, whose fulfilment it can only await as it makes this movement. In the most literal sense creaturely occurrence is only preparatory, i.e., it is engaged in a process. The creature itself cannot decide either why it moves or whither it moves. This decision belongs to God who rules the creature. It is His action which determines the world-process in its true and definitive form. This is in a sense the vertical relativisation of creaturely occurrence. God co-ordinates the various events and the various activities and effects of individual creaturely subjects. He allots to each one its own place and time and function in relation to all the rest. And this means that we can speak of the significance of any one thing only in the light of its connexion with all other things. The individual thing is as it were a word or sentence within a context. It is indispensable to this context. But only within this context does it say what is really intended. Only within this context can it be read and understood rightly. And this is in a sense the horizontal relativisation of creaturely occurrence.

But we must be more precise. The twofold relativisation of creaturely occurrence has reference to its relationship to the rule of God. It is God who arranges for each creature its end and ends. Thus He subordinates all creatures to Himself. And under Himself He co-ordinates all the ends, and therefore all the activities and effects of all creatures into a totality. To this extent all creaturely occurrence and all creatures are relegated to a position of lowliness and dependence and relativity. This means that in themselves they are nothing, and that of themselves they can neither mean anything nor do anything. God is the "yonderside" of all creaturely being and activity from which alone the light and life and power of creaturely occurrence can derive. In relation to God the creature is lowly and dependent and relative. But this position of lowliness and dependence and relativity in relation to God does not involve a degradation or depreciation or humiliation of the creature. To be lowly before God is its exaltation. If it is nothing without Him it is everything by Him: everything, that is, that He its Creator and Lord has determined and ascribed and allotted to it; everything that He will continue to be for it, and to execute with and by it. And since this is [171] the optimum of light and life and power, making possible its own value and dignity, it is really everything. If we are to understand the divine world-governance rightly, there is one idea that we can never resist too strongly, one notion that we can never reject too sharply. The fact that God causes His will and His will alone to be done in all things, does not mean that the ruling God is an oppressor who grudges it to the creature even to exist at all, let alone to have its own value and dignity over against him. It is the glory of the creature to be lowly in

---

[EN494] nexus of circumstances and actions

174

relation to God. For when it is relative to Him, it participates with all its activities and effects in His absoluteness. To be able to serve Him alone with all its activities and in all its joint-effects, to be in His hands and under His control only as a means, an instrument, the clay of the potter—this is its direct and original glory. It is exalted in this necessity; it is rich in this poverty; it can go forward on the basis of this humiliation. To exist in any other way but in this relativity towards God would mean misery and shame and ruin and death for the creature. Its full and perfect salvation consists in this subordination to Him, and in this subordination in the co-ordination with its fellow-creatures which is ordained by Him. That this is the case, and the reason why it is the case, will become clearer when we turn expressly to the substance and centre of the divine world-governance.

We must not obscure the positive sense of the relativity of all creaturely occurrence by ignoring the fact that God and God alone is the One in relation to whom the relativity exists. It is from a misunderstanding of the second and horizontal form of this relativity, of the co-ordination of all creaturely occurrence in the divine world-governance, that danger may threaten. We could substitute for the divine work of this co-ordination the very human idea of a cosmic relationship which curves in upon itself. We could substitute for the King and Father who co-ordinates the individual to the whole the abstract idea of the whole itself, the idea of the universe as co-ordinated by God. We could substitute for the dependence of the individual creature and its activity upon God the idea of its dependence upon this *universum*EN495. The first and vertical dependence of the creature in its direct relationship to God could in a sense merge and disappear into the second and horizontal. Its subordination to God could be forgotten in favour of its co-ordination with the creature. Everything depends upon this not happening; upon our understanding the second and horizontal dependence in its connexion with and as a consequence of the first, as a second factor which has its basis in the subordination.

For if the misunderstanding does arise, the individual creature with its action can never be more than a part or organ or function of the whole. It can never be more than an integrating moment, a point of transition, in the existence and history of this whole. It can have its own right and glory and determination only from this whole, only in the course of this history and process, only as a contribution to its development. Its activity and effects, therefore, are only stages in this higher creaturely history. Its task is to serve this history in its own place. Its distinction is to be able to do this in its own way and at its own time and place. Its destiny is to be a particle and function of this whole. And now let us consider whether we could just as easily recast our earlier statements and say that it is the glory of the creature to be lowly in relation to this universal whole; whether the positive sense of the dependence of the creature could be maintained if it were referred only to its co-ordination with other creatures, its being in relation to that whole. Obviously this would be the case only if the whole were itself God, and its life and development were the life and activity of God, granting and guaranteeing a certain honour and freedom to individual creatures and their actions in spite of its superiority to them. But no concept of a creaturely whole, not even that of a whole co-ordinated by God, can ever take the place of God Himself. Even if we think ourselves capable of forming such a conception, it will not lead us by a long way to the knowledge of the God who is the Creator, and therefore the Lord, and therefore the King and Father of the creature. For any creature, to be lowly in relation to this universal whole could mean only to be absolutely less than this whole. For the individual creature, to be subordinated to this whole, and therefore to be lowly and dependent and relative in relation to it, could mean only degradation, depreciation and humiliation. To be ruled by this whole, to be subject to it, to exist and work only because of it and in the service of its aims and ends at this or that [172]

EN495 totality

175

time and place and in this or that way, could mean only the suppression of the individual creature. Why? Because the whole itself is only a creature. To be sure, it is the sum and substance of creation and its activity, and it is therefore an all-powerful creature. But it is still a creature, with no claim to rule either itself or its individual moments or particles, to determine either itself or individual creatures, to be beneficent towards these creatures, or to give them value and honour. The totality of creaturely being and occurrence has need that someone should do this to it. The totality of creaturely being is in no position to do it either to itself or to its individual constituents and their movements. No matter how comprehensively or deeply we understand the life-process of creaturely being, it does not have within itself or by itself the power to do this. It may well be powerful, and power in its own sphere can be achieved only at the expense of the individual moments and stages of its course and development. In the context of this totality individual things can only be small and not great, dependent and not exalted, poor and not rich. And the totality cannot give to them that which it does not itself possess, but of which it has absolute need. We cannot, then, attempt an equation of this kind. Schleiermacher was not the first to undertake this false switching of the doctrine. We can find it here and there in the older Protestant theology. It passes almost unnoticed, and yet the danger is clear. Let me quote as an example *Syn. pur. Theol.*, Leiden, 1624, where we read in *Disp.* 11, 18 f. that it does not belong to the providence of God that each individual thing *ad finem particularem sibi convenientem dirigatur*[EN496], but only that it should attain *absolute*[EN497] the goal *qui toti operi congruit*[EN498]; just as when we burn wood in the house, we do not do something which corresponds to the particular purpose of the existence of wood, but something which corresponds to the purpose of the house in general. The divine world-governance has to be compared to the *providentia*[EN499] with which the father rules his house and the king his country. The *bonum commune*[EN500] is more important to it than the *bonum singulare*[EN501], so that he has to pay more heed to the well-being of the community than to that of the individual. When we consider the objects of the divine *gubernatio*[EN502] there is a difference between those *quibus Deus providet propter seipsas*[EN503], and those *quibus providet propter aliud*[EN504]; just as in a house there are the things about which we are concerned for what they are in themselves (e.g., the family and the family property), and things like tools and vessels which are important only *ad horum utilitatem*[EN505]. In the universe as a whole there are some things which belong *essentialiter*[EN506] to its perfection and therefore must not be destroyed, and others which can and necessarily do perish and therefore last only as long as they have to do in the interests of the first group. This is a type of argument which is very enlightening and most dangerous in its amiable brutality. It is most dangerous because its brutality is far more noticeable than its amiability. And the reason for this is that between the free governing will of God subordinating and co-ordinating all things and individual creatures and their existence there is interposed quite independently an all-embracing third factor, the house or state, *totum opus*[EN507], the *universum*[EN508], the

---

[EN496] be directed to the particular end appropriate to it
[EN497] absolutely
[EN498] which suits the work of providence as a whole
[EN499] providence
[EN500] common good
[EN501] individual good
[EN502] ruling
[EN503] which God establishes for their own sakes
[EN504] which He establishes for the sake of something else
[EN505] for their usefulness
[EN506] essentially
[EN507] work as a whole
[EN508] totality

communitas[EN509], in the interests of which and in relation to which the individual is reduced to a mere means, and in the light of which one thing may be and act *propter seipsum*[EN510] and the other only *propter aliud*[EN511], the one being permanent and the other transitory. It may easily be seen that a divine world-government of this type will inevitably result in the unequivocal abasement of the individual creature or at any rate the majority of individual creatures. This matter is of the greatest practical importance. At the end of the thread which [173] begins here there lies in the ethical sphere the political or economic totalitarianism which has caused us so much anxiety to-day both in its Western and also in its Eastern forms. To avoid this result we must not start along the road which leads to it. The forces at work in this conception of the divine rule are the motives and logic and law of an immanent hierarchy of power and value. The articulated whole is greater and more important than its component parts. Its life is greater and more important than that of the parts. And if this is the case, then amongst the parts themselves there arises the further distinction between those which are more important and necessary for the whole and those which are less. The former can and perhaps will rise up and assert themselves, achieving honour and attaining their own particular ends in so far as they are advantageous to the whole. But the latter can only sink into obscurity, rendering their service to the whole at the proper time, but disappearing like the Moor when they have fulfilled their obligation. It is obvious that countless beings are in this second case, existing only to be sacrificed at the last for the life and progress of the whole and the favoured few. It is all very well for those who for the sake of the whole belong to that earlier class, continuing as its heads and bearers and representatives to the glory of the whole. But it is impossible to equate this much too primitive ordering of the world and society with the divine world-governance.

For if the kingdom of this King means order, if it is, therefore, a kingdom of righteousness, then this means that His plan and will, His co-ordinating of all the activities and effects of all His creatures, does not encroach too much upon any one of them, not one being simply used and then dropped and trampled underfoot. If the ruling of God consists first and foremost in His subordinating of all things to Himself, this means that without prejudice to their mutual relations He deals with each one in a direct and immediate encounter and relationship with Himself. There is not one of them which His rule does not abase, but there is also not one of them which being abased by Him is not exalted. There is not one of them which His rule does not co-ordinate and fuse with others into a single whole, but there is also not one of them which is made only to suffer by this relationship, which is not comforted and gladdened by it, seeing that God Himself created it. For this is what distinguishes the totality which is raised up and sustained and maintained by the divine governance from the unholy hierarchy of a universal collective whole. It is the totality of the freedom and right of each individual. It is the totality in which each individual has to the full its own honour. It is the totality which has its own honour in the fact that no person or thing which it comprehends and orders has simply to do its bit and then to be sacrificed. It is the totality in which each individual moves towards and is certain of its own goal even as it serves the common goal. In this whole there is nothing which at its own time and place and according to its own function is simply instrument, material, cannon-fodder, in the fulfilment of this or that development, or the establishment of this or that *bonum commune*[EN512]; which in practice, then, is merely a means to further the ends of certain favoured creatures, a ruling class within this whole. But as each individual with its own being and activity is co-ordinated with

---

[EN509] community
[EN510] for its own sake
[EN511] for the sake of something else
[EN512] common good

all other individuals under God and according to the will and plan of God (and certainly not without this subordination and co-ordination), by this very fact it has its own independent significance and validity, its own independent value and dignity, being granted that which is good, which is indeed the very best, for it, attaining its own individual ends, and in this way the common end of all individuals. It is in loving and ruling each individual creature that God loves and rules them all. He loves and rules them, therefore, in their inter-dependence, their mutual association. But on this account He does not love and rule them any the less but to the highest degree possible in their particularity and singularity.

[174]   We have to admit that at this point the older Lutherans had relatively a better insight and happier touch than the older Calvinists. They were not so anxious to interpret the individual activity under the divine in terms of the concept *instrumentum*[EN513] (or more commonly, with Thomas Aquinas, *medium*). It was and is legitimate to use these concepts so long as it is clear that it is God Himself who directly and immediately holds these *instrumenta*[EN514] or *media*, which means that their own honour is not merely safeguarded, but constantly ascribed and accorded to them. But the concepts necessarily involved danger once the direct relationship to the lordship of God was obscured, once the notion of a universal whole was interposed between God and the creaturely individual, once the creaturely individual could and indeed had to be understood as a mere instrument and means in the service of this third factor, the universal whole. We have to admit that what the *Syn. pur. Theol.* says on the point does tend at least to obscurity in this respect.

    On the other hand, it was of value that the older Lutherans (e.g., Calov, *Syst.*, III, 1659, 6, 1, *qu.* 2, and Quenstedt, *Theol. did. pol.*, 1685, I, 13 *sect.* 2, *qu.* 1) laid particular stress upon the thesis that the divine world-governance extends to all things and to each individual thing, and therefore *ad singularia et vilissima quaeque*[EN515]. They were again wrestling with Democritus and Epicurus, but also with Aristotle and a text ascribed to the Latin father Jerome; with the view that some things and events are too small, too insignificant, too unimportant, indeed too futile, for us to be able to suppose that the Godhead will in any way be interested in them. *Minima non curat praetor*[EN516]. Will God really concern himself with the growth of caterpillars in the grass sprouting in the province of Saxony in any given year? Or with the thread hanging from the beggar's coat? Indeed, He does, they quite rightly answered, with a reference to Augustine (*S. 6 in Matth.*): *Videte, quia minima non contemnit Deus; nam, si contemneret, non crearet;*[EN517] and of course to all the texts in which we are told that God clothes the grass of the field (Mt. 6^{30}), that He feeds the ravens (Ps. 147^9), that He does not allow one sparrow to fall to the ground without His will (Mt. 10^{29}), that He numbers even the hairs of our heads (Mt. 10^{30}), that He keeps all our bones (Ps. 34^{20}), that He knows our downsitting and uprising (Ps. 139^2). The saying in 1 Corinthians 9^9 did cause a little difficulty, for expounding Deuteronomy 25^4 ("Thou shalt not muzzle the mouth of the ox that treadeth out the corn") Paul asks: "Doth God take care for oxen? Or saith he it altogether for our sakes?" But it was rightly perceived from Psalm 36^6 that God does take care for the ox ("O Lord, thou preservest man and beast"), and the saying of Paul was rightly explained within the whole context of the Old Testament as a prophecy of the events and the ordering of events attested in the New. What was meant is that although God takes care for the ox with one kind of care, and in some sense a "typical" care, with the other and true care He is concerned for the preachers of the Gospel with whose sustenance the apostle is inci-

---

[EN513] instrument
[EN514] instruments
[EN515] to things both particular and common
[EN516] The boss is not concerned with the details
[EN517] You see that God does not despise little things; for if He did despise them, He would not have created them

dentally dealing in the context of 1 Corinthians 9. The final reply to the objection was a counter-question: What does great or small mean to God? Both small and great, both what appears to us to be mean and what appears to us to be important and outstanding, are alike the work of God and His possession, and therefore worthy to be ruled by His wisdom and to be used in some sense in the fulfilment of His purposes.

It is clear that the older Reformed divines could not and indeed did not differ from this view. But if we take these texts and the whole insight seriously, our thinking cannot be along the lines to which some of the Reformed seemed to approximate rather too closely. Nothing, however small or insignificant, can be understood simply as a means to fulfil the purpose of a greater whole, and therefore of other better-placed creatures. Quite irrespective of its being in relation with the whole, indeed quite irrespective of this relation, we have to ascribe to each creature its own immediacy towards God and therefore its autonomous validity and worth. The command in Mt. 18[10] not to despise one of these little ones thus takes on the [175] character of a basic principle which apart from its direct meaning in the Gospel can be applied indiscriminately and consistently to creation as a whole. Even amongst the older Lutherans we do not find the resultant repudiation of the contrary opinion in the form in which it is required, so that although their answer to the question did in fact provide a useful stimulus to further thinking, they did not provide any proper safeguard against the false ideas which threatened at this point.

But it is now time not so much to leave or abandon the formal consideration of the divine ruling which has so far engaged us as to complete it by turning to the material content of what we have just said. What we have said demands completion in this way. When God rules all creaturely occurrence as King and Father, what does this really mean? What is it that actually happens? What do we mean when we confess God as Lord over all things, when we confess God alone, God in Himself, God in His transcendence over all immanent contradictions, God as the One who subordinates all things to Himself, and therefore co-ordinates them one with another, God as the One who is and does these things in the same immediacy both to the whole and also to the individual? How do we arrive at the point where we can confess the reality and unity and exclusiveness and totality of such a ruling, and God Himself as such a Ruler? Where are we to turn to find the assurance that what we have said is actually the case? And finally, what does it mean for us to fulfil this knowledge? What is it that the Christian community says both to its own members and to all other men when, in and with its message, and as an integral part of the truth which it proclaims, it has to tell them that God is the Father who exercises His lordship in this way over and with all creation, that in this way He is the Almighty, the Creator of heaven and earth? The Christian community confesses this truth as something which is well-founded and not unfounded. It is a truth which could not be perceived or confessed at all unless its foundation were known. And in dogmatics generally, and therefore in the present context, it can be affirmed as something which is well-founded and not unfounded. And all that we have said so far has been said in the light of the fact that it has this solid foundation. It is this which has guided us in all that we have said, both in general and also in detail, pushing us forward in one definite direction, and keeping us on the right lines. It is this which has enabled us to grasp the very idea of the divine ruling, to think it through with a tolerable order and consistency, and to express it, so far as we can say this of any idea. But so far we have not examined the solid foundation which we have had constantly in view. So far we have not expressly related the idea to the reality which distinguishes it from a mere idea, and it may be an empty one. No order or consistency can distinguish it from a merely empty idea. It is distinguished in this way only as its relationship to this foundation, to the reality envisaged in it, is expressly revealed. It is only as the [176] community sets in this relationship its confession of the Father, the Almighty, the Creator of heaven and earth, only as each individual member of the community sets in this relationship his perceiving and confessing of this God, only as dogmatics sets in this relationship its thinking about Him, that the thinking and perceiving and confessing become an activity filled with real meaning.

> The weakness of the older orthodox theology was that in all its doctrine of the divine providence, and of the creation and man, and earlier of God and the election of grace, it believed that it could dispense with this relationship either entirely or almost entirely. It thought and spoke about the divine ruling as about an idea. With all its divergence from individual philosophical systems, its development of the concept was far too like the philosophical development of a concept. In spite of the testimonies from Scripture, it was content with what was basically a quite formal and abstract consideration of the subject. It did not make it at all clear to what it ought really to be looking as a Christian theology, and more often than not it did not even look there, but somewhere else. This was the root of all its uncertainties and deviations, of all the dangers to which it more or less openly exposed itself as it proceeded, and above all of the insipidity or colourlessness of all its thinking to which we drew attention at the outset. The One who is described as King in Holy Scripture is acknowledged to be such, but He does not act as such. At any rate, it is not at all clear that He controls dogmatic thinking concerning Himself. At many points He seems in fact not to control it. What does control it, and what is passed off as the authority which controls the whole universe, seems rather to be the concept of a supreme being furnished with supreme power in relation to all other beings. And the credibility of what is ostensibly said about the rule of God seems to depend upon the existence of this being. With regard to this, we may say: 1 that the existence of such a supreme being is itself highly doubtful, and therefore the credibility of a doctrine of God's rule based upon it can only be very conditional; and 2. that such a doctrine of God's rule cannot be a Christian doctrine because the God of Christian teaching is certainly not identical with that supreme being. If we are still under the shadow thrown by this twofold difficulty, it is high time that we moved away from it.

The Father, the Almighty, the Creator of heaven and earth, about whose lordship over all things we have been speaking, is the King of Israel. There in one normative biblical concept we have the solid foundation of all that we have said, the foundation which we have now to unfold, and to which we have now to relate all that we have said. The King of Israel is the King of the world. It is His will that is done in the ruling of all creaturely occurrence. It is He who is the Lord over it. It is He who is transcendent over all contradictions. It is He who subordinates all things to Himself, and co-ordinates them one with another. It is to Him that we must look if we are to have assurance that everything really is as we have described it. And a knowledge of this matter means a knowledge of Him which presupposes and includes and involves everything that is necessary for a knowledge of Him. The fact that it concerns Him, the King of Israel, is what distinguishes all that we have so far thought and said about the divine ruling from a merely empty idea, or from the uncertain and in any case unchristian idea of the power and activity of a supreme being. If it [177] concerns the King of Israel, we are on solid ground and under sure leadership. The King of Israel is the God who rules all things.

At its simplest, this is the definition with which we have to fill out our hitherto formal consideration. And again, we can elucidate the definition most clearly and simply by saying that the God of Israel, and therefore the God who rules all things, is the Subject whose speaking and acting is the source and also the object and content of the witness of the Old and New Testaments. To put it in another way: The King of Israel is the One who according to the witness of the Old and New Testaments spoke the "I am," and in speaking it actualised it for seeing eyes and hearing ears by acts of power within the created cosmos and human history. The concrete name "the King of Israel" covers both the Old Testament and New Testament forms of the spoken and actualised "I am" in which we have to do with the Subject of the divine world-governance.

It may be noted that with this definition and its elucidation the idea of the divine world-governance, whatever may be our attitude towards it, does at least cease to be a mere idea and is related to a reality. The form of the idea acquires concrete substance. The colourless idea takes on colour. And this takes place when it is seen that in the idea of the divine world-governance the Subject God bears this concrete name. To apprehend and affirm the idea we have to think of definite periods in human history as this name leads us. And we have to think of definite places—the land of Canaan, Egypt, the wilderness of Sinai, Canaan again, the land on the two sides of Jordan, Jerusalem, Samaria, the towns and villages of Judaea and Galilee, the various places beyond in Syria, Asia Minor and Greece, and finally Rome. We have to think of definite events and series of events which according to the witness of the Old and New Testaments actually took place at these periods and in these places, relating them always to the spoken and actualised "I am." And then necessarily we have to think of the concrete Scripture which bears witness to these events, the text of the Old and New Testaments. And if we cannot apprehend and affirm the idea of the divine world-governance, then quite concretely this means that we stand in a negative relationship to these events which took place at definite periods and in definite places, to this reality, and to this concrete Scripture. Belief or unbelief in the divine world-governance, whether we do or do not apprehend and confess it, is no longer a matter of the right or wrong development of the idea, but of the right or wrong relationship to this reality to which the idea has reference, and therefore to these definite events as according to the equally definite witness of the Old and New Testament Scriptures they took place at definite periods and in definite places. For the Subject who speaks and actualises the "I am" in these events, the King of Israel, is the God who rules the world.

[178]   Thomas Aquinas (*S. theol.*, I, *qu.* 103, *art.* 2) postulates and in his own fashion tries to prove that the Subject that rules the world and directs it to Himself as the one supreme end and goal is necessarily *aliquid extra mundum*^{EN518}, a *bonum*^{EN519} or *principium extrinsecum a toto universo*^{EN520}. We can and must accept this postulate. For if the Subject that rules the world is not recognisable and actually recognised as something distinct from the world, how can it really be a Subject that rules the world and posits itself as the goal of all world-occurrence, and how can it be recognisable or recognised as such? But we may question whether this quite justifiable postulate ought to be filled out by the particular concept of God which Thomas presupposes and uses in his own demonstration. For this concept of God, the concept of a being in Himself, quite independent of all other being and to that extent absolutely superior to it, is indeed an attempt to point away beyond the world. But the reality of this supramundane being cannot be reached by an attempt of this kind. For the only reality that we can point to in this concept is that of the world as it attempts to transcend itself, so that even in such an attempt it is still the world and not this *principium extrinsecum*^{EN521} which might as such be the Ruler of the world and recognisable and recognised as such. We thus have a concept of God which demands proof of the existence of God. If it is to be recognisable and recognised as a being which is different from the world and therefore qualified to be its Ruler, something more is needed and something more must be perceived than the attempt of the world to transcend itself in this concept. What is needed is that the being itself should transcend the limit and self-knowledge of the world, and thereby demonstrate itself. For the idea of the world-governance of such a being can only have substance, the power postulated by Thomas, if by its own initiative and activity and revelation it actualises and makes perceptible the reality of its supramundane being over against the world, thereby demonstrating itself in the midst of the world. This supramundane being can make itself present in the world only by free grace. And it is the source and object and content of the biblical witness that this did actually occur. Of course, this witness does not refer us to the so-called natural proofs of God's existence in which Thomas found support at this critical point. It witnesses to the very intramundane and temporal and spatial "I am" as the work and revelation of grace in which the *principium extrinsecum*^{EN522}, which can as such be the World-ruler, has actually demonstrated itself to be such; intramundane and temporal and spatial as opposed to the concept of God as an extramundane reality.

This is why in the biblical witness the divine world-governance is related to the King of Israel. From a philosophical standpoint the naivety with which it does this is highly objectionable. But it is in this naivety that its real strength lies. For it does not find any difficulty in the counter-question whether this supramundane being who as such can rule the world really exists. No second postulate is needed to fill out the first. No resort to natural proofs is needed to fill out the second postulate, and by means of the second the first. The outfilling is itself the starting-point. The basis is the intramundane self-demonstration of the extramundane God and World-ruler. And dogmatics has to take over this naivety and strength in its own thinking and utterance. There is no alternative if it is to be Christian thinking and utterance. If we are really to have a World-ruler, one who is capable of world-dominion as a *principium extrinsecum*^{EN523}, we have to relate the matter to the King of Israel.

---

^{EN518} something outside of the world
^{EN519} good
^{EN520} principle that is extrinsic to the universe as a whole
^{EN521} extrinsic principle
^{EN522} extrinsic principle
^{EN523} extrinsic principle

In the Old Testament form of the spoken and actualised "I am," the King of Israel is the Lord who made a covenant with the twelve tribes of Israel, thus making them one people and His own people. "I am the Lord thy God, which brought thee up out of the land of Egypt, the house of bondage" (Ex. 20²). In this event He is the One who initiates the history of this people, and in all that follows He is the One who directs and fulfils it. He does this in such a way that He separates it from other peoples and keeps it as a people to serve Him. To that end He gives it His Word as commandment and promise and warning. But in return, from the very outset and in the whole course of its history, He experiences at the hands of this people only a lack of recognition, confusion with the idol-gods of the nations, ingratitude, disobedience, unfaithfulness and backsliding. The One who elected Israel has to be and is content continually to be rejected by Israel; to be its despised and rejected King. And by that very fact Israel is itself delivered up, putting itself in the sphere of the legitimate wrath of its King. Hence its history is simply a series of the predicted and inevitable judgments of this King. But he is still its King. The unfaithfulness of Israel calls down upon it the judgment of its King, but it cannot alter His faithfulness. He is still faithful and gracious to Israel, confirming his election and calling, even when He chides and judges Israel. He does not cease to separate and keep and sanctify and bless this people. Nor does His Word cease. His prophets rise up continually and pronounce it. And there is always a remnant which, even in its solidarity with the people in sin and judgment, perceives that the King reigns, remembering that He has done so in the past and confident that He will do so in the future; which pays heed to His Word and recognises in the adversity of the people the judgment of its King; which humbly acknowledges His judgment to be just and even in judgment recognises His grace, and therefore outside and alongside His judgment the continuance of His favour; which on this account can still rejoice even in its isolation, praising the King on behalf of the whole people; which sets its hope upon Him and has therefore a living hope. This is the kingly rule of God according to the Old Testament witness: a history which is clear in itself, yet very obscure; a history which is a whole in itself, yet obviously incomplete ; a history of the presence of God at its most actual, in a form which apparently cannot be surpassed in directness, and yet a history only of the expectation, implicit here and explicit there, of a future towards which it is only moving.

And in the New Testament form of the spoken and actualised "I am," the King of Israel is the same Lord of the same covenant: except that now he illuminates the obscurity which dominated the history of covenant in its Old Testament form, removing the incompleteness of it and fulfilling the expectation; except that now, in utter discontinuity with all that Israel has been and accomplished, He Himself in free grace directs to its goal the covenant which He had instituted and faithfully maintained and which Israel had constantly broken. "I am—the way, the truth, and the light" (Jn. 14⁶). Now the King Himself comes,

[180] and He comes from Nazareth in Galilee, from the place where the Old Testament obscurity was most pronounced and backsliding and the divine judgment most evident. Hence the sayings: "Can any good thing come out of Nazareth?" (Jn. 1[46]); "Shall Christ come out of Galilee?" (Jn. 7[41]); "Search and look: for out of Galilee cometh no prophet" (Jn. 7[52]). And yet from that very place there has come a good thing, *the* good thing; there has come a Prophet, *the* Prophet of whom all the other prophets were the forerunners—even though he was born at Bethlehem, as the son of David and heir of David's throne. From this place there has at last come the Israelite who does that at which the whole history of Israel aimed, repaying faithfulness with faithfulness to the King and Lord of the covenant. And late as it is, and only in the one man, is not this the true being and achievement of Israel? Indeed it is, and to the extent that there lies in this One Israel's justification in the day of judgment. But Israel will reject this last and true Prophet from the company of His loyal predecessors—reject Him more consciously and drastically than any of the others. It will remain only too true to the attitude in which it always despised and rejected its King. "Jesus of Nazareth, the King of the Jews" (Jn. 19[19]), will be the pagan irony to which Israel will deliver up the One in whom it is justified. And by this attitude Israel will prove that its justification is in no sense its own work, but only His kingly mercy, the remission of sins, the fulfilment of its yearning with the answering of the prayers of the remnant, not the acknowledgement of what is finally revealed to be its own righteousness. No: in the person of the one loyal and righteous man, the one true Israelite—and this is the new feature in the New Testament witness—King Yahweh Himself has come into the midst of His people on behalf of His people, to turn this people to Himself, to confirm in His own person its election and calling, to vindicate His kingly honour. Hence the confession: "Rabbi, thou art the Son of God; thou art the King of Israel" (Jn. 1[49]). He is the King whose faithfulness to Israel has triumphed in the fact that He Himself has become flesh in the one Israelite. He is the King who in the person of the one Israelite has Himself achieved the faithfulness which His people owed Him. He is the King who judged the people in the crucifixion of the One who is His Son, but in so doing, Himself fulfilled the Law and justified His people. This is the King of Israel according to the witness of the New Testament, and this justification of Israel by Him is His kingly rule. And now the New Testament community, whose foundation is a part of the object of this witness, is the community of this King of Israel; the people which consists of those who have seen His glory in the new and absolutely clear and full and definitive form of the one Israelite, and who have found in Him both their own salvation and the salvation of the whole world. It is this community which from amongst Jews and Gentiles He has called to faith in Himself by His own Word and Spirit, which in its weakness has put itself in the position to rely only upon His grace, and to praise His grace in its life and

[181] by its witness, both with and without words. This New Testament community is the new Israel: Israel, because those who are gathered within it live by the

justification which has come to Israel in this One; the new Israel, because even if they are Jews they cannot do this on the basis of their birth and circumcision as Jews, but only on the basis of the fact that the King of the Jews has Himself come on His people's behalf and called them, only because in this coming on His people's behalf He has come on behalf of the whole world. This is why the people and possession of the King is the community not of the Jews only but also of the Gentiles; the catholic, the ecumenical, the universal Church; a community which is destined to be a shining light to the whole cosmos, knowing what the world does not know, and looking forward to the culminating revelation of the King and therefore to the end of all His ways.

This is the "I am" spoken and actualised in world history according to the witness of the Old and New Testaments. Concerning the mutual relationship of the two forms we can say only this. In the Old Testament it is primarily the question of an all-powerful Word which has been declared. The King reveals and proclaims His election and will and love and command. He does, of course, confirm these things by what He does in the history of His people. But the characteristic relationship of His people to Him seems to be decisively fixed by the "Hear, O Israel," and the specific servants of God in the midst of Israel are the prophets who mediate His kingly calling and Word. As against that, in the New Testament it is predominantly the question of an all-powerful act which has come to pass. The King Himself has come; He has brought a sacrifice for His people, and in this way He has demonstrated Himself to be the Victor. In so doing He does, of course, speak and teach and command. But the beholding of His glory seems now to be the decisive thing in the relationship of His people to Him, and His specific servants are now the apostles who carry the news that He has appeared, who tell what has occurred, and does occur, and has yet to occur. Thus in the Old and New Testaments, and in the movement from the one to the other, we see the King of Israel treading always the one path. In His movement from the one to the other He has in a sense His own history, but in both He is obviously one and the same, so that in both His Word and act belong together. In both the ascendancy which marks Him as a King is the ascendancy of His free grace. How free it is, is shown in the Old Testament by all that makes it so obscure and incomplete, so much a witness only to expectation, with the shattering demonstration of the contrast between the faithfulness of the King and the unfaithfulness of His people. How much it is grace is shown in the New Testament by all that in contrast to the Old makes it so obviously a witness to fulfilment, with its comforting demonstration of the way in which the faithfulness of the King has itself overcome the unfaithfulness of His people. But in both it is both free and also grace, just as in both it is both [182] Word and act. And in both it is supreme and royal. According to Old and New Testaments alike the "I am" is an act of government.

But the phrase "an act of government" is far too weak and casual and relative to describe that which all the biblical witnesses saw and to which as prophets and apostles, and to some extent as both, they all tried to bear witness. The great "I am" as a royal Word and act, as the irruption of the supremacy of free grace to which they testified, is far more to them than an individual act of government beside which, and independent of and perhaps superior to which, there might be other acts of government by other subjects, or beside which we might have to see and expect other acts of government by the same Subject, but this time of a completely different and perhaps totally antithetical character. No: in the act which those witnesses heard and saw, with its definite character of free grace, there takes place the one rule of the one Subject, to which all other in some sense ruling subjects and their power and rule are absolutely subordinate, which is indeed normative for all other rule by the one Subject. All actual rule in this world can be only the rule of this one Subject, and therefore a rule which has the one form and purpose peculiar to this Subject. The fact that the Old and New Testament witnesses were wholly and absolutely claimed by what they heard and saw of the King of Israel who met them in this Word and act of His is sufficiently clear of itself. But we must look further, and we see that for these witnesses other kings, if there are such, cannot possibly be the rivals of this One, for the throne at whose steps they stand is uniquely exalted. And again, they quite definitely do not reckon with the possibility that this King might display a different character, or that different acts of government might proceed from this throne. In His encounter with them, He and His rule claim them totally because He alone is in a position to do so, and because in this encounter He allows them to see Him as the One who will be the same at all times and in all circumstances. The King of Israel attested in the Old and New Testaments is a King who is absolutely superior as compared with all other kings, and absolutely consistent in Himself. For the biblical witnesses that which is peculiar to His kingdom, the supremacy of His free grace, which the Old and New Testaments attest as the meaning of these particular events, is something which undoubtedly stands behind and above all things, behind and above world-occurrence in general. There is no other who in fact rules as the King of Israel rules, and outside this particular history the King of Israel does not rule differently or with a different purpose than He does within it.

[183] This is the insight which must be the filling out and substance of the Christian doctrine of the divine *gubernatio*[EN524]. And we are again faced with a basic insight without which a Christian doctrine of providence as opposed to a mere scheme of things would not even be possible, and in the light of which we have already considered the sustaining and accompanying activity and will of God in and with and over world-occurrence. The rule of God as opposed to the control and outworking of a natural or spiritual cosmic principle is characterised by the fact that it is here in the particular events attested in the Old and New Testaments, in the "I am" spoken and actualised by the King of Israel, in the covenant of free grace instituted and executed, promised and fulfilled by Him, that it has the centre which controls and is normative for everything else.

[EN524] ruling

3. *The Divine Ruling*

The power which rules the world is the power which is active and manifest here as the power of this King. There is no other power equal to this power. And as His power it is never different in any way from this power. To understand the divine governance we have to observe a twofold rule.

1. We have to look at world events in general outwards from the particular events attested in the Bible, from God's activity in the covenant of grace which He instituted and executed in Israel and in the community of Jesus Christ. The particular events do not take place only for themselves, but as the inner basis of all creaturely occurrence. They take place as the fulfilment of the meaning of this occurrence, as its preservation and deliverance and glorification and manifestation—an anticipation of what the totality of heaven and earth, and what man on earth and under heaven, is one day to be according to the will of God. These particular events are not a final end, but an original and pattern of the general events. They are not an end in themselves, but a ministry in and to the whole of God's creation. Already in the Old Testament the King of Israel is secretly the King of all the nations and of the whole earth. In the New Testament His coming on behalf of His own people means that He is active and manifest as the Lord of a community of Jews and Gentiles, as the Light of the world. Therefore when we have to do with the particular history of the covenant and salvation as it took place to and in and of Jesus Christ, we cannot make it into a private history. For if we did, we should be denying the fact that in this history, if we hold to the biblical testimony concerning it, we are dealing with the one act of rule which as such embraces and determines all other events over and above its own fulfilment, which even in its particularity is the centre of a circumference, of all creaturely occurrence both in heaven and on earth. We cannot deny this; we cannot try to think abstractly of the events described in the Bible, of the supremacy of free grace as it is there spoken and actualised, without completely misunderstanding, or worse still denying the majesty and sovereignty, the "I am," of the King of Israel, as it was perceived and clearly enough extolled by the biblical witnesses

2. We have to look back from the world events of nature and history, both far and near, both above and below, to the particular events which are attested in [184] the Bible, to the history of the covenant of grace from the promise which initiated it to its final fulfilment. The general events do not happen for their own sake. They do not form a self-contained and self-motivated whole as contrasted with the particular events. There is no such thing as secular history in the serious sense of the word. What we have tried to describe as such abstractly, the history of created reality as such, occurs concretely only as an outward platform for the fulfilment of the particular events. The general events have their meaning in the particular. It is only as the particular events take place that they are preserved and delivered and secretly filled with glory, and move towards the revelation of this glory. In the particular events the divine will and plan for them is anticipated. They are not, therefore, a final end, an end in themselves; they serve rather as the copy and reflection of the particular

187

events. In the Old Testament the nations have a place only as instruments of the will of God for Israel, and in expectation of their appointed salvation as it is to be proclaimed in Jerusalem. The earth and all that is in it is important only because in its totality it belongs to the Lord who comes from Zion. And in the New Testament the Gentiles who have come into the community have no glory of their own (Rom. 11^{17}), but are only engrafted branches which are borne by the root Israel (not the reverse). And the earnest expectation of all creatures waits for the manifestation of the sons of God (Rom. 8^{19}). For the very same reason that we are not allowed to make the history of the covenant a private history, we are also forbidden to make universal history private over against it. If we did, we should have to reckon with other and rival Kings, or with an inner instability of the King of Israel. Again, and from a different angle, we should be denying the public nature and claim of what did occur, and does and will occur, in the history of the covenant and salvation to and from and in Jesus Christ—in the greatest particularity, to be sure, yet not apart from but at the very centre of creaturely occurrence. We should be failing to recognise that in all creaturely occurrence—however far it may seem to be from the "I am" of the Bible—we have to do with the circumference of this centre. We should be forcefully wrenching away that circumference from the supremacy of free grace which rules it from this centre. Again, we should be betraying the most central content of the prophetic and apostolic message. We should be acting as if the King of Israel had not spoken or acted, as if an act of government had indeed taken place, but not *the* act. And that is something which we cannot allow from this standpoint either.

We can now define our position in relation to two conceptual distinctions constantly met with in the older theological doctrine of the *gubernatio*[EN525]. On the one hand, a distinction is made between a *providentia generalis*[EN526] and a *providentia specialis*[EN527], and on the other between a *providentia ordinaria*[EN528] and a *providentia extraordinaria*[EN529]. By *providentia generalis*[EN530] is meant the divine government of the whole world-order as such, and by *providentia specialis*[EN531] the government of the Church and the faithful and men generally. By *providentia ordinaria*[EN532] is meant the divine government as it occurs within the framework of what we can recognise as the laws which underlie the cosmic events of nature and history, and by *providentia extraordinaria*[EN533] the divine government in so far as it takes the form of miracles.

From a different standpoint, these distinctions might be applied to the two spheres of which we have just been speaking—the activity of God on the one hand in the history of the covenant and salvation, and on the other in history generally. But the order in which the

[185]

[EN525] ruling
[EN526] general providence
[EN527] special providence
[EN528] ordinary providence
[EN529] extraordinary providence
[EN530] general providence
[EN531] special providence
[EN532] ordinary providence
[EN533] extraordinary providence

concepts are brought up makes it clear that there is something wrong. For if we are on the right track in relation to the divine world-government, that is, if we are on the track indicated to us by the Bible, we shall have to reverse the order, i.e., to move from a consideration of the *providentia specialis*[EN534] or *extraordinaria*[EN535], i.e., salvation history, to that of the *providentia generalis*[EN536] or *ordinaria*[EN537], i.e., world-occurrence in general; and then back again from the latter to the former. In fact, the general with its recognisable laws has been treated as if it were the norm, and the particular (this particular) as if it were only a single application, or from a different angle, a single infringement of the norm. We can explain this procedure only on the presupposition that the subject of the whole activity was thought of in terms of a speculative supreme being and not of the God of Holy Scripture. In this connexion we may add that simply to bring the two spheres under the one concept *providentia*[EN538], to reduce them to single common denominator, is a confusing levelling down of the problems involved. Certainly the concept "providence" can be used in a wider sense, and we can then say that the divine government of this particular sphere, the divine control of the history of salvation, is also an act of divine providence. But it is certainly something more and something quite other than a particular instance of general and orderly world-governance corresponding to the norm, or even an isolated case contradicting it. The whole concrete difference between these particular visitations and the general as it dominates all Scripture is that in the one case we are dealing with the centre, in the other with the circumference; in the one with the controlling original, in the other with the subservient copy; in the one with the particular as it is normative for the general, in the other with the general as it stands under the law of the particular. And this difference is a vital insight which is obscured when the two spheres are brought equally under the one master-concept *providentia*[EN539]. But further, if we restrict this sphere of the particular only to the Church, or to men generally, or, from another angle, to miracles, then we are obviously missing the decisive thing, the history of the covenant and salvation, to which even the divine miracles belong as representative of its particularity, and in the light and context of which the history of the Church, and the life of the individual Christian, and in connexion with the Church and Christianity the life of all men in world history generally acquires a central importance. But it is not the Church or Christianity or humanity which constitutes this centre, this primary and particular sphere upon which the significance of the second and general sphere is grounded. It is not miracles, not the miracles of the Bible or any other miracles. It is the activity of God to and in and of Jesus Christ, the activity of the King of Israel as the object of the biblical witness. Therefore we have to make several important reservations with regard to the traditional distinctions. And if we do make them, we shall depart widely from the sense in which the distinctions were introduced into the older theology. But if we are not prepared to make them, it would be better to abandon the distinctions altogether.

We maintain, then, that the King of Israel is the King of the world and the Subject of the *gubernatio*[EN540]. The fact that God rules means that there rules the supremacy of the free grace which according to the witness of the Old and   [186]
New Testaments irrupted into the world in the promise and fulfilment, the

---

[EN534] special providence
[EN535] extraordinary providence
[EN536] general providence
[EN537] ordinary providence
[EN538] providence
[EN539] providence
[EN540] ruling

institution and execution of this covenant, in the Word and act of this King, as he went His own way. This same is God: "Christ Jesus is his name, The Lord Sabaoth's Son; He, and no other one, Shall conquer in the battle." There we have the clearest expression of the Christian faith in the divine world-governance. And the Christian idea of the matter is not an empty idea, or an idea which can be filled out in a variety of ways. When we think of the divine governance we are not thinking of an empty form, of a general and overriding order and teleology in all occurrence. We are not looking either up above or down below. We are simply looking at the Old and New Testaments; at the One whom Scripture calls God; at the events which Scripture attests in their relationships the one to the other; at the incursion of the supremacy of free grace which Scripture records; at the Subject who is active in this incursion; at His inconceivable but manifest act of election; at the faithfulness which He demonstrates and maintains; and, at the very heart of these events, at Jesus Christ on the cross; at the One who was not crucified alone, but two thieves with Him, the one on the right hand and the other on the left (Mt. 27[38]); at the One who accepted solidarity with all thieves both Jew and Gentile; at the One who is King over them all and on behalf of them all. It is from this point, and in this sense, and according to this purpose as it is active and revealed in these events, that the world is ruled, heaven and earth and all that therein is. This is the Christian belief in the divine world-governance. The history of salvation attested in the Bible cannot be considered or understood simply in and for itself. It is related to world history as a whole. It is the centre and key to all events. But again, world history cannot be considered or understood simply in and for itself. It is related to the history of salvation. It is the circumference around that centre, the lock to which that key belongs and is necessary. And in view of this relationship we must give up trying to develop the idea of a general kingship of God, and turn to his kingship in the Old and New Testaments, in the light of which we can again consider and understand His kingship in general. Without this substance and form the doctrine of the divine world-governance might, and necessarily would, be erroneous, or remain an empty scholasticism.

Why is it that God rules alone? Why is it that He alone has the right and the power and the wisdom to rule, when the rule of others can lead only to oppression and confusion? Why is it that God is so indispensable as the Subject of this rule? Why is it that there cannot be any collateral or counter-government? Our answer is that it is because He is the One who in, His freedom is gracious, and in His grace free; He alone is the One who can elect, and who can confirm His election by giving Himself; He alone is the faithful One who cannot be wearied or thwarted by any unfaithfulness. He alone is the fountain of mercy, the eternal Father of the eternal Son. Similarly, He alone is the source of the Holy Spirit, the only One who has true power. He alone is capable of a transcendent Word and a transcendent act. In all this He is absolutely unique. In all this He

[187]

is high above all idols and dominions and powers. And in all this, and in this way, He is God as the King of Israel. It is as the King of Israel that He is the only Ruler of the world, and can be known as such.

Why is it, and in what sense, that God makes and posits Himself the goal of all creaturely occurrence? Why is it that it is the blessing of all blessings, and the true glory of the creature, to promote His glory? Why is it that the guiding and direction of all things and events to Himself can be understood only as an act of the supreme and divine self-seeking? Our answer it that it is because He Himself, the Son of the Father and the Father of the Son, is love, and in His Son, as Creator, Reconciler and Redeemer, He is love to another, to the creature which needs His love, which can live only by His love, which may and must live by this love. The glory of God is in His being as the One who loves eternally. The greatness of His glory is in the fact that His love is actualised. And it is actualised in the fact that He does not abandon the creature to itself; that He does not direct it to other ends, but to Himself as the one end; that He wills that He Himself should be its end and blessing. And it is as the King of Israel that He is God in virtue of that love. It is as the King of Israel that He is and may be known as the One who in asserting Himself, in gaining the victory, in triumphing, gives Himself; who is therefore active and revealed in this way as the great and radical Benefactor.

Why is it that there belongs to Him that transcendence over the universal antinomies of necessity and contingence, of law and freedom? Why is it that He rules not only over these antinomies but also in and through them? Why is it that He is not fate and not chance, and yet both—the One who implacably orders all things, and the One who freely disposes in all things? Our answer is that He is over these antinomies, and in His own way in them, because in Himself He is both valid law, and also in favour of the highest individuality and the richest concrete life; because in His own most proper reality, which is above law—which is a reality self-conditioned and free in itself—He has willed to turn to the creature and to speak and act towards it (and finally to speak and act as Himself one creature with others); because in this reality He has in fact spoken and acted towards it. It is in the almightiness of His mercy and in the mercy of His almightiness that He is above and in these antinomies. And it is as the King of Israel that He acts and manifests Himself in this way, that He is both unity and life, that He is almighty and merciful in an unfathomable and incomparable, a truly incomprehensible and yet manifested divine union of the two, in the union in which He overlooks and controls and is thus superior to all the tensions which these antinomies necessarily mean for the creature [188] and creaturely thinking, in which the antinomies can only serve him. We can never be deceived or go astray in the matter if we look at what the King of Israel actually says and does.

And why is it the case that God orders creaturely events, that from all eternity and yet also at every moment He is Himself both the Planner and the plan, the *ordinator*[EN541] and the *ordo*[EN542]? The answer is that in the supremacy of His free grace, in His zeal for His own glory and therefore in His love for the creature, in His transcendence over and in the contradictions of the world, He has pursued a definite course, executing His eternal will in a temporal history, moving from promise to fulfilment, from Word to act, from grace to judgment, and back to a new and inconceivably greater grace, and yet through it all remaining exactly the same. The One who speaks and acts in the greatest freedom is inexorably caught up in the execution of His own project, and the One who executes His own project is the One who continues the most free Lord of His own will. It is thus, then, that God orders, i.e., that the King of Israel is seen to order: always according to an eternal necessity, and yet always with a surprise; always with freshness; always on the basis of incalculable presuppositions; always with the most unexpected results; but really ordering; really planning from stage to stage; manifestly proceeding according to a plan which since it is this plan could not be more strictly determined or appointed. Do we really understand this? All that we can do is to perceive the fact of it as a fact, and to understand that the King of Israel is both the Planner and the plan, the Orderer and the order of His own Word and act. We cannot for a moment doubt the fact that He is, and if He is the God who rules the world we cannot for a moment doubt that His rule is an ordering.

What is the nature of the relationship between the rule of God and the operations of His creatures? It is true that He directs them all to one goal and subordinates them all to His own operation. It is also true that He does not suppress them in their distinctiveness over against His own operation, but affirms and honours them. We have already stated the fact, and as far as possible explained it. But on what basis can we properly state and explain it? Is there not an intolerable contradiction at this point? Are we not faced again by a question which is wearisome because of its age and yet still a burning issue— the question of the relationship between the freedom of God and our freedom, between the freedom of God and that of the creature? With all its wearisomeness the question will flare up again and again as long as hazy notions prevail concerning who or what we mean by God, as long as we answer the question in another way than the Christian. But where God is at work in the supremacy of His free grace, where the King of Israel is active with His Word and act to and by His people as opposed to the world at large, there we really [189] see the two in a single relationship, not in a unity of tension, but in a relationship which is inwardly calm and clear and positive. Manifestly God wills and determines and effects all things in this relationship, so that all creaturely activity and effects have to strive wholly and unceasingly towards Him, adjusting themselves to His plans and purposes and executing His commands: Israel itself and the nations; the good and the evil; the sun and its heat and the sea

---

[EN541] ordainer
[EN542] order

with its waves; the stars of heaven and the grasshopper in the fields. Where is the creature which ever does anything different or differently from that which the will of God has ordained for it? And yet it is still the case that all creaturely activity has its own meaning and determination; that Israel itself and all other peoples live out their own individual history; that all men, the obedient no less than the disobedient, think and speak and act according to the manifest desire of their hearts; that the desert is dreary and the night dark; that the sea roars and honey is sweet; that bread sustains and wine makes glad the heart of man; that everything is and acts as it does. It has to be noted that, although miracles are ultimately unexpected and inexplicable as series of creaturely actions and effects directly initiated by God Himself, they do not involve any setting aside of such actions and effects. In the particular occurrence whose Subject is the King of Israel, God is of course absolutely the Almighty. But we cannot overlook the fact that men—and not only men—are also there over against Him, with their own particularity and activity, with their own being and action. And they are there not merely like chessmen—let alone like chessmen already out of the game—but all of them, from Moses and Paul to Judas Iscariot, from the cedar of Lebanon to the hyssop that grows on the wall, are there with their own individual being and the individual activity which corresponds to that being. And self-evidently everything depends on men and other creatures, on their individual actions and effects. It is with them that almighty God is concerned in His own almighty work. This is the case even in the history of salvation. It does not offer any solution at all to the technical problem raised. If we read the Bible with a desire to find any such solution, we shall find that it has nothing to say. But it offers us something far greater and far better, the fact of a relationship between the Creator and His creatures, between His freedom and their freedom, which is still clear and positive in spite of the existence of this problem. If we look at this factual relationship, and therefore at the rule of the God of Israel, we see that it is actually true that in the world-goverance of God everything has to be and is absolutely under God, and yet everything attains in freedom to its own validity and honour.

But is it true that in subordinating everything to the one end the divine rule involves the co-ordinating into a single whole of all the activities and effects of individual creatures, the establishment of a horizontal relationship and order? [190] Is it true that in spite of this coordination there is no question of a suppression or conjuring away of the creature, of the individual creature in its existence as such, but rather of its exalting and glorification? We have already stated the fact and made some attempt to explain it. But unless we give a clear and Christian account of who and what we mean by God in this connexion, there must always be doubt whether these things are not really incompatible. When we turn, however, to the history of the covenant and salvation as attested in the Bible, we have to do with a totality of creaturely being and activity co-ordinated by God in face of which no such doubt can ever arise. The people of Israel with

whom the Yahweh of the Old Testament entered into covenant, and the community of the New Testament which has Jesus Christ as its Head (in relationship to this King, and ruled by Him), are no chance conglomerations of individuals, but wholes, and indeed in the strict sense a single whole, with a common guilt in virtue of their solidarity in obligation and responsibility, but also with a common justification and sanctification. This fact has often been misunderstood both in theory and in practice, but exegetically there is not the slightest doubt about it. On the one hand, we have the election and calling of the people (the twelve tribes, and their individual families, and the members of these families in all their generations, but all of them bound together like a single man). On the other hand, we have the one Holy Spirit of the one Lord as the bond of peace which embraces the whole community, so that they are not like many men, but only one. And in both cases the meaning and result are the same. The supremacy of free grace has created in this history a historical cosmos, a living but perfect unity, a body. But we must beware of trying to follow through this thought to its logical end. "This body" is not a collective whole in which the totality is everything and the individual nothing. How sadly we should misunderstand this body if we did not perceive that in both the good and the evil the whole has only the form of particular individuals, and that individuals are always this whole before God. Where can we see the people more clearly in its common sin and need and with its common promise than in Deutero-Isaiah? And where are the people surprisingly addressed as such in words which in every page, and rightly so, have been received and accepted and passed on as the most powerful of all words in the individual and personal cure of souls? Who ever addressed the community of Christ so consistently as a unity, a body, as Paul did? And yet who but the same Paul saw this body so fully represented in his own apostolic but highly individual person? It is true, of course, that the history of the covenant and salvation as it occurred under the rule of the King of Israel, and with this history the Bible, does not offer us any solution to the technical problem which arises, any formula which will reveal to us how the individual and the community can properly co-exist. But it offers
[191]   us far more. It shows us the fact. They are together, and together in such a way that there is no need to safeguard the individual against the community or the community against the individual, to defend righteousness against freedom or freedom against righteousness. If we cling to the actual fact as it is attested in the Bible, if we think in the light of this fact because in it we see the one true God at work, we shall see that in the divine world-governance it is actually the case that all things are coordinated, that in this very fact each individual receives its own kingdom, and that in this fact again all things are co-ordinated.

At all points, then, to fill out the idea of the divine world-governance along biblical and Christian lines is to make it concrete, to actualise and verify it. If we think of it as filled out in this way we are not considering the empty framework of a mere concept of God, but a form, a face, a history. We are as it were caught up and forced to tread a definite path. We are not concerned with an empty idea, but with something real. And this means that our thoughts can no longer roam about freely. We are taken out of the sphere of vacillating opinions, and at all these different points we are led to the definite conclusions indicated.

But this is not all. For it is only when we can presuppose this filling out along biblical and Christian lines that the idea of the divine world-governance becomes a practical idea: an idea which illuminates both individual life and the life-process generally; an idea which gives direction; a significant idea. If it is really the King of Israel, the Lord of the covenant; if it is really God in Jesus Christ, who is the Subject of this governance, then even the concept of the world-occurrence to which it relates signifies something much more than a mere mass of things and events, which in spite of all its variety lacks finally either contour or direction. World-occurrence is no longer the endless wavebeat of a sea which has neither shore, colour, nor form, but is everywhere the same, flowing out of itself and flowing back into itself. It is no longer the basically uninteresting and even boring *universum*EN543 of monads all of which in principle have the same status and form, a *universum*EN544 to which our thinking merely adds the basically uninteresting and even boring truth that both in its totality and in each of those monads which have the same status and form, it is directed only by God the chief Monad.

It is to be noted that if God Himself has no form nor face nor history, if in the name God we can only look at the empty framework of a concept of the original being and activity of a chief Monad, then the truth that God rules the world is at bottom a dispensable and superfluous luxury. We have to represent world-occurrence as in some sense a self-ordered unity. And to this unity and order we give the name of the divine governance. If the concept God is an empty one, it may well give greater solemnity to what we say, or to our feelings as we say it, but in practice it will not make the slightest difference to the sig- [192] nificance or lack of significance of the unity and order. For all practical purposes they would have no significance at all, and even if our apprehension of them were correct, it would still be unimportant. A thought is not important because it is a correct thought. In any case, a unity and order which embrace the whole world uniformly can only be a theoretical idea, whether the unity and order are immanent in the world or imposed by God. If the idea is to have any practical significance, i.e., a significance which determines the existence of the man who conceives it, it must acquire this significance elsewhere. It will probably have to be added by the man himself as he adopts a practical attitude towards that immanent or transcendent unity and order, and his own peril. Any importance that it has will be due to himself and to the measure of importance that he attaches to it.

EN543 totality
EN544 totality

But if the King of Israel is God, and therefore the King of all occurrence, the idea of the divine world-governance is not only clearly differentiated from that of a unity and order immanent in the world, but as such, as a distinctive idea of the divine world-governance, it has a practical and not merely a theoretical significance. It is not only correct; it is also important in itself. It is not an idea that we can only think, and then have to give to it a practical significance; it is an idea that is practically significant in itself. It determines human existence. It is an idea by which we can immediately live, and, if we really think it, must live. World-occurrence under the rule of the King of Israel is more than a mass of events which may perhaps be self-directing or may even be directly and uniformly ordered by God but is still lacking in either contour or direction. If the King of Israel rules, then of course this means that each thing and everything takes place in a uniform order as He directs it. But it means more. It means that all occurrence has a definite form. There is direction in the all-embracing unity. And this means that there is a first and a last, an above and a below, a foreground and a background. It means that the unity and order involve a definite disposition and economy. And while it is the same King who rules all things on the basis of this economy, things cannot be both above and below, both great and small, both first and last, at one and the same time. On the basis of this economy there is a continual differentiation within that occurrence. There is an advance and a corresponding withdrawal. There is an illuminating and also an obscuring. There is authority and also subordination. On the basis of this economy occurrence acquires the character of a motivated history. It is still the case that in the kingdom of this King there is a purpose behind every individual thing as such, that nothing at all is lost, or exists and acts merely for the sake of something else. Indeed, it is on the very basis of this formative disposition and economy that with all its particularity the individual thing can exist and act in immediacy towards God. But the individual thing receives its [193] particular dignity and value on the basis of a formative economy which assigns to all things a place and time and function. And this means that the true image of the cosmos which this King rules, and of the unity and order which He gives to world-occurrence, is not the image of a sea but of a river which has its source and course and estuary. It is certainly not that of a globe, on whose surface and in whose interior any one point may in principle be exchanged for any other, since all of them have exactly the same function in their own place, and the only difference between them is that they happen to be this or that point and not another. An image of this kind would be basically uninteresting and even boring, whether accompanied or not by the corresponding concept of God as an empty framework. It is an image to which the form and significance of any kind of life—we will not ask what—would have to be added and read in theoretically by the existential decisions of man himself. But the true image of the cosmos which is ruled by this King is undoubtedly that of a natural structure, a living plant perhaps, or some other organism, in which the various parts, root, stem, branches, leaves, buds and fruit are all mutually ordered, in which the presence of all the others demands that each one should have its own place and function, in which they all have a different place and function and are therefore different the one from the other. Or else it is the image of a human work of art, a building for example, in which the plan and purpose and meaning of the whole, to which all the parts must conform, is revealed in both the individual significance and also the indestructible variety of the parts.

In 1 Cor. 12$^{14-26}$ Paul uses a well-known image to describe the relationship between the community and its individual members as they are endowed with various gifts of the Spirit. Trait for trait, the image is normative for a description—not of the concept of an empty framework—but of the cosmos which is ruled by the living God, the King of Israel. We must allow Paul to speak for himself: "For the body is not one member, but many. If the foot shall say, Because I am not the hand, I am not of the body; it is not therefore not of the body. If the whole body were an eye, where were the hearing? If the whole were hearing, where were the smelling? But now hath God set the members (ἔθετο τὰ μέλη) each one of them in the body, even as it pleased him. And if they were all one member, where were the body? But now they are many members, but one body. And the eye cannot say to the hand, I have no need of thee: or again the head to the feet, I have no need of you. Nay, much rather, those members of the body which seem to be feeble are necessary: and those parts of the body, which we think to be less honourable, upon these we bestow more abundant honour; and our uncomely parts have more abundant comeliness; whereas our comely parts have no need: but God tempered (συνεκέρασεν) the body together, giving more abundant honour to that part which lacked; that there should be no schism in the body; but that the members should have the same care one for another. And whether one member suffereth, all the members suffer with it; or one member is honoured, all the members rejoice with it."

But if this image, and not that of the sea or globe, is normative for our understanding of the cosmos which God rules and of universal occurrence as He directs it, this means that we can never think this thought without a Word [194] being addressed to us. We cannot linger before the picture of the God of Israel ruling the cosmos as we would before the picture of the universe directed by an indefinite authority which might just as well be God as anything else. We cannot merely consider it, having to discover for ourselves any unity and order which it may have, and to work out for ourselves the practical bearing of that unity and order. For if the idea of the divine world-governance is concretely filled out as we have suggested, then at once we are caught up in the divine economy and disposition. We at once begin to have dealings with this King, with the Lord of this history, with the will of this Lord and King, with the supremacy of this free grace. We at once find ourselves in a concrete relationship with this concrete act of government as the act which is decisive for all events and therefore for our own life and existence and activity. In advance of all our own opinions and attitudes we see ourselves questioned and invited and called. And we know that with all that we are to be and to do we will always give either an affirmative or a negative answer. For good or evil we have to answer individually to this Lord of the world who is our Lord. We are not at one of those neutral points on a globe which in principle are identical and interchangeable. In virtue of the formative economy and disposition of the One who rules the world, we have our own definite time and place and function. Whether it be far or near, above or below, in the foreground or the background, whether we accept it with a good grace or a bad grace, it is at any rate different; it is the function which is assigned to us; and we are in a definite relationship to what is specifically willed with us and through us by the One who is Lord of the world both in general and in particular. There is no room for the uninteresting and even boring idea of a unity and order which arise in the process of events either with or without God. The idea of the divine world-governance is no longer a theoretical and speculative idea. It is a practical ("existential") idea. We cannot think about the relationship between the Creator who rules and the creaturely world which is ruled by Him without thinking about ourselves, without thinking about ourselves as a definite factor within that economy and disposition, i.e., within the history of that relationship. The very fact that we think the thought means that we have begun to put it into effect in our own particular sphere. If we think the thought, we cannot alter the fact that, if the King of Israel is the Lord of the world, He is also our Lord, and therefore He is thinking of us and laying claim upon us. We cannot think the thought without understanding the Word of God and being caught up in the work of God; without seeing in the election and calling of Israel our own election and calling; without seeing in the unfaithfulness of Israel our own unfaithfulness; without seeing in the faithfulness of God His unmerited faithfulness to us; without seeing in Jesus Christ the Saviour who came down [195] and was manifested and died and rose again for us; without seeing in free grace the reality to whose service we are pledged and by whose glorifying we can live—we who are called here and now, and have cause for gratitude, being indebted for our very selves. The very fact that we fill out the idea in a biblical and Christian way means that the divine world-governance necessarily becomes an event in our own lives and that we have to recognise and affirm it as such. Even as we think the thought we ourselves are the creature which is ruled by that ruling Creator, and we recognise and accept ourselves as such. If the King of Israel really is for us the Lord of the world, and therefore the Subject with whom we have to do when we think this thought, then necessarily the thought is for us concrete and actual and true in all its parts, and more than that, it acquires this immediate practical significance.

As we have tried to understand the divine world-governance as the rule of the King of Israel, we have frequently referred to it as a formative economy and disposition. By this we mean only that all world-occurrence receives from this ruling Subject its goal, thus acquiring a unified line and direction, and also that this Subject gives it a context, the interconnexion of individual events, the significance of their sequence, of the way in which they mutually cause and condition and limit and overlap each other, of the way in which they follow and accompany and are mutually related to each other. And it is by means of this context that the King gives form and character to world-occurrence. That is why we cannot possibly compare world-occurrence as it takes place under the divine rule with an amorphous and self-diffusing mass, but only with an organism or building.

What this context is, is revealed to us in the history of the covenant and salvation to which the Bible bears testimony. It is grounded in the free election of grace. It has its beginning here in the form of the particular and sacred work of God in the creation of the world. It continues with the reconciliation of the world to God as it was foretold in the history of Israel and accomplished in Jesus Christ. And when the interim period of the proclamation of this work is over, it will culminate in the perfecting or redemption which consists in the general revelation of the creative and reconciling act of God. It is in this that we find true economy and disposition. It is here that creaturely occurrence acquires line and direction, and meaningful sequence and context, and therefore form and character, by the rule of God. It is in the name of Jesus Christ that this economy is comprehended. This name, which is present at both the beginning and the end, is the centre which reveals the economy. It is in this name that it really consists. But at every point in this particular and sacred work, at the beginning and middle and end, we find that its concern is with the world. It is the world which God created in His grace. It is the world which He loved and reconciled in His Son. It is the world which He will finally perfect in Christ. And the opening event in this particular sacred history is the calling into being of a special people, a holy community, whose existence is not an end in itself, but something which has to testify and proclaim to the world the Word of the King to it and the work of the King for it. And this means that the context, the economy, the disposition is not only revealed in the history of the covenant and redemption whose centre is Jesus Christ. In a hidden form it is also present and active in world-occurrence generally. The two spheres are distinguished only by the fact that in the one case it is hidden and in the other it is revealed. From this particular, sacred history we see that even world-occurrence generally had its beginning by the grace of God the Creator, that it was decisively altered and conditioned by the love which appeared in Jesus Christ and was authenticated by His death and resurrection, and that it moves towards its own perfection and therefore to the end of the age in the still future revelation of Jesus Christ. The existence of this particular, sacred history means that we can no longer think of world-occurrence generally as a raging sea of events which has neither form nor direction. World-occurrence is something formed, and it is formed indeed according to the sense revealed in this history. Its unity and order are identical with the unity and order which were manifestly achieved in this history. Its Lord is identical with the One who is called the Lord in this history, and therefore with the King of Israel.

But of course this does not mean that the lordship and economy can be directly seen and demonstrated in world-occurrence as such. The history of the covenant and salvation in which the King of Israel rules, in which His plan and will and acts take place and are revealed, does not cease to be a particular history, a history which is not continued or repeated outside its own sphere. It

[196]

is from this history and this history alone that we learn that world-occurrence generally stands under the same lordship and has the same relationship, because the King of Israel is its King too. If we will accept it from this source, we will progressively confirm that it is actually so. We shall not discover that it is so, but confirm it. Instructed by this history, accepting what it reveals, we can have a prior assurance of the presence of this context, of the existence of this line and direction in world-occurrence generally. On this basis we can count upon the fact that all occurrence really has form and character, that there is purpose and unity and order in all things. And we can do so according to the same sense and in virtue of the same formative economy and disposition as were revealed and active in Jesus Christ. From the very outset, then, we can acknowledge only Him as the Lord of all occurrence, as the One who is decisively at work behind and within its relationships and movements, behind and within the sequence of its events. With a certainty which is absolute we can count upon the fact, and only upon the fact, that even where there is no trace of a

[197] particular or sacred history everything does move from the gracious creation of God, by way of the reconciliation accomplished in Jesus Christ, to the final revelation. And how could it be otherwise? For the conclusions already reached from the knowledge of Scripture and of the revelation to which it bears witness cannot be a general conclusion. With all boldness we shall venture to apply this conclusion concretely to all kinds of relationships and developments in world-occurrence generally. And in all of them we shall find that it is concretely confirmed. But the power or force of our knowledge will always be that of the revelation which is fulfilled in the particular and sacred history. It will always be that of the presupposition with which we approach and view world-occurrence in the light of this revelation. The measure of the certainty of our knowledge will be determined by the extent to which it really derives and is illuminated and directed by this revelation. Only in the light of it can we accept the conclusion as self-evident, or venture with such boldness and joy and certainty to reckon even in world-occurrence generally upon the sole lordship of the One who directs the creature from grace to grace. And the very consolation and help and support and counsel which, as the answer to this venture, we again and again receive in the midst of world-occurrence in the form of surprises, or it may be quiet perceptions and insights, the discovery of definite traces of this context—all these can be true only as we already have elsewhere, in His own direct revelation in that particular and sacred history, a knowledge of the King of Israel who creates this context. For if we did not know Him already in this revelation, how could we ever perceive Him in world-occurrence as a whole?

For the way in which He creates the context in world-occurrence does not reveal Him to us, but conceals Him from us. In world-occurrence He can be revealed to us only in the light of the particular occurrence. It is true that the divine governance does give rise to an economy and disposition in world-occurrence generally. And it is true that this economy and disposition are identical with the economy and disposition of the saving events of biblical history which culminate in Jesus Christ and derive from Him. But it is not at all the case that this economy and disposition can be understood directly from world-occurrence itself, as though this occurrence were a second Bible. It is not at all the case that we have this economy and disposition before us in the form of a handy system of world-goverance, or of certain easily recognisable features in such a system. In world-occurrence it is a question only of the hiddenness of God and of the ruling power of God. We can and must expect the removal of this hiddenness by the revelation which He has already given to us, but we cannot achieve it ourselves. Even the history of the covenant and salvation is not yet complete. It will be complete only when we can see the full reach of the grace of God and of His love for all creation in the revelation of what He has already done for it as Creator, in the reconciliation effected in Jesus Christ, [198] and therefore in the revelation of this context. But from that which the history of the covenant and salvation has already revealed and demonstrated we have seen and learned that the King of Israel, Jesus Christ, is Lord of all. Like all other created things, however, we have not yet seen and learned the way in which He is Lord of all, the extent to which this economy and disposition are executed and revealed in world-occurrence generally. The plan of God and this context are concealed from us even when we venture to acknowledge Him as Lord. Even in the perceptions and insights which are from time to time vouchsafed to us, they are not so clearly revealed to us that in the light of them, in the light of our own ventures or of the understanding which is given us, we can enter fully into the thought of the divine world-goverance. We are always referred back to the one and only Bible, or to its content, this one particular and sacred history. And we must and can content ourselves with this. For to come to know the Lord of all occurrence; to have the revelation of His free grace as the secret of the cosmos which is ruled by Him; to be absolutely certain that there is no such thing as secular history, i.e., history apart from or opposed to this economy; to have the courage and joy and certainty of the knowledge that there is one, this One, who occupies the seat of power; to risk again and again the venture of that confirmation; to give ourselves the consolation and help and support and comfort that are so necessary to us; in a word, to have our eyes opened, and to be able occasionally to see at any rate the traces of this rule—for all this it is enough if we have the one Bible with its witness to the history of the covenant and salvation, and there is no need to supplement it by looking for a system, or the features of a system, which underlies the context of world-occurrence. Indeed, it is much more likely that if we do discover such a system, we shall merely check and disturb and hinder if not completely mislead ourselves, in the true and serious application of what has been discovered already without any assistance that we can give. It belongs to a right understanding of the divine world-governance that we should be content with the form in which it is revealed to us here and now, i.e., with its biblical form. It belongs to a right understanding of it that we should be aware of the fact that in its other and complete, because direct form, it is here and now concealed from us.

But we shall fall short of completeness if we do not throw one definite light even on our assertion of the provisional hiddenness of the divine world-governance, and therefore of the formative economy and disposition of world-occurrence as such. There is in this occurrence no second revelation of the divine world-governance, no second Bible. The first is quite sufficient, and it has to suffice us. But as we consider it we cannot deny that within world-occurrence as such there are certain constant elements which do indeed belong to it; which in themselves and as such do not constitute a further revelation, or a continuation or repetition of the one revelation; from the existence of which we can no more deduce the How? of the divine rule than we can from that of any other elements in world-occurrence; but which have all the same a special character and function in this regard. By their special nature they stand in a special relationship to the history of the covenant and salvation, and therefore to that one revelation of the divine world-governance. We can and indeed have to say concerning them that their existence and activity and the effects which they produce are as it were a permanent riddle in relation to history as a whole, and that in the last analysis they can be explained only when we can consider them from the one distinctive place. In some sense they point to the fact that world-occurrence is bordered by this one distinctive place. To this extent they are signs and witnesses that world-occurrence is really ruled from this place, i.e., by the One who at this distinctive place is called God. Of course, it belongs to the very nature of these elements that their character as signs and witnesses to this fact can easily be overlooked. As signs and witnesses they will inevitably be overlooked if they are not considered from this one place. They will be seen only as elements like others. The riddle of world-occurrence will be so much greater. But why should there not be these mysteries like so many others? Why should they not be ignored like so many others? Even if they can be explained only from the one distinctive place, this does not mean that there is a general compulsion to acknowledge that all occurrence is bordered by this place, or that the One who is called God there, the King of Israel, is the Ruler of the world. The existence of these special elements does not even give us an indirect systematic indication of the divine world-governance, the critical material for a systematic apologetic or a philosophy of life and history. But at the same time it does belong to the nature of these elements that we can consider them as signs and witnesses to this God. They have no advantage in other respects. In their creatureliness, and with their activity and its effects, they are no dearer to God than other creatures. But they do in fact stand nearer than all other creatures to this centre of all creaturely occurrence, this centre of the history of the covenant and salvation which is enacted at the heart of the whole. And when we see their particular proximity and affinity to this central event (and we certainly cannot see it except from the event itself), we also see that away from this centre, in the midst of world-

[199]

occurrence generally, they do not prove to us, but they do testify and confirm and demonstrate, from where and by whom that occurrence is ruled. They do not tell us how it is ruled. They affirm that the Ruler and His work are here and now concealed. When we ask concerning His economy and disposition they refer us back to the one source of all true knowledge in the matter, and they also refer us forward to the promised consummation. But as signs and wit- [200] nesses they do affirm that the One who rules is the Lord of the history and the covenant to which the Bible bears testimony—the King of Israel. And they do not affirm it as it may occasionally be affirmed by other elements in world-occurrence, or to the extent that there may be similar perceptions and insights—if not with a final, at any rate with an all but final certainty—in the experience of all men. They affirm it according to their special character as constant elements in world-occurrence, as universal and objective historical contexts of this kind. Of these signs, too, it may be said that only those who have eyes to see will see them, only those who have ears to hear will hear them. And yet they can be heard and seen at all times and in all places. They do not penetrate the hiddenness of God as it is penetrated in the history of the coven-ant and salvation. But within world-occurrence, in the sphere where God is hidden, they are standing, permanent, objective reminders that the penetra-tion did take place at this point, that it will take place again and again from this point, that the economy and disposition of world-occurrence can be seen at this point. We shall not do justice to the problem unless we consider these special elements in all their different forms. I shall mention the most import-ant of them, in each case adding what seems to be most necessary by way of comment and explanation.

1. The history of Holy Scripture. We are thinking now of its origin and trans-mission, and its exegesis and influence in the course of history generally. Cer-tainly we cannot say that from this standpoint it sheds any compelling, universal, direct or necessary light upon its content, i.e., the occurrence of that particular and sacred history, and therefore the King of Israel as the Lord of world-occurrence. For there is no doubt that these aspects can be con-sidered and explained as simply the result of a particular epoch in the reli-gious development of mankind, or even as the result of certain peculiar superstitions and delusions, or it may be of the most serious and profound experiences and insights of the human race, according to the standpoint of the individual observer. And this certainly does not mean that they can be regarded as the result of a demonstration of the world-governance of the One concerning whom this Scripture speaks. We cannot say more than that the history of Holy Scripture can also be considered quite differently from this standpoint. But this we can say. We can take up the position which man neces-sarily occupies according to the content of this Scripture. And then we can receive and accept its witness, and the Old and New Testament message of the Word and work of God to which it bears testimony. It can then be the case that as we encounter this witness we encounter God Himself and His gracious and

compelling existence, and that we are claimed and liberated and captivated by it. It can then be the case that in consequence we are men in whose lives the governance of this God—far from being the governance of a particular god in his own sphere, or the power of a particular idea—has actually shown itself to be the governance of the world. Clearly, the history of Holy Scripture can be considered from quite a different angle on this presupposition, and we may think that on this presupposition it has to be considered from this quite different angle.

[201]

We can see this already in relation to its origin. If we accept the witness of Holy Scripture, then implicitly we accept the fact that, quite irrespective of the way in which they were humanly and historically conditioned, its authors were objectively true, reliable and trustworthy witnesses. It is not merely that we recognise their opinions to be good and pious, or appreciate their part and significance in religious history. We perceive rather that it pleased God the King of Israel, to whom the power of their witness is pledged as to the Lord, to raise up these true witnesses by His Word and work. In this fact, at the very beginning of the history of Scripture, and at the heart of world-occurrence, even while the fact itself is a moment in occurrence generally, what we see is not merely a moment in occurrence generally, and in religious occurrence in particular, but a trace of the governance of God as the one and only true God, a trace of this God as the Lord of all world-occurrence.

And this is what we also see in the continuation of this history, the rise, completion and transmission of the Canon of the Old and New Testaments. Certainly it is not a history which is apart from the developments and complications which affect all human history. Certainly it is not a history which is preserved inwardly from the follies and errors and oddities of all human history. It is a history which is not accidental but necessary in its whole course and sequence. It is true history, not a perverted history. It is a history whose necessity and truth have constantly to be recognised, understood, tested, and actualised. And as such it is a history which can be interpreted in many different ways at different times. But however it is considered and interpreted, it is a history whose meaning persists and maintains itself. It is a history which gives rise to constant questioning, but which constantly puts more important questions on its own account. From this angle again, what we see is not a trace of creaturely occurrence but of the plan and will which rule this occurrence—the plan and will of the One whose Word and work are the subject of the Scripture whose peculiarity is so much emphasised.

And this is also what we can and must see in the history of exegesis which begins already with the history of the text and Canon and necessarily returns again and again to this history. Here, too, we are not outside the sphere of world-occurrence generally, but inside it. Here, too, we see the powerful and far-reaching effect of the various languages and racial characteristics, the politics, economics, philosophy, scholarship, artistic sense, faith, heresy and superstition of the different ages, the individual talents of the various individual [202] readers and exegetes. And here, too, we must give sober consideration to all these factors: how it was all a help or a hindrance; how it was that such singular honour came to be paid to the Old and New Testaments, and what they had to put up with; to what extent men faithfully reproduced the teaching of Scripture, and to what extent they wilfully read their own teaching into it; how again and again Scripture was continually discovered and forgotten, esteemed and despised; how at all times it was continually understood and misunderstood. Should our estimate of this history be an optimistic or a pessimistic one? If our attitude to the content of the texts which we are considering is the attitude of that original freedom and constraint, there can be no doubt at least that we shall always see in that history a history of their own self-exegesis. And this means that we shall never look upon the prophets and apostles as merely objects for the study and assessment of later readers; they will always be living, acting, speaking subjects on their own account. The fact that they have spoken once does not mean that they have now ceased to speak. On the contrary, they take up and deliver the Word afresh in every age and to every people, at every cultural level and to every individual. And they do it in such a way that what they have to say is far more acute and relevant than what may be said or thought about them. What are all the commentaries and other expositions of the Bible but a strong or feeble echo of their voice? If we are in that direct relationship to the Bible, then in the last and decisive analysis we shall not consider the history of biblical exegesis in the light of what took place outwardly. On the contrary, we shall consider the history of its outward experiences in the light of its own continually renewed and for that reason always surprising action, as a history of its self-declaration and self-explanation in the midst of that general occurrence to which it belongs and within which it constitutes its own life-centre and origin in virtue of its affinity with the divine Word and work to which it testifies. It was not merely a rhetorical flourish when at the time of the Reformation Scripture was gladly described and magnified as *dux*[EN545] and *magistra*[EN546], or even as *regina*[EN547]. The fact is—and it does not make the slightest difference whether it is recognised or not—that in all ages Scripture has been the subject of its own history, the guiding, teaching, ruling subject, not under men but over men, over all the men who in so many ways, and with such continual oddities and contradictions, have applied themselves to its exposition. And for this reason its history is in this respect too— those who have eyes to see, let them see—a trace of the ruling God whom it declares. It has a concealed but not a completely hidden part in His kingly rule.

[EN545] leader
[EN546] teacher
[EN547] queen

And finally, we have to consider the history of its influence or effects. At this point we touch upon the second of the special historical elements about which [203] we shall have to speak in a moment. What happened to that witness? What is happening to it now? What does it actually accomplish in the world in which it is spoken and transmitted and continually expounded? In this respect, too, we have to consider it in the sequence of all the other factors of world-occurrence and their effects. Let us take as an illustration the well-known theory that what we call Western Christendom is a hybrid product deriving from biblical Christianity on the one hand and Graeco-Roman antiquity on the other. But how many other causes do we have to mention side by side with the Bible, some of them oriental and some occidental, some of them spiritual and some very strongly material? If we have not already done so, we shall have to accustom ourselves to thinking of the historical effect of the biblical witness as one effect among many others. And when we do this, we cannot be too serious in reckoning with the fact that what we have to do with here—we need only think of what we call Western Christendom—is a historical effect which is very much diluted and distorted, and which in addition is always restricted in power, and constantly threatened with extinction. In a genuinely historical investigation it can even be asked whether one day this force will not be exhausted and lost like so many others. But what is this force, the influence of the Bible in world history? If we consider it in the light of the influence which we know as an event in our own lives, then we know it as a wonderful election and calling which we cannot explain merely as a possibility of our own. To our own astonishment we find that we are added to the people, the Church, the community of the King of Israel. We find this particular influence of the biblical witness in the quite extraordinary existence of this community and its commission in the world. And in face of this influence we can only be amazed, first that we are not excluded from it, that we can be aware of it in our own lives, and then that we are not alone in this experience, but can publicly share it with so many others both past and present, both far and near. It claims our whole attention to take this influence seriously, and gratefully to do justice to it. And this means that we have neither the time nor the energy for general historical considerations. We have a prior claim and commission within and in face of all other occurrence. And we shall not experience any surprise at the way in which the influence of the biblical witness is necessarily diluted and distorted and threatened as seen against world-occurrence generally. This fact will not cause us any anxiety or despair. We shall be well enough aware of it from the way in which this influence is diluted and distorted and threatened in our own lives as members of the people of God both individually and corporately. Far from despairing, we shall be ashamed, and do penance, and pray, and work, not only for ourselves, but for the whole people of God. And we shall remember that it would be something far more strange if this high and solemn thing were something triumphant in the midst of world-occurrence, if it were an enormous and undiluted and unequivocal success, if it were something popular. We know [204] that all the influence of the biblical witness can itself have only the form of a witness, the witness of most inadequate creatures. By our commission and its execution we shall not cease to aim at what the Church either is accomplishing or could accomplish by means of it. And there can be no mistake as to the influence which—with all the ambiguity and weakness of that which results from it—the biblical witness does actually have, and always has had, and always will have—in the fact that new witnesses are called out and new confessing communities are assembled by this witness. In the vast ocean of other influences we shall be aware of the fact that at all times and in all places this calling out and assembling has taken place and still does take place. And we shall not look at this influence merely as one among many. We shall not weigh and evaluate it optimistically or pessimistically in relation to the others. In this influence, in the power of the prophetic and apostolic witness at all times and in all places to call out and assemble, we shall again find traces of the One with whom that witness has to do, of the One who is manifestly present as King not only in this influence, but everywhere and always.

2. The history of the Church. We have necessarily had to touch already on this second sign and witness within world-occurrence. The Church is a result. It is a result of Holy Scripture. It is built upon the foundation of the apostles and prophets. To that extent it belongs to the history of Scripture. But it obviously has its own history in that there takes place within it the transmission and exegesis and effective operation of Scripture both amongst and also by means of others outside the circle of the first witnesses. Called out and assembled by those first witnesses, others enter upon the scene. We now live in the last time to which they pointed in their message, i.e., the time of the expectation of the final and definitive and universal revelation in the return of Jesus Christ of the reconciliation of the world which God has already accomplished in Him. This last time is the time of the Church. The Church is the communion of saints, i.e., the fellowship of those who by the self-revelation of the King of Israel to which Scripture bears testimony are personally called: called out of the world; called into the community; called to faith in the kingdom of God and to the proclamation of this kingdom. Church history is the history of this fellowship within world history generally. And it is one of those special elements in world-occurrence which point to the divine world-governance.

We make contact at this point with the older doctrine of *providentia specialis*[EN548] as it appears particularly in the preservation, direction and confirmation of the Christian Church. The special protection and preservation of the church is referred to, for instance, in *Questions* 51 and 54, and most impressively in *Question* 133, of the *Heidelberg Catechism*, where in the commentary on the second petition we have the words: "Preserve and increase thy Church; destroy the works of the devil, every power that exalteth itself against Thee, and [205] all wicked devices formed against Thy holy Word, until the full coming of Thy kingdom,

---

[EN548] special providence

wherein Thou shalt be all in all." And a passage from F. Burmann's *Syn. Theol.*, 1671 (I, 44, 88) will show in what form the Dutch theology of the 17th century believed that it could discern and estimate the controlling of divine providence in this special sphere: "The Church has no cause to be ashamed of its lot right up to our own days. It is still illuminated by the light of the Gospel. Liberated from its Babylonian captivity, it can breathe freely amongst pious kings and magistrates. Tested in conflicts, it has not been destroyed, and the conflicts have merely revealed the truth the more clearly. Never has the Gospel triumphed more gloriously over error than in our own epoch. The heat of persecution has been tempered, and by the grace of God many enemies of the Church have been converted. And almost everywhere God maintains civil order, providing that peace should always follow strife. He also adds his blessing in the economic sphere, so that the generation and instruction of a holy posterity is assured. Similarly, there are both higher and primary schools in which those things are taught which pertain to God and are beneficial to the race. And even to-day God raises up prophets from our sons and Nazarites from our young men. Therefore, although the Church still sighs in many places by reason of its heavy adversity, we have every cause to render our thanks to God for so great benefits." We shall have to pursue the matter rather more deeply than this, even if in the last analysis we come to the same conclusion.

We think of the remarkable claim with which the Church exists. We think of its capacity for resistance and renewal. Again, it is not as if the Church were in a position either to proclaim directly or to prove to the general satisfaction its own status as the communion of saints and thus the lordship of God in world-occurrence which it believes and proclaims. It is true that its time, the last time, exemplifies the presence and lordship of the King of Israel. The fact that He sits on the throne is the revelation with whose particular form this time begins and to whose universal form it moves. But even the last time is still time. It is a perishing but an even more powerful old aeon. It is the time when the glory of God does not yet fulfil all things, when, the rule of God is over all world-occurrence and yet concealed by it, when we walk by faith and not by sight. Even the Church belongs to this time and is under its conditions. It is not a continuation or repetition of the biblical revelation. It is not a breaking-through the order and disorder, the progression and the pauses and retrogressions of world-occurrence generally. It is nowhere unequivocally distinguished from this occurrence. It can be perceived—and will be perceived only—as one phenomenon among many others. Its history allows of this even more than that of the Bible. And this is true even of the greatest periods and purest forms and most promising movements and developments and achievements in the history of the Church. Perhaps it is too summary a judgment to describe this history as "a medley of error and violence." But basically we cannot dispute either this or similar verdicts, unless we are in a position to look at [206] it from a different angle. "As secular history, Church history (F. Overbeck) is at all events a very tempting programme and one that seduces by reason of its consistent honesty." We can only say that there is no compelling reason why the consideration of Church history in its solidarity with world history generally should be regarded as the only possible way of considering it. Like the history of the Bible, it can also be considered in the light of the presupposition that the observer and critic himself is not outside the Church but inside it; that he is one of those who are called, called out and from and into; that he is one of those who on the strength of the biblical witness can and must believe and proclaim the lordship of the King of Israel; that he is, therefore, one of those who are both liberated and bound. And in the light of this fact it may be that he really begins to know what Church history is about, and what it has been about from the very first. It may be that he really begins to know with whom and with what we are confronted in this sphere, and will be continually confronted in the ever-changing constellations of history. He can really begin to experience joy and terror at the greatness of that which takes place in the events and relationships, the movements and pauses of Church history, i.e., the Word and work of God constantly seeking new realisation from generation to generation. To some extent he can begin to know the great decisive characters of this history, not from outside but from inside, in the knowledge of his own solidarity with them. He may, therefore, find himself in the situation in which he has to think of the historical sphere of this community of faith and proclamation not merely as one among many others, not merely in its entanglement in the problematical character of all similar spheres, but in and for itself, as a special and strangely isolated sphere. And in this isolation he will have to see a trace of the divine world-governance, of the same divine world-governance under which he finds himself in his own existence, and of which he is therefore a personal witness. And if we consider it from this always possible standpoint, we have to say something rather more about Church history than that it is merely a part of secular history.

And first we have to consider a remarkable claim of which the Church, if it is the true Church, is always and necessarily aware when it thinks of the significance of its own history in the midst of occurrence generally. For if we ourselves belong to the company of those who are both liberated and bound, then we know that it is the character of our time to be the last time. As the recipients and bearers of the good news of the resurrection of Jesus Christ we are awaiting the return of Jesus Christ. And this means that we cannot think of the time between these two events as infinite, or empty, waiting to be filled in one way or another. It is a time which is limited, which is marked off for a definite filling, which shares a very definite meaning and purpose. And we know that this filling consists in the believing of the Gospel and its world-wide proclamation. It consists, then, in something which is the work and gift and task of the [207] Church. Hence we know that all other events, however great and important they may be, however glorious or terrible they may be, are still co-ordinated with, and subordinated to, this one purpose of the time. And this means that we know what is the really urgent and necessary thing in all possible circumstances. We see the utter insignificance of Church history in the midst of the other events of our so-called era. But we also understand the claim which has always been advanced by the Church for the importance of its history. We are not ashamed of this claim, nor do we reject it. In theory, and above all in practice, we have to confess that Church history does actually have priority over all other history, that with all its insignificance and folly and confusion in history generally, it is still the central and decisive history to which all the rest is as it were only the background or accompaniment. We shall be most careful in our concrete applications of this insight, because we know that it can be maintained only with the demonstration of the Spirit and of power. But we cannot give up our insight that our time as it is still given to us is the time of the Church. And in its fulfilment we are faced by Church history as a continuous trace of the One in whose name the Church offers its most modest and equivocal service, which is still the highest service of all.

Furthermore, we have to consider the capacity for outward and above all inward resistance which the Church has continually shown in the course of its history. The fact that it is in time, and in history generally, the fact that it is indeed one element in history generally, means that in all the expressions of its life, at every stage and in every form of its history, it has to wrestle with the overwhelmingly oppressive and powerful strangeness and even hostility of all other elements in that history. It has always had to believe in the world what the world does not and cannot believe. It has always had to proclaim to the world what the world does not want and is not able to receive. That this is the true situation of the Church no one is more fully aware than the one who is called to the Church, who is himself one of those who are both liberated and bound. He knows the overwhelming opposition of the world to his Lord, as the Old Testament bears dramatic witness to it in the relationship between Israel and Yahweh. He knows it in the most intimate way from his own Israelitish heart and mind and will and life. But in the most intimate way he also knows the more powerful resistance which is already offered to all the turmoil and strangeness and hostility of world-occurrence. He knows the almighty faithfulness of the King of Israel. And it is the wonderful operation of this faithfulness which he obviously sees in action in the Church. He does not see there indomitable character, or inerrant ideas, or infallible courts or institutions. What he does see is all the power of the assault of that strange and hostile element, and in face of it all the human pusillanimity and compliance

[208] and helplessness and weakness which have always appeared in a more unfavourable light in the Church than in any other sphere. He sees that continually real dangers were not recognised as soon as they should have been, and others feared when they might coolly have been ignored. He sees that clever and pious folk who were apparently sound and living members of the Church have gradually or suddenly gone to pieces and become a target for contempt and scoffing. He sees that with the passage of time lights which had once been bright have become dim and eventually been extinguished. He sees so much apparently undeserved and inexplicable and meaningless suffering on the part of the community and its members, so much unjust and yet triumphant persecution, so much crude or refined repression, so much sacrifice and destruction. But understanding only too well his own outer and inner

involvement as a member of this Church, he not only sees all this, but he also understands it. And this means that he will not be too greatly shocked at it, or too full of criticism and complaint. For he also sees that in and through it all the Church has continually resisted, that it has continually been snatched from its anxieties and preserved at the last from a complete submergence in its temptations, that suddenly or after a period its wounds have been healed, that its Babylonian captivities have ended, that its enemies and persecutors have one day vanished from the scene, that it has continually been raised up from the dead to newness of life. He sees in its history something persistent and persisting—a continuity. Certainly he does not deduce it from the insights and capacities and piety and good-will of the men who take part in this history. Nor does he deduce it from the soundness of the majority of Christians, or from particularly Christlike personalities, or from the dogmas and institutions of Christianity, or from the Christian cultus. He sees the equivocal nature of all these things, and yet he sees also this something persistent and persisting in them. This is why he cannot fail to give thanks for all these things, for the life of the Church, for the faith of the people of God, for what is given to him by individual leaders and teachers, for the constant power to enlighten possessed by the dogmas and institutions of Christianity and the Christian cultus. In spite of inevitable criticism, his thinking about them will be basically positive. For he knows that even in their weakness and proneness to evil they could and can be the instruments of this resistance and signs of this persistence; just as he himself as a bound and liberated member of the Church, irrespective and in spite of his own merits, and quite inexplicably in the light of his own weakness, can also resist in his own thoughts and decisions, in his own heart as a believer. That which persists, that which resists, is simply the power of the divine call. Or primarily, it is simply the power of the living Word of the prophets and apostles. At every other point in this matter we can and must set a question-mark. But the divine call, the living Word of Scripture, does persist and resist; it does actu ally win through in the Church. The divine call is the Church's enabling: [209] the power of resistance which in spite of all its outer and inner wretchedness it has continually displayed in its history; the power to remain what it is; the power to believe again and to take up again its task of proclamation in spite of its defeats and declensions and difficulties. If we are to see our way clearly at this point, we must see this divine Nevertheless. And if we do see it, we shall see in Church history the trace of that supremacy of free grace. We shall see that it is supremacy even in the midst of world-occurrence. And we shall also see the King of Israel, and therefore Jesus Christ, as the One who is Lord of all.

Furthermore, we have to consider the power of renewal which the Church has continually and no less clearly manifested in the course of its history. In relation to other elements in world history, the Church often appears either to be age-old—the curious remnant of a magical epoch, or of some other age which has long since disappeared—or else relentlessly to be growing old. It is indeed old, and there is nothing to be ashamed of in that fact. For the fathers boasted that in the true sense its existence began even in Paradise. But the point is that this Church which to its glory or shame we have to call old has continually displayed its capacity in some astonishing fashion to become new—far more new than all the novelties of secular history. Again, of course, we know this renewing in the most intimate way, as an event in our own lives. For if in our encounter with the Word of God we have really begun to live as members of the Church, then we know something of the goodness which is new every morning; we know something of the way in which the inward man is renewed day by day; and, knowing this, we know something of the secret of this renewal of the Church. We cannot deduce it from inherited human factors, although in this case, too, we have to reckon with them, and reckon with them observantly and thankfully. If we were to look only to these factors, the total picture would be only of a confirmed old age, or a relentless ageing of the Church, just as humanly speaking the total picture of the life of the individual Christian can only be of his growing old. But we can also think of the work of God's Word in the Church, remembering that the Church is the place where His honour dwells. We can think, for example, that the prophets and apostles are always in its midst as living subjects speaking something new. Then we shall see that it does not merely persist and resist, but that it is in fact made new. Then we shall see that Church history is not merely one of restorations but also of reformations. We shall know the Church not merely as *perpetua mansura*[EN549], but also as *perpetua reformanda*[EN550]. We shall see that if it has any power its *manere*[EN551] is always a *reformari*[EN552], that its triumphant *manere*[EN553] consists in its *reformari*[EN554]. And then perhaps we shall ask whether the processes of deformation, the distortions and disturbances which are caused in

[210]

the Church by human error and ill-will, must not be regarded as necessary reactions against what have come to be dominant over-emphases, or as beneficial challenges to a new and better faithfulness. The fathers were perhaps right when along these lines they tried to find a positive meaning even in the existence of heresies and schisms. Certainly, if we are members of the Church participating for ourselves in its daily renewal we learn to be amazed at the economy which rules in its history, not merely modulating and correcting but constantly reviving, so that it seems to be ordained that a secularised Christianity should always be followed by the counter-thrust of a vigorously eschatological, a narrow and restricted by that of an open and free, an old-fashioned by that of a modern, an intellectualised by that of a practical, a naive by that of an instructed, an indolent by that of an active, an over-busy by that of a contemplative, a clerical by that of a lay, and a too popular by that of a healthily

---

[EN549] enduring forever
[EN550] forever being reformed
[EN551] enduring
[EN552] being reformed
[EN553] enduring
[EN554] being reformed

authoritarian. These have all been actual renewals. They have not been accomplished without new errors and apostasy, but from the standpoint of the basis of the Church they still have to be recognised as necessary renewals, in which the Church as a whole has come to life again, in which we can on the whole, therefore, recognise a guiding of the Church, a guiding which does not ever desire its death, but always its life. And if we do not fail to see this, we shall not fail to see a trace of the divine world-governance in the Church which is also a trace of the divine world-governance as such.

3. *The history of the Jews.* It may well be said that of all the phenomena so far mentioned this is the most astonishing and provocative. At this point we are almost tempted to speak, not of an indication of the world-governance of God, the God of the Bible, but of an actual demonstration of it, as the physician of Frederick the Great did to the king. But we shall not do this. For it is not impossible to consider the history of the Jews, like that of the Bible, without coming to the conclusion that the world has a ruling King, and that Jesus of Nazareth is this King. This is something which can be proved only by its own self-demonstration. But even as an indication not only of the matter itself but of its self-demonstration, the history of the Jews has a very special cogency. It is easier to turn away unenlightened from the history of the Bible and that of the Church than from this history. And it is harder with this history than with the others to be content with a view which does not accept the theological insight and explanation. Yet even at this point we cannot actually see any more than we can at the others. All that we can do is to begin to think along rather unusual lines.

With the fall of Samaria in 722 and the disappearance of the ten Northern tribes from biblical and secular history, in practice the Jews, or the two Southern tribes, became Israel, and Israel became the Jewish people. From that point onwards the content of the Old Testament is the particular and provisional history of this people with God, or rather of God with this people. The question is one of a provisional history. It is one of the tortuous history of a much threatened people, which is still this people, and as such has this history. The judgment overhanging it had not yet been fully executed. Even the temple which the Babylonians destroyed in 586 was built again in 520 under Zerubbabel. The people went into exile, but they returned again to take up their own life in their own country. The second violation of the temple by Antiochus Epiphanes in 168 was followed in 165 by a second restoration. To this period according to the usual reckoning there belong the last and most recent portions of the canonical Old Testament. In the first century the Canon was fixed and closed in its present form, and the temple was destroyed a third time, and a third time—and now more gloriously than ever—it was re-established. It was in this form that Jesus Himself saw it, and it was at the end of this development, which was no longer a development, that He who was Himself a Jew visited His people: this people which was still Israel and yet only representative of Israel; this people which still had the consciousness of its divine election and of the divine covenant established with it, but which strictly speaking had the consciousness only of their written documentation. For what had really happened after 722, or before? And what was going to happen? Who were these Jews, and what was to become of them? It seems that even amongst the surrounding nations there had already been a good deal of speculation on this point. (Cf. for what follows, Kurt Emmerich, *Die Juden,* 1939.)

[211]

After the death of Jesus there was a significant interval of some forty years—a kind of final period of grace, a last opportunity for repentance. Then the real history of the Jews began with what was to be the final destruction of Jerusalem and the temple by Titus. On this point there is no doubt at all in the witness of the New Testament. The definitive destruction of the old form of Israel was the negative side of the death of Jesus as a saving event, the shadow thrown by that event in the wider sphere of world history generally. The connexion between the two is a whole subject in itself. What is quite indisputable is that after this double event there is on the one hand no continuation of the history of the covenant as a history of God and this one people to the exclusion of all others, and on the other a particular history of the Jews within world history generally, a history which is no longer provisional but has all the marks of being final. The die is now cast. From now on the Jews will be that which they became in the year 70. And what is that? What have they been during these last 1900 years? What are they still to-day? This is the problem with which we are now faced.

We may begin with the simplest and most impressive factor. The die is cast, but this did not mean that they disappeared like the ten tribes. It did not mean that they were destroyed as their then enemies intended. They outlived the Roman Empire to which they were then subject, just as they have notoriously outlived other empires since. They are still there. This is in itself a highly astonishing fact. We have to remember how small they were. We have to remember how unfavourable the conditions were for their continued existence. We have to remember what had become of the powerful nations which had once been [212] their enemies, the one-time Assyrians, Babylonians, Persians and Syrians, not to speak of the lesser peoples which had once been their neighbours and oppressors. They had all long since lost their identity. We no longer know any of them as they once were. But in spite of the destruction and persecution and above all the assimilation and interconnexion and intermingling with other nations the Jews are still there, and permanently there. And how active and prominent they are!—an isolated element in history; a leaven which maintains itself and in its own way succeeds amongst other elements; not often loved or even assisted or protected from outside by the others, but quite the reverse; usually despised for some obscure reason, and kept apart, and even persecuted and oppressed by every possible spiritual and physical weapon, and frequently exterminated in part; yet always and everywhere surviving; again and again demonstrating its continued existence by the fact of it; again and again winning for itself an involuntary respect. The only thing that has been missing is something that we have seen in our own days—the Jews (or at any rate many of the Jews) actually living again in Palestine, claiming and setting up and establishing a new state of Israel, and this quite irrespective of the conflict between East and West which threatens the stability of the rest of the world and its culture. In the shortest possible time it has produced the most striking results, culturally, diplomatically, and against all expectation militarily. It seems to have behind it—and we could not say this of all states—an enthusiastic and self-sacrificing youth. Not from any point of view can we ignore or make light of the existence of this state. And in it all its representatives have displayed in an astonishing way the very qualities which distinguished the Jews as far back as the time of Jeremiah, and again in that of Judas Maccabaeus, and the defenders of Jerusalem against Titus, and Bar-Cochbar, and similar figures from their distant past. There they are again, there they are still—the remarkable, representative remnant of Israel. It ought not to be so. In the year 70, in that destruction of Jerusalem which corresponded in so sinister a way to the death of Jesus, it was clearly not intended that it should be so. Jews as Jews were not meant to have any continued existence. They were not meant to have any perceptible existence. But they always have had, and they still have to-day; and to-day genuinely so, and directly after what was apparently the worst disaster in all their history, completely eclipsing all previous disasters. There they are, actual witness to Old Testament history, actual members of the race to which Jesus Himself belonged and without which there would never have been a New Testament or a Christian Church. There they are, the "librarians of the Church," as Augustine called them, because the Old Testament without which even the Church cannot live is ultimately the book of their books, and originally their sacred Canon. There they are, not as antique-dealers, but as a constantly self-renewed actualisation and demonstration of the man who in virtue [213] of these books was God's partner in the covenant upon whose fulfilment the Church is founded. For if we hear of man before God either in the Old Testament or in the greater part of the New it is this man, Jewish man, who is meant. And if any of us wish to identify ourselves with man before God in the biblical sense, we have to identify ourselves with this Jewish man. Both inside and outside, outside and inside the Church, this Jewish man as such is incalculably present, forcing us to take note of him in world history. And seeing there is this Jewish representation, are not the ten lost tribes there as well? Is not all Israel always present unrecognised? When the name of the new state jumped so surprisingly from the language of the Bible and the Church, the language of Canaan, right into the modern newspaper, did it not express a solid fact and not merely a presumption?

We speak of the Jews, and yet in the strict sense we cannot say with any certainty who and what we really mean by the term. Even if we accept the equivocal expression, it is impossible to prove conclusively that the Jews form a single race. If the Jews do belong to a race, it is to the Semites to which their former enemies also belonged, and to which the most bitter of their modern enemies belong. And from the biological standpoint it is impossible to point to any specifically Jewish characteristics within the generally Semitic. The physical traits which were once regarded as specifically Jewish are all characteristic of the Semites as a whole, and not only of the Semites, for the same features can be found just as clearly amongst Mediterranean peoples with quite a different origin, and even within the so-called Aryan peoples. The idea of a specifically Jewish blood is pure imagination.

Again, there is no particular speech which marks off the Jews as Jews. In those branches of Judaism which have held fast to the religion of Moses Hebrew has been preserved as a cultic language, or as the language of theological scholarship. And in certain well-defined areas of Jewish life degenerate forms of Hebrew have been preserved as the common speech. And to-day in connexion with Zionism and its fulfilment in Palestine there are Hebrew newspapers and the beginnings of a Hebrew literature. But this does not mean that the overwhelming majority of Jews have thought and spoken in Hebrew throughout the centuries, or that they do so to-day. In the modern state of Israel, Hebrew has again attained to a place of honour, or rather it has been artificially given a place of honour, but even there its obvious character is that of an Esperanto introduced for the purpose of mutual understanding between people who speak so many different languages. It is merely a confirmation that the Jews as such have no mother-tongue.

[214] Again, we cannot speak of a specifically Jewish culture. What the Jews have always achieved in this sphere has been by way of an outstanding and peculiar contribution to the formation and more particularly to the development and purification—and often to what for other reasons, and not through any fault of theirs, turned out to be the dissolution—of the culture of other peoples. So far they have never produced a specifically Jewish culture in the sense in which we can speak of specifically German and French and Italian and English cultures. They have never given a recognisably Jewish character to culture generally, as the Americans are doing to-day, and as the Swiss did formerly. It has yet to be seen whether or not something of this kind will happen in Palestine. But it has not happened so far.

Again, for a long time now the Jews have obviously not been marked by a common religion. There is the Jewish Synagogue, but for many years the Synagogue has not been identical with the Jewish people or representative of it. And who can say whether even the Synagogue, so far as participation in the life of it does characterise some Jewish circles, does really continue along the orthodox lines of the older post-exilic Judaism, and not according to one of the many Liberal re-interpretations of the Law, as actually happened at the time of the assimilation, when it more or less consciously adopted the modern philosophy of the *Goyim*[EN555]?—not to speak of the fact that Jews can be pantheists or atheists or sceptics or even good or bad Christians without ceasing to be Jews. With all their veneration for the Jewish past, the authorities and people of the state of Israel—and with good reason—do not seem even to have thought of regarding any religion, whether Mosaic or otherwise, as constitutive for its inauguration.

[EN555] gentiles

Finally, even the concept of the history of the Jews as we ourselves have made use of it is a most ambiguous one. Since the year 70 there have been many different and disconnected histories of the Jews, that of the Polish Jews, the Spanish Jews, the Portugese Jews, or the German Jews. There has, of course, been the history of the Jewish Synagogue and its various ramifications, the history of its scriptural exegesis, its worship, and its piety. There have been the histories of countless Jewish groups and individuals. There have been the histories of Jewish movements and undertakings, as, for example, modern Zionism. But there has never been a connected history of the Jews as a single community, a history which itself has helped to form this community. In the individual histories there has been much that was common to all of them, but at no point did the common element produce that which is essential to the history of a people—a common movement from the past to the future. Even that which is taking place in Palestine is provisionally only the work of a comparatively small proportion of Jewry as a whole. It is still an open question whether the overwhelming majority of the others will want to participate in it. And even if they do, it is still a question whether they will be able to do so, considering their numbers in relation to the particular spatial, climatic and economic factors.

Since the same peculiar circumstances obtain in relation to a common physique, language, culture, religion and history, there is every justification for what is admittedly a perverse question: Are the Jews really a people at all? Certainly the question is not at all an impossible one. In respect of all these criteria there is need of clarification when we speak of the Jewish people. And no such clarification is possible. The Jews are really and perceptibly there, and in face of this fact we cannot easily deny that they are a people. But when we say this, we have to realise that strictly speaking we do not know what we are saying. As the history of this people was determined in the year 70, it seems to consist in the fact that the people then took up its existence again, and yet ceased to be a people in the usual sense of the term, and has never been one since. It necessarily continues to exist in this unique way, as a people which in the usual sense of the word is not a people. It necessarily has history which strictly speaking is non-historical; the history of a guest and alien and stranger and exception amongst the nations, with the eternal Jew, perhaps, as its legendary pattern. [215]

What we have seen, then, is the mysterious persistence of the Jews, and their even more mysterious existence in world history. Surely the providential significance of their history must be immediately apparent to everybody. And yet we have to say that even here there is no question of a "must." It is possible either to overlook or to deny this significance. In the light of what we have seen the possibility is a singular one, but it is still a real possibility. The historical facts can carry a very different message without any detailed differences in the way in which they are seen and assessed. It is obvious that the Jewish question as a whole does not have to everyone the same acuteness as we have found in it.

Even the fact of the continued existence of the Jews to which we first referred does not have to be regarded as quite so astonishing as we pictured it. And the question who and what are the Jews can be put in a far less penetrating and emphatic way than we have put it. The perplexity in which we find ourselves cannot be denied, but at any rate it can be concealed, perhaps with the help of different pretexts at one or other of the points that we have touched on. Certainly it is possible to dispute our own conclusion that the Jews have to be understood as a people which is not a people. And this conclusion is in fact disputed: not only by the champions of what is in principle a relativist view of history, to whom *a priori*[EN556] the existence of any such paradox is necessarily uncongenial; but also by those who are passionately involved in the question, by the Jews themselves, who will certainly protest against having to exist in the last resort only as the strange shadow of a people among other real peoples; and also by anti-Semites and philo-Semites, who if our view were correct would have to admit that they were fighting either for or against a shadow, and who are certainly not prepared to make an admission of this kind. As against the view of Jewish history which we have developed, those who regard it from these different standpoints can conclude only that it is not at all perplexing, and that the people is not at all shadowy, as we have suggested, but that in their own way the Jews are a normal phenemonon in world history generally, and that it is wrong to ascribe to them any special or providential significance as compared with other peoples. And none of them is at a loss for restrictive or attenuating explanations of the historical facts to which we have alluded.

[216]

It will be as well to accept this possibility at once. But we do not propose to make use of it ourselves. In face of a historicism which is in principle relativist, in face of the Jews themselves, in face of anti-Semites and philo-Semites, we maintain that when we deal with the phenomenon of the history of the Jews we are dealing with a problem *sui generis*[EN557]. We maintain that within world history generally the Jews are a people in the distinctive way which in the last resort we can describe only as negative. We maintain that it is only as a people of this kind that they have a history. But we have to admit that when we say this we are considering and assessing them from a standpoint which it is not within the powers of everyone to adopt. Certainly we cannot speak of any necessity to consider the matter from this standpoint. It is a question here, and categorically so, either of knowing or not knowing. It is a question of the inseparably interrelated message of the Old and New Testaments. It is a question of the divine electing and calling of this people as it culminated and was fulfilled in Jesus Christ as the King of Israel. It is a question of the faithfulness of Yahweh in face of the unfaithfulness of this people. It is a question of the supremacy of His free grace towards this people as it was revealed and actualised in that One. It is a question of the saving event of His death and its meaning for this people.

[EN556] unconditionally
[EN557] in its own category

It is a question of that event in whose shadow the history of the Jews began in the year 70. To those who know all this, the history of this people and its continance and being in the midst of other peoples will always be a miracle and a riddle. They cannot think of this people merely as one people among others. They are amazed that it does exist, but they are no less amazed that it exists in this way, as a people which is not a people, and has no true history. And they see in this special history a trace of the divine world-governance, and they see that the world-governor is the One whom the Bible calls God, the Lord who is called Yahweh in the Old Testament and Jesus of Nazareth in the New. But again, those who do not know this, and perhaps will not know it, can only reject this view, thus leaving it an open question whether the history of the Jews should not be regarded as the normal history of a normal people incorporated as such in world history as a whole, either after the manner of historical relativism, or according to the proud self-understanding of the Jews themselves, or the interpretation of their opponents or sympathisers. And from one or other of these standpoints they will deny that in the history of the Jews we [217] are confronted with a particular manifestation or trace of the divine providence in the Christian sense of the word. We freely allow that we ourselves made use of the first and not the second possibility when we regarded and represented the history of the Jews as something inexplicable, as a great question-mark. We claim indeed that that history is explicable, but only in its inexplicability, only as a question-mark interposed into world history. And we make this claim because and to the extent that we are able to view the matter from the standpoint of the Christian message. For it is only as we ourselves know this message, only as we know it in such a way that we are committed by it, that we are forced to start our thinking at this point and at no other, and can and will see the history of the Jews as we have here represented it. Seen from this point, the history of the Jews does necessarily take the form of an *aporia*, a riddle, as we have represented it. Seen from this point, it does so necessarily; although necessarily, as we have granted, only as seen from this point.

The Jews, the remnant of Israel, did not disappear from world history in the year 70. As a submerging minority amongst other peoples, they alone of all the great and small nations which once surrounded them continued an inexplicably and unprecedently active and visible life, a life which they are still energetically continuing to-day. It was in that year indeed that they really entered world history for the first time. And from the standpoint of the Christian message the reason for this is that God's decree in His election of this people and covenanting with it is an eternal and unshakeable decree. The people was an unfaithful people. From the very first it willed to be a people like others, to have a king and a history like others. But this could not alter the faithfulness of God, and it has not altered it right up to the present time. It was not altered even by the provisional judgments and finally the definitive judgment which in the year 70 ended its existence in identity, or at any rate similarity, without her peoples. How could it be altered by the judgment in which God finally ratified

His grace towards this unworthy partner by Himself taking its place, the judgment of Golgotha? Far from turning aside from His people, far from allowing
it to fall, in the One who died for His people and for all men God not merely
turned towards it but accepted solidarity with it. His appointment and constitution of Israel as the bearer of light and salvation to all nations are actualised
in the death and revealed in the resurrection of the One who is the remnant of
the Jewish remnant of Israel, and who definitely died and rose again on behalf
of this remnant, indeed of Israel as a whole. What it involves to be the unfaithful and disobedient Israel, and the unfaithful and disobedient remnant, of this
faithful and gracious King, is worked out and manifested in the judgments
which continued all through the earlier history of Israel and finally culmin-

[218]   ated in the events of the year 70. Progressively, and at last completely, these
judgments and this final judgment whittle away that which Israel and the Jews
had allowed to become a snare to them—their identity, or at any rate their
similarity with other peoples. Those who according to the word of the prophet
had willed to be "Not my people" now became "Not a people." They can be a
people now only as the people of God, only on the basis of His election and
grace and long-suffering. At the very moment when salvation comes, and
comes of the Jews, Jerusalem and the temple fall—the Jerusalem and temple
of the Jews who even in that saving event remain only too true to themselves in
their unfaithfulness. But their election and the covenant which God made
with them do not fall with the fall of this external glory. How could they fall
when they were actually confirmed both by the act of salvation and also by the
act of destruction? And since the election and the covenant still stand—not
removed but fulfilled in Jesus Christ—the Jews also stand in world history. This
is the secret of their continued existence, which seen against the message of
the Old Testament is not in a sense a historical riddle, nor an accidental miracle, but the declared mystery of God, the mystery of His faithfulness and
grace, of the constancy of His will and decree. It is not to their race or language
or culture, and least of all to their Mosaic religion, but to the faithfulness and
grace of God, that they and the world owe the fact that they are still there: the
descendants of those who murmured in the wilderness and set up the golden
calf; the people who did not hearken to their prophets and later adorned their
sepulchres; the people who finally rejected their Messiah and delivered Him
up to the Gentiles; and yet the people to whom God had sworn and has kept an
unchanging faithfulness; the people to whom He never denied His witnesses
and succour; the people whose history He fulfilled by Himself becoming one
of them, and as an Israelite, a Jew, maintaining the covenant which they broke
and ratifying the promise; the people from whom this Israelite, this Jew, came
forth, to be the Saviour of the world. It is because they are this people that the
Jews are still there with their own particular history within world history generally: a people which is no people, and as such is *the* people, the people of God;
a people which has no history, and as such, with all the problems which it raises
in world history, has the only truly human history, the history of man with

God. It is because the Jews are this people that it is true of them right up to our own day: "He that toucheth you toucheth the apple of my eye" (Zech. 2⁸). But no man can touch the apple of His eye. Therefore the Jews can be despised and hated and oppressed and persecuted and even assimilated, but they cannot really be touched; they cannot be exterminated; they cannot be destroyed. They are the only people that necessarily continues to exist, with the same certainty as that God is God, and that what He has willed and said and done according to the message of the Bible is not a whim or a jest, but eternally in earnest, and the theme of creaturely occurrence in all ages. The history of the Jews is the embodiment of this theme of all world history. Hence derives not merely the explicability but the necessity of the proofs of existence which they have continually displayed, the power of which has manifestly not decreased but increased with the passage of the centuries, and which are still being displayed to-day with a likeness to the situations attested in the Old Testament which is almost uncanny. And the historicists and the Jews themselves and their opponents and sympathisers must ask themselves whether in the last analysis it is not futile to try to explain it all from any other standpoint. But if we do see and explain it from this standpoint, with all its necessity, then we perceive that what confronts us is the trace of the divine world-governance in all creaturely occurrence, a trace in which we recognise at once who it is that exercises the divine control. [219]

But from this standpoint, and in the light of the biblical message, we can also understand the enigmatical being of the Jews in world history, and in all its enigmatical character. Who and what is the Jew? We can now answer that the Jew is the man who belongs to this elected people. Because this election is still valid, he is therefore a man who continues right up to the present time. He is a man who always participates in it. But we have to add that he is a man who belongs to the people which from the very first has shown itself to be unworthy of the election; which has always supposed that it ought to have elected its own king rather than be elected by Him; which again and again has looked upon its election as a favour shown towards it in virtue of its own electing; which for this reason could easily and readily elect other kings, perhaps at bottom preferring another king; which for this reason rejected its King when He appeared amongst it, ratifying His grace but also quite definitely endorsing His claim to lordship. The Jew, therefore, belongs to the elected people, but he also belongs to the people which is unfaithful to its election. It is for the sake of the election that this people, and the Jew himself, persists and lives, but it is also for the sake of its unfaithfulness that it persists and lives, that the Jews exist as they actually do exist, that they are not a people, that this is the form in which they have traversed world history since the year 70. It is not in vain that they are a people ordained as bearers of light and salvation to all nations. It is not in vain that they are the holy remnant of Israel. It is not in vain that they are the human servant of God. It is not in vain that they are the people of the Jew Jesus of Nazareth who died on Golgotha laden with their sin and the sin of the whole world. It is not in vain that they are represented by this One. What man is in the light of the divine election and calling, how he is an object of the free grace of God, what is his relation to it and in what capacity he is judged by it—it is this whole shadow of the history of the covenant and salvation and its fulfilment which the Jews embody and reveal. Let it be understood: not in spite of their election, but because of it, on the basis of it. It costs something to be the chosen people, and the Jews are paying the price. Everything has to fall away that makes a man great and glorious in himself, all the pride of his own religion and culture and language and race. Living only by the grace of God, he is not allowed anything of his own by which to justify or adorn himself, or to vindicate himself and make his way in world history as a whole. All that he can do is simply to be there. He cannot be overlooked, or banished, or destroyed— for the grace of God holds and upholds him—but he is not allowed the glory which counts in world history generally. He is everywhere the minority. He is everywhere the guest and stranger. He is always the one who has no home, no city, no temple. How can he have, when the judgment of God is necessarily active and revealed in him together with the grace of God? Abraham was a stranger in the land of promise. Moses was a stranger to his own people. So were the prophets. The foxes have holes, and the birds of the air have nests, but the Son of Man hath not where to lay His head. The elect of God, whose very existence proclaims light and salvation to the world, but in whom the judgment of all flesh is also active and revealed, will always and necessarily be strangers in the world, with no home of their own. In this sense, too, the Jews are the elect of God.

And obviously the Jews are not merely strangers, but in their strangeness they have always been looked upon with disfavour. They have been unloved and despised and hated. Why especially the Jews? What is the reason for anti-Semitism, directed only against these particular Semites? How can we explain the strange disease from which every non-Jew seems to suffer in one form or another, the disease which can affect whole masses of people and break out so terribly, as it did in the Middle Ages and even more so in our own days, and can then be suppressed and forgotten, only to break out again like the plague? What is it that we have against the Jews? We cannot explain it merely by the few not very pleasant traits which we customarily attribute to them. All peoples have their unpleasant characteristics. Why is it that, although we are indignant at the unpleasant characteristics of other peoples and yet pardon them, we can never pardon those of the Jews? Why do all peoples react against the characteristics of this particular people as though they were something unusual? Is it not as though the enigmatic nature of the whole being of the Jews in some way affects other peoples at this point, so that an enigmatic attitude is forced upon them? It is pure illusion to suppose that on account of their characteristics the Jews are objectively worse, or harder to tolerate, than other peoples; that quite deservedly they give rise to a greater aversion than other peoples. And this means that we cannot understand anti-Semitism merely as a disease. It cannot be denied, however, that in fact the human race does suffer from this disease, and it must also be asserted that with all the available rational and moral argu- [221] ments we cannot overcome the disease. It is explicable (i.e., meaningful, as the meaningless thing which it is), only if as strangers, even as a people which is no people amongst other peoples, the Jews are still the elect of God, whose humanity shows up in a different and special and more penetrating light than that of other men, even though they themselves are neither better nor worse than other men. What is it that we see in the Jews? What is it that incites us against them? What is it that fills us with horror? What is it that can lead us to those most shameful and damnable outbreaks? If we are going to explain it theologically, and therefore radically prevent it, two things have to be said.

It is a source of annoyance to us—whether consciously or not makes no difference, for whether we are aware of it or not this is the one thing that really annoys us about the Jews—that in the Jews and their habit of life we have held out before us, and we recognise only too clearly, our own. The Jew as a Jew is neither better nor worse than other men. But in the Jew we have revealed and shown to us in a mirror who and what we all are, and how bad we all are. Even in this respect the Jew pays for the fact that he is the elect of God. The mercy of God to all man has been manifested in him, in this people. The Word and work of God in which salvation appeared to the whole world were actualised in the history of this people. God Himself was made flesh of our flesh in a member of this people. Hence it is revealed in this people what man is, man in his relationship with God, man before the judgment seat of God, sinful man: the man who resists and opposes the grace of God; the man who counts it too mean a thing to live only by the grace of God; the man who wants another king instead of this King; the man who does not want to be elected by God, but wants to elect God, and secretly wants to be his own god; the man who wants to preserve and help and save himself by his own efforts, taking to himself all the glory. And is this only the Jewish man? Not by a long way. This is every man, without exception. But what every man is before God, as the object of His mercy, is revealed in the Jewish man (as elect man) in a way in which it is not revealed in any other. How finely it is suppressed and concealed in the former neighbours and enemies of Israel, the Amalekites, Philistines, Moabites, etc., the Egyptians and Assyrians and Babylonians, and later the Greeks and Romans! How finely it is still suppressed and concealed in the British and French and Germans, and above all the Swiss. How easily, with our usual one-sided anger and hatred, we can ascribe to one another the characteristics and failings which are common to us all! How easily, after our momentary quarrels, we can again understand and acknowledge and approve one another, and even find one another interesting and likeable! Why? Because the evil in man—the true evil in his relationship with God and therefore with his fellow-men—is not at all revealed in the habits and bad habits of these other peoples. [222] It is undoubtedly there. But who is to tell? Who is to recognise the primal revolt of man against God and his own nature? Who cannot cloak over this revolt? And who can see through the cloak in the case of these other peoples? Who can see right through to what they really are—enemies of grace, and as such necessarily enemies of one another? Who can see right through to man himself as the enemy of the human race? If we are to know this, we must first know that there is such a thing as enmity against the grace of God, and therefore against man; that there is such a thing as sin. And if we are to know this, we must first know ourselves. But the nations and the individual members of the nations do not know themselves; they do not know what sin is. They can fight with one another and they can treat with one another. They can make war and they can make peace. There can never be real enmity between them. There can never be anything like anti-Semitism. There can never be that original and unconquerable aversion which they all have to the Jew. Why to the Jew? Because that which is suppressed in them is not suppressed in the Jew; that which is concealed in them is not concealed in the Jew. The Jew is the man from whom the cloak has been torn off. The Jew stands before us as that which radically we all are. In the Jew there is revealed the primal revolt, the unbelief, the disobedience, in which we are all engaged. In this sense the Jew is the most human of all men. And that is why he is not pleasing to us. That is why we want him away. That is why we want to remove this alien element from our midst. It is the very fact that we know him only too well which makes his strangeness repulsive. That is why we are so critical of the Jews. That is why we make them out to be worse than they really are. That is why we invent the absurd notion of a Jewish race, which we invest with every conceivable unpleasant characteristic. That is why we ascribe to the Jews as such every possible crime. Our annoyance is not really with the Jew himself. It is with the Jew only because and to the extent that the Jew is a mirror in which we immediately recognise ourselves, in which all the nations recognise themselves as they are before the judgment-seat of God. That is what we can never forgive the Jew. That is why we think we have to heap hatred and contempt upon the stranger. And obviously it is because they are this mirror that the Jews are there. The divine providence has arranged it that the Jews should still be there, and continue to be there, and no anti-Semitism, however refined or crude, can ever alter the fact. Because they are the elect people of God they have to be there openly and visibly. And because their election is a pattern of the election of all peoples, of the whole of the human race, this mirror cannot be taken away and must not be taken away. All men have to look in this mirror and see themselves as they really are, and confess that their cloaks are only cloaks, and that in reality they too are mani-

[223] festly the enemies of God. It is obvious that it needs more than the existence of the Jews actually to reveal this fact to men and to the nations. It needs the Gospel and faith in the Gospel; it needs their ingathering into the community of Jesus Christ, if men are to read and understand the sign and testimony which is given them in the existence of the Jews, and are actually to be convinced that they too are the enemies of God, enemies to whom He has turned in the supremacy of His grace and not according to their own merits or

deservings. Otherwise it is natural that the existence of the Jews should merely prove to be an annoyance, a source of irritation. But the objective meaning of the irritation and annoyance, the objective truth of the sign and testimony which has here been given to man, is not in any way dependent upon whether they perceive and understand it as such. It is still the case that the sign and testimony is given to them with this meaning and this truth. And the fact that it is given is proved by the non-Jews themselves when they are so annoyed and irritated and estranged and offended, when they cannot let the matter rest. It is clear that they know well enough that something unpleasant is being said to them at this point. They cannot deny the existence of the point. They cannot deny that they are in danger of hearing this unpleasant thing even though they have not already heard it. They must always return to the point, like a criminal to the scene of his crime. Their anti-Semitism betrays them, even though they may not know what it is that they are trying to do, or actually doing, when they are so obstinately anti-Semitic. In face of this trace of the divine world-governance, they do the most perverse thing conceivable, but in so doing they make it only too clear that they have come across this trace and cannot evade it. This is the first thing that we have to say from the theological standpoint.

The second is this. It is a source of irritation to us—and again it makes no odds whether we are conscious of it or not—that in the actual existence of the Jews, in their strange being as a people which is not a people, we are positively confronted with the fact of God's electing grace, with the fact of His mercy as the sole and mighty basis of human existence. And by our irritation we confirm that we do not really like this fact. It annoys and irritates us that the Jew is undoubtedly there as he has been there for 1900 years. It annoys and irritates us that he obviously can be there, even in and in spite of the unfavourable historical situation in which he is placed, even though he is not marked by any of the things which normally make possible the existence of a people as a people, even though he is not protected by the qualities which normally differentiate other peoples the one from the other, constituting them individual peoples and giving them a right of domicile, a claim to a place in world history. Even when it had a certain similarity with other peoples, how pushed about this people was!—first into Palestine, then down into Egypt, then into the wilderness, back again into Palestine, and so on right up to its great and final [224] dispersion among all the nations. And what an existence it has since had in all the different groups and individual members of these groups!—an existence which defies all outward and inward probability. But it still does exist, and it can still be perceived. Is it really possible to exist as the Jews have existed? Well, this is what they have done, and in doing it they are obviously a mirror, a mirror of the election of the divine grace and mercy on whose basis they were clearly able to do it. And not on any other basis!—that is what annoys and irritates us so much from this standpoint. In their persistence the Jews are absolutely exceptional, and they obviously surpass us. We ourselves have to exist in the normal way, and we are content and even proud to have an assured place and an assured path. But we see only too clearly that placed in the same unfavourable conditions we could never have achieved a similar persistence. There are plenty of examples to prove it. It took only a century for the Frenchmen who emigrated to Prussia to become Prussians, and in some cases ultra-Prussians; and when the Swiss settle in America they immediately become Americans. Now the Jew himself can become a German, or a Swiss, or an American, but in so doing he never ceases to be a Jew, either in his own consciousness or consequently in that of others. In this respect the Jews can do something which we cannot do. And this fact irritates us, and the more so because we cannot explain why they can do it. In existing in so strangely relative and unrooted and uncertain a fashion, and yet doing it with such unparalleled persistence, they remind us painfully of the relativity of our own existence. Both phenomena are comprehensible from the standpoint of the divine election. If they are the elect people, and if they continue to exist by the divine grace and mercy, it is quite comprehensible that they should exist without any other root or security. And it is also comprehensible that they are able to do it with this persistence, that they are obviously preserved in a way which cannot be said of other peoples. The one phenomenon is explained by the utter freedom and unmeritedness of the divine mercy, by the glory which God wills to lay up to Himself. The other is explained by the force and omnipotence of His grace. But supposing that their existence is not an end in itself, a final end? Supposing that as the elect people in the midst of others they are the mirror of the election of all peoples, of the whole race? What a close and unwelcome reality we see in this one people! For in this one people we perceive that if the divine election is a fact, and if it is the secret of human existence, the basis upon which all peoples and all individuals live, then what remains to us of all our assurances, of all that we imagine we can think and boast of as our own? Are these qualities of ours of any more lasting worth? Do we not exist far more dangerously than we either know or will admit? In this respect, too, is it not the case that the existence of the Jew reveals something which is otherwise con-

[225] cealed?—that no one, neither people nor individual, really has a home in world history, that no one is finally secure, that we are all pushed about, that we are all eternal strangers, since it is only in God that we are finally at home and secure. To us, the *beati possidentes*^{EN558}, the history of the Jews seems to convey something of this sort. And it is hardly surprising that we do not like either the message or those who deliver it. One of the reasons why we become anti-Semites is because of the anxiety aroused in us by this elect people and its fate. That is why we have a compelling desire that the mirror should be removed. And supposing we add the second fact, the uncanny persistence of Jewry in its very character as not a people? Supposing we realise that these Jews, stripped of all the things with which we think we can console ourselves, can still do that which we have been proved in practice incapable of doing, still

---

EN558 possessors of blessedness

remaining what they are even in destruction and dispersion, even in their long-continued exile through the centuries? Supposing these Jews have achieved in practice the very thing which other peoples devote so much energy to achieving, and at the last achieve only paritally and imperfectly, i.e., the practical demonstration of genuine national identity and independence? How irritating—and the more so the more we are feverishly concerned about our own nationality—to have to see nationality attained in the history of this people almost playfully, without any effort and against all expectation! Is it anything but sheer envy that has always enlisted the frightful support of nationalism against these Jews, this impotent not a people? What is it that we see in this mirror of the election of the Jewish people? Why is it that we are so unwilling even to be told that it is the elect people? Why is it that we ransack Christianity for proofs that it is no longer so. But obviously, if it is so, if this people which is not a people is the people of God, if in all its world-historical weakness it is still the true people, a nation without equal, then what becomes of the rest of us? And what a frantic sin is all other nationalism! From the existence of this people we have to learn that the elect of God is not a German or a Swiss or a Frenchman, but this Jew. We have to learn that in order to be elect ourselves, for good or evil we must either be Jews or belong to this Jew. And who among us is really willing either to learn this or to admit it? Yet it is a fact, and perhaps the wild fury of the anti-Semite is more perspicacious at this point than the gentle humanitarianism of those who are not patently guilty of the sin. For in the existence of the Jew we stumble upon the fact that the divine election is a particular election, that we ourselves have been completely over-looked in the particularity of this divine election. What the history of the Jews tells us is that the divine election is the election of another. Our election can be only in and with this other. If the grace and mercy and long-suffering of God are to be to us, if we are to remain, to persist, to be preserved, we cannot possibly avoid this other, for the goodness of God can be to us only as it is first to him, and to us only in and through him. And who is this other? The Jew? So we believe and suspect, and we hate and oppose the Jew as the rival who has eclipsed us and to whom we are unwilling to concede this superiority. But really it is the one Jew Jesus Christ who is looking out upon us from the desolation and persistence of the existence of the Jews. He is this Other who is for us. He is the one Elect as the new Head of the whole human race. It is true, of course, that He actually looks at us face to face only when we first encounter Him in the Gospel, in faith, in His community. It is true that only indirectly does His face meet us in the history of the Jews, agitating us in all this Jewish question. It is true that He Himself and His Word and Spirit are necessary if we are to perceive and understand this sign and testimony and not grossly to mis-understand it. But the sign and testimony is there—we have only to under-stand aright our own irritation at the Jews and we shall perceive it at once—and it is a sign which speaks of the election, which speaks of divine grace, which speaks of the One who was Himself a Jew, and outside whom there is

[226]

salvation in none other, but in whom there is fulness of salvation for all men of all nations. The sign and testimony of the history of the Jews is waiting for open eyes and unstopped ears. But it has been set up in the midst of world history, as a manifestation of the kingdom of this One, and therefore of the One who is the Lord of all world history.

4. The limitation of human life. We now make what is apparently a quite illegitimate leap. For what is the connexion, and how can we conjoin into a single series the history of Scripture, the history of the Church, the history of the Jews—and then suddenly, the limitation of human life? The first three are all concrete historical sequences with a definite content, and in virtue of their distinctive character all three stand in a clearly recognisable relationship to the history of the covenant and grace. But in the latter we have a general and formal condition of human life of which we can immediately add that it is a condition of all life. All life has to be lived as limited life. How, then, can we be dealing with a further sign and testimony to the fact that all world-occurrence is occurrence controlled by God, by the God of the Bible, by the King of Israel? Are we not deviating from the centre from which our thinking must start and to which it must return? Are we not leaving sacred history for the great and dark and always equivocal sphere of creaturely occurrence in general, which needs the light that may perhaps fall on it from sacred history, but which has no light of its own in virtue of which it can take its place with the elements already mentioned and tell us something about this sacred history, and about the One who is the active Subject in this history, and as such the ruling Subject in all occurrence?

By way of introduction to this pressing question, we will say this. Let us assume that at this point, in this arrangement which is no doubt very general and formal and embraces not only man but all life, in the fact, then, that all [227] men have to live within a definite limit, we really have to with a sign and testimony of the divine world-governance, the governance of the holy and gracious God of the Bible, the King of Israel. Let us suppose that this arrangement is in fact one of the characteristic or significant elements in world-occurrence, one of the traces which it is always and necessarily rewarding to contemplate as traces of the divine Lord of the world. If we make this assumption, then this trace has one specific advantage over all the others so far mentioned. For it can be contemplated directly. We have always to be made aware, and to be aware, of the fact that there is a history of Scripture and a history of the Church and a history of the Jews. They are indeed objective facts. Even if they do not enable us to give any specific proof, we can always describe them as such and to some extent discover them to be such. But we have to describe and discover them specifically. Even as facts they can in themselves remain concealed from countless numbers of men, simply because they do not lie within their orbit of vision, and perhaps never come within their orbit of vision. And they are never present to any of us so continuously and naturally and self-evidently that they can always speak to us. But if we have one of these signs and testimonies in human life itself, in its limitation and conditioning as the passage of a definite space of time from the beginning to the end, in its prolongation from the one to the other, then we are dealing with a fact which—whether we think of it or not—is at any rate constantly present to all of us, because it directly concerns the basic determination of our own existence. Even if I have never heard of Scripture or the Church or the Jews, or even if I have heard of them only as a concept which makes very little impact upon me, or even if they have not been present or spoken to me for some time past, it is still the case that I myself am a sign and testimony of the divine world-governance, and I myself am always present to myself: I myself, who am somewhere on the way between the beginning and the end, and conditioned by both; I myself, who once was not, and one day will be no longer; I myself, with my own individual life characterised by its individual limitation; I myself as the object of this disposing. And the fact of my limitation does not affect me any the less definitely and movingly, any the less decisively and personally, because I know that it extends not merely to me but to all men, and indeed to all living creatures. That I am a particular form of this general truth only makes it more relevant to me; it certainly does not make it irrelevant. That the truth is a general one does not alter the fact that, in so far as it is particular to me, it affects me and is undoubtedly present to me.

For example, in the well-known syllogism: All men must die; Caius is a man; Therefore Caius must die, the first proposition does not make the last untrue or irrelevant, but merely emphasises the truth and relevance which quite apart from the syllogism it still has for Caius himself.

If in itself and as such the limitation of human life is one of these distinctive [228] elements in world-occurrence—distinctive as an indication of the divine world-governance—then this means that in fact, and irrespective of whether he considers the fact or not, each individual man as such is a sign and testimony in this respect. His own individual life—the fact which is to him only too close and perceptible, the element in world-occurrence which he knows most intimately—is as such a sign and testimony which will speak to him in this respect even if he has never heard of Scripture or the Church or the Jews, even if he is unable to appraise their significance, even if in their significance they are not actually present to his consciousness. Always and in all circumstances we are conscious of ourselves. And therefore if the limitation of human life does belong to this series, its unmistakeable advantage as a sign and testimony to the divine world-governance is that it is always before us in a way which cannot be said of the others.

It is not my own inspiration to introduce the theme at this point, but I am simply following the curious and specific doctrine which the older theologians regularly introduced into their discussion of divine providence—the doctrine of the *terminus vitae*[EN559], i.e., the temporal goal and end of life as God has foreordained it for each individual with all its outer and inner circumstances. Many of the older theologians (as, for instance, D. Hollaz, *Ex. theol.*

[EN559] limit of life

acroam., 1707, I, 6, *qu.* 8) expanded it into a doctrine of the divinely ordered *ingressus, progressus et egressus*[EN560], and therefore of the divine conditioning of human life generally. But the accent was always upon the *egressus*[EN561], and therefore upon the frontier of life which is still before us. In all that they said on the point we can sense the atmosphere of an age to which the thought of death was on the one hand more familiar and self-evident, but on the other more pressing and serious; an age which in this respect showed itself to be far wiser than many. They had continually before them the saying in Ps. 139[16], which tells us about the eye of God which sees all our days, and the book in which they are all written; or in Ps. 31[15]: "My times (destiny) are in thy hand"; or in Job 14[5], which tells us that "his days are determined, and the number of his months are with thee, thou has appointed his bounds that he cannot pass." It is surprising that they did not think of other Old Testament passages, as for example Genesis 9[5f.], in which murder is forbidden because the blood, that is, the life of man as created in the image of God, belongs to God and must therefore be sacred to man, seeing that it is not his affair but God's to desire and will and encompass the end of a man. But at least they did face with a proper awe this fact of the limitation of human life, and in the single, concrete application and form of this general disposing, the death of the individual at his appointed hour, they saw a particular overruling of the divine providence, and one which called for particular notice and honour. The conflict between the Reformed and Lutheran groups came to the surface on this issue. The former spoke of a *terminus immobilis et fixus cum omnibus suis circumstantiis*[EN562] which God had appointed for each individual life, and in which it was naturally arranged that in the divine decree everything would be seen and foreordained which in his freedom man himself might contribute to the shortening or lengthening of his days (cf. F. Burmann *Syn. theol.*, 1671, I, 44, 8 f.). As against this, the Lutherans could allow only an absolute foreknowledge on the part of God, but they regarded His will and decree as partly conditioned by the course of nature which God had ordained, by the free conduct of man, good or bad, rational or irrational, and also by prayer, by which the *terminus*[EN563] already proclaimed and appointed for man can be deferred, as is [229] shown by the story of Hezekiah in Isaiah 38[1f.] (cf. D. Hollaz, *loc. cit.*). But the really remarkable feature is that they were all at one in regarding this appointment of a *terminus*[EN564] as a particularly important mark of the overruling of providence. It is this hint which we are following. But as we do so, we shall try to evaluate more precisely than they did the specific content of the thought which was in their minds.

The proposition that God sets a term to the life of man, so that it begins at one moment only to end at another, is one which belongs to the sphere of theological anthropology, i.e., to the nature of man as God created it and saw that it was good (cf. *C.D.*, III, 2 § 47). We shall not labour this point in our present context. Our concern now is with the fact that this natural limitation, as it is willed by the Creator who is also Lord of the creature's history, takes on the form of actual events in the individual life, first at the beginning of this life, and then at the end, i.e., that we were all born, and shall all die. For the moment we shall leave aside all evaluation of the two events, for example, whether it is good to be born and bad to die, or perhaps the reverse. We shall

---

[EN560] beginning, development and ending
[EN561] ending
[EN562] a limit that is fixed and immovable in every detail
[EN563] limit
[EN564] limit

simply claim that taken together the two events do constitute the outline of the disposing or limitation of the life of all of us. Our life is like the small medi-aeval town whose main street and side streets and back streets all stemmed out from the one gate and led back again to the other, the whole city being sur-rounded by a moat which on both sides formed a connecting link between the two gates and the towers above them. All of us are on the one way from birth to death. We live within the limits imposed by this fact. Whatever happens in our life between birth and death is only an open or secret variation upon the one theme which is imposed upon us by this basic disposing. Some of the variations are apparently, and it may be actually, decisive, and some are less important. Some are determined by our own individuality and some by our environment. But our coming and going, our rising and falling, our increasing and decreas-ing, our establishing and fulfilling, are all of them imposed by this basic dispos-ing. The question which we have now to answer is that of the significance of the fact that this twofold limitation is the basic disposing of our human life.

And first we have to assert that the past event, our birth, and the future event, our death, are not in the least like permanent towers, just as a city with its permanent buildings and thoroughfares is a poor image of what actually takes place between birth and death. There is a moment when a man begins to be, and there is another when he ceases to be—and who can know with cer-tainty when either moment will be? In both these moments there takes place something absolutely unpredictable, something entirely new, something that was never there before. The new factor may be the Here which is given to us once and for all in our birth, or it may be the Yonder which meets us irresist-ibly in our death, but in either case there is a change. And what are all the changes and novelties which take place between as compared with these first [230] and last events? Measured by these events, are not all the other events in our lives conditioned by the fact that they take place between these two? either as a development subsequent to birth, or as a decay preparatory to death; and all of them probably both a development and a decay, a decay and a develop-ment; all of them both repetitions of the new fact of our birth and anticipations of the new fact of our death. These two events condition and characterise all that lies between them. They are in sequence with all other events, but as the first and last in the sequence they are unique and incompar-able. And what is it that makes them so? Obviously the fact that in the life of the individual they reflect the two great acts of God at the beginning and end of all things, the creation and the consummation. Obviously the fact that in them the individual participates in the mystery of the origin and goal of all creation, its limitation by God, its derivation from God, and its movement to God. And it is because man is the one creature who is called by God to receive the revelation of this mystery and to be aware of this derivation from God and movement to God, and in this knowledge to be responsible to God, that the disposing and limitation of his life, his birth and death, are "events" in a unique and emphatic sense of the term.

We claim further that in both these events, if in a reverse direction, there is a sharp conflict between the spontaneity of life, in which we know and understand and fulfil ourselves as the free subject of all our knowing and willing and doing and suffering, and the lordship by which sovereign disposition is made concerning us. The first event is primarily an act of that lordship. Before any question of spontaneity arises, without my being consulted, without my being able to do anything about it, it simply happens to me that I am as it were liberated for individual life, for being as an I. And the last is also an act of this lordship, for when I have made some use of the freedom given to me—perhaps made use of it to destruction as in the paradoxical case of the suicide—it is irrevocably taken from me, and again there can be no question of spontaneity. This is how I actually live. This is how I am actually enclosed both behind and before as though by unavoidable brackets: first called to the sphere of spontaneity, and then called away from it; first kindled as a self-illuminating light, and then extinguished. It is I who live, but both in my birth and in my death it is made clear that to live is something which I myself cannot take, or give, or maintain; something which is ordained and given to me. It is I who live, but in so doing I do not belong to myself; I am indebted to the power which ordained that I should live within the limits laid down not by myself but by that power. It does not make any difference whether we call the ordination permission or command; as permission it is command, and as command permission. And it certainly does not make the slightest difference whether we find it [231] acceptable or otherwise. Obviously it is not for us to interpret it in either the one way or the other. Either way it is an ordination, an act of lordship, which encloses our whole life and to which we owe its spontaneity. That there are divine decrees—and whatever its nature, a divine decree is one that is necessarily made and executed—is something which is revealed in our lives by the fact that they are disposed and limited. In the knowledge of our life and death, and therefore of the lordship which disposes concerning us, we know in fact—even though we do not know what we know—the decree of God which affects us, yes, us personally: the decree which we cannot escape; the decree in whose omnipotence we are safe; the decree by which we are held.

We continue that it is these two events which give to human life its character of once-for-allness. In all the other events of which this life is made up and by which it is characterised, this character is to say the least equivocal. We have here the only thing which a man possesses absolutely alone, in the greatest possible disproportion and isolation as against that which is possessed by all other men and all other creatures. All other things he possesses only as in some degree he participates in a disposing and order which are either general or determine the life of his particular environment. In all other things he is engaged in various kinds of continuations and repetitions and variations of his own existence. In all other things there is a general or particular uniformity in his life. But in the two events which happen only once even in his individual existence, his birth and his death, he is utterly himself, absolutely original, and absolutely alone. The individuality and originality which may characterise other events in his life are only relative, being conditioned by the fact that he proceeds from the absolutely original event of his birth, and returns to the absolutely original event of his death. But these two events, his birth and his death, he does have entirely to himself, even outwardly, even in relation to his general and particular environment. In neither of them was he represented, or could be represented, by another. They take place only once. And in the once-for-allness which is established by them he exists not merely for himself but for all other creatures within the context of world-occurrence generally. It is these events which define for man his particular place and function; the function in which, in spite of the well-known saying, he is in fact irreplaceable, indispensable, and non-interchangeable. His function may be extremely unimportant. His coming and going and all that lies between may outwardly be very ordinary. But the greater or lesser importance of his coming and going, and the attention which he claims, hardly matter as compared with the fact that he actually is, that in the midst of all other men and all other creatures he has his own personal life, he who never was before, and will never come again. He is not merely *a* man; he is this particular man. And who is to say what he really is or is not for others, and in the context of world-occurrence as a whole? All that is certain is that this whole would not be the whole without the [232] once-for-allness in which, isolated from all others and yet associated with them by these two movements at the beginning and end of his life, he is this particular man. The eternal singleness of God Himself is reflected in the small creaturely once-for-allness of this life of his which has a single beginning and a single end. And who is to say that it really is so small? Who is to say whether the singleness of God is not reflected quite differently, and far more clearly and significantly, in this creaturely once-for-allness than appears either from his importance or the attention which he claims? The only certain point is that this singleness of God is reflected there in a way which is itself peculiar and once and for all. The only certain point is that in the once-for-allness of his birth and death, and in virtue of the disposing and limitation of his life— whether he is aware of it or not—he himself, this particular man, does have to do only with God, who is also primarily and originally for Himself, isolated and unique, in the fact that He alone is worthy of confidence, that He alone can lay claim to obedience, that He alone persists where everything in human life with its desire for greatness and importance and indispensability can never be anything more than a continuation or repetition or variation of the divine claim and the divine promise.

We continue that it is these two events which always make human life into a history. The brackets by which we are enclosed and held are not the same. The acts of lordship under which we stand and which determine the once-for-allness of our existence are not the same. The one is a giving, the other a taking. The one is a calling to, the other a calling away. The one is an establishing, the other a completing. And the order of the two events is irreversible.

The path from the one to the other can be traversed only in one direction. The life of man has a definite upward thrust from birth and a definite downward drag to death. Neither physiologically nor psychologically is it possible to separate the two forces. From first to last their operation seems to constitute only the one movement. And there is no reason to regard the one (most likely the upward) as positive and the other (most likely the downward) as negative. In all respects our life is the co-operation of these two forces. Without being asked either to separate or evaluate them, we undoubtedly live at a stage in the movement which is determined by them. And in so far as I am caught up in this movement from my beginning to my end, my life becomes my history—we might almost say my drama—in which I am neither the author nor the producer, but the principal actor. I did not place myself in this movement, nor do I maintain myself in it. But I myself am in this movement. Between my birth and my death the freedom is given to me to be myself in this movement, in this ascent and descent. To be in this freedom is to live. Therefore my life consists

[233] in the possibilities offered by this movement. They will all have something of the character of ascent, and they will all have something of the character of descent. At one and the same time I will always be coming and going, receiving and wanting, called and called away, summoned and discharged, working or resting, waking or sleeping. But in the contrariety set up by my beginning and end I am continually choosing and deciding, now grasping and making use of this possibility, now of that, now being caught up in the movement away from birth, now in that towards death. For a large part of our life, of course, we are simply and necessarily asleep, and therefore we have constantly to decide simply to sleep again. Even this fact shows very clearly that in our life's drama the choice of the second possibility is in its own time and place just as inevitable as that of the first. But like a real drama, this drama has its time. A history without an end would not be a history. The lordship under which we live, and the once-for-allness which it gives to our life, have provided that it should be a real history with both a beginning and an end. In a single moment, the beginning of the movement means the beginning of my wrestling with the possibilities which it offers, and in a single moment its ending means the ending of this wrestling. My birth and my death characterise it as a true history, in which something interconnected takes place, which in its totality acquires and assumes the character of a definite decision. It is a question this time of overriding decision how I fulfil my role, i.e., along what lines, with what consistency or inconsistency, according to what law or with what disregard of law, I continually choose between ascent and descent, receiving and wanting, doing and resting, waking and sleeping; what form it will all have when it is finished; who and what I myself will become and will have been in the whole course of my wrestling. This is the crucial question at every stage in my life's history, which is constituted a totality by this disposing and limitation. Even from this standpoint I am always dealing with God in this limitation of my life. For the overriding decision in my life-history—who and what I really am as I am caught up

between birth and death—is obviously not my own decision, but is controlled by the One who, limiting me as He did, is so vastly superior to me, and, limiting me in this way, causes my life to be so once-for-all before Him. This One is the King of my life's history. And since my life is constituted by my birth and death, and moves in terms of that ascent and descent, and is peculiar to me in my wrestling with the two, the question of its overriding decision is that of the reflection or promulgation of the divine sentence under which I stand. I live. I am caught up in that wrestling. And whether I realise it or not, this means that I am delivered up to His hands, to His severity and His mercy. It is as He decides that it will come to pass. If I can hope at all, I can hope only in Him.

And now finally it is in virtue of these two events that we are witnesses of world-occurrence generally. In virtue of these two events, that is, in the limits [234] fixed by them, in the freedom given within them, and on the basis of the peculiar possibilities offered by them, all world-occurrence in heaven and earth takes place for us. Here and now, in the history which is our wrestling with this two-fold movement, all world-occurrence has its effect upon us, and actively and passively, in action and in contemplation, both moving and also moved, we participate in it. Knowing ourselves, we know heaven and earth. Proving ourselves in the tiny place which is seriously allotted to us and the short hour which is seriously accorded us, we prove creation as such and as a whole. We are not merely the pawn in a secondary theatre of action, but the responsible person on the spot at the very heart of things, the one who decides what creation is to become. For what do we know of creation except as we know ourselves between birth and death, ourselves in our once-for-allness, and therefore all the thousand and one open or secret relations and connexions, similarities and identities to some or many or all other creatures in which we are what we are? And how can we know ourselves without knowing what it is that binds us to these others, without therefore knowing them? We live, i.e., we have experience of ourselves, i.e., we wrestle with that upward and downward pull, and as we do so, in the course of our lives we encounter these others and have experience of them too. Our eyes may be open or blinkered, our ideas clear or hazy, our actions decided or undecided, but they are all there for each one of us, and we wrestle with them, and experience their influence upon us, and exercise our own influence upon them. In the history of our life there takes place *in nuce*[EN565], but very truly, all history. And far from cutting us off or isolating us, the limitation means that we are laid open to the whole; that our existence is given solidarity with that of heaven and earth; that we are given a stake in the law and the promises, in the peril and the preservation, of all creaturely reality; that we participate in its life and are responsible for its nature and continuance. And if in virtue of those two events we are the witnesses of all world-occurrence, and all occurrence is under the dominion of that Lord who is the Creator of all things, then this means that in virtue of

[EN565] in miniature

235

these two events we too, and—*hic Rhodus, hic salta*—we especially, are confronted by this Lord at every step on the way from the one event to the other. For we are certainly not outside the existence of heaven and earth, nor can we escape it. So, too, we are not outside and we cannot escape the lordship of the One who created heaven and earth. And the divine will and decree concerning the whole reality posited by and distinct from Him is His divine will and decree in respect of each individual man, the will and decree which will be fulfilled in the life of each individual.

[235] To sum up, the commonplace fact of the limitation of human life has from every standpoint the same high significance. It testifies—and since we ourselves live the life which is bounded by these two events, we too testify—not merely to a higher being, but to God; not merely to a divine nature, but to the activity of God; to a God who does a new work in which He is the almighty Lord, in which He is unique, in which He is the Judge of men and as such the Ruler of all things. In our movement from birth to death we are the sign and testimony to ourselves of this Lord of life and death, of the lordship of this God. And who is this God? We must not forget to concede that as we can easily miss the history of Scripture or the Church or the Jews, so we may easily miss this history of our own life in its most significant limitation, the *terminus vitae*[EN566]. We may easily be insensible to the question raised by it and blind therefore to the corresponding answer. We may perceive neither God Himself nor the activity of God which characterises His Godhead. We may see only the commonplace fact that we come and go. It may be all in vain that we are a sign and testimony to ourselves. But it is certainly not in vain when we already know the God whose activity we do in fact denote and attest by living this limited life. It is necessary already to have heard His Word if we are not to miss the fact which confronts us, if we are actually to understand ourselves, if we are actually to understand this basic determination of the history of human life, if we are actually to understand the most ephemeral of all things. Once again, if it is a question of the knowledge of God, it is a question of recognition. And that we do recognise Him presupposes that He has given it to us to know Him in His Word. By calling the limitation of human life a trace of the divine world-governance, we dare to presuppose that God has given it to us to know Him in His Word, so that we are now able to make this recognition. And if we can do this, then the question, Who is the God who is the Lord of life and death? cannot remain unanswered, or receive varied answers. The bit of world-occurrence which is identical with our own life obviously speaks with a special and continuous power and a quite exceptional intimacy about the One who is the active Subject of sacred history, the history of grace and the covenant, and as such the ruling Subject of all occurrence; about His new work, His lordship, His singleness, His judgment and His mercy to all His creatures. In the limitation of our life we recognise the faithfulness in which He has pledged Himself

---

EN566 limit of life

to the unfaithful, the supremacy of His grace, the severity and goodness of the King of Israel. In the bracket which encloses us behind and before we recognise the hand of His in which we are held, and in which we are both secure and free because it is the hand which preserves all creatures. Necessarily we have not to miss this hand. We can recognise it with thankfulness. We can know and experience the great freedom which is given to man in his limitation by these two events. And for this knowledge and experience is it not enough that in this limitation we are put in exactly the same place as that of the Son of God when He went the short and narrow way from the cradle to the cross? Yet in this [236] limitation He rose again from the dead, and in the same limited being He will return in glory. As the man who is limited as we are He now reigns at the right hand of the Father. Living in this limitation, we are like him. That is why the limitation declares to us a great freedom. Certainly it cannot mean more than declaration. But it can mean declaration, and it does mean it if we have heard the Word of God. That is why we esteem it the closest visible trace of the One who is the King of Israel, and as such the King of the cosmos.

But in the witness to this King in world-occurrence generally there is one constant element which is more important than any of those so far mentioned. We have seen how the fourth element is quite distinct from the first three. But the one to which we now refer is distinct from all the others. It does not stand in any possible sequence with them. It can only be opposed to them. And we can do it only allusively, in the form of a preliminary introduction of a whole context which we have not so far touched on but which has its own special place in the framework of the Christian doctrine of the Creator and creation, and will therefore require a more specific enquiry and statement (in § 50). It is simply a question of the existence and function of the beings which with a surprising frequency in Holy Scripture, and consistently in the traditional language of Christianity, are referred to as angels. This is not the place at which to do more than introduce the problem in so far as it is significant for the present discussion, *non ut diceretur, sed ne taceretur*[EN567]; for it is a fact that in this respect, as a sign and testimony of the lordship of the King of Israel in world-occurrence, the existence and function of angels, if rightly understood, not merely surpasses but includes all other elements. Angels are the sign and testimony κατ' ἐξοχήν, *par excellence*, the sign and testimony which stands behind and above all others. That is why, if we were to list the others but omit this, our list would not merely be incomplete but unsatisfying, for the power of all the others—apart from the self-attestation of God—depends upon the power of this sign and testimony. It is therefore indispensable that we should give a preliminary indication of the way in which we shall fill the gap.

All too easily we forget that God created not only earth, but also heaven. With the cosmos which we can comprehend and approach and at bottom control, He created the higher cosmos which we cannot comprehend or approach or control. All too easily we forget that heaven is the higher cosmos because, although it is created, it constitutes that side of created reality which is much more closely related to God, and to that extent nearer and in a closer affinity to Him. And all too easily we forget that world-occurrence does not cease with the earthly events which we can understand as natural history or the history of man, which we experience directly because like ourselves they too are earthly, but that with the earthly events there is also a heavenly occurrence which we do not understand in the least, and

---

[EN567] not in order to speak, but in order not to remain silent

which as such is directly related to the earthly events both in its original and essential affinity to the determinative lordship of God and also in its absolute difference from them. All too easily we forget that, just as earth and man upon it are under heaven, so earthly occurrence takes place under the powerful determination of heaven. What is the source of this heavenly occurrence? The aim of God, the object of His election and activity, is upon earth and not in heaven. It is an earthly history, the history of the covenant and salvation, which begins with the creation of the universe and constitutes the central part of its history. It is the lower cosmos, this world of ours, which is the scene of the magnifying of God's mercy for the greater magnifying of His glory. For this reason the Son of God does not become a heavenly

[237] creature, but He becomes flesh, man, an earthly creature. In the history of the covenant and salvation, and in all the divine world-governance, it is a matter of the will of God being done on earth as it is done in heaven, always, and without any particular forethought, as befits the character of heaven. God has no independent goals and ends in heaven. There did not need to be any specific heavenly occurrence merely for the sake of heaven. This occurrence arises only as in the divine relationship to earth, heaven, the higher cosmos, is the throne or dwelling-place from which God sets out to establish on earth His own order and glory, and therefore that of earth as well. According to the stricter biblical interpretation it is by this invasion of God for the deliverance and government of man and His world, our lower cosmos, that heaven is set in motion, and a heavenly occurrence arises which precedes the earthly. God arises in power to come to us, to come to the place where we are, to speak to us, to act amongst us and with us, to interest Himself in us and in our needy world, the lower cosmos, both as King and as Lord. But since He is still God, and heaven is still His throne, it is inevitable that heaven and all the higher cosmos, both in its incomprehensibility but also in its affinity with Him, should follow the movement which He Himself makes, imitating and accompanying it, adoring and extolling His will and Word and work amongst us in the lower cosmos, standing by and supporting His activity, His forceful striding down from above to below. Where God Himself is, heaven is also there to serve Him, as a sign and testimony. That is why (in Matthew at any rate) the kingdom which comes to us is called the kingdom of heaven. In coming to us, it rends heaven apart. It sets it in motion. It changes its structure. And in coming to us, it brings heaven with it. It brings the higher world down to the lower. It is the kingdom in which the kingship of God means that the forces of what is in principle the unseen and heavenly world assume form and enter the earthly world and become active in it and real factors in its occurrence. In their being and function they cannot for a single moment or in any one respect be separated from the Word and work of God, or be autonomous over against the will of God. They are truly active and glorious to the extent that they fulfil His will. Naturally they have to be distinct from God, but like the totality of heaven and earth they are only the creatures of God, and they are real factors only to the extent that they are absolutely under His lordship. But they also have to be distinct from all earthly factors. Within the earthly they are heavenly factors with all the high incomprehensibility of heaven, participating in that proximity and affinity to God which finally distinguishes the higher cosmos from the lower.

Speaking in a preliminary and provisional way, these factors are angels, i.e., heavenly messengers ordained to service, or heavenly servants ordained as messengers, in the plurality corresponding to the fact that heaven develops its apparently rigid unity into flexible richness in virtue of the concrete will and work of God (both in itself and to the world). But they are the heavenly world as it is set in motion by God and with God. That is why they do not belong to a doctrine of the creature, and are never even considered in the biblical story of creation. They do not exist at all as man does, not simply because they are heavenly, but primarily because as heavenly beings they are distinct and special creatures, acquiring and enjoying their being and function only in and with this invasion and Word and work of God.

They belong essentially to the Word and work of God, to the covenant and saving activity and rule of God in the creaturely world, to Jesus Christ, the Prophet, Priest and King. They are still creatures, but as heavenly beings, as beings which belong to the Word and work of God, they stand side by side with man and all other creatures, and also above them.

And it is in respect of these two characteristics that they are the primary sign and testimony of the world-governance of the King of Israel—which is our concern in the present context. Therefore of all that has to be said concerning them we shall select only that which [238] is immediately apparent in the Scriptures of the Old and New Testament. Obviously their being and function is everywhere presupposed, but they actually appear, and are described as active, only when it is a matter of declaring the Word and work of God Himself as fulfilled in speech or action. They are as it were the luminous border of this Word and work, marking it off from world-occurrence generally. This is how they appear, for example, on the margin of the events of Advent and Christmas, or of the Easter incidents during the forty days, or of the prospective *parousia*. On this margin, or as they themselves form this margin, they are watchers, calling and speaking and singing, and when the time comes sounding the trumpet to awaken all those who are asleep or half-asleep. But they are all this as the sign and testimony of the One who is the Lord and Master of all things and over all things. And they are the primary witness because they belong to this higher cosmos, and belonging to it, in their being and function they take precedence over the lower, over all the prophets and apostles, over the whole Church, over the Jews, over ourselves and our witness to ourselves. The other signs and testimonies are there only because they are there first. Therefore we cannot really compare any of the divine constants in world-occurrence with this constant, this chorus of angels in heaven which accompanies the Lord on his way.

It is true, of course, that we can miss the angels. We can deny them altogether. We can dismiss them as superfluous, or absurd and comic. We can protest with frowning brow and clenched fist that, although we might admit that there is a God, it is going too far to allow that there are angels as well. They must be questioned or completely ignored. There are, therefore, even Christian and theological systems in which there is no place for angels. We have to be careful that they are not the very systems in which there is no place for the other constants either. For if we do not know anything of the primary sign and testimony, how can we know anything of the secondary? If we cannot or will not accept angels, how can we accept what is told us by the history of Scripture, or the history of the Church, or the history of the Jews, or our own life's history? And since it depends upon our acceptance of these secondary signs and testimonies whether or not our own system includes within it the living God, we have to ask ourselves whether a system in which there is no place for angels, and therefore for the primary sign and testimony, will not at bottom be a godless one. Where God is, there the angels of God are. Where there are no angels, there is no God. And whatever our system may be, it is comforting and good that the world and its occurrence should not be without God and the angels of God, that our lower cosmos should not be without the encounter and contact with the higher cosmos set in motion by the Word and work of God. The worse for us if we are not aware of it! For if this is the case, it is a fairly sure symptom that we have not heard the Word of God and that we are not aware of the work of God. Just as the Word and work of God wait to be heard and received by us, so the heavenly cosmos and the angels wait to be perceived and considered by us. And in the meantime they offer us their services even though we are not aware of the fact, or do not remember it, for there can be no doubt that the Word of God is true, and His work proceeds, even though we are not, or even before we are, thankful for it. That side by side with and high above all other sign and testimony, these primary and supreme signs and testimonies to the divine world-governance do in fact stand in their office, and wait on their office, is the preliminary fact concerning angels of which we have to take cognisance in the present context.

4. THE CHRISTIAN UNDER THE UNIVERSAL LORDSHIP OF GOD
THE FATHER

We have now given an outline of what we are required to believe by the Word
of God concerning the great objective reality of the activity and rule of God
the Father as Lord of the creature, concerning His divine preserving and
accompanying and ruling of the creature, and the basis and meaning of its
history. But our sketch would be incomplete if in conclusion we did not
expressly consider the creaturely subject which participates in the divine lordship, not merely from without, as a creature which is preserved and accompanied and ruled by Him like all other creatures, but in some sense from within, as
a creature which not only experiences this rule in practice but perceives and
acknowledges and affirms and approves it, which is in fact thankful for it and
wills to cleave and conform to it. So far we have tacitly presupposed the existence of such a subject, and all our propositions and their elucidation are based
upon this presupposition. In our final discussion, when we listed and
described the constant traces of the divine world-governance in all creaturely
occurrence, it was particularly clear, and we had constantly to draw attention
to the fact, that although these traces can be seen they can easily be missed. It
is only a certain kind of subject which can see them. The precondition was
particularly clear at this point, but in reality the same precondition governs all
theological propositions, including the doctrine of providence as a whole. But
who is the subject, and what is his specific nature and attitude, to whom the
conservatio, concursus[EN568] and *gubernatio*[EN569] as we have described them are
not empty concepts, but who has actual knowledge of them? We cannot avoid
trying to give a right answer to this question, not merely in order to reveal in
conclusion what is the basis of our knowledge of this whole matter, but because
a right answer to this question is calculated to put the whole matter in a light
which is absolutely indispensable if it is to be perceived aright.

The doctrine of providence—at any rate as we have understood and presented it—is with all its elements an integral part of the Christian confession.
Therefore the subject to which we were referring is the living member of the
Christian community, the Christian. We will not at this point try to explain how
this subject is constituted, and how far there can be and is a Christian community, and a Christian as its member. What concerns us now is that the Christian alone is the creaturely subject which can join in a confession of the divine
providence because it knows this providence, because it participates in the
divine world-governance in this special and inward way. What concerns us now
is the Christian as the point from which all that we have said in the matter can
be understood as actual reality. We are enquiring into the specific being and

---

[EN568] preserving, accompanying
[EN569] ruling

attitude in which the *conservatio, concursus*[EN570] and *gubernatio*[EN571] are just as   [240]
visible to the Christian in the developed form of the divine operation as are
happenings on the street to a man looking out of a window. We are asking how
it is that this self-evident manifestness of the divine lordship is both possible
and actual in the Christian community.

We can best begin by making the simple assertion that even the Christian is
only a creaturely subject, and that in solidarity with all other men and creatures he stands therefore wholly and utterly under the universal lordship of
God: with the same disadvantage that this means for every man or every fly,
that he cannot be his own lord; but also with the same advantage, that he does
not need to be anxious concerning his own preservation or way or end. The
Christian, too, is upheld by God without being able to do anything towards it
or about it. He, too, has in God an almighty Companion who embraces his
whole being, whose activity sovereignly precedes and accompanies and follows
his own activity. He, too, can only let himself be ruled. What, then, distinguishes him from the others? In the first instance, only the fact that with all its
consequences he accepts and affirms the fact that he is only a creaturely subject like the others, that in this respect there is nothing to distinguish him from
them. Of all creatures the Christian is the one which not merely is a creature,
but actually says Yes to being a creature. Innumerable creatures do not seem to
be even asked to make this affirmation. Man is asked. But man as such is neither able nor willing to make it. From the very first man as such has continual
illusions about himself. He wants always to be more than a creature. He does
not want merely to be under the universal lordship of God. But the Christian
makes the affirmation that is demanded of man. This is his distinction. It is the
distinction of renouncing all claim to distinction. He makes the common confession of what all creatures really are, sometimes without even being asked,
sometimes in defiance of their own wrong answers. The Christian, therefore, is
the true creature. All the virtue and activity, all the joy and worth of the Christian must begin with this simple fact, and must finally lead back to it. It is
important to assert this at the very outset. The glory of the particular relation
and attitude of the Christian to the universal lordship of God consists in the
fact that it does not give occasion for any glorying in self. It begins and ends
with the laying aside of all claim to self-glory. The height of the Christian in
this matter is always the depth—and it is no height at all, but a very real
depth—of the reality with which he can and may and must and will stand
towards the fact that as a creature he is in no sense superior to other men, or to
the dust under his feet, but can exist only under the universal lordship of God.
Whatever advantage he may have over other men—and he really has a very big
advantage—he has it only under the continually present and actual presupposition that as a creature he has no advantage at all.

[EN570] preserving, accompanying
[EN571] ruling

[241]   How is it that the Christian of all men attains to the reality of acknowledging this fact? Our answer can be the very simple one that he sees what the others do not see. The world-process in which he participates in solidarity with all other creatures might just as easily be a vain thrusting and tumult without either master or purpose. This is how many see it. But the Christian sees in it a universal lordship. The lordship might just as easily be that of natural law, or fate, or chance, or even the devil. This is how many see it. But the Christian sees in it the universal lordship of God, of the God who is the Father, who is the Father to him, his Father. He sees the constitutive and organising centre of the process. What makes him a Christian is that he sees Jesus Christ, the Son of God, in the humiliation but also in the exaltation of His humanity, and himself united with Him, belonging to Him, his life delivered by Him, but also placed at His disposal. And seeing Him, he sees the legislative, executive and judicial authority over and in all things. He sees it as the authority of God. He sees it as the authority of the Father. He sees himself subjected to this authority as the one who is united with and belongs to the Son. Only the Christian sees this centre of the world-process. Only the Christian sees at this centre, as the One who has all power in heaven and on earth, the Son of God, and through Him God the Father, and on the circumference himself as a child of the Father for the sake of the Son. The whole Christian community is simply a gathering together by the Word which tells us this and explains and reveals it to us; a gathering together of those whose eyes are opened to the fact of it. Only the Christian is a member of this community, i.e., one who is gathered together with others by this Word, one whose eyes are opened to this fact. There are some creatures which do not need to have eyes for it because even without seeing it they are carried along by the power of this order and are secure in its peace. There are other creatures which have eyes for it but they will not and cannot open them. But the Christian has open eyes. That is why he has the reality freely and joyfully to confess his creatureliness and his consequent subjection to the universal rule of God without reserve and without claim. What he sees at that centre and on that circumference is not something which frightens him, something which he has to reject. God the Father as the ruling Creator is obviously not an oppressor, and Christ as a subject creature is obviously not oppressed. There is nothing here which need frighten him. There is nothing here which need cause him to flee or rebel. To be wholly and unreservedly under the universal lordship of God, to be wholly and unreservedly a creaturely subject, is not in any sense a constraint, a misfortune, an outrage or a humiliation for the man who as a Christian can see actualised in Jesus Christ both the lordship of God and also the subordination of the creature. For him all attempts to evade this fact are purposeless, and the illusion by which it is

[242]   obscured or avoided is superfluous. If the relation between the Creator and the creature is the relation which he can see in Jesus Christ, then existence in this relation is the existence which is to be truly desired, an existence in the highest possible freedom and felicity. To have to confess this is not an obscure

law, but a friendly permission and invitation. It is not unwillingly but spontaneously, not grudgingly but gladly, that the Christian will affirm and lay hold of this relation and his own existence in it. Hence the reality does not cost him anything. He does not have to force it. He does not have to struggle to attain to it. It comes to him in the same way as what he sees comes to him. And this means that he does not screw himself up to a height when he is a real creature. It also means that there does not arise any claim or merit on his part just because he confesses so unreservedly what other creatures and other men cannot and will not confess. The fact that he does so is not a kind of triumph for his individual honesty. Other people are just as honest, perhaps more so. He is simply made real by what he sees. And as such he is simply availing himself of a permission and invitation. He is going through an open door, but one which he himself has not opened, into a banqueting hall. And there he willingly takes his place under the table, in the company of publicans, in the company of beasts and plants and stones, accepting solidarity with them, being present simply as they are, as a creature of God. It is the fact that he sees, and that which he is able to see as the centre and the circumference, the Creator and the creature, which constitute the permission and invitation and open door to his peculiar reality.

To summarise provisionally, we may say that in virtue of what he (and only he) can see, the Christian is the one who has a true knowledge in this matter of the providence and universal lordship of God. This providence and lordship affect him as they do all other creatures, but he participates in them differently from all other creatures. He participates in them from within. Of all creatures he is the one who while he simply experiences the providence and lordship of God also consents to it, having a kind of "understanding"—if we may put it in this way—with the overruling God and Creator.

In practice, of course, he is faced every day afresh with the riddles of the world-process, with the precipices and plains, the blinding lights and obscurities, of the general creaturely occurrence to which his own life's history also belongs. Of course he can only keep on asking: Whence? and Whither? and Why? and Wherefore? Of course he has no master-key to all the mysteries of the great process of existence as they crowd in upon him every moment in a new form, to all the mysteries of his own existence as a constituent existence in the historical process of all created reality. On the contrary, he will be the one man who knows that there is no value in any of the master-keys which man has thought to discover and possess. He is the one man who will always be the most surprised, the most affected, the most apprehensive and the most joyful in the [243] face of events. He will not be like an ant which has forseen everything in advance, but like a child in a forest, or on Christmas Eve; one who is always rightly astonished by events, by the encounters and experiences which overtake him, and the cares and duties laid upon him. He is the one who is constantly forced to begin afresh, wrestling with the possibilities which open out to him and the impossibilities which oppose him. If we may put it in this way, life in the world, with all its joys and sorrows and contemplation and activity, will always be for him a really interesting matter, or, to use a bolder expression, it will be an adventure, for which he for his part has ultimately and basically no qualifications of his own.

And all this is not because he does not know what it is all about, but just because he does know. All this is because he has an "understanding " with the source from which everything derives, from which directly or indirectly everything happens to him; the "understanding" of the creature with its Creator, which is, for him, that of the child with its father. One thing at least he does not need to puzzle about. About this one thing he has no need to enquire, to be always on the look-out for new answers, new solutions. For he has learned once and for all who is this source, and what basically he can expect from it, and what will always actually come from it. But how the decision is reached, and in what form everything will come as it proceeds from this source, he is as tense and curious as a child, always open and surprised in face of what comes. Yet whatever comes, and in whatever form it comes, he will see that it comes from this one source. However, strange it may seem, however irksome in the form in which it comes, he will approve it as coming from this source. He will always be, not perhaps able, but at least willing and ready to perceive the positive—and in the light of its source the most definitely positive—meaning and content of what comes. He will always be willing and ready—again a daring expression—to co-operate with it instead of adopting an attitude of supercilious and dissatisfied criticism and opposition, or, if it were possible, retiring sulkily into a corner as a sceptical spectator. He will always allow everything to concern him directly, and, with all the dialectic of his experiences and attitudes, he will ultimately and basically allow everything to concern him positively. Ultimately and basically he will always be thankful, and in the light of this thankfulness he will look forward to what has still to come. He will always know both what was intended and what is intended. He will always be the child having dealings with its father. This is the knowledge of the Christian in matters of the divine lordship. There is nothing arrogant about it. It remains within the bounds of the reality in which the Christian can know himself—know himself as a creature under the lordship of God like all other creatures. It is in a sense only the [244] reverse side of this reality. Naturally the confession of the providence and universal lordship of God is not the same as the expression and product of this Christian knowledge. It is rather an answer to the Word of God. It can be understood only as an echo of the call of this Word, not as a human or even a Christian achievement or acquirement. But obviously, where the Word of God is really heard, this Christian knowledge will also arise as a historical determination of the existence of the hearer. Obviously, too, the confession of the providence and universal lordship of God will inevitably be cold and formal in the heart and on the lips of anyone who misses this Christian knowledge, who does not know what it means for him personally when he speaks of the divine preserving, accompanying and ruling, to whom the matter arises only in a distant and alien height and not in his own sphere, not in the form of a historical determination of his own existence. In relation to everything that went before, the question of the Christian subject is a kind of controlling question: Understandest thou what thou readest? Have you reached the point where both in your heart and on your lips the doctrine of the divine providence is not the type of speculation in which you are interested only as a more or less clever spectator, but where you are affected and laid hold of by the object of the doctrine itself, where you have therefore apprehended and understood it from within?

This Christian knowledge has nothing whatever to do with mere speculation. Nor have we to think of it as a kind of insight or perception which has been miraculously implanted in or imparted to the Christian as the one who sees, and which has now passed into his possession. It is nothing at all if it is not an exercised science or craft. Certainly it is given to him, not as a supernatural quality, but as a capacity which is actual only as it is used, which is not in any sense magical, but absolutely free and natural in its exercise. And it is, of course, the highest knowledge, but because it is the highest, it is a knowledge which claims not only his eye and intellect, but the whole man. Its reference is to a relationship, to the relationship effected between the operation of God the Creator and the totality of creaturely occurrence as overruled by Him. It is, therefore, an attitude, but a dynamic attitude, in which the Christian, being totally claimed, participates in the operation of God and creaturely occurrence: contemplating to be sure, but active as well; perceiving, but also working; and both in such a way that it is quite impossible to separate the one from the other, because proceeding from the one he is always leaping along the way to the other. It is all perceiving and understanding and knowing. But, as we had to add at once, it is all affirming and approving; it is all a willingness and readiness to co-operate; it is all thankfulness. If the divine providence and lordship are reflected in the Christian as in pure glass, if the Christian knows them in such a way that this "speculation" takes place, then this obviously means that the occurrence which proceeds from God and embraces heaven and earth is repeated in the narrow sphere of his own creaturely existence, of [245] his own thoughts and will and deed, of his own life. The providence and universal lordship of God are not merely true to him, but in this repetition they are actual. How they are actual to him it will now be our task to indicate and explain.

They are actual to him in faith, in obedience, and in prayer. These are the three forms of this dynamic and totally Christian attitude. We shall find all of them more or less impressed on all expressions of this Christian attitude, and we shall recognise them fully and clearly. And we can test our own attitude by the simple but sure standard whether it seeks to express itself in these three forms; whether any one of them is lacking; whether it is straining to express itself equally and fully in all three. If it does, but only if it does, it is the Christian attitude. And if it is the Christian attitude, none of the three must be omitted or stunted, none must obscure or absorb the others, none must try to replace or crowd out the others. If only one of the three is completely missing, our attitude is not a Christian one. Even though the other two may be intact, or perhaps strongly developed, it is still definitely not a Christian one except in appearance. And we must note that in faith, as in obedience and prayer, it is not a matter either of pure theory or of pure practice, but always of the step or leap from the one to the other, from seeing to doing, from knowing to acting. When the Christian believes and obeys and prays, all doubt or debate concerning the precedence of the one over the other is transcended. To dispute concerning the more contemplative or active nature of Christianity, or the respective merits of waiting and hasting, of grace and freedom, of comfort and exhortation, or however else we may express the antithesis—all this is superfluous. In none of its three forms does the Christian attitude know anything of such abstract antitheses. Antitheses of this kind are always relics of a wrongly speculative approach to the divine providence and lordship. As they are truly considered in the dynamic and total form possible only in the Christian life, and as they are repeated in this subjective sphere, the divine providence and lordship render all such antitheses superfluous. From first to last the truly Christian attitude is a knowing of God in His own Word, and this means that from first to last it is a doing according to the rule of this Word. This applies to faith no less than to obedience and prayer. Therefore we cannot possibly understand the three forms as three parts of the Christian attitude which limit and complete each other, so that the Christian first believes, then has to obey, and finally must pray; or first believes, then has to pray and finally must obey; or first obeys, and then has to pray and finally must believe. We should note that divisions of this kind lead immediately and necessarily to the position in which we are dealing with a law, in the fulfilment of which the Christian attitude must then consist. The Christian attitude—the Christian knowledge

[246] which comes from hearing the Word of God—has nothing whatever to do with a law of this kind, no matter how the sequence may be formulated. The Christian attitude is the being of the Christian as graciously awakened by the Word of God which always gives and always demands. It is his being in the freedom of the Gospel, not his being under a law. But seen in this freedom of the Gospel each of the three forms is also the whole; each of the three forms include the other two within itself.

We are bold to make the comparison that, as the three trinitarian modes of the divine being do not limit and complete each other as parts of the Godhead, but are the one God in a threefold identity, so that each of the modes includes the other two within itself and is within the others, so the faith and obedience and prayer of the Christian are the one Christian attitude, and they are all individually that which the others are as well. If faith is really the faith of the true Christian attitude, it is also obedience and prayer, and on the same presupposition obedience is faith and prayer, and prayer is faith and obedience. Yet the distinction, i.e., the peculiar emphasis and standpoint and even life of faith and obedience and prayer is just as indispensable as is the distinction between the modes of being in our confession of the triune God, for the unity and totality of the Christian attitude is never actual or visible *in abstracto*[EN572], but only in the three forms. A reversion either to the neglect of any one of the forms in favour of the others, or to the totalitarianism of any one at the expense of the others, cannot be justified on the score that we consider them to be identical in essence, just as in trinitarian teaching the doctrine of the *perichoresis* of the three divine modes of being cannot mean that ultimately we are returning to the modalistic heresy.

On this presupposition and with this reservation we shall now expound the three forms of the one Christian attitude to the divine providence and lordship, and therefore the three forms of one and the same Christian knowledge at this point. We will take them one after the other, but in the most intimate connexion the one with the other, first faith, then obedience and then prayer.

1. Faith is the receiving of the Word of God as such. It is the lively confidence in which the Christian perceives and acknowledges the Word as a Word from God and a Word spoken to him, and in which he affirms it to be such, a Word from God and a Word spoken to him. Faith, therefore, is the source of the Christian attitude. As compared with obedience and prayer, it has no primacy in value or importance, but it has a primacy in order: not necessarily a primacy in temporal order; but necessarily a primacy in actual order. In faith in Jesus Christ a man becomes a Christian. In faith, God in Jesus Christ is his Father, he himself in Jesus Christ is the child of God, and he becomes the particular creature which participates from within in the divine providence and universal lordship. In faith, the particular relation and union which God has established on earth between Himself and His people actually attains its goal on the manward side. Therefore everything which goes to make up the Christian attitude is really grounded in faith and is a form or work of faith.

This is not the place, however, in which to speak fully or in detail of the [247] origin and nature of faith.

We may dismiss briefly, on the one hand the idea that faith is a magical quality imparted to man and enabling him to surpass the nature given him at creation, and on the other the idea that it is an activity which man produces of himself simply by exercising a capacity which belongs to him by nature. The true source of faith is the Word of God. Faith, therefore, is a new activity which man cannot of himself decide to undertake, and which he has no power of himself to undertake. When it takes place, faith is a historical determination of human existence, a determination in the history of salvation. But—in opposition to the first view—it is an awakening of man to his own activity, an activity which as such is not merely within the sphere of his own creaturely nature, but corresponds at every point to the highest natural determination of his creatureliness; just as the incarnation of the Son of God, which is the great

---

[EN572] in the abstract

pattern of the origin of faith, means not only a completely unmerited liberation of human nature, but also and for that very reason a restitution of its highest creaturely determination.

We may also dismiss, on the one hand the idea that faith is a blind subjection to a law imposed upon the will and understanding from without, and on the other the idea that it is a conviction of the truth and importance of certain objective facts, a conviction which is established and attained by man himself, and then, and for this reason, chosen and adopted by man himself. As opposed to the second idea, faith is, of course, an arrest and commitment in which man is set free from his own caprices and acquires a Lord whom he must follow. It is a new and strange light shining upon man from above. But—in contrast to the first idea—it not only shines upon human life, and therefore the human will and understanding, from without, but it also illuminates them from within. It does not close our eyes, but opens them. It does not destroy our intellect and compel us to sacrifice it, but it sets it free just as in a definite sense it captivates it, i.e., for itself. It does not break down our will, but sets it in free movement; just as the incarnation of the Son of God, the pattern of the nature of faith, is actual and visible not only in the perfect obedience but also in the perfect sovereignty of the activity of Jesus Christ.

The reality of faith transcends these antitheses. It includes them. Faith is altogether the work of God, and it is altogether the work of man. It is a complete enslavement, and it is a complete liberation. And it is in this way, in this totality, that it is raised up and lives as it is awakened by the Word of God.

And it is in this way that the Christian participates in faith in the divine providence and world-governance. In the first instance his faith is simple and direct—a participating in Jesus Christ and in His work of grace and salvation.

[248] Jesus Christ is in fact the Word of God by which faith is awakened. The Christian lives by Him, and holds fast to Him. In its first and decisive moment his faith is a confidence in what took place and was revealed in this One, in the kingdom of God in Him, in the uniting of God and man accomplished by Him, in the reconciliation of the world with God actualised by Him, in the fatherhood of God and the sonship of man proclaimed by Him. As faith in Him, as faith in the power and obedience of the Holy Spirit, it is Christian faith. And as such, in a movement arising from this first movement, it as it were raises itself and reaches out and becomes confidence in the fact that what occurred in Jesus Christ has precedence over all other occurrence; that all other occurrence is subordinate to it, having in this occurrence its origin and goal, its norm and standard; that to the one Jesus Christ all power is given both in heaven and in earth. It is as he participates in Jesus Christ in faith that the Christian participates in the divine providence and universal lordship. The same Holy Spirit who first led him into the narrower and central sphere now leads him out over its periphery into the wider circle. The distinction between the two movements is clear. Believing in Jesus Christ, the Christian enters into a given presupposition, and now he draws out the deductions implicit in that

presupposition, but implicit only as deductions. In the former case, faced with the particular occurrence in Christ, his faith is a confidence which is both related to and based upon a definite objectivity. In the latter, faced with crea-turely occurrence generally, it is a confidence which ventures out from this basis without any such objectivity. In the one case, it is a light kindled by the light, and in the other a light shining in the darkness. In the one case, it receives the assurance and encouragement and promise which it does not receive in the other, but by which it has to live and conquer. In the one case, it has the character of a present certainty, in the other, of a certain hope. But in both cases it is the same. In both it is altogether the work of God and it is altogether the work of men. In both it is the complete enslavement of man and his complete liberation. It is never present in the one case and not in the other. It cannot participate in Jesus Christ without participating in the divine provi-dence and universal lordship. Again, it cannot participate in the latter without participating in Jesus Christ. It is always our striding from the one to the other: from the place where God is revealed to the place where He is hidden; from the Here with its Therefore to the There with its Nevertheless.

In the present context our interest in faith is in respect of the second move-ment in which the Christian is faced with creaturely occurrence generally: not lost and helpless and defenceless, for in faith he participates in Jesus Christ; but only in the power and protection of that participation. He is called to participate in the divine providence and universal lordship, but it is only as the one who participates in Jesus Christ that he is empowered and equipped to do so. For the rest, he is actually confronted with the world-process in which he [249] cannot expect to meet fresh revelations. The Word alone which he has heard can make it possible for him to accept there too the ruling hand of God, there too the plan of God which is now being executed, there too the active mercy and omnipotence and wisdom and goodness of God, there too the faithfulness of God both generally and in detail. The Word alone can open the eyes of the Christian to the signs and testimonies of the presence and purpose and help-fulness of God, signs and testimonies which are real but hidden, which always need to be re-discovered. The Word alone by which he has known God can enable him to recognise God there. The Word alone can prevent him from creating either on a large scale or a small his own arbitrary and arrogant or it may be despairing or sceptical scheme of things; from indulging in, or perhaps surrendering to, his own unsubstantial vision of a self-subsisting and self-motivated universe in which there is no place for God; from becoming a hea-then either secretly or openly, either in theory or in practice. The Word alone can hold him over the abyss and lead him across the waves. And the Word alone can give him the necessary courage and patience, and cheerful heart. And by this Word the Christian is awakened to faith. In faith he lays hold of it. In faith he assents to it and affirms it. In faith he holds to the Word and main-tains it in face of everything that the world-process can produce, and above all in the face of his own unsettled heart which so consistently opposes and contradicts it. That is why we can and must say that faith alone must make it possible. In faith alone the Christian must have open eyes and see. In faith alone he must despise and dismiss all false systems. In faith alone he must be held over the abyss and be led through the waves. In faith alone he must be courageous and patient and cheerful. In faith alone; for how may he or can he or ought he to be willing and ready for all these things except in faith?

But in faith the Christian does all these things. And it is not a matter whether his faith is greater or smaller, stronger or weaker, more instructed or simpler. These are secondary questions. It is a matter whether his faith is a real faith and not a faith only in appearance. It is a matter whether as a real faith it is the source of the whole Christian attitude. And whether it is a real faith depends upon whether it is participation in Jesus Christ, and whether it draws out the deduction implicit in this fact. To put it in another way, it depends upon whether it really draws upon the Word, and is nourished by the Word, and allows itself to be directly and constantly renewed by the Word. If it does not do this; if in one sense or another the faith of the Christian is faith in himself, possibly an introverted faith in the power and seriousness of his own affirmation of the Word, or very commonly faith in the truth and beauty of Christianity; or if it is merely borrowed or assumed, a faith which is the imitation of what [250] we believe is faith as perceived in others, then we need not be surprised if it is not the victory which overcomes the world. But to the extent that in some measure or form it does do what is essential to it as faith, participating in Jesus Christ and drawing out the deductions involved in this fact, even if we cannot describe its achievements as perfect or brilliant, it is at least the Christian's participation in the divine providence and universal lordship. And the Christian, the creature which knows first of all that it can only lie in the dust before God, is the man who in faith, even if it is only a pitiable fragment of faith, is with God, and therefore not under or in but above all the wind and waves of world-occurrence. He is with God as a child of the Father and heir of His glory, and here and now a free lord of all things. He can see even where there is nothing to see. He can laugh at false systems and visions even when they are so strong. He can stand and proceed even when his neighbours and he himself expect to see him fall into the abyss. He can be courageous and patient and cheerful even where not just appearances but the massive whole of reality forbids him to be so. He bids defiance, not in an artificial spasm of religious overexertion, but because in believing he is himself defied, and therefore maintained both against himself and against this whole. He himself has a Lord, and therefore he can and may and must bid defiance and himself be lord with him. From the Therefore there follows at once the Nevertheless, and what is still lacking, what he still awaits, awaits ardently but not anxiously, is simply the revelation of his own Lord as the Lord also of world-occurrence, or, to put it in another way, the revelation that his Nevertheless is also a Therefore.

But that is what it means—at any rate in this respect—to live by faith. The just, the Christian, will live by this faith of his.

By this time it should be clear why it is so important that we should maintain that faith is altogether the work of God and altogether the work of man; that it is the complete enslavement of man and also the complete liberation of man. If it were not all these things, it would not achieve what it does achieve. It achieves it in so far as it is all these things.

If it were not the work of God on man, how could it exalt man as it does? How could it mean his participation in Jesus Christ, and therefore in the divine providence and world-governance? How could the creature grasp at such a thing for himself, or maintain it once it had been given? How could the creature believe of himself, and live by his faith? What an Icarus-flight faith would be if it were a venture undertaken by man in his own strength! But with God, and as God gives Himself to man by awakening faith, nothing is impossible. Awakened and moved by God, man can and does believe. But again, faith must also be the work of man if it is really to find him and affect him as the work of God on him, and not merely to hover above him as a kind of hypothesis. If the Christian did not himself believe, himself trust, himself make that first and [251] second movement, himself be caught up in the step from one to the other; if in all these things he were merely the spectator of God, how could it ever be said of him that he could personally recognise the revealed God even in His hiddenness, that as a child of the Father he could find his way about the house of the Father, that with God he could be the lord of all things? In this respect he would find himself left on one side, with fine thoughts about the things which might be, but are not for him. But the gift of faith consists in the fact that man himself can believe, that man himself can really accomplish the whole work of faith, that man himself therefore, can really live by his faith.

The importance of the second assertion will also be clear. Faith must consist in a complete enslavement of man. If he believes, he necessarily acquires a Lord; he necessarily begins to exist in what is for him a new and strange light. He cannot remain in the world as he was before. He must be separated and consecrated to participate in Jesus Christ and the divine providence and lordship. He must accept the fact that the Word of God disposes concerning him, and demands obedience. If he did not do this, how could he ever come to the point of clinging to it and being borne by it? How could he ever be made by it the friend and confidant of God who recognises Him even where He is now hidden? How could he ever be made by it courageous and patient and cheerful? How could he be a free lord over all things with the Lord, if he himself either could not or would not have a Lord? How could he see light in the darkness if he himself had not come into the light? If he will not lose his life, he cannot gain it. Therefore faith must always consist in the fact that in Christ he not merely sees himself questioned in the most radical possible way, but he must constantly abandon himself for lost in favour of the One who has found him. But the faith which consists in this is also the complete liberation of man.

In the very fact that he is so completely challenged, he is completely established. His being as a creature is not humiliated but supremely glorified by the fact that in faith he experiences this separation and consecration; that in faith he acquires a Lord and comes to stand in this new and strange light. Again, he would not have acquired this Lord, or come to stand in this light, if his creatureliness had not been revealed by faith, if in faith he had not become alert, one who sees accurately, and thinks keenly, and wills with decision, and acts with knowledge and energy. How could his faith be the victory if it were not also and at all points the warfare, if he were not willing to wage this warfare as a free man, enlisting and participating in it not with more, but certainly not with less, than the whole man? How could he believe from the heart, and be comforted and established in his heart by faith, if his whole being—for the heart is the whole man—were not thereby made free to live freely? Faith, then, must always consist in this summoning of the whole heart and soul and mind and strength of man. The Christian is always the man who is challenged in this sense.

[252]

From all that we have said, it will be immediately apparent that faith as such contains within itself obedience. The very essence of Christian obedience is subjection by emancipation, emancipation by subjection. And is not this the essence of all obedience? But does not all other obedience suffer because of its vacillation between subjection to tyranny and emancipation to anarchy? In Christian faith obedience occurs without being enmeshed in this unholy tension. As included in Christian faith, on both sides it is a critical and genuine obedience. In faith as trust in Jesus Christ, and by implication as trust in the fatherly rule of God in world-occurrence, obedience is not merely necessarily included in it, but it is necessarily included in this genuine and critical form. Faith lives by the Word. The Christian lives by his faith in hearing the Word, but only in really hearing it, only in living by hearing it, only in being obedient to it. Trusting the Word means entrusting himself to it, surrendering himself to its keeping, and therefore to its direction. He would not be trusting it if he did not do this. And if he did not trust it, he would not really believe. And then it would not be at all surprising if what he regarded as his trust in the Word of God were not justified by his life within world-occurrence; if he failed to make the second uprising and outreaching movement of faith; if he were not capable of the Nevertheless at the place where God is not revealed but hidden. If he really believes the Word, if he really trusts in it, then he has surrendered himself to its direction, and in so doing he has already become obedient, and genuinely so.

In the same way faith includes within itself prayer. Christian prayer means thanksgiving and praise, then confession and intercession, and then again thanksgiving and praise: all directed towards God; all offered to Him; all spread out before Him; all commended to Him with absolutely empty hands; all with the intention of committing oneself wholly and utterly to Him. Such prayer is included in faith. Faith itself cannot be without prayer, for, as we have already maintained, faith is neither a possession which is transferred to the Christian from without, nor is it a conviction which he has reached from within, but it is an act which is creaturely by nature, which fulfils itself in those two movements, but the fulfilment of which is anything but self-evident, needing the awakening of man by the Word of God. Therefore it is inevitable that in faith, in the fulfilment of this act, God is always a surprise to man, and man a surprise to himself. Man stands amazed before the divine goodness which gives him the freedom for this act. And he stands amazed before all that it shows him—the fatherhood of God, his own sonship, and the right of sonship in the house of the Father as the Father confers it and he himself receives it. It is in this inevitable surprise that the faith of a Christian as such is also prayer—the [253] prayer of thanksgiving and praise. Again, he stands amazed before the unmerited gift that he himself is actually enabled to believe, to believe this. And he can never understand how it is that he is able to do so, to receive this unmerited gift. Indeed, the more freely he can believe, and the more fully he receives in faith, the more he is conscious of his own inability and unworthiness, his own incapacity. It is in this surprise that his faith as such is prayer—the prayer of penitence and confession of penitence towards the great God who has done such things towards man, and still does so. And again, the Christian stands amazed before the nearness of God, and the superabundant wealth of all those things which call him to faith, and which as the gift of God are calculated to appease his hunger, to cover his nakedness, to make good his deficiencies. He stands amazed at the fact that he has only to ask and to knock, like a child at the nearby and trusted door behind which the Father dwells, and he can believe and live again in faith in the participation in Jesus Christ, and then in the divine providence and universal lordship. And again, it is in this surprise that the faith of the Christian as such is prayer—the prayer of the petition and intercession in which faith ventures to ask about the God who is so near to it and about his benefits which are so near to it, and when it is heard, again receives comfort and blessing, and above all is again given the freedom to be real faith, thus again turning to praise and thanksgiving. This faith would obviously not be the Christian faith if at its deepest level it were not this great surprise in which in and with the two other movements inwards and outwards—and the step from the one sphere to the other is unheard of in its Whence? and Whither?—man did not make of himself the movement of prayer, which is a pure movement upwards. For what is this movement in which the Christian can proceed so absolutely from God if in every respect, and therefore in all the inward possibilities of prayer, it does not of itself lead back to God, so that each individual act of faith is at bottom always an act of prayer?

So much for faith both in itself and in its relation to obedience and prayer. Faith constitutes the Christian attitude. To that extent it is the first form, and we shall have to consider it together with the two others, at which we have already cast a preliminary glance. The Christian believes, and in relation to the divine providence this gives him the knowledge without which all thinking and utterance on the subject is futile. In faith, the Christian has knowledge of the divine providence.

2. Obedience is the doing of the Word of God, the alert response in which the Christian justifies it against himself, against all men, against the whole world, and in which the Christian himself is justified. For the justification of man consists in his having and using the freedom to justify the Word of God. This is what is demanded by the Word of God; this is what it claims man for. And man hears it—really hears it—not merely by accepting it as the imparting of information, but by surrendering to and satisfying its claim. In this respect, the activity of the Christian is obedience, the second form of the Christian attitude, and one which again in its own way includes the whole. In believing, a man becomes a Christian; in obeying, he is a Christian. In doing what he has to do as a man who in Jesus Christ has come to know God as his Father and himself as a child of God, the Christian is the creature which not merely contemplates the work of the divine providence and lordship from without, but co-operates in it from within. What we have particularly to emphasise in this connexion is that the Christian attitude to the divine work does not consist merely in looking at it, but in co-operating with it. The same really has to be said of both faith and prayer. But this is the special feature of the whole Christian attitude which we have to note and describe when we speak of its character as obedience.

In the present context we cannot fully expound the question of Christian obedience: Christian works; active Christian righteousness; the Christian life in sanctification. What we can do is to draw two lines of demarcation on the two different sides.

On the one side, Christian obedience is certainly not an achievement which gives the Christain a claim or merit, which enables him to attain or keep for himself a position of advantage in man's relationship to the judgment and promise and assistance of God. And on the other side, Christian obedience is certainly not an achievement which can be either chosen or avoided; something which he may equally well achieve or not achieve. As opposed to this second view, it is the *obligatorium*[EN573] under which the Christian is placed by the very thing which makes him a Christian, the necessary content of being as a Christian. But in opposition to the first view, it is so because it is only the fulfilment of a direct obligation, not related to any claim and not carrying with it any distinction for the one who discharges it. It is the direct expression and manifestation of a life for which he will have no claim to thanks and for which he least of all will expect either gratitude or reward.

When the Son of God, who was sent by the Father, does the Father's will on earth, and fulfils it to the end, what advantage or reward or honour does He get because of it? He does the will of the Father simply because He is the Son. To be sure, He does do it, and He has no

[254]

EN573 obligation

choice not to do it. He does it necessarily. He would not be the Son of God if He did not do it. This is the great pattern of Christian obedience as we have to consider and understand it according to this twofold demarcation.

Again, on the one side Christian obedience is certainly not under an outward law. It is not in any sense the fulfilment of a written or unwritten code. It has nothing whatever to do with the maintaining of Christian standards or the setting forth of a Christian way of life. For it comes from the Holy Spirit, who is [255] the Christian's only Master. But on the other side, because it does come from the Holy Spirit, it is the very antithesis of human whims and caprices, of free-lance fancies and opinions, of conduct based only on sentiment or resentment. For the Holy Spirit rules the Christian, in a conflict in which the Christian's own spirit must always give in and be beaten. The Holy Spirit speaks by the Word of God, binding the Christian to its commands and directions. And ultimately He is the Spirit who is given not as the Spirit of the individual but as the Spirit of the whole community. He leads the Christian in the fellowship of this community, and He orders his actions to obedience within the framework of this fellowship and its mission and service. Yet while we have to remember this on the one side, on the other we have to remember, too, that in His divine authority, on His own basis, and within the limits of His own nature, the Spirit is the free Spirit of God, moving where He Himself wills, demanding of each individual his own individual obedience, demanding of each individual an obedience which is always new, and leading the community as such into new situations and laying upon it new tasks. Therefore there cannot really be any external statutes by which Christian obedience may ever be defined or determined absolutely.

Once again the divine pattern must be normative on both sides. In His procession from the Father and the Son, the Spirit is a particular Spirit, the Holy Spirit. He is always a Spirit of love and peace and order, but now He is the Spirit of the love and peace and order which according to the eternal mystery of the unity of Father and Son will always be a mystery in the ways and works of the Spirit in the created order, and therefore in Christian existence. The Spirit can never be observed or imprisoned by the creature, and therefore by the Christian, but in all His majesty He will always be a free Spirit and therefore the Holy Spirit.

It is in the obedience which has this basis that the Christian participates in the divine providence and universal lordship. But first we have to consider this obedience in the direct form in which it is simply his participation in Jesus Christ; in the kingdom of the grace which is revealed and active in Him. The Christian is used in this kingdom. When he is incorporated into this kingdom he is enlisted for duty and service. He is given a commission. He is directed to a particular path. That he himself should be delivered and saved is not the final meaning of the grace shown to him in Jesus Christ, or the final aim of the Christian life. He is delivered and saved as he acquires a Lord and a task. He is delivered and saved to the glory of God and for co-operation in the execution of the kingdom which God has purposed. He is bound to this Lord and established for the sake of this Lord. And it is because his obedience is obedience to

[256] this Lord that at one and the same time it is so necessary and so voluntary, so bound and so free. The fact that it proceeds from the Holy Spirit means concretely that it is one of the movements in which the lordship of Jesus Christ as the Head of His community is expressed and reflected. The Christian is a member of this community, and therefore his activity is one of the movements which Jesus Christ its Head induces in His body and its members. Christian obedience is therefore the submission of the individual Christian, as a member, to the directions given by Jesus Christ to His community. It is following Jesus. And this means that the obedience of the Christian begins at the cross of Christ where it is decided what man is to be as he belongs not to himself or to an alien power but to God, and what the world is to be as it is not lost to him but loved by Him even in its lost condition. The individual and the world as a whole really begins there. But the Christian who knows what really happened there does what has to be done now that the world as a whole and the individual come from there. As we said at the outset, he justifies the Word of God. This means concretely that he justifies the decision made in Jesus Christ, in the death of Jesus Christ. He takes his stand on this decision. He acts as it demands. This is his obedience. And he is constrained to it by the Holy Spirit, who seeing that he is a member of the community, seeing that he is enabled to believe, indwells and controls him. This is the meaning of the personal sanctification and discipline and purpose to which he is made subject. And this is also the meaning of his incorporation into the life and service of the community and his responsibility for its inward development and outward mission.

But from the first movement of obedience there spontaneously arises a second, which is again an uprising and outstretching movement. The Lord of the community, who as such is the personal Lord of the Christian, is also the Lord of world-occurrence generally, in which the Christian participates at every step, not passively only, but at his own time and place and in his own way actively as well. In the one case the Lord is revealed, in the other He is hidden. But in the latter case no less than the former He is the Lord. Therefore in the latter case no less than the former the Christian can be obedient to Him. Hence the wider sphere of world-occurrence generally is not a sphere in which the Christian is any the less claimed, or not claimed at all by Jesus Christ. In this sphere, too, he has to respect and attest the decision which was made in the death of Jesus Christ, and to justify it by his conduct. It was a decision which was made for all men and for the whole world, and therefore in the case of the Christian for the totality of his being in all its dimensions. This means that he is claimed not only in the religious sphere but also in the secular; not only in the spiritual but also in the physical; not only in the ecclesiastical, but also in the political and economic and academic and aesthetic. Here, too, the difference between the two movements is clear. We might say that the one is centripetal and the other centrifugal, or the one direct and the other indirect, or the one [257] basic and the other deduced, or the one original and the other the copy. But here, too, our first task is to see that they belong together, and to see how they belong together; to see that Christian obedience consists in a single step from the one to the other, so that the Christian can never be engaged exclusively in either the one or the other. The distinctness of the two movements of obedience is conditioned by the fact that God, Jesus Christ, as the Lord of creaturely occurrence, is revealed to him in the one, in the Christian community and his personal life as a member of it, but hidden from him in the other, in world-events generally. But the homogeneity of the two movements is conditioned by the fact that in both cases it is the same Lord and the same claim is made upon the Christian. This means that there is no place for dualism, and that from the very first it is impossible either to neglect or to omit the second form of Christian obedience.

In this context our concern is with the second form, in which consciously or unconsciously, voluntarily or involuntarily, directly or indirectly, on a small scale or a great, the Christian does actually participate in the course and process of creaturely and universal occurrence as a whole. Our concern is with the second form in which the Christian is called obediently to participate in the lordship of God in this more general sphere, and therefore—and this is the real problem of obedience—to participate in it actively, justifying by his conduct that which God Himself is doing in this sphere. Now it is clear that only in a direct participation in Jesus Christ, only in discipleship, only in the life of obedience as a member of His community, is the Christian equipped to do this. At this former point he has to learn to know what will be the bearing of his subjection to the will of God at the latter. At this former point he has to become so familiar with the life and authority of the Holy Spirit in the Word of God as to be able at least in some measure to differentiate Him from all other spirits at the latter. At this former point he has to accustom himself to obedience to Him, and exercise himself in this obedience. Any gap in his development, his schooling in active righteousness, in this inward sphere will necessarily avenge itself at once in a refusal to exercise it in the outward. And the smallest faithfulness at this point will be confirmed a hundred-fold at that. But it is, of course, with the equipment that he receives at this point that he must manage and succeed at that. In that sphere, in world-occurrence generally, he will be confronted with all kinds of clear or less clear ordinances and regulations, with all kinds of general rules which interfere with his actions, with all kinds of generally or fairly generally recognised principles which demand both his respect and on sufficiently concrete grounds his compliance. But in that sphere he will not encounter the Holy Spirit in the Word of God. He will not encounter any absolutely binding directions, any divine commands which he can and must observe unconditionally as one who knows both the utter freedom of the subject and the utter subjection of the free man. He will [258] not encounter anything which can be compared even remotely in its unequivocal authority with the will of God as it is actualised and revealed in Jesus Christ. In this respect, he will never find solid ground in that sphere. It is only of the Holy Spirit whom he has received and by whom he is controlled that he is governed at all and not carried one way by this current and another by that like a ship without engine or rudder. It is only of the Holy Spirit that he can take heed when he hears His orders. It is only of the Holy Spirit that he can learn to understand situations, to recognise opportunities, to choose possibilities and to distinguish them from impossibilities. The situations and opportunities and possibilities and impossibilities of the world-process with which he is called upon to wrestle do not as such contain within themselves or proclaim any divine and infallible Word. In the midst of them he can direct his path only with a provisional certainty. It is only the Holy Spirit who can command him, giving the orders and prohibitions which he must and can obey. It is only the Holy Spirit who can really guide him. It is only the Holy Spirit who can give him a good conscience both before and after his actions. It is only the Holy Spirit who can so bind him to his path that he is really bound, and so liberate him that he can tread this path in real freedom. It is only the Holy Spirit who can give him the light for right decisions and the power to make them. It is only the Holy Spirit: but that is to say, it is only the pure and unbroken Word of God accompanying him where God Himself is hidden; or, from the standpoint of his own attitude, it is only the obedience which he has learned in the school of Jesus Christ and brought out from that school, and to which he can remain faithful in all his decisions. Whether he actually is obedient is measured by the extent to which his obedience is this obedience. It may conform to all the other ordinances and regulations and principles and claims with which he is confronted, or it may be in opposition to them, in a completely isolated opposition to them, but at any rate it is not obedience to other lords, but to the Lord who has at this point the only claim to his obedience because He is the only true Lord. And in relation to the divine providence and governance in world-events, what he does in this obedience is the active righteousness, the good work of the Christian, his life and activity in sanctification.

The Christian actually achieves this obedience. We do not overestimate him when we say that. We naturally reckon with the fact that what he does is only more or less obedience—usually less. Even here there are really substantial differences between an enlightened and an unenlightened obedience, between an obedience which is clearly directed in its origin and one which is not, between an obedience which is bold and one which is timid, between an obedience which is pure and one which is obscure. But however substantial these differences may be, they are only side-issues compared with the question [259] whether it is a real or only an apparent obedience. And whatever else we may have to say about it or against it or for it, this question is decided by whether as a participation in Jesus Christ this obedience is founded and induced by the Holy Spirit, the wisdom and power of the Word of the one true Lord. We may grant that in the actions of a Christian many other lords may constantly exercise dominion side by side with the one who is really Lord. If only the Christian is not entirely unspiritual! If only he is not a complete stranger in the school of Christ! A little that is spiritual can make its way against much that is unspiritual. A little real obedience—even with all the scandal that there is so little of it—can counter-balance and make good a great deal of disobedience. If only it is there in some degree and in some form, then with all its ambiguity and brokenness we can say of the conduct of a Christian that in his decisions and activity, in what he does and accomplishes, he becomes and is a real factor, an active element in the hidden governance of God, along the positive line of this hidden governance. This fact is not altered in the slightest by his being under the lordship of God, by the creatureliness of his conduct. Grasping at the divine sceptre is the very last thing that the Christian will attempt if he is living in obedience. With all other creatures he is still in the dust before God, and the more real his obedience, the more he will be conscious of the fact. But it is still the case that to the small extent that he is obedient, at specific points and in specific ways he is posited and used in the service of the divine lordship, in the fulfilment of the positive divine will. On earth God has in every age elected and created and preserved His community as the people of His own beloved Son, willing both to have and to rule them as His peculiar possession within all other occurrence. And in the last analysis He does not do this in vain. It is not an indifferent matter or an idle pastime that by the Holy Spirit of His Word He establishes their existence as individual members of the community, and determines their decisions and activities. The particular purpose of God rules in all these happenings according to the particularity of the happenings. His community has its commission, and in this community there are commissions for the individual members. And it is in the execution of these commissions that in the midst of world-occurrence Christians are compelled to obedience; that by the commands and prohibitions of the Holy Spirit of the Word of God they are led to recognise and distinguish between the various situations and opportunities and possibilities and impossibilities, selecting some and rejecting others; that they are empowered and consecrated to an active righteousness, to good works in this world. All this is not really for their own satisfaction or profit, or to supply here and there a pious flourish at the wonderful conjunction of events. In the midst of world-events, in all the necessity and obligatoriness, the constraint and freedom of their obedience, in all the poverty of its execution, in all the shame which they heap upon themselves and their Lord, Christians are the children of God, and as such they are the true and proper servants of God, not hired servants, employees, but natural servants, by whose activity God wills at a specific time and place to accomplish something specific in the context of His own activity; something which will attest His kingdom, or recall the revelation which He has already given, or declare this revelation as it has still to be completed. It is as these creaturely acts of attestation, recollection and declaration take place within world-occurrence that the positive will of God is done in this sphere. And as the Christian is obedient, and to the extent that he is obedient, he is used to this end, and is in the service of the will, the positive will of God, and of the divine providence and world-governance. For this to be the case, it is not necessary

[260]

259

that he himself should sit in the counsel of God. It is not necessary that he should understand the context, the pragmatics, of the will of God, even as it concerns a single week, let alone years and centuries. It is not required of him, and he himself does not need, to know the great line of the divine purpose for the kingdom, or to be able to assign as it were to himself and his activity their function in the strategic plan of the divine world-governance. He can and indeed he must leave all these things to God. All that he has to do is to listen. But as he does listen, and to the extent that he does, he has his function in the divine world-strategy, doing at some point the duty which is allotted to him as a soldier and servant. Why he has to do it, what he accomplishes or does not accomplish by it, why he was used and posited in this service, he will one day learn when a great light is shed on all things. But all that concerns him here and now is that his work is not really in vain, that he is in this service, and that he has his duty to do, whether he does it well or ill. He is always a very unimportant creature with other creatures. From the point from which he and all other members of the community may come he is referred only to the Holy Spirit in the Word of God. He is a modest creature, and a modest member of the people of God. But as such he is directed to this place; he is posited and used in it; he is given his own particular commission at this point in world-occurrence; he is equipped for it in his own particular way. All that is required of him and all that he needs is faithfulness. And as in some measure and form he is faithful, he has a part—and in all its lowliness a glorious and active part— in the divine providence and world-governance.

Looking back, we can now repeat that the demarcations which we made at the beginning of the discussion were not superfluous. The obedience of the Christian is wholly necessary, but it can never be an acquisition; and, while in this obedience the Christian is not under any statute, he is subject to the strictest authority.

Christian obedience is not an acquisition but a free achievement. It can [261] never look for thanks or merit or reward because in itself it proceeds from what is the highest and at bottom the only acquisition that man can ever know: from the election and call which constitutes a Christian; from participation in Jesus Christ; from the gift and operation of the Holy Spirit. The Christian can obey only as he comes from the acquisition which has accrued to him, not as he seeks some further acquisition. He thanks God for the fact that he is a Christian, but he cannot expect any thanks for it. He obeys as God has made Himself meritorious on His behalf—what further merit is to be expected? He has his reward in the fact that he is a Christian, and that as such he can obey. This reward, which precedes and follows all his own achievement, is now hidden and will one day be revealed. But the man who participates in it has no time to look for any other, because all his time is taken up in simply obeying on the basis of the reward already received in secret. The obedience which he has to exercise in the inward and practise in the outward sphere would obviously be null and void if he could and did maintain it in another way. But to say this is to say already that its free achievement is also necessary. Real obedience has passed the point where there is a possible choice of disobedience. Christian obedience is real obedience because in it this choice was excluded at the source. From the very first it consists in the recognition that God is justified: justified in the incomprehensible mercy of His movement towards man; justified in His claim upon man; justified in His will to determine and direct him by the Holy Spirit in His Word. In the light of this recognition the Christian can do no other. He achieves obedience knowing that it has to be achieved. If it were otherwise, if he could disobey, he would *ipso facto*[EN574] be denying his own origin and being; the thanks which God can claim for the fact that he is there at all; the merit which God has gained for him; the reward which he has already received from God. He is under a personal obligation to God: personal, for this is what makes his obedience a free achievement; and an obligation, for this is what makes it a necessary one.

And now, to take up the second demarcation, Christian obedience is not under any statute, but takes place under the sole authority of the Holy Spirit in the Word of God, because as real obedience it has only one Lord, because all ordinances and regulations and rules and principles and claims which are encountered by it in the world-process lack the unconditional majesty and validity which might make respect for them a real and genuine obedience. Authorities of this kind can enslave and liberate man only in appearance. And it is a dangerous error if we believe that we have to render them an absolute reverence or compliance. Their majesty and validity are really conditioned, that is, they are measured by the supremacy of the one true Lord, and their recognition or non-recognition is decided by His sentence. If the Christian does recognise them, it is for the sake of this one Lord, because this Lord orders him to recognise them within their own limits. Often enough it can and will happen that in obedience to the same Lord he will not grant them this recognition but will have to oppose that which they enjoin. He would not be obedient to the one true Lord if he were not prepared to do this. He remains free either way, but in this freedom he is under real authority. Having the sovereign choice either to comply or not to comply, as a child and also a servant (or better, a slave) of the heavenly Father, he is wholly at the disposal of the will of his Father; he is merely an executive instrument; he is simply caught up in the fulfilment of the function allotted to him. In this very freedom he no longer asks: Why should I do this? What will be the outcome of it? What do I stand to gain by it? He no longer tries to sit in the counsel of God. He no longer wants to be master and servant at one and the same time. If this were what he wanted, it would be a sure sign that he has not completely escaped the dominion of false gods and their decrees, that he has not yet entered the sphere of true obedience. It is only submission at this point which makes him a free man; his own whims and caprices can only unfit him to be so. And as a free

[262]

[EN574] by that very act

261

man, he has to make the most definite submission and observe the strictest discipline.

In this respect, too, we have to bear in mind the unity of the Christian and therefore the relationship of Christian obedience to Christian faith and Christian prayer. In obedience as we have described it faith is necessarily included. We have seen already that as the work of God to man and man's own work faith is translated into an event, an action, a real human existence, only in virtue of the fact that it contains within it obedience, that faith itself is at root an act of obedience. It is only too true that while faith alone is the basis of the Christian's standing, yet without works, without its translation in obedience into an event or action, it would be dead. But in the case of obedience, too, everything depends upon the fact that it contains within it faith. Only as the Christian believes does he participate in Jesus Christ and the community of Jesus Christ, and therefore in the divine providence and lordship in world-occurrence. Only as the Christian believes is it true that he begins his whole life at the cross of Jesus, where the decision of the love of God for him and for the whole world was made. Only as the Christian believes is he summoned to justify the will of God in the one sphere and also in the other. It is as he is able to believe that he enters the school of obedience to which he can then be true and upon which he can bring honour in the realm of creaturely occurrence generally. The command and the power to do this, and the courage to dare it, are the command and power and courage of faith, without which the whole undertaking would simply be a gamble leading inevitably to failure and collapse. It needs a particular confidence to make this venture; and this confidence is quite simply

[263]   the confidence that Jesus Christ is Lord of all, and that it is His will that we have always to consult and His interests that we have always to represent. It is not at all self-evident that Jesus Christ is this, that no other lords can dispute His title, that no fate or chance or laws or principles can vie with Him or permit the Christian to turn to anyone else or to meet any other commands but His. To say this, we have continually to utter that Nevertheless, not merely with heart and mouth, but also in deed. To say this, we have always to venture that run and make that leap in a sphere where everything seems to be obscure and where—apart from what the Christian brings with him from this school—it remains always equivocal and uncertain. In this sphere the Christian finds himself in the sphere of the hidden God. He needs a confidence that the one light of revelation will give light and prove reliable even where apart from it there is no light. He needs a confidence which endures, a confidence which renews itself, a confidence which in a sense is new every morning. For the situations in which the Christian has to obey are many, and are constantly changing, and make necessary new insights and new decisions in which he can hardly do other than begin again and again at the beginning. Above all, he needs a confidence to be always alert and ready for such beginnings. Even the little obedience that the Christian can always bring is in fact surrounded by so much of his own weakness and folly and even wickedness, by so much shame,

that he has good reason constantly to grow weary of himself, to despair of himself, to abandon himself as utterly unworthy and unfitted to execute his commission, and even to relinquish this commission. In all this he would be utterly lost if it were not for the fact that he is upheld by the assurance that for him, too, there is divine mercy, that he, too, will be forgiven, and that because of this he cannot be weary. He needs Jesus Christ to forbid him to despair of self. He needs to have it impressed upon him that no severity of judgment under which he may see himself authorises him to surrender instead of fulfilling (well or ill, with good report or bad) the function which has been allotted to him in the divine plan. For God in His grace and also with His claim is all the closer to him the more clearly he sees with what fulness he is under the divine judgment. But the confidence which he needs is at all points the confidence of faith, without which there can be no Christian obedience. And to this we must add that the authoritarian Commander and Leader to whom the obedience of a Christian is due is the Holy Spirit and none other. Upon this depends the fact that it is an achievement which is both free and also necessary, which is completely free from all regulations and for that very reason completely under discipline. But there are so many spirits. Above all, there is the spirit of the Christian himself, to which we have to attribute far too great a readiness to substitute itself for the Holy Spirit, and which can far too easily lead the Christian into enterprises which have really nothing to do with obedience and in which he will fulfil anything but the purposes of the kingdom of God and be [264] anything but a dutiful servant of the Lord. Advisedly, then, we have referred again and again to the Holy Spirit of the Word of God. This would imply that the Holy Spirit is not an indefinite or inarticulate spirit, not a vague nor even a vigorous compulsion this way and that, the understanding of which is finally left to the conceits and caprices of the Christian himself. The Holy Spirit is holy in the fact that He does not come from us but to us, and that He does not come to us from our own environment but from above. The Holy Spirit is the wisdom and power of the Word of God. And so Christian obedience differs from an uncontrollable compulsion in the fact that following the guidance of the Spirit means obedience to the Word of God. But this brings us back again to the source of the whole Christian attitude in faith. For we have defined Christian faith as a knowledge and acknowledgment of the Word of God as a Word spoken by God and to us. The Word of God—and in this it is obviously different from all other words—is Jesus Christ Himself in His own work and revelation. The obedience of the Christian means that he gives himself to this specific Word and to the wisdom and power and guidance of this Word. He does not listen to the voices and promptings either of his own heart or of that of others, but only to what the Word itself says, and to what it says to him here and now. But this means that he must return constantly to his faith, to the place where he personally is bound by the Word and made free by it to be truly obedient. If he does not do this he will inevitably go astray at every slightest step. And the Holy Spirit whom he obeys outwardly will be a sinister figure under whose guidance he can only do harm to himself and others, and certainly fail to fulfil the task with which he has been entrusted. The power of his obedience can be only the power of the confidence in which he gives himself afresh to the protection of the Word of God and in which he will continue afresh under this protection. In the power of this confidence, and therefore in the power of faith, but not otherwise, he will be a man constrained by the Holy Spirit, and therefore an obedient man.

And now we must consider the relationship of obedience to prayer. That Christian obedience includes prayer means first that prayer is the most intimate and effective form of Christian action. All other work comes far behind, and it is Christian work, active Christian righteousness, the doing of the will of God, the fulfilling of the function allotted to the Christian in the discipleship of Jesus Christ and the service and execution of the divine purpose of the kingdom, only to the extent that it derives from prayer, and that it has in prayer its true and original form. When the Christian wishes to act obediently, what else can he do but that which he does in prayer: render to God praise and thanksgiving; spread himself before God in his weakness and sin; reach out to Him with all that impels him; commend himself to Him who is his only help; and again, and this time truly, render to Him praise and thanksgiving. This is

[265] Christian obedience *in nuce*^{EN575}. In it there takes place the one thing necessary, the one thing that is demanded of the Christian, the one service that is required of him. For everything else is included in this one thing. It is perfectly true, within limits, that prayer is the renewing and inward empowering of the Christian, a breathing of the soul, and so forth. But it must not be forgotten that prayer is also the true and proper work of the Christian. And the greatest Christian business is only idleness if this true and proper work is not done; while again, if outward appearances are not deceptive, the most active workers and thinkers and fighters in the divine service in this world have at the same time, and manifestly, been the most active in prayer, and obviously they have not regarded this activity as a waste of time. And on this point we have also to say that the problem of obedience, like that of the permission and necessity of faith, sets the Christian at a place where if his willing and doing is genuine, if it proceeds from faith, it must pass over into this particular form of willing and doing, passing over into prayer, ending and also beginning afresh in prayer. The Christian himself can never simply presuppose that he has the light and the power for genuine obedience. And the faith in which alone he can be obedient is not something which is so readily accessible that he has only to give himself a jolt and he will believe afresh, and in this faith be obedient afresh. In faith, he is dealing directly with God Himself in His freedom and majesty. But in prayer he presents himself to God, the God whom he can always avoid in his activity, but to whom he must always present himself if he is to have a genuine and effective faith and therefore to be capable of a bold and effective obedi-

---

^{EN575} in miniature

ence. In prayer, he makes use of the freedom to answer the Father who has addressed him, or, to put it in another way, to go to meet the Father from whose goodness he proceeds, or, to put it in yet another way, to give direct and natural expression to his great surprise that God is his Father and that he is the child of God. In all its forms prayer is this answering, this going to meet, this direct expression of the truth of the situation in which the Christian finds himself as a Christian. When he prays, he puts himself in the position in which faith and obedience can always begin again at the beginning. As this primitive movement, prayer, which is the basis of all other activity, is included in obedience. It is itself the act of obedience *par excellence*, the act of obedience from which all other acts must spring.

3. Prayer has just been described as a primitive movement. Indeed, in this third form of the Christian attitude we are dealing with the simple and basic form of the first two. Prayer is the primary thing in faith as well as obedience. Basically, faith is prayer, and obedience too is prayer. Yet we have still to distinguish a third form, and to this form we must now give more specific consideration. For we shall not do justice to the essence of prayer in this context if we simply think of it as included in faith and obedience as the basic form of both. [266]

When we touched upon it earlier we described it as the sequence of praise and thanksgiving, confession and penitence, petition and intercession, and again praise and thanksgiving—all side by side with or following one another as seen from a distance. This description was not incorrect, but it is insufficient. What is lacking when we think of prayer in this way is a centre; something which makes it prayer as opposed to faith and obedience. On this view, it could easily merge into those first forms of the Christian attitude. But prayer has and is a form of its own, a form which as such includes within it the other two just as it is included within them. The sequence of acts which we provisionally described as prayer has in fact a centre, one specific act which constitutes the whole, from which all the rest proceeds and to which it returns, from which alone it receives its meaning and power.

To do justice to what takes place in Christian prayer we must not try to bring it under the one denominator of praise and thanksgiving, or more comprehensively, worship. This is a possibility which might well have suggested itself already from the fact that we deduced prayer from the great surprise which is also the source of faith and obedience; the great surprise of the Christian in the situation in which he finds himself placed by the Word of God and in which he can be a Christian. From this surprise there results very simply a worship of the One who has made this situation and who determines and controls it as the Lord; a humble astonishment at the mystery of it; a praising and an honouring and magnifying of God because He has turned and revealed Himself to man in His Word, and because of the form in which He has done so; a prostration before His incommensurable greatness; a thankfulness for His incomprehensible favour; a praising of His glory and unmerited goodness.

But the very situation which the Word of God has made for the Christian, and therefore the surprise which it evokes, and therefore the worship of God which results, have all a definite direction and colour, a distinctive Whence? and Whither?, which will prevent us from stopping at this point and seeking here the very essence of prayer. The Christian situation is not the abstract one of that which is great encountering that which is small, of that which is exalted encountering that which is lowly, of that which is holy encountering that which is defiled, of majesty encountering creatureliness. It is this; but it is it in a very concrete form. And that is what distinguishes our surprise in this particular situation from the general surprise which might easily be nothing more than idle gaping. That is what distinguishes Christian worship from a general glancing upwards, from mere reverence at the presence of the numinous, which in a form which is more religious than Christian and more aesthetic than religious might easily be nothing more than the sterile reverence of rapture or terror. To do justice to the specific element in Christian worship we must not try to understand prayer systematically, as it were, as worship, as praise and thanksgiving. This element can never be lacking. And in practice prayer does both begin and end at this point. But it is not at this point that we shall understand the factual order and essence of prayer.

[267]

Again, to do justice to prayer we must try not to bring it under the one denominator of confession or penitence. The Christian's surprise at his situation does have this element or aspect. It is a knowledge and acknowledgment of the judgment under which he stands. Therefore Christian prayer is inevitably a confession of his own weakness and inability and unworthiness, of the whole lost condition in which he is discovered in the sight of God. It is an indication that his utterly empty hands are the only offering which he can bring before God and spread out before Him. To pray in the Christian sense means fully and unreservedly to admit and confess to God all our wretchedness. To pray in the Christian sense means to renounce all illusions about ourselves, and openly to admit to ourselves our utter need. The man who will not do this will never pray. The Pharisee in the temple had a heart which seemed to be full of praise and thanksgiving, but he did not do this and therefore he did not pray. We must necessarily pass through this humiliation if our worship of God is not to be self-deception and pretence before God. But again, we must not try to understand prayer at this point. The Christian situation is not the abstract one of the lowliness of man before God, although this forms part of it. Nor is the Christian situation the abstract one of man's horror of himself, although this is included within it. Christian prayer, therefore, is not exhausted by this self-humiliation of man before God. This act must not be lacking in it, but even in this act it has a particular character, a particular direction and purpose, in which it is distinct from a general wretchedness which might be merely pitiable, or from a general self-abasement which might be only that of lassitude or despair or scepticism. The way of prayer does, of course, lead us to this impasse. Prayer does include penitence. But there is no point in trying to understand the essence of prayer in the light of this fact. The short prayer of the publican in the temple was natually a prayer of penitence, but in its decisive content it was something more, and something different.

There remains prayer as petition. And the question arises whether worship and penitence and petition (the centre of all prayer not being found in the latter) are not equally important and urgent and characteristic in the equality in which we have provisionally considered them; whether they do not form a sequence, the end of which always brings us back again to the beginning. In practice this may well be so. But in substance it is not so. In all languages the word prayer is itself against it. For it speaks only of petition as the constitutive element in what takes place in prayer. It shows us that while prayer is a matter [268] of worship and penitence, it is not so in the first instance. In the first instance, it is an asking, a seeking and a knocking directed towards God; a wishing, a desiring and a requesting presented to God. And the actuality of prayer is decidedly against not merely a precedence of the other two elements but even their equality with petition. The man who really prays comes to God and approaches and speaks to Him because he seeks something of God, because he desires and expects something, because he hopes to receive something which he needs, something which he does not hope to receive from anyone else, but does definitely hope to receive from God. He cannot come before God with his petition without also worshipping God, without giving Him praise and thanksgiving, and without spreading out before Him his own wretchedness. But it is the fact that he comes before God with his petition which makes him a praying man. Other theories of prayer may be richly and profoundly thought out and may sound very well, but they all suffer from a certain artificiality because they miss this simple and concrete fact, losing themselves in heights and depths where there is no place for the man who really prays, who is simply making a request. But the first and decisive argument against the subordination or equality of petition is the actual text of the Lord's Prayer, the substance of which is quite clearly and simply a string of petitions, pure petitions, in which the elements of worship and penitence have, of course, their place, which begin and end with worship, but which in themselves and as such are neither adoration nor confession, but simply petition. If we are to understand the essence of prayer, we may well be asked to follow the Lord's Prayer. And in the present context, in our survey of the divine providence and universal lordship and the Christian attitude to it, it is essential that we should speak of prayer in detail, because in the first instance—and this controls and includes everything else—prayer, or praying, is simply asking.

And now let us try to understand materially what it is that is primarily and properly surprising in the Christian situation. It is not simply that God is so great and holy and rich, nor is it simply that in comparison man is so small and unworthy and poor. Both these things are unmistakeably clear and surprising to the Christian, but they are only the complement to that which is primarily and properly surprising—that by His Word this great and holy and rich God draws so near to the man who is so small and unworthy and poor; so near, indeed, that in perceiving Him man can only worship, and in perceiving himself he can only abandon himself; but above all, so near with the nearness of Father and child that in face of Him man now finds himself in the nearness of child and Father. At bottom, it is this nearness which surprises him, and it is from this that there derive all other things which surprise him both in the heights above and the depths below. This, and this alone, is the specifically Christian element in the Christian situation. This is the content of the Word of God by which the Christian finds himself placed in this particular situation. This is the content of the revelation of God in Jesus Christ whose attestation is the task of the Christian community and in the knowledge and acknowledgment of which the Christian is a Christian, a member of this community, participating in its faith and sharing the responsibility for its service in the world. It was for the direct nearness between God and man as between Father and child, and child and Father, that Jesus Christ was born a man and crucified. And this nearness is the light of His resurrection. And when the Christian prays, he does what he has to do in answer to the Word and work of the Son of God. He makes the first available use of the freedom which is given to him by the amazing fact created in Jesus Christ. But this first answer certainly does not consist of thinking high thoughts about the glory of God and deep thoughts about his own unworthiness, and then making the movements which correspond to these thoughts. It consists in simply turning to the God who has drawn so near to him, and to whom he himself has been brought so near, with the intention that God should give to him, and that he should receive from God, all that is necessary to his situation; that he should receive from Him that which, as he clearly perceives in this situation, only God can really give to him. The freedom of his situation is that he sees the majesty of God, that he also sees himself and what he lacks and what is against him, but that he does not need to be in any way anxious about these things. He does not need to be afraid to draw near to God so that he who is so small and unworthy and poor may receive from Him something, yes much, yes everything. Nor does he need to be afraid to lift up himself to tell God who is so great and holy and rich what it is that he wishes to receive from Him. Something has happened in Jesus Christ, and something has been said in the Word of God, which makes this twofold fear unnecessary. The Christian is able to ask. The mystery that God is the Father of man and man the child of God is a mystery which has been revealed to him. And so he does ask. He says that which corresponds on his side to this happening and this revelation. He takes God as God gave Himself and showed Himself to the world and to him, as a Helper and Giver and Deliverer, as the source of all blessing and power and enlightenment and hope, in short of all the things that he himself lacks, but which God who has drawn so near to him, and is bound to him, will not keep to Himself but will allow him to enjoy as well. It is true that God does not allow any part of Himself to be taken from Him. But how if He gives Himself? If He does, it is even more true that

He does allow Himself to be taken. And God will not allow anything to be taken from Him, not one of all the things that He possesses, and that is everything. But how if He gives man all the things that He possesses when He gives Himself? Is it not even more true that He allows everything to be taken from Him, from His own hand? The Christian is able to take because God gives him [270] Himself and all that He possesses. "He that spared not his own Son, but delivered him up freely for us all, how shall he not with him also freely give us all things?" (Rom. 8^{32}). Thus the most intimate thing in Christian prayer, and therefore in the whole Christian attitude, is the fact that the Christian both may ask and actually does ask. In the praying of a Christian there is no impudence; no forgetting of distances; no arbitrary transcending of the antithesis between the one side and the other, between that which is above and that which is below; no self-seeking. On the contrary, he is doing that which corresponds and answers to the situation in which he finds himself placed by the Word of God. He does that which he is not merely permitted but commanded to do in this situation, seeing that he is obviously placed in this situation in order to do it. We may note that in so doing he makes the most genuine act of praise and thanksgiving, and therefore worship; and again, that in so doing he makes the most genuine act of penitence. By coming before God as one who asks he magnifies God and abases himself. And this is what God desires of him. This is how God would have him act. In so doing he meets the attitude of God Himself towards him. The true worship of God is that man is ready to take and actually does take where God Himself gives, that he seeks and knocks in order that he may really receive. This receiving is Christian prayer in all its centrality as petition. In this form it does not derive from the self-will of the Christian himself, just as the freedom which is given him is not the freedom of self-will. On the contrary, it derives from what the Christian receives from God, and from the command which is given with this gift. As petition, it is the human fulfilment of this receiving. It is really the basic form of Christian obedience. But we must reverse the proposition. The basic form of Christian obedience consists in the fact that on the basis of what God is and has for him man does not look upon God as so great and himself as so small that he dare not ask; he looks upon God as so gracious and himself as so genuinely accepted by God that he not merely must in some way dare to come to God as a suppliant, but he may actually do it as the most natural and necessary expression of his life.

If we are to understand the essence of prayer, we must try to be clear concerning this asking. And to do this we shall have to take rather a strange and apparently circuitous path. For however difficult it may sound, the hearing really precedes the asking. It is the basis of it. It makes it real asking, the asking of Christian prayer. It makes it the third and decisive form of the Christian attitude. That is why we said above that prayer derives from what the Christian receives. It is simply the human fulfilment of this receiving, the direct expression of the life of the one who stands amazed at what God is and does for him;

[271] amazed primarily, not at the majesty of God compared with himself, not at his own lowliness as contrasted with this majesty, but at the fact that God is actually for him, and that God acts for him. That is the point where we must begin. It is there and there alone that we can understand why prayer is permitted and commanded to man as petition. It is there and there alone that we can understand why together with faith and obedience, and including both, prayer is an integral element in the whole Christian attitude.

Of all the things that are needed by man, and needed in such a way that he can receive them only from God, that only God can give them to him, there is one great gift. And to all the true and legitimate requests that are directed necessarily to God, there is one great answer. This one divine gift and answer is Jesus Christ. It is Jesus Christ because in Him it came about that God concerned Himself in the world and man, and in so doing He turned upon the world and man the fulness of all blessing. It is in relation to Him, in and with His election as Mediator, that the world and man are created. It is as the Son and Word of God became flesh, man, creature, that God pledges and covenants Himself to the world, and at the heart of the world to man, accepting solidarity with him and accomplishing his deliverance, and directing upon him His own eternal glory. In Him God has constituted Himself personally the Lord and Guardian and Helper and hope of the world and man. In Him, in His own beloved Son, in His Word which is a Word of salvation and peace, He controls all occurrence, upholding it, accompanying it and ruling it. In the fact that Jesus is there, the world is already helped, and everything that creation needs, and at the heart of creation man, is already provided. In the fact that He is there, the name of the One from whom all things derive and to whom they return, who has moved all things, is declared and revealed and proclaimed as the name of the God who is the Saviour of the world, who is not without or against the creature, and does not work without or against it, but absolutely and utterly for it. Therefore He is the one great gift and answer in which all that we can receive and ask is not merely determined but actually given and present and available for us.

And Jesus Christ is not an isolated form or figure. To Him there belong those who are elected in and with Him, His own people, who by the Spirit of His Word are called to faith in Him, and by faith to obedience to Him. In its historical form He has called forth this body by the message of His prophets and apostles. This body of His is the community, His community, the Christian community, His people. He has given Himself to this people as the Lord, and revealed Himself as the Lord. He has shown Himself to this people as the One He is in order that there may be an office and ministry of witness at the heart of creation; in order that His light may shine in this world even before and up to His final manifestation before all things and on behalf of all things; in order

[272] that the recollection and hope of the divine love may have a concrete location and content. And in this respect He is present now in His people. In Him, it has present within it the one great divine gift and answer. In Him, it knows the

name of the One who is the beginning and end of all things, the Lord of all occurrence. In Him, its Creator, the Preserver and Ruler both of itself and of all creation, is actually and personally present within it as the Saviour, so that it looks to Him, it lives in communion with Him, holding fast to Him and fixing all its confidence on Him. This people is born for Him and gathered to Him in baptism. It is nourished by Him and for Him in the Lord's Supper. It is continually called and upheld and enlightened and guided by His Word. It lives, therefore, in the presence of the divine gift and answer which takes place in Him. And this means that it does not lack anything from its Lord. In Him, it possesses already all the grace and hidden glory which God has ascribed and applied to the creature. In Him, it has found already its home, its citizenship, its inheritance: found them in heaven; and indeed above all heavens, in the immediate proximity of the throne of God, of God Himself. From God it looks back and down upon all that is not yet ordered, all that is not yet solved, all that is not yet liberated, all the disturbances and obstructions and confusions and devastations which we still find in the world-process, all the darkness which still tries to obscure and actually does obscure for us the fatherly rule and determination under which this process stands. In Him, it already sees it unobscured. In Him, it already lives by all the goodness and wisdom and perfection of this rule. In Him, it already breathes at the heart of God. It would not be the Christian community if, as it knew about Jesus Christ, it did not also know about this Already, if in all the weakness and imperfection of its creaturely existence, but looking always to its Lord, and always in faith, and by faith in obedience to Him, it did not really live in this Already, in the full presence and receiving of the divine gift and answer. How could it, and how would it be the witness to Him, the light which He has kindled in the darkness, if it did not know about it and live in it, if it could not bear witness to it? It can only be a matter for concern—and we must not allow the protestations of a humble realism or a realistic humility to conceal or justify the fact—if things are otherwise; if it has nothing to say to the world, or only something lame and halting to say to the world, about the full divine gift and answer which is already actualised and present; if it is not very sure about this matter even so far as it applies to itself. It is precisely about this matter that the living Christian community is absolutely and unconditionally sure. It proclaims it with a loud and not a broken voice.

And the Christian whose attitude we are now considering is a member of this Christian community, the body and people of Jesus Christ. All that we have said in relation to Jesus Christ, and in company with Him the Christian community, also applies to the Christian personally. He personally is baptised into [273] Jesus Christ, and can receive His body and blood, Jesus Christ Himself, in the Lord's Supper, to live by Him and with Him. He personally can hear His Word, to experience its truth for him. He personally is made responsible for the community's mission in the world. It is for him that Jesus Christ is who He is; for him that the name of God the Creator of heaven and earth is made known;

for him that God is present as Saviour and also as the gracious Lord and Guardian and Helper and all his hope. It is he who can live in this world and participate in the events of this world in the full knowledge that God has taken up its case, that He has finally affirmed this world, that He has pledged Himself to it, that He has entered into covenant and accepted solidarity with it, that He has taken it into His own service. It is for him as a Christian, i.e., as one who has personal knowledge of the prophetic and priestly and kingly office of Jesus Christ, as one who by his membership of the community participates in this office, that world-occurrence is clearly and palpably not abandoned to its own devices, but preserved and accompanied and ruled by God, that it is preserved and accompanied and ruled by Him for good, for salvation, and in goodness and mercy, and that it is moving forward to eternal glory. It is he who in the Lord of the community, who as such is also his Lord, is dealing with the one great gift and answer which have already been manifested for him, which are already clear and palpable. And what does he not have, what can he possibly lack, when he can have Him? What can disturb or hinder or confuse or devastate him in life as a Christian and a man when he can live with Him, in communion with Him? What need is not already met in Him, what difficulty is not already removed in Him, what help is not already present in Him, what word of comfort that he needs is not already spoken in Him, what direction that he awaits is not already given in Him? In Him, he has already attained, he is already at the goal, and he can look back and down upon all his distress as already alleviated, all his complaints as already redressed, all his questions, however they may engage or consume or agitate him, as already answered. And let it not be said that this is to maintain too much or to speak too highly. No formulation can be too bold or far-reaching except when it is made by one who is not yet a Christian or no longer a Christian, except when it is made by one who secretly separates himself from the body of Jesus Christ, from the community which is elected and called by Him, except when it is made by one who perhaps separates the community and therefore himself from Jesus Christ instead of seeing and understanding both himself and the community as they are in Him. And if there is anyone who does do this he ought not to pretend that it is honesty but recognise it as his own weakness. In the honesty which he owes himself as a Christian he will not make separations of this kind, but rather

[274] be amazed and horrified that he has not yet realised in what fulness the divine gift and answer is already present and near to hand, and with what joy he can avail himself of it, and in what thankfulness he can acknowledge the fact.

And Christian petition, the meaning of which we are trying to understand, is simply the taking and receiving of the divine gift and answer as it is already present and near to hand in Jesus Christ. In this gift and answer we have to do with the will of God not only over but with the creature. We have to do with His covenant with man. We have to do with His grace directed towards man as an autonomous being distinct from Himself. We have to do with His work, which in man has an animate and not an inanimate subject. We have to do with His

Word, which man can hear and answer. In short, we have to do with the freedom in which man himself can live. In this freedom the Christian takes and receives that which God is and does for him, that which God offers him. In this freedom the Christian asks. For what can all that great and divine gift and answer be to him if he does not take and receive? It is destined for him, and therefore for one who takes and receives. But how can he take and receive that divine gift and answer except by asking for it? The only possible status of the creature in this matter is that of one who asks. Appropriating, using and enjoying is nothing but a continual and continually renewed asking. It is only in asking that it is not something strange and novel and unattainable to him. Asking is the only thing that he can do, the only spontaneous response that he can make. When he asks for it, when he says to God: I have not, and Thou hast; Therefore give me what Thou hast and I have not, he acknowledges and magnifies God Himself as the Giver, and he honours the divine nature of that which he is able to take and receive. And when he asks for it, he also perceives and confesses that he himself is a weak and unworthy partner of God, that he is most inadequate in his taking and receiving of the divine gift. In asking for it, he fears God and loves God. Again, in asking for it, he takes up towards this God a position which he alone may and can take up. But in doing this, in entering into a suitable and therefore a right and profitable relationship to the gift and answer already given and present, it comes about that he can actually take and receive it, so that God attains His end with him as the Saviour. The Christian asks, and by this asking the doors are opened wide, and the gates are lifted up, that the King of glory may come in.

To understand this Christian asking as such, it will be our best plan to follow the same order as when we spoke of the divine gift and answer. The first and proper suppliant is none other than Jesus Christ Himself. The Gospels tell us that He taught His disciples to pray, and that He did so by repeating a prayer with them, by being their Leader in prayer. This fact is of decisive practical importance for the meaning and character of Christian prayer. As the Son of God, He was the divine gift and answer, but as the Son of Man He was human [275] asking. In Him, God interceded for the creature, pledging and offering and imparting Himself to it in all His divine wealth. And in Him, the creature entered into the right and profitable relationship to God, and He became the first One properly to take and receive the divine gift. He himself was the King of glory who comes in, but He Himself was also the man who opened wide the doors and lifted up the gates in this world. He is the revelation of the name of God, the name of salvation, but He is also the man who hallows this name, who according to the divine revelation confesses the glory of God and the shame of man, and in so doing proves and demonstrates that He is the man who is elected and favoured and blessed and exalted and glorified by God, the representative man, the One who brings deliverance and bears salvation for the whole race. For what the man Jesus did was the very thing that He told us to ask for in the first petition of the Lord's Prayer: He hallowed the revealed name of

God. He took up towards God the relationship that man must take up because God is the merciful Saviour. He justified God, and in so doing He allowed Himself to be put in the wrong. He acknowledged the holiness of God, and in so doing He acknowledged the transgression and misery of man. He submitted Himself to God in all the fulness of a free and loving childlike obedience, and in so doing He was content to suffer the punishment of human sin, and to be delivered up to death because of it. Jesus Christ asks, that is, He takes up towards God the position of One who has nothing, and has claim to nothing, who has to receive everything, and to receive it from God. He trusts in God that He will in fact receive it from Him. He trusts only in God, but He trusts in God fully. He entrusts everything to Him. This is how He lives. This is how He loses His life. This is how He gains and saves it. As a Suppliant and nothing more, as One who in His supplication takes seriously both the holiness of God and the transgression of man, He is already heard and answered. His life is a life which is controlled and upheld by the grace of God. It is revealed by His resurrection to be a life which is delivered and glorified by God. God Himself has moved towards man. In His person the salvation which God has intended for man and the glory which He had predestined and promised to man are made event and presence. Man is caught up in the whole fulness of God. And all this is because He asks, because in all His actions as a man He is only and altogether a Suppliant. Naturally, as the Son of Man He is only and altogether a Suppliant because as the Son of God He is Himself altogether the divine gift and answer. It is, therefore, the love and power of God Himself which breaks through and gains the victory in the existence of this man by becoming a single request. God triumphed in this man. But He did it because this man actually asked, and asking took and received; because this man sought, and seeking found; because this man knocked, and as He knocked, it was opened to Him.

[276] In this way God triumphed in the asking, and therefore in the individual being and work of this man. And because it was in the individual being and work of this man, it was only by this man that the name of God was hallowed, only by this man that the response to the divine gift and answer became event and reality on the human side, not merely objectively but subjectively. It was, therefore, by this man, as He went through the narrow archway of asking, that the doors were opened wide and the gates were lifted up in this world. This man prayed. He prayed to God for His unspeakable gift.

And we may now add that He is not alone in doing this. He did not do it for Himself. For Himself, He did not need to confess either the glory of God or the transgression of man. In His own person He did it for others, and first of all for His own people, for all those who believe in Him, and who believing in Him can obey Him, because He Himself has called and empowered them to do so, because in this calling and empowering He has willed to send them forth into the world. God's target when His Son became flesh was the world, just as His target when He made the world was His Son's becoming flesh for its salvation. And so in the asking of the Son of Man, in His existence as the one great Suppliant, and as the One who in asking receives, the target was the world. But because it was the world, it was primarily others who can and may and will ask together with the Son of Man. It was primarily His community as the assembly of those who can ask, and who can therefore receive. For His community is the assembly of those whose eyes are open to the fact that in this One the target of God was the whole world, and primarily themselves, and that in Hun and with Him they too, as they are assembled by His Word, are elected to ask, and therefore to take and receive, and in this way to be His witnesses to the world. The Christian community sees and knows that this One did not pray for Himself but for them, that they might be His witnesses, and that they might keep themselves as such. The Son of God became the Son of Man, and passed through the narrow archway of asking, in order that He who takes and receives the divine gift and answer might be the Representative and Substitute for all others. There must always be this taking and receiving. But this taking and receiving is beyond the will and capacity of men. It had, therefore, to be done for men. Thus the existence of the Son of Man in which it was done was not merely petition but intercession, i.e., petition on behalf of those who cannot and will not ask for themselves, and therefore of themselves are not in any position to take and receive. But this mighty intercession has already taken place. The community which is elected with Him and called and assembled by Him knows by the Holy Spirit of His Word that it has already taken place. And now this community is called to Him, called into His fellowship and communion. He Himself is in the midst of it. He has attached Himself to it, and it has attached itself to Him. It is constituted by the fact that it knows and acknow-   [277] ledges and affirms His intercession as that of the great High-priest, that it is posited on this basis, that it cannot posit itself on any other. It accepts the fact that the gates are opened for it too, that its incapacity and unwillingness are now at an end, that there has been created and made available for it the freedom to be able and willing, the freedom to ask. The Son of Man teaches it to pray, and therefore to ask. It allows itself to be taught by Him. And as He prays with it, it can now pray with Him. How can it accept that intercession of His by which it lives, how can that intercession ever be made for it or revealed to it, if it will not accept and learn and practise this lesson, the lesson of true prayer, if it will not pray with Him? Naturally, it will always be aware that it needs this lesson, not once, but continually. It will always be aware that it cannot do anything without Him, that it cannot pray unless He prays with it. Therefore it will never regard it as its own work, as a human achievement, if by asking it is able to be true to its election in Him and its calling by Him. It will never ask except "in His name." It will never regard its asking except as the gift and work of His Holy Spirit, something with which it can honour Him alone, without any glory at all for itself. But just because it holds fast to Him, just because it asks in His name, and therefore expects everything from His intercession and nothing at all from its own asking as such, just because in its own asking it relies entirely on the gift and work of His Holy Spirit, it can never be idle—for there is no stronger incentive than the knowledge of the real grace of God. Therefore it will not allow its Lord to be alone in prayer, but it will be at His side with its own asking, however imperfect and perverted and impotent this may be compared with His. And both with heart and mouth the asking of the community which is elected together with Him will be a true and genuine asking, because and in the very fact that it is merely a repetition of His petition, that it is enclosed in His asking, that it is associated with it, that it lives by its seriousness and power, that it is related to the gift and answer of God present within it. It is in this that it has its own seriousness and power, that it is prayer which is answered, even though it is made with all the imperfection and perversion and impotence of all things human. It is in this that it is a real taking and receiving of the fulness of God actual and present in Him. It is in this that the community participates in Him, in His life as the Lord. It is in this that it really is His community. It will ask, therefore, as for the one thing needful: that it may really be His community; that it may not be in vain that it is founded and maintained and ruled by Him; that it may not be in vain that it is separated from the world and sent out into the world. It will ask for His love, that in a new way it may be united within itself; for His Word, that in a new way it may hear and know it; for His witness, [278] that in a new way it may be effective both in its life and on its lips. It will ask for all that it requires as His community, and therefore as the light of the world which He has kindled. It will certainly not ask for its existence as such, as though that were an end in itself, but for its existence in His service, for its existence in the carrying out of His commission, for its existence with Him and for Him, the One who by His own existence with it and for it revealed Himself so gracious and mighty towards it. It cannot exist at all except as it goes with Him through the narrow archway of this petition for its own existence. Like Him, it lives only and altogether as it asks, as it asks with the recollection that He has asked for it. Like Him, it can keep and gain and save its life only as it risks and loses it in a confession of the glory of God and the sin of man. If it could keep it in any other way it would not be the Christian community. There is no Church which is not an asking Church, a Church which is continually asking for its own existence as such. But the real question is its existence in the service of its Lord. And for this reason its asking, too, is at the deepest level intercession. As it asks for its own existence, it asks for the world from which it is separated and into which it is sent. It knows that help can be given to the world, but actually is given, only by the divine gift and answer for which it asks and which asking it takes and receives. It sees that as yet the world does not know this, and it sees how the world suffers from the lack of this knowledge. And it sees, too, that its own task is to tell the world what the world does not know. And when it asks it does what the world does not do. It does it for the world, on behalf of the world. But how could it presume to do this if it were dependent on its own capacity and willingness, if it were not supported by the intercession of its own Lord, an intercession of which its own petitions are simply the repetition ? It is in this repetition that it is really at His side, above all in the sense that in it it finds its own part in the divine gift and answer which is made to Him, its own part in the fulness of the Godhead which dwells in Him. For the God who answered the request made by His Elect, the God who answered Him as in obedience to Him He humbled Himself even to the death of the cross, is the very same God who answers the request made by those who are elected with Him, His brothers, His community. He is the very same God who answers this request as it is brought to Him in His name and with reference to Him and in full confidence in Him by those who as members of His body live by Him and with Him as their Head. It is as the Church asks in the name of Jesus—however little it may do so—that it exists as a true Church. As it does so, it receives all that is necessary for its existence as such. Its existence as a true Church is to be the light which is kindled by Him and which constantly burns and shines by Him. Therefore as it asks in His name, it is continually at His side in the sense that it acquires a part in the fulness of grace directed upon Him, an active part in His ministry. For the Church there can never be any question of anything more or anything other than the ministry of witness. [279] It can never usurp the place of its Lord. It can only be at His side. The existence of the community is not an extension of the incarnation. But it can be and it is a witness to it. It is a true confessing community, confessing Him, and therefore confessing God to the world by asking in His name. In asking, it attests and confesses Him, not only because it receives that which equips it for its office and activates it, i.e., the Holy Spirit, and together with Him unity in love and the light of knowledge and the capacity for obedience, but also in the simple sense that over against the world it is the most powerful witness to Jesus Christ, the most powerful recollection of Him, and the most powerful intimation of His coming: a community which is gathered around Him in petition; not therefore in wealth but in poverty; not with self-consciousness but with humility; not triumphantly but with the most profound modesty, and yet also a determined and joyful expectation; looking to Him, and in Him to God; expecting everything from God, and from God everything. By its very existence this community speaks of Him. And it is only as it does speak of Him by its existence that it can and will do so in other ways as well. It is as an asking community—and basically perhaps only as this—that it is really a new phenomenon in the cosmos; something which can be understood, if at all, only in the light of its origin in Jesus Christ and relationship with Him. And from this standpoint, there is a third sense in which we can say that in its asking it is at the side of its Lord. As it repeats His petitions, as it asks with Him, it is together with Him before God. It participates not only in His prophetic but also in His high-priestly office and work. Again, this is not in the sense that it can continue or amplify or complete His intercession on the world's behalf, for this is unnecessary, since His work is quite complete and sufficient in itself; it is in the sense that it attests His asking even before God, that there at the heart of the cosmos it can confirm the fact that His name is already hallowed, His kingdom has already come, His will is already done on earth, and the whole cosmos is caught up in a movement whose end is the meaning of its creation and preservation and of all that occurs within it. Thus the asking community stands together with its Lord before God on behalf of all creation. Not merely is the fulness of all divine giving and receiving present within it, but as it prays there takes place within it something which does not take place anywhere else in the world, where this asking is neglected, or denied, or completely wanting. The asking of this community anticipates as it were that of creation as a whole. It gives voice and expression to the groaning of creation. We can say that whatever may be already present in the world, although unnoticed by it, of the divine gift and answer, of the blessing of the gracious patience of God, is there as an answer to the asking of the community, which is a repetition of that of

[280] Jesus Christ. Because the community asks, the world in its godlessness is not simply godless, but God finds in the world and has in it a partner, and the history between Himself and the world—which is not merely a history of judgment but also of salvation and grace—moves forward to its ultimate goal.

And each individual Christian as such is a member of this asking community. In the framework and context of its asking he, too, is both called and empowered to ask. His asking belongs essentially and necessarily to this context of the asking of Jesus Christ Himself and therefore of His community. It is the prayer of Jesus Christ, the Lord's Prayer, which he will repeat in some form or other whenever he asks. And even as his personal and individual asking it will be a We prayer according to the unequivocal direction of the Lord's Prayer. The We are the members of this community, and behind them, not praying but groaning together with them, all men and all creatures. In the fellowship and discipleship of the asking Lord, and in the assembly and sequence of the asking We, it is, of course, a matter of the personal and individual asking of the individual Christian. It is up to him. It is he with his personal sin, but also with his personal union with the supplication of Jesus Christ, who is responsible for the community. Upon his crying to God as one who is poor and modest and humble after his own fashion, everything depends. And everything depends upon his receiving from God that which has already been prepared for him, and for the whole community, as the divine gift and answer. He can and must pray for himself: that the name of God may be hallowed by him, and therefore by his genuine praying, which will itself always be supplication; that the kingdom of God may be set up, and therefore the lordship of God in his own life; that the will of God may be done in his life, in his free thoughts and words and actions; that he may have the daily bread which is necessary if he is to continue to exist both as a creature and as a man; that he may be forgiven the particular guilt which separates him from God; that he may be guarded against his own particular temptation; that he may have all the things which he does not have and of himself cannot have, but can have only from God. He can and must ask these things for himself. How else can he really ask for them? But he asks for them in this order. He would not really ask for them if he did so in such a way that this order was broken. With the whole community he asks in the name of Jesus, on the basis of His intercession, attaching himself to Him, standing at His side. Therefore in his own prayer he cannot disregard or deny or crowd out the true and proper Subject of prayer who recites the prayer before him. In his own prayer he can desire only to serve and follow Him. In his own prayer he will leave the initiative to this first and proper Subject of true prayer, of the prayer which is heard and answered even as it is offered. And as the Christian follows his Lord with his own most personal and individual petitions, they become holy petitions, petitions which are heard and answered, petitions in which the divine fulness is grasped and received as they are presented to God. But as the Christian prays in this way, his petitions cease to be private petitions, and the more so the more directly they relate to his own needs. They are prayed in the chamber in secret, but they are the petitions of the community. And this means that in the concrete form of his own most personal concerns, the Christian brings before God the concerns of the community ; that there—in his life as a member of the community—he may help and rectify and save, proving himself an heir of glory. What the Christian needs, what he can and must legitimately desire for himself both physically and spiritually, including the nature and course and effect of his environment both far and near, and his own relationship to it, is that he himself in each specific situation, and also those around him, should be equipped and usable and ready in the service which Jesus Christ has assigned to His people, and in which they can have their salvation and glory. Therefore in his own form—and it may be a very improbable and external and worldly form—the Christian will pray that he and those around him may be kept worthy and may be able to may remain cheerful in that service. This is what he most legitimately needs and desires for himself, and this is what he also receives as he asks for it in the name of Jesus. From this it will be seen that the asking of the individual Christian includes intercession not merely as an optional extra, but if it follows the order of the Lord's Prayer, and therefore of We prayer, essentially and necessarily. If he prays in the name of Jesus, if therefore he prays after Jesus, then like Jesus he prays for the community. If he prays in the name of Jesus, he can never pray more earnestly for himself than when as a member of it he prays for the community, asking that it may be ordered and equipped for the service laid upon it, that it may discharge it conscientiously and cheerfully, and that it may have the Holy Spirit as the power behind its continuance and work. And because the community lives in its members, the asking of each member as such is necessarily an asking for the others. The particular asking of each individual Christian has its place in that of the community, in the framework and context of it. Therefore all ask for all, and each for each. For in the service of the community each knows that the other is used in the same service, and that no one else is capable of this service apart from the divine gift and answer. And the true and only good that each can wish for the other is that this part in the divine gift and answer may not be denied but may come to him from God, and that on the basis of it he may fulfil his role in the service of the community. But

[281]

since in each case this is something which only God can answer, no one can pray for himself, and therefore for the community, without praying for others, and indeed for all others who come within the orbit of his vision and under-[282] standing. And when he really does this, he will in fact be also praying for those who are outside, for those who do not so far pray, or who no longer pray, but can only groan. He will, in fact, pray for all men and for all creation.

And this is Christian prayer. It is human asking according to this order. In the name and service of Jesus Christ, in the context of the asking of His community, it is the petition of the individual Christian, with its basis and reference in the divine gift as it is directed to that community and to each individual in the same Jesus Christ, in the divine answer which is already given. It is the prayer which as petition of this kind is the taking and receiving of the whole fulness of this gift and answer. It is (1) primarily and centrally an asking. It stands (2) in a basic relationship to the divine answer. And it takes place (3) in this order. These are the three elements which are essential for an understanding of Christian prayer. We shall touch later on the last of these, which gives to prayer its particular importance in the present context. But first let us consider briefly the relationship of prayer to the two other basic forms of the Christian attitude.

It is apparent at once that Christian prayer can only be the prayer of Christian faith. It is human asking in confrontation with God; asking in which man turns to the One who confronts him and expects from Him the fulfilment of his request. The asking of which we are now speaking is not a yearning sigh or cry addressed into the void, into the mystery of a supposed transcendence in which man finally runs up only against his own limitations. That God does actually hear this sighing, that there is a definite answer and gift even for the creature which merely sighs, is a subject apart. The asking of Christian prayer, however, is something more and other than this sighing or groaning. In Christian prayer as the prayer of Christian faith man transcends his own limitations, for in his asking he turns to the God who has posited and given Himself as the One who confronts him. It is because we had definitely to describe it as a taking and receiving of the divine fulness that we had first of all to speak of the divine gift and answer and only then of its character as asking. Christian prayer is participation in Jesus Christ; participation, basically, in the grace which is revealed and active in Him, in the Son of God; and then only, and on this basis, participation in the asking of the Son of Man. Christian prayer is life in and with the community of Jesus Christ; life primarily and basically out of and in the fulness of the Spirit and the hope which Jesus Christ imparted and continually imparts to them in His Word and in baptism and the Lord's Supper; and then only, and on this basis, co-operation with Him in the service to which it is commissioned. Christian prayer is the preservation of the existence of the Christian as a member of the body of Christ which is His community ; the [283] preservation, primarily and basically, which is freely granted to him; the supreme freedom which is given him as a child of God, by God's only Son; and then only, and on this basis, the fulfilling of the duty to which it is committed by this freedom. In prayer, the Christian is dealing with the merciful God. To be able to pray, he must be awakened and called to prayer by God. He must receive and appropriate the childlike freedom to believe in Him. And this means that God must set him in fellowship with His Son, gathering him into the community of His Son and making him a living member of it. In this freedom, he prays, and therefore he asks, and he can do it as we have described—in the fulness of the divine presence, and therefore with a strong assurance that he will be heard even as he asks. It does not need a great faith to do this. It needs only real faith. But without faith the Christian cannot pray, just as without faith he cannot be a Christian at all.

On the other hand Christian prayer is just as self-evidently related to Christian obedience. We will not labour the fact that the prayer of the Christian to God is the basic act of the obedience engendered in faith. We will simply think of the order in which his asking takes place and affirm that in asking he places himself within this order. His asking, therefore, is not a capricious act which derives from his own needs and desires. It is related—and how else could it be so joyful and assured?—to the divine gift and answer already present in faith. In asking, he follows the law by which this fulness is showered down upon him. He asks therefore—and how else could he arrive at this point?—not in his own name, nor relying upon the power and force of his own asking, but in the name of Jesus and in conjunction with His asking. Therefore, although he prays for himself as an individual, he does not pray private prayers. At his own place and in his own way, according to his own part in the community, he prays the prayer of the community, the common prayer of all Christians. Praying for himself, therefore, he prays with and for all other Christians, because he prays for the service and work of the community; and in so doing he prays for all men. In this way he prays obediently. If he were to pray in any other way he would fall away from faith; he would not really be dealing with God; he could not pray with any assurance of exaltation; his prayer would again be a mere sighing at closed doors and windows; and in the last resort he would again be alone with that supposed transcendence. The fact that he remains obedient in his praying means that he keeps to this order and therefore to the point. And as he does so, his asking always becomes as such taking and receiving. It is only natural that a disobedient asking should disintegrate like an unbelieving asking, and that there should be no answer to either the one or the other. And it is equally evident that the obedience in which Christian prayer keeps to this order and to the point should be simply the obedience of faith, of the evangelical faith of the free children of God. If Christian prayer is made in this obedi- [284] ence, then from a dead work it will continually and necessarily become a living, from an unprofitable work a fruitful.

In conclusion, our treatment of Christian prayer would not be complete if we described it as a living and fruitful work but were merely thinking of something which is no doubt very important but takes place entirely within the

Christian himself as he prays in the obedience of faith. There are certain theories of prayer which finally amount to little more than an understanding of prayer merely as the highest form of religious or Christian self-edification, a living and fruitful dialogue between the Christian and himself. By thinking of it centrally as petition, and understanding it wholly in the light of the divine gift and answer, and therefore strictly in that order, we have necessarily parted company with theories of this type, and tried from the very outset to bring out its objective bearing. In our whole study of the Christian under the world-governance of God the Father, it was, of course, our very first task by way of general elucidation to make it quite clear once again that there is a creaturely subject, the Christian man, who recognises the relation in which he and all other creatures are placed, who participates in the great events of the divine world-governance inwardly as well as outwardly, who is in sympathy with this governance, and who has a real knowledge of the whole matter. But we could not describe this Christian knowledge as a mere seeing and knowing. On the contrary, the knowledge of which we spoke presented itself in the guise of a particular attitude—the attitude of Christian faith, Christian obedience and Christian prayer. And as we tried to understand this attitude in the form of prayer we were led far beyond any idea of a merely subjective basis of our knowledge of the objective events of the divine world-governance, far beyond any idea of a merely subjective reality. There can be no doubt that at this point too—as at every point in our description of the Christian attitude—we find ourselves at the very heart of creaturely occurrence and therefore under the universal lordship of God. But it must not be overlooked that in this supreme form of prayer the whole Christian attitude, although it has its place below as a creaturely movement within all creaturely occurrence, does also point upwards, above all the immanence of the creaturely subject, above all the supposed transcendence within this immanence. It does so because in this supreme form it has the character of petition, of an asking which has to be understood in the light of the divine gift and answer, of an asking which is done in this order. And even less must it be overlooked that occurrence in this higher sphere, far above all creaturely occurrence and therefore above the Christian attitude even in the form of prayer, inclines as it were towards this attitude, merging into and fusing with it, so that although the Christian attitude is still a creaturely movement it acquires a share in the universal lordship of God, so that that lordship has a place and is actualised not merely in the higher sphere but also in the attitude of the Christian. Not that the creature itself, man, the Christian, could do this. Not that the Christian could of himself secure a share in this high matter. He simply believes, he simply obeys, and even his prayer is simply an asking. Not that the universal lordship of God has ceased to be wholly and entirely His own work. The creature, man, the Christian acquires a share in the matter simply by believing, by obeying, and finally and supremely by praying, and therefore by asking. The share is given him by God. It is a share which is quite incomprehensible from his own standpoint.

[285]

He cannot deduce it from his own capacity or volition and activity. It is not in any way effected or conditioned. Yet it is still a genuine and actual share.

It is a genuine and actual share in the universal lordship of God. The will of God is not to preserve and accompany and rule the world and the course of the world as world-occurrence in such a way that He is not affected and moved by it, that He does not allow Himself to converse with it, that He does not listen to what it says, that as He conditions all things He does not allow Himself to be determined by them. God is not free and immutable in the sense that He is the prisoner of His own resolve and will and action, that He must always be alone as the Lord of all things and of all occurrence. He is not alone in His trinitarian being, and He is not alone in relation to creatures. He is free and immutable as the living God, as the God who wills to converse with the creature, and to allow Himself to be determined by it in this relationship. His sovereignty is so great that it embraces both the possibility, and, as it is exercised, the actuality, that the creature can actively be present and co-operate in His overruling. There is no creaturely freedom which can limit or compete with the sole sovereignty and efficacy of God. But permitted by God, and indeed willed and created by Him, there is the freedom of the friends of God concerning whom He has determined that without abandoning the helm for one moment He will still allow Himself to be determined by them. There is no autonomous and rebellious counter-activity of the creature in opposition to the eternal activity of His own will and action; but on the model of His own will and action there is an individual activity of the creature which is planned and willed and demanded and made possible and actual by His own eternal activity, since it is included within it. There is no divine surrender to the creature, but in the very fact that God maintains and asserts himself as King and Lord there is a divine hearing—on the basis of the incomprehensible grace of God an incomprehensible hearing—even of the creature which is sinful. The grace of God to sinful man is that He encounters him as the hearing God; that He calls him not merely to the humility of a servant and the thankfulness of a child but to the [286] intimacy and boldness of a friend in the immediate presence of the throne, His own presence; that He not merely permits but commands him to call upon Him in the definite expectation that He will both hear and answer, that his asking will have an objective as well as a subjective significance, i.e., a significance for his own will and action. The will of God is done even as the creature calls and presses and prevails upon it to be done. It is done as the converse with the creature established by this will is entered into by the creature in the form of this calling and pressing and prevailing. It is done as God participates in the creature, and enables it to participate in Himself, and in the purpose and direction of His works. It is done on this condition. And in this way it triumphs as the sovereign will of God which is living even in its divine sovereignty.

This is what takes place in what we have described as the Christian attitude, and ultimately and supremely as the asking of Christian prayer. We do not rightly describe even Christian faith and Christian obedience if we do not think of them as a human co-operation in the doing of the will of God. To be sure, it is a co-operation here below under the universal lordship of God. But none the less it is a real co-operation. And this is absolutely and unequivocally the case in the supreme form of the Christian attitude, which is prayer as petition. In obedience the Christian is the servant, in faith he is the child, but in prayer, as the servant and the child, he is the friend of God, called to the side of God and at the side of God, living and ruling and reigning with Him. To be sure, he is only a suppliant. He acts only as a suppliant, and as a suppliant down below, under the universal lordship of God. It is only as a suppliant that he is called to God's side. It is only as God stoops down to him and sets him there that even as a suppliant he is actually called to His side, and is there and can live and rule and reign there with God. It is only as God has intervened for him, with the fulness of the divine gift and answer to him, that he can actually present his request to God, that as a suppliant he can actually be the friend of God. It is all the divine condescension of grace, and there can be no question of human possibility or attainment, of human right or merit, of human autonomy or presumption. But grace is creative and active in the sphere where a man can believe and obey and finally pray as a Christian. And grace is creative and active to make it possible for a Christian to be actively present in the divine lordship as the friend of God: present not merely as one of many objects nor as a spectator or critic; but present as a subject, which in its own place and within its own limits has an actual voice and responsibility in the matter.

[287]   It is clear that we cannot understand this except within the order apart from which we cannot say anything worth while about Christian prayer, or even faith and obedience, because apart from it they would not exist at all. Originally and properly the Christian who is at the side of God and has His own voice and responsibility in the divine rule is the one Son of Man, Jesus Christ. It is He who sits at the right hand of the Father Almighty. It is He who with God is the Lord and King of all things. It is to Him that there is given all power in heaven and on earth. It is His asking which is answered, which is the work of the creature which includes within it the fulness of the divine presence and gift, and therefore helps to determine the divine will and action. Far be it from us to ascribe to the Christian creature, and his piety, and the strength of his faith, and the seriousness of his obedience, and the depth and fervour of his prayer, the power to rule and reign with God. Without Christ there are no Christians and there is no Christianity. But by and with Christ there are Christians and there is a Christianity, and it is to these that we refer. There is a discipleship of Christ. There is a faith in Him, and through Him in God. Likewise there is an obedience to Him. Likewise there is prayer or asking together with Him, and on the basis of His asking. Likewise there is a participation of the Christian not merely in His prophetic and high-priestly but also in His kingly office. In Him God came to our side and entered into our humility. And in Him we are set at God's side and lifted up to Him and therefore to the place where decisions are made in the affairs of His government. And this is what takes place in Christian

faith and Christian obedience and Christian prayer. We are set there; we are lifted up to that place. To deny this or to question it is just as fatal as to deny or question the full humanity and creatureliness of the Christian's activity. It is not the Christian in and for himself, but the Christian in Christ, who is at God's side and has a say and a part in the place where those decisions are made. It is not the Christian in himself, but the Christian in Christ, who is the servant and child and also the friend of God, and as such a free lord with him over everything.

In relation to this order we have also to say, of course, that he is all this as a member of the body of Christ and therefore as a member of His community. He is it in the most personal sense. He can lead his own life in this freedom, and he has to lead it in the responsibility which it involves. But he cannot do it as a free-lance. He personally is called to God's side. But he is not called as it were in his private but in his official capacity. And it is his personal but not his private needs and demands and petitions which can there confidently await an answer and determine the will of God. The friends of God are the creatures to whom He has given His grace and also a definite commission in the world. It is for the sake of His business, and therefore—because His business concerns the whole of creation—for the sake of creation as a whole, that God calls them to [288] faith and obedience and also to prayer. It is in their official capacity in this respect that He allows Christians a voice and a part in the formulation and execution of His will. This share in the kingly office of His Son, and therefore in His lordship, is not granted to the I in isolation, but to the We of those who are gathered to His people and service, and to the I within the We. The individual can expect and experience an answer in so far as he believes and obeys and prays as a member of this people, as one who is called to this service. If he is not this, or if he thinks that he ought to believe and obey and pray in some other context, he need not be surprised if he is left groping in the void. But the moment he does it as a Christian, and therefore as a member of this community, he will be amazed at the fulness of the divine answer in which he participates.

Presupposing that it is done within this order, we can never rate too highly the objective significance of the Christian attitude, even if we are thinking only of the individual Christian as such. Nor can we reject too strongly those theories which seek to restrict the significance of prayer to the subjective sphere alone. If this presupposition can be made, then whenever the Christian believes and obeys and prays there does not merely take place a creaturely movement. But concealed within the creaturely movement, yet none the less really, there moves the finger and hand and sceptre of the God who rules the world. And what is more, there moves the heart of God, and He Himself is there in all the fulness of His love and wisdom and power. We then find ourselves at the very seat of government, at the very heart of the mystery and purpose of all occurrence. The subjective element, which ultimately can never have more than the form of a bloodless and impotent asking, of hands which are empty although stretched out to God, conceals and contains and actualises the most objective of all things, the lordship of the One who as King of Israel and King of the kingdom of grace holds all things in His own hands, and directs everything that occurs in this world for the best: *per Jesum Christum, Dominum nostrum*[EN576].

[EN576] through Jesus Christ our Lord

INDEX OF SCRIPTURE REFERENCES

INDEX OF SUBJECTS

INDEX OF NAMES